The Moment of Astrology

Geoffrey Cornelius is a consultant astrologer with a background in philosophy and divination. He is a former President of the Astrological Lodge of London, and a co-founder of the Company of Astrologers. He has been active in UK astrological education since the 1970s, is one of the original band of pioneers of the subject both in adult education and at university level. He currently teaches Cosmology and Divination in the Mysticism and Religious Experience MA programme at the University of Kent, where he is engaged in post-graduate studies in divination.

The illustration on the front cover is anonymous, sixteenth-century Venetian, reproduced by permission of the Phillips Collection, Washington D.C. It is a small furniture panel, 12 × 19.5 cm, in the style of Giorgione (1477–1511), and known as 'Father Time and Orpheus' or by the earlier title 'The Astrologer'.

The musician has been considered to represent either Apollo or Orpheus. Infrared analysis reveals an underdrawing showing the musician placed near two deer confronting each other, which favours the Orphic interpretation. The buck is visible in the painting, but the hind has been covered by the figure with the hourglass. The angelic musician plays the lira da braccio, the instrument used by Marsilio Ficino in his invocations. This suggests that the astrologer times the planetary hours for the musician, commencing the day with the first planetary hour at the moment of dawn (see on-line dox reference for further discussion).

THE Moment of Astrology

ORIGINS IN DIVINATION

Geoffrey Cornelius

FOREWORD BY PATRICK CURRY

THE WESSEX ASTROLOGER

Published in England in 2003 by
The Wessex Astrologer Ltd
4A Woodside Road
Bournemouth
BH5 2AZ
England

www.wessexastrologer.com

ISBN 1902405110 Revised and expanded 2nd edition
(Previously published by Penguin Arkana as ISBN 0140193693)

A catalogue record of this book is available at the British Library

Typeset by John Saunders Design & Production

To the Student in Astrology

Acknowledgments

Many friends and colleagues in astrology have helped me with their insight and inspiration, and I have endeavoured to refer to particular contributions where appropriate in the text and notes. Special thanks are due to clients and former students for their permission to use case histories; and to the Astrological Association, publishers of the *Astrological Journal*, for their permission for me to reproduce Charles Carter's discussion on horary astrology.

Acknowledgments are due to the Warburg Institute of the University of London, on account both of the courtesy and efficiency of the library staff, and the intellectual generosity of Dr. Charles Burnett. The importance of this institution for the scholar in astrology can hardly be overestimated. Likewise, the helpers at the former Urania Trust Astrology Centre in Camden gave unstinting service in searching out some of the treasures in the unrivalled collection of twentieth-century astrological materials held in the libraries of the Astrological Association and the Astrological Lodge.

I would like to express my gratitude to all those who made comments on all or a substantial part of the first edition in its preparatory stages: Robert Chandler, Patrick Curry, Jane Farrer, Angela Voss, Vernon Wells, and Graeme Tobyn. Both Angela Voss and Graeme Tobyn have given invaluable guidance on Latin texts which form part of my background research for both the original and this revised edition. A word of thanks is also due to Melanie Reinhart, for being at the right place at the right time to give this book a nudge into manifestation, to Christopher Hedley, whose herbal strategy helped me on the hidden paths and ways, and to Kirk Little for his valued observations and his encouragement of the second edition.

On the editorial side, Erin Sullivan and Robin Waterfield made vital contributions to the original shape of the work. As copy editor for the first edition Christine Collins showed patience and perception, and I have been especially fortunate in the careful attention given to this second edition by Margaret Cahill at The Wessex Astrologer.

My last word of thanks must go to Maggie Hyde, whose untiring support, critical acumen and symbolic perception have sustained me through the seemingly interminable process of giving expression to both first and second editions of *The Moment of Astrology*.

Contents

Foreword   xiii

Preface to the Second Edition   xvii

Introduction   xxi

 1 The Scourge of Astrology   1
 2 An Anti-Astrology Signature   22
 3 Science and the Symbol 1: Humpty-Dumpty   42
 4 Science and the Symbol 2: Two Orders of Significance   59
 5 Ptolemy's Broad Shoulders: The Moment of Astrology in the
   Western Tradition   81
 6 The Question of Horary   98
 7 Katarche:The Line of Descent from Augury   124
 8 Horary Revived   144
 9 Some Genius or Spirit   167
10 The Unique Case of Interpretation   184
11 Appearances: The Symbol in Context   203
12 Images of Birth   230
13 Images of the World   256
14 The Fourfold Symbol I: Divination and Allegory   277
15 The FourFold Symbol II: Water into Wine   292
16 Astrology as a Gift of the Soul   303

Appendix 1 Pico's Disputations   333
Appendix 2 The NCGR-Berkeley Double-Blind Test   338
Appendix 3 Charles Carter on Horary   347
Appendix 4 Frankland's 'Missing Father'   351
Appendix 5 Ashmole on Astrology   359
Appendix 6 Reworking Sibly   361
Appendix 7 Case Study: Stella   369

Index   381

List of Figures

1 Marsilio Ficino   5
2 Pico della Mirandola   9
3 An Anti-Astrology Signature   27
4 Astrology on trial   29
5 Venus times the publication   32
6 Lilly: fish stolen   99
7 Carter: Is there anything in horary astrology?   114
8 Neptune rises at the Mercury-Jupiter perfection   119
9 Frankland: missing father   121
10 Lilly: gentlewoman and the aged man   149
11 Should we accept the offer for the house?   157
12 Elizabeth II   191
13 Margaret Thatcher   192
14 Arthur Koestler   197
15 Commencement of a weekend course   210
16 Dead sheep and flamingo   213
17 Physic without astrology is like a lamp without oil   217
18 Mr. B.   225
19 Diana - version I (Libra)   233
20 Charles   234
21 Diana - version II (Sagittarius)   236
22 Death of a Princess   244
23 Diana - Adrian Duncan's rectification   246
24 Sibly's 'Revolution of America'   265
25 United States Declaration of Independence   268
26 The hermeneutic cross in the cadent houses   279
27 Functions of the symbol in divination   281
28 Lilly: If Presbytery shall stand?   313
29 The geography of an astrological coincidence   352
30 What should I do about the pregnancy?   373
31 Stella   377

Foreword

PATRICK CURRY, Ph.D.

This is an extraordinary book. I believe that within the astrological tradition, it is the most important since the great flowering of European astrology more than three hundred years ago. Indeed, Geoffrey Cornelius can fairly lay claim to have broken the mould first cast by Ptolemy in the first century A.D., which subsequent and even modern astrologers – despite their theoretical, technical and statistical pyrotechnics – have but extended and refined.

Lest there be any misunderstanding, let me quickly add two things. First, he has not done so alone but working closely together with his colleagues in and around the Company of Astrologers, especially Maggie Hyde and Gordon Watson. Hyde's *Jung and Astrology* (1992) is in many ways a companion to this volume, and a worthy one.

Second, *The Moment of Astrology* is radical in the proper sense of a return to roots. But that does not mean hankering after an impossible return to the lost golden past. Like any good revolutionary, Cornelius builds on what has gone before, and one of his book's chief virtues is the way it has actually taken on board modern and recent developments in other fields – psychoanalysis, science, philosophy – without losing sight of astrology along the way. Astrologers have been despised for so long that their tendency to ignore the rest of the intellectual world is understandable, if lamentable; but the corollary of such battered self-confidence is that having raised their heads and gazed around them, they are too quick to trade an exchange between equals for willing subjugation.

Cornelius can hardly be said to rush in, but much of this book will make uncomfortable reading for astrology's current angels. Indeed, one of its pleasures for me is the way he politely but firmly closes off, one by one, all the principal avenues by which modern astrologers have escaped into wishful thinking. Nor, by the same token, does he shirk intractable ethical questions. Such rigour means demanding reading, but any practising astrologer will be encouraged to persevere by the strikingly precise and subtle horoscopic interpretations that run throughout the text.

Unavoidably, of course, the same interpretations may pose a problem for the non-astrologer. But he or she too, I think, will find encouragement in the obvious integrity and courage of Cornelius's approach. Indeed, as he excavates and brings to light the missing cultural and epistemological category, or dimension, of divination, such a reader may even have the most to learn. For his principal claim, simply put, is that astrology is an ancient but still living tradition of astral divination. One might even say the Church fathers were right about it all along, in their judgment, if not their hostile valuation: astrology really is a pagan, implicitly polytheistic, pantheistic and/or animistic practice.

I have already said, however, that Cornelius writes in no spirit of nostalgia. So let me try to place my claim in some broader historical and intellectual contexts. I write independently, of course, so he cannot be held answerable for my views; but my own work on the history of astrology, in *Prophecy and Power: Astrology in Early Modern England* (1989) and *A Confusion of Prophets: Victorian and Edwardian Astrology* (1992), has led me in very much the same direction. These remarks are not meant to be definitive,or to summarise what follows them. Their point is to help the reader understand why this book is not only about the moment of astrology in its actual practice, but also its present moment as a tradition: including the past that had made it so, and its as yet undecided future. For in this respect too, 'destiny is negotiable'.

Katarchic omen astrology – the ancestor of horary astrology – died out (or was pushed) about eighteen centuries ago. The arguments between 'magical', 'rational' and later 'scientific' astrologers have been going on almost as long, but both sides have always agreed in denouncing horary. Taking his cue from this history – along with his indispensable experience as a practising astrologer – Cornelius seizes on katarche and horary not in an act of antiquarian perversity but as the key to the suppressed divinatory dimension of astrology. And as he gently but persistently tugs on this seemingly tiny thread, it is marvellous to behold the entire millennia-long astrological tradition gradually unravel.

First to come unstuck is that machine for destroying astrological effects (principally by eliminating the astrologer) called scientific research, which some are still trying to perfect. Next is the principal astral orrery of the twentieth century, psychological astrology. Roomier, more soft-edged and 'humanistic', it began life as a spiritual and karmic model under the wing of Theosophy, before it was unevenly and uneasily secularised by the followers of Jung, beginning with Dane Rudhyar. It still retains 'archetypal', 'transpersonal' and 'esoteric' versions. Finally, almost apologetically, the original 'machine of destiny' itself (in Cornelius's marvellous phrase) grinds to a halt. Devised by Ptolemy, perfected by Aquinas and finding its apotheosis in John Addey's harmonics, this one has managed to succour astrologers and wrongfoot their opponents for centuries, not least through skilfully alternating between a magical (neo-Platonic) version and a rationalist (Aristotelian) one. Indeed, the Ptolemaic theory has proved so durable and successful that any astrologer outside its one final and ultimately non-negotiable Order – the key that unites all these variants – has long been almost unimaginable.

I have no wish to be unkind, or (least of all) to patronise. Astrologers have always had to consider how to survive, as well as develop and extend their tradition; and to succeed as they have took not only brilliance and perseverance but a necessary element of compromise and adaptation. But the time has now come, it seems, when other truths about astrology can be voiced.

Why now? It does not diminish Cornelius's efforts to note that they coincide with a more general cultural and intellectual sea-change. Broad strokes here are not only unavoidable; they are what matter most. So let us note that this book appears at a time whose only generally agreed-upon description (notwith-standing bitter disputes about its precise meaning) is 'postmodern'. Its key realisations are those of 'anti-essentialism' – that identities (of any kind) are not inherent or transcendentally given, but vary with time, chance and context; and 'relativism' – that every statement (including of course this one) unavoidably embodies the perspective and assumptions of the one who makes it, and the contexts in which appears. Its guiding philosophy is that of Richard Rorty's 'liberal irony', which rejects the philosophical obsession with objective Truth beginning with Plato, and admits the contingency of its own ideals; its politics those of Laclau and Mouffe's 'radical and plural democracy', using the 'logic of articulation and contingency'.

These positions mark a radical break from the attributes of modernity; its love of all-encompassing 'grand narratives' and worship of progress, its restless search for 'foundations', and its contempt for the local and particular in favour of the universal, and for the 'merely subjective' and personal. We can now see how universalism requires enforcing when dissenters see things differently; and how objectivism and rationalism are actually the particular point of view of a privileged and powerful few. With the fall of European communism came the end of the ultimate modernist dream become nightmare. Nothing, it now seems clear, necessarily or automatically means anything; and no longer can any one thing be seen as the key to everything.

Of course, all this is exhilarating, but it signifies no starry-eyed New Age. Nor does Cornelius indulge in such wishful thinking; thankfully, for example, he doesn't try to convince us that quantaum physicists now believe the stars to be God's daisy-chain. The modernist monologic of capital, funded by the IMF, World Bank and transnational companies, still drives the global ecocide sometimes described as 'development'. And older forms of Blake's 'single vision' are also abroad again: nationalist essentialism and its obscene 'ethnic cleansing', and theologically sanctioned murder in the name of religion. All the more important, then, that the wisdom of the new insecurity is recognised, and its voices – however puny, tenuous or 'peculiar' – be heard.

Their message, although never so fresh, is actually a very old one; it has been called 'beginner's mind'. The contrasting attributes of modernity, too, partake of a much older attitude. Astrologers ought to recognise it, having been on the sharp end for many centuries. Its roots are clearly discernible in the institutions which have long been their bitterest enemies: in rough order of antiquity, the Christian Church; modern science and its apologists; and professional intellectuals taking their mandate from the Enlightenment. Now the interesting thing is that all these groups have always managed to set aside their own serious differences in order to attack astrologers, often using the identical terms of abuse (for example, 'superstition'). This historical fact reveals their profound common ground: namely, monism. Science and the Enlightenment borrowed the Christian commitment to monotheism wholesale, secularising it from one universal God into one universal and objective truth, or way of finding truth. The latter still requires policing. (The activities of the Committee for the Scientific Investigation of Claims of the Paranormal, or CSICOP – aptly pronounced 'psicop' – are more blatant but less important in this regard than the power of patronage through research funding and publication.)

Of the three groups, scientists have probably had the greatest impact on modern astrology – both positively, as a powerful and eminent model to be imitated, and negatively, through their hostility. I have already mentioned several contemporary philosophers, under the loose umbrella of postmodernity. But the most important for astrology, by virtue of his matchless insight into modern science – 'that most recent, most aggressive and most dogmatic religious institution' – is probably Paul Feyerabend. His *Farewell to Reason* (1987) makes it very clear why we must 'either call gods and quarks equally real, but tied to different sets of circumstances, or we altogether cease talking about the "reality" of things and use more complex ordering schemes instead'. And in the scheme pertaining to astrology, its proper place is not under the microscope or in the bowels of a supercomputer, but alongside intuition, prophecy, meditation, the art and literature of mythopeoic imagination, the insights and values of feminism and ecology ... and, I would add, humour.

This company marks no plunge into mere subjectivity, let alone irrationalism. As Cornelius makes quite clear in the case of astrology, the point is not to replace but to complement and correct our narrowly purposive and instrumental consciousness. Gregory Bateson called this process the 'recognition of and guidance by a knowledge of the total systemic creature', and identified it as 'the sacred'. We might equally call it 'the sane', for without it there is neither sanity nor sanctity.

Astrologers, however, have not just been on the receiving end of the commitment to monism. As this book shows, their own practice too has long been constrained by one universal and effectively divine Order. Indeed, their own treatment of horary uncomfortably mimics that of astrology as a whole by its mainstream critics. That is why the kind of astrology this book presents – one centred on personal participation in a unique situation, following a divinatory logic with a symbolic attitude, and open to multiple perspectives or truths – is, as befits its subject, so very timely. The meeting of contemporary postmodernism and ancient paganism (for want of a better shorthand) is an auspicious one.

Many astrologers will therefore find it an inexplicable relief after their customary confinement. And few will miss the dream (itself increasingly a nightmare) of being able to stand outside astrology and ascertain its truth by waving a scientific wand that separates wheat from chaff. But some rather more cherished notions are also part of the price; astrology as something continuously happening 'out there', for example, which the astrologer-as-magus need only tap into (and what a feeling of power that can confer!). Nor can it any longer be talked up as a universal language (or algebra, or code) of life, whose potential validity and relevance is therefore necessarily also universal. Those are the delusions of the old order.

But note that I am not arguing (nor, if he is wise, will Cornelius) that his 'take' on astrology is truer or more real than others. That is to play into just the wrong hands, whose game assumes that astrology is something out there that will hold still long enough to be 'objectively ' analysed by those in the know. For exactly the same reason, it is also to invite the creation of a new orthodoxy.

No, the point is that a divinatory model is more useful; elegant, liberating and, not least, humble. It cannot succeed in taming and automating 'the phenomenon of astrology', or even explaining it (whatever that may exactly mean). Nor does it offer any technical solution; it is quite possible to practise horary astrology, for example, as a kind of idiosyncratic antiquarianism, following the letter of tradition alone. But the approach taken here has this cardinal virtue: it takes something that merely leaks out of the interstices of the various machines of destiny (even the tightest) and 'allows' it to happen. It turns the moment of astrology from a problem to be explained into the starting-point of analysis; and analysis itself into an activity that facilitates the moment.

Or that *can* facilitate it. A symbolic attitude or divinatory logic is doubtless far from a firm and objective foundation on which to ground a discipline. But that chimera is also part of the old game, whose futility is now increasingly clear. Precisely one of this book's virtues is to abandon it, and recognise that in art as in life, there are no guarantees; that all knowledge is suffused and delimited by mystery, and all initiative by dependence. That is why it contains no simple answers. It is also, for the reasons I have mentioned, quietly but deeply subversive. In short, this is a book for people who look to astrology – as Jung noted of the *I Ching* – neither for facts nor power, but wisdom.

Preface to the Second Edition

This edition of *The Moment of Astrology* involves substantial emendations to the original published in 1994 by Penguin/Arkana, as well as minor corrections and the updating of some bibliographical references. The order up to and including Chapter 12, 'Images of Birth', follows the first edition; details of major changes within these chapters are given below. Chapter 13, 'Images of the World' is wholly new, and extends the argument for horoscopy as a mode of divination from natal to mundane astrology. The following two chapters on the Fourfold Symbol are little changed from the original.

The final chapter 16, formerly 'Synderesis of the Stars' and now called 'Astrology as a Gift of the Soul', has been completely reworked. As often happens with last chapters, the book in its original form was at this point abandoned rather than completed. I have dropped the lengthy discussion of a violent death prediction; this was in its time a powerful piece of astrology for me, but I was never happy about its status in the book. The interested reader can find this material on-line in the dox file (see below). In its place is an introduction to one of the most important themes to have come to the fore in the last few years, namely the renaissance hermetic understanding of the nature of astrological judgment, profoundly reinterpreting the old dictum 'by you and by the science'. Along with ideas of the fourfold symbol, more no doubt needs to be explored here, but this would take our thesis well beyond the bounds of the current text.

Returning to the earlier part of the book, important amendments have been made to Chapters 4 and 7. Chapter 4, 'Science and the Symbol 2', has been extensively revised to cope with the sorry tale of the most recent phase of research into Vernon Clark-type trials, and the questionable statistical inferences drawn from them by Geoffrey Dean and others. The analysis of Shawn Carlson's widely-reported NCGR-Berkeley test of astrology has been relegated to Appendix 2. I was loathe to dispense with this altogether as it remains a model of bad science, quoted even today as 'evidence' in the case against astrology, and a chilling reminder to research astrologers tempted to trip gaily to their doom down the same barren path. On a more cheerful note, Chapter 7 on 'Katarche' includes a new section on the origin of the decumbiture, indicating the sacred and divinatory roots of this traditional method. Chapter 11, 'Appearances', carries a discussion on Graeme Tobyn's wonderful orange-omen, which was only briefly treated in the first edition. Chapter 12 carries forward the sad tale of Diana, Princess of Wales, to include the astrological symbolism at her death in 1997.

The appendices have been placed in a new order, with only minor corrections. Two additional appendices appear; one for the NCGR-Berkeley test already mentioned, and another for a discussion on the origin of the Sibly horoscope for the U.S. Declaration of Independence. This latter should, I hope, help to lay to rest the historical debates about this important horoscope.

On-line dox: web-based document extension and reference

The concept of a web-based extension (dox) is ideal for a book of this type. This allows an easily-accessible means of maintaining references, corrections, and additional materials or discussion. The on-line dox file for *The Moment of Astrology* is located at: *www.astrodivination.com*

Regular updating cannot be guaranteed, but it is intended to maintain the dox file long-term as a source of occasional reference. In the event of failure or change of address, please check for a link from the Company of Astrologers site (currently *http://coa.hubcom.net*) or The Wessex Astrologer site (*www.wessexastrologer.com*).

A note on technical conventions adopted in this edition

My chosen house system is Topocentric, which gives results within a degree of the Placidus cusps for intermediate houses. The horoscopes from Lilly and Culpeper are given with Regiomontanus cusps. Modern horoscopes show the true node. Secondary progressions employ progressed MC by solar arc in longitude.

A change in my methods since the first edition has been my decision to experiment with the Part of Fortune calculated differently by day and by night (day horoscope fortuna = asc + Moon - Sun; night horoscope fortuna = asc + Sun - Moon). Up until recent times the modern approach, like that of Lilly, has been to take the same computation by day and night. The revival of classical astrology methods pioneered by Project Hindsight has encouraged a closer look at the difference between day and night figures, however, and this is one illustration of that influence. To maintain consistency with the first edition, the day fortuna has been noted in cases of night horoscopes.

Introduction

THIS work is a review and critique of the conceptual foundations of Western astrology. It also offers a radical reinterpretation of the main part of astrological practice, by considering horoscopy in the light of divination. By the term 'Western astrology', I refer to the stream of practice and theory that has come down to us through the transformation of archaic celestial omen-watching into the purified cosmic conception of Classical Graeco-Roman astrology. This tradition was transmitted and further transformed through the imagination of the Arabs, and passed on into late medieval and renaissance Europe. On this great stream the little boats of modern European and American astrology still ply their busy trade.

A marvellous history is no guarantee of future survival, and the secure place astrology once held in the scheme of science has gone for ever. Over the last three to four hundred years astrology has fallen from grace, and the recent upsurge in popular and psychological forms is only of superficial significance compared with astrology's more fundamental decline. The pressure of change as our subject stumbles into the modern world has exposed weaknesses in its conceptual foundation which were always there, but which in my view now seriously impede creative and intelligent development.

I start this review by using negative rather than positive method, reminding the reader of attacks on astrology, ancient and modern. It is five hundred years since Pico della Mirandola's highly publicised scourging of astrology, and over fifteen hundred years since the shrewd and formidable critique by St. Augustine. In modern times we have had to face the censure of 186 scientists – including 18 Nobel Prizewinners – in the 1975 *Humanist* attack. It would be unwise to treat these occasional assaults as aberrations, as they signify a much wider and ongoing struggle over the credibility of astrology. However, my main concern is how astrologers answer these criticisms, and I am afraid that the answers commonly given, even amongst ourselves, present a rather sorry and unconvincing case.

Chapter 1 opens with Pico's attack, not so much because of its substance, but because of its context in Renaissance philosophy. Pico is usually taken to prefigure the modern scientific and humanist stand, but just as significantly he marks out the rupture between astrology and Renaissance magic. This leads us back to the attitude of Pico's mentor, Marsilio Ficino. In Ficino we see the possibility of a different way of theorising about astrology, a magical and poetic interpretation running counter to the orthodox tradition. Ficino refers to certain phenomena of astrology that are incapable of expression in the orthodox theory given by our classical tradition.

Pico's attack is a good starting point for another reason altogether. If we are to believe later accounts, the most dramatic answer of the astrologers to his challenge was the prediction of his death. This famous story reveals a dilemma which strikes to the heart of our practice, and the problematic question of the ethic of judgment and prediction is taken up as a thread throughout the text.

On the side of positive statements about astrology, the primary theme is that the main body of astrology's practice, and especially the interpretation of horoscopes, is properly to be understood as a form of divination. It is divination despite all appearances of objectivity and natural law. It is divination despite the fact that aspects of symbolism can be approached through scientific method, and despite the possibility that a few factors in horoscopy can arguably be validated by the appeal to science. If this thesis is correct, it follows that the philosophical investigation of the greater part of astrology requires a way of description that is appropriate to the phenomenology of divination, and some preliminary steps in this direction have been outlined here.

The question of divination is virtually never addressed by astrologers, even though it is such an obvious descriptive tag for the discerning outsider to the subject. This suggests a long-established blind-spot in the way we perceive our practice, and something awry in the way we describe it to others. I have written this book in the hope of putting to rights our faulty descriptions and opening our vision to things we have not up to now been quite able to see. In so doing, I have woven together a complex pattern of ideas which have engaged my attention, and the attention of a group of colleagues, over many years. A brief outline of the history of these studies will, I hope, give the reader another line of orientation to the text.

Several major themes taken up here were first published in the quarterly journal *Astrology* between 1978 and 1986. The central argument, which begins with a critique of the Ptolemaic model as the foundation of Western astrology (Chapter 5), was first put forward in a series of six articles entitled, as is this book, 'The Moment of Astrology'.[1] Other unpublished material, including more recent developments in my thinking, has now been woven into the text.

These years, 1978 to 1986, are significant in marking out the development of a new way of approach to the description of astrology. This arose initially amongst a leading group in the Astrological Lodge of London, and later, after a period of ideological and political fissures and storms, in the Lodge's offspring, the

Company of Astrologers. During this period there occurred the distinctive emergence of what Patrick Curry has aptly termed 'hermeneutic astrology'.[2] Hermeneutics is the study of meaning, and of how we arrive at our interpretations of things. In the context of astrology, the term implies a turning away from the common taken-for-granted assumption that a fixed astrological meaning is simply 'there', in front of us, as some sort of fact of nature. The hermeneutic inquiry in astrology reveals the essential dependency of the meaning of symbols on the act of *interpretation* of that meaning. Seen in this way, horoscope interpretation involves something other than a supposed pre-existent meaning waiting to be decoded, and depends both on the context in which meaning is sought, as well as on the intentionality of the one making the interpretation. This has become best known in the description of 'takes' (Chapter 11), where we may say that a particular line of interpretation constitutes a 'take' on a horoscope.

This whole way of approach to the description of astrology owes much to two primary sources of inspiration. One is the phenomenological hermeneutics of Martin Heidegger, and the reader familiar with his work will be able to trace this influence in certain stances I adopt. However, I make no claim for completeness or for consistency in this project, and the steps I have taken are of the most rudimentary nature. I have made no attempt to bring out the specialised philosophical problems involved, as these would burden the text without necessarily adding much for the practising astrologer.

The other prime source, apparently antithetical but in some ways complementary to everything Heidegger stands for, is Carl Jung. Jung's ideas on divination and synchronicity, and his treatment of the nature and interpretation of symbol, form outstanding reference points for the astrologer and are important features in my argument. This aspect of the description of astrology, and its application to practice, has been thoroughly developed by Maggie Hyde in her pioneering work *Jung and Astrology*.[3]

Since the early days of this new approach, incorporating both a phenomenological (Heideggerian) and a symbolic (Jungian) hermeneutic, I have become aware of the possibilities for the description of astrology inherent in the Four Levels hermeneutic of medieval Christianity. This suggests the description of astrology as a divinatory allegory, with practical interpretation being a type of allegorical method (Chapters 14 and 15). Once again, the reader is advised not to seek a smoothed-out consistency and fit between these very diverse ideas.

The hermeneutic approach as a whole is sometimes, wrongly, equated with an anti-science stance. What it will certainly effectively counter is *scientism*, the inappropriate extension of scientific method to phenomena and domains of experience which cannot be reduced to objective and positive assertions of a literal nature. Far from having to reject the findings of science, by freeing astrology of presuppositions derived ultimately from the Ptolemaic model, it is possible to utilise and interpret results from purely scientific research in astrology to bring to light facets of the astrological phenomenon. This has been indicated in Chapters 3 and 4, and represents an overview of the broad conclusions that we should draw from the whole spectrum of statistical investigations, from the Vernon Clark experiments to the findings of the Gauquelins. The results of this research point fairly unambiguously, in my opinion, to the need to logically distinguish two orders of meaning and significance in astrology. Further, a close study of various research results begins to indicate the functioning of an irrational or 'psi' component, and the effect of this is illustrated in some depth in the peculiar breakdown of the NCGR – Berkeley double-blind test of astrology (Appendix 2).

This overview of existing research therefore supports the proposal put forward here for a division in astrology between two distinct orders, Natural and Divinatory. The present work is concerned almost wholly with the description of divinatory astrology, i.e. judgments from horoscopes, but the existence of another type of astrological revelation in the natural world, and commensurable with scientific method, is nowhere denied. However, it would go beyond the useful scope of this current project to attempt a grand theory or 'equation of the orders' to tie the whole show together. In fact, it is the attempt at a total conception that so frequently undermines the capacity of theories of astrology to describe anything useful about the actual phenomena we encounter.

An important part of the task I have set myself centres on a critique of the foundation of the false defences of astrology, and in particular the rationale given to us by Ptolemy. This has been adopted virtually without further reflection by the whole tradition of astrology down to the present day. To get to the deep roots of the Ptolemaic solution for astrology means taking up anew questions of time, objectivity, and the interpretation of symbol. All of these issues are involved in the seemingly innocent question, 'What *is* the moment of astrology?' This book is a challenge – and an invitation – to modern astrologers to take up this question and look again at the foundations of our mysterious and beautiful Art.

NOTES

1 'The Moment of Astrology' series of articles in *Astrology Quarterly*, published by the Astrological Lodge of London: Part I, vol. 57, no.3, Autumn 1983; Part II, vol. 57, no.4, Winter 1983/4; Part III, vol. 58, no.1, Spring 1984; Part IV, vol. 58, no.2, Summer 1984; Part V, vol. 59, no.1, Spring 1985; Part VI, vol. 59, no.4, Winter 1985/6. Part VII was never produced.

'An Anti-Astrology Signature' appeared in *Astrology*, vol. 52, no.3, Autumn 1978; and a list of typographical errors in the original article, together with correspondence from Norman de Gournay and my reply, in vol. 53, no.1, Spring 1979.

2 Patrick Curry, 'An Aporia for Astrology' in *Radical Astrology* papers (Radical Astrology Group, London, 1983).

3 Maggie Hyde, *Jung and Astrology* (Aquarian Press, London, 1992).

1

The Scourge of Astrology

The writings of astrologers... intrude everywhere; they corrupt philosophy, adulterate medicine, weaken religion, strengthen idolatry, destroy prudence, pollute customs, blight the heavens, and make men anxious, unquiet, and unfortunate in all things.

Pico della Mirandola[1]

THE demise of Astrology as a significant component in the intellectual life of the western world is part and parcel of the cultural shift that occurred between the fifteenth and eighteenth centuries. This period opens with the Italian Renaissance and closes with the Scientific Enlightenment. In fifteenth century Europe the astrological world-view 'intrudes everywhere', entering into almost every area of inquiry and belief. The astrology of particular judgments from horoscopes (judicial astrology) had always had its doubters, but the fundamental conception of a continuous pouring down of stellar influence was virtually unquestioned by critic and practitioner alike. Yet by the end of the 18th century astrology in any shape or form had been all but wiped out as a credible intellectual endeavour, its serious study confined to a small minority perceived as eccentrics.[2]

The present-day survivors marooned on the little island of modern astrology sometimes talk as if the ship never went down, and the subject is just as secure as it always was. A few look back to a golden age when the masters of the Art really knew what they were doing, and the modernists look forward to the new era, just around the corner. These comforting illusions can be maintained only if we are blind to our history. The small gains in credibility achieved here and there in the twentieth century revival are flotsam and jetsam in the sea-change of the modern imagination. The debate for and against astrology has gone to and fro over the centuries with the astrologers in the main being pushed further and further back, until we come into the modern era with few plausible arguments at our disposal.

In the course of this saga there have been dramatic incidents that epitomise the struggle. The most outstanding of these are two great attacks on astrology. The first, written in 1493-4, is the *Disputations against Divinatory Astrology* by Giovanni Pico della Mirandola. The second, in 1975, is the *Objections to Astrology* by '186 Leading Scientists'.

The wider cultural context of these assaults is crucial to understanding them. Taken at face value, they are both humanist critiques of astrology. Pico's text represents the culmination of a line of criticism from the great philosopher of the Renaissance, Marsilio Ficino. The criticisms expressed by Pico are drawn in large part directly from his mentor's unpublished attacks on the 'vulgar' astrologers of his day. The modern attack by the 186 scientists is all the more significant for being orchestrated to celebrate the one hundredth anniversary of the founding of the Ethical Humanism movement in the United States. Behind Pico stands Ficino and the brilliant project of Renaissance magical-religious humanism, and behind the 186 scientists we discover modern rationalistic humanism. However, despite some significant conclusions in common these two anti-astrologies turn out to have very different motives and foundations. While much effort is devoted in modern astrology to answering the reservations represented by modern science, I believe the earlier critique is more significant for us to answer. The stance of Pico, and more especially of Ficino, raises the most important of all questions for astrology. The implication of their critique, and the response of astrologers to it, forms the substance of this chapter.

MARSILIO FICINO AND THE RENAISSANCE CRITIQUE

Pico and Ficino both attacked the astrologers, but here we are presented with an immediate dilemma. Both these men are the archetype of the Renaissance magus – but why should *magicians* attack astrology? Even more puzzling, Ficino is an accomplished and learned horoscopic astrologer. One of his most influential and popular works, the *Three Books on Life*, consists in its major part of the medical-magical-astrological text 'On Obtaining Life from the Heavens'.

To unravel this puzzle we need to start with the background of Ficino's thinking. The rebirth of the learning of classical and high antiquity, and a restoration of its honoured place alongside Christianity, has come to give meaning to the term 'renaissance'. Under the patronage of the Medicis, Ficino had transformed the intellectual horizon of fifteenth century Europe. In 1463 he had published his translation of the *Corpus Hermeticum*. These mystical-magical texts, attributed to the dawn of history and the legendary Hermes Trismegistus

('Thrice-Greatest Hermes'), are now known to date from around the second and third centuries AD.[3] They had an extraordinary influence in the Renaissance and are the foundation of European hermetic occultism.

Many of the dialogues of Plato had only recently become available through Byzantine sources, and Ficino was the vessel for this transfusion of classical learning into European culture. He completed his translation of the works of Plato from the Greek into Latin in 1468, and went on to translate several neo-Platonic philosophers, including Plotinus. Based largely on the false authority and antiquity accorded to the *Corpus Hermeticum*, Ficino rehabilitated the magic of 'ancient Egypt' as the source of a wisdom tradition from which, so he believed, later Platonic and Christian revelations flowed. These texts were in large part responsible for the rise in status of magic from its dark medieval image to being central to the life and expression of the renaissance philosopher.

Early studies in medicine and the influence of his father's profession as a doctor are reflected in Ficino's celebrated medical treatise *Three Books On Life*, completed in 1489.[4] The third of these books offers a system of natural magic applied to practical medicine. In the European tradition, natural magic is in large part a branch of applied astrology. It has always had a close relationship with medicine, and this connection is probably best known to us in modern times through herbalism.[5] Natural magic refers to practices designed to employ the hidden virtues or qualities in all things, plants, gems, animals etc. The astrological *is* the system of those correspondences. Hence natural magic utilises astrology – and in European culture it is hardly conceivable to be a natural magician *without* being at the same time an astrologer.

There are several orders of magic, although in distinguishing them there is always an overlap in intentions and practices, well illustrated by Ficino himself. However, *natural magic* may be distinguished from forms that involve ceremony (*ceremonial* or *ritual magic*) or invocation of Intelligences (*celestial* and *daemonic magic*). Ficino's natural magic can be illustrated by his approach to the counter-balancing of negative planetary influences. Saturn, rising in his own natal horoscope, is the signature of the melancholy of the philosopher. Its depressing influence should be balanced by the Three Graces of Sun, Jupiter and Venus and this could be achieved by making use of their correspondences in music, colour, herbs and talismans.

Music was at the heart of things for Ficino and his views on astrological music therapy are discussed in the *Books on Life*. In the practices of the Platonic Academy which he gathered around him, the Orphic Hymns constituted a system of invocatory planetary music. These hymns were almost certainly combined into ritual,[6] which in principle takes them beyond natural magic. The employment of talismans, which Ficino rather cautiously discusses and clearly practised, also takes us to the limits of natural magic, where it borders on the realms of celestial and daemonic Intelligences.

Ficino lived and breathed astrological symbolism and he knew and honoured astrology's traditions and authorities. He cast and consulted horoscopes for himself and his friends, conducted his practical, cultural and magical affairs in accord with the heavens, wrote a treatise on medical astrology, and showed himself technically conversant with the subject. He was in every sense an astrologer. Yet he attacked the astrology of his day and fully concurred with Pico's similar critique. Why?

THE NEO-PLATONIC REFORM OF ASTROLOGY

It is clear from the *Three Books on Life*, as well as from other writings, that the type of astrology which Ficino wishes to promote is a reinterpretation of the practice of his day in line with hermetic tradition and the teachings of Plato. This project may justifiably be termed *neo-Platonic astrology*. It represents the integration of the craft of astrology with both the mystical Platonism of Plotinus (third century AD) and certain elements of hermetic occultism. Its practical emphasis appears particularly strongly in the fusion of natural magic and medical astrology. The purpose is the healing of bodies as well as the healing of souls.

A few ideas taken from the early chapters of the third of the *Three Books on Life* – 'On Obtaining Life from the Heavens' – will serve to indicate the richness and scope of this neo-Platonic astrology. Ficino observes that the whole cosmos is animate, which is demonstrated not only by the arguments of the Platonists but also by 'the testimony of the Arabic astrologers'. The foundation of astrology resides in the working of the World Soul (Anima Mundi), who contains in herself the 'seminal reasons of things'. These 'reasons' reflect or correspond to the *Ideas* in the Divine Mind; but for the Ideas to become materially manifested, they have to be brought to birth in the womb of the World Soul. She is the mother of all things, and she works through the virtues of the stars and planets. This therefore is Ficino's rationale for the signatures in the horoscope of birth:

> When the [World-Soul] gives birth to the specific forms and the powers pertaining to the species of things below, she makes them through their respective reasons with the aid of the stars and the celestial forms. But she produces the endowments peculiar to individuals... not so much with the aid of celestial forms and figures as by the location of the individual stars and the relation of the motions and aspects of the planets...[7]

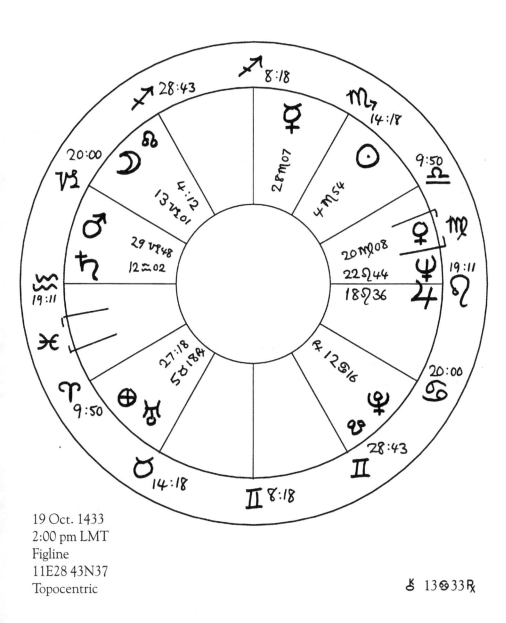

19 Oct. 1433
2:00 pm LMT
Figline
11E28 43N37
Topocentric

FIGURE 1 Marsilio Ficino

But mankind is not simply passive with respect to such heavenly gifts. Through the knowledge of astrology we can draw these gifts to ourselves. Here is the prescription for natural-astrological magic:

> No one should doubt that we ourselves and all things which are around us can, by way of certain preparations, lay claim to celestial things... those things which pertain to any planet should be sought and performed precisely when it has dignities... in its day and hour if possible, also when it is in its own house or in its exaltation or at least in its triplicity...[8]

So we obtain things from Venus through her affinities in 'carnelian, sapphire, lapis lazuli, brass (yellow or red), coral, and all pretty, multicoloured or green colours and flowers, musical harmony, and pleasant odours and tastes'. These benefits are enhanced by employing the natal horoscope:

> The specific rule for an individual would be to investigate which star promised what good to the individual at his nativity, to beg grace from that star rather than another, and to await from any given star not just any gift and what belongs to other stars, but a gift proper to that one.[9]

The difficulty of holding hard and fast with our original distinctions between the orders of magic is apparent: 'to beg grace from that star' cannot fall far short of direct invocation of the Celestial Intelligence of that star – in other words, of prayer. Lest we should be carried away by these gifts of magic, Ficino cautiously and wisely exhorts his reader 'by no means to ever attempt anything forbidden by holy religion'.

THE ATTACK ON DETERMINISTIC ASTROLOGY

It is only a minority of modern historians whose intellectual studies are informed by an intimate experience of the symbolic attitude to life, and fewer still who have any comprehension of the particular phenomenology of astrology. Both these capacities are required for any reliable assessment of the complex question of Ficino's attitude to the subject of astrology, the motives that led him to write his own *Disputation against the Judgment of Astrologers* and the basis of his explicit support for Pico's attack.[10]

When it comes to discussing magic and astrology Ficino was usually cautious in making statements that might offend the Church. There were perilous consequences for the charge of heresy. He sometimes withdrew behind the authors he was translating and commenting on, quoting rather than unequivocally committing himself to a dangerous opinion. The astrologer will not be much surprised to see the dominance of the Scorpio and Capricorn placings in Ficino's horoscope: Saturn rising with a political 11th house Moon in Capricorn, and the mysteries of the 9th house Mercury well hidden. He kept his opinion obscure when discretion required obscurity.

It is reasonable to infer that Ficino was developing and changing his views throughout his life, as well as testing them against his chosen authorities. His attitude to conventional astrology may well have been less explicitly critical before he began to study the neo-Platonic philosophers in earnest, above all Plotinus, who condemned the false logic and fatalism of the astrologers of his day.

The most striking feature in Ficino's approach is, put most simply, that he was a 'free will' astrologer, and his attack is on 'fate' astrology. Far from being a repudiation of horoscopic astrology, his project was one of sublimation, 'the incorporation of astrology into natural magic'.[11]

In terms of categories that will become clearer to the reader later in this book, Ficino exemplifies the struggle to express a divinatory and katarchic ('initiative') astrology within the limiting bounds of our tradition's Aristotelian – Ptolemaic model. This traditional model was being falsely and illogically interpreted to allow exact *deterministic* judgments by some astrologers – the 'petty ogres' that Ficino so heartily loathed – spoken with the certainty of oracular decisions. As the reappraisal by Angela Voss has shown, to understand Ficino we need to distinguish divination from determinism:

> ...the use of astrology as a basis for divination was... upheld by Ficino as its most legitimate application. His attack fell on those who abused the transformative potential of the divinatory moment by wanting to reduce it to a pseudo-scientific rational norm.[12]

This insight provides the touchstone to discern Ficino's motives in the various arguments he brings forward about astrology. His criticism broadly follows on two main lines already established by Plotinus. Firstly, he criticises the false logic of stellar determinism, both applied to the tiny contingent details of life but more significantly when applied to the human soul. In repudiating this determinism, Ficino hunts down the astrologers by deconstructing their logic. Their certainty in particular judgments cannot be justified by any appeal to the Aristotelian physics that they take for granted. This weakness in the astrologers' position will be discussed in the next section on Pico, who follows the identical critical method.

For Ficino, astrology is not science; it is 'poetic metaphor, not reason or logic'.[13] He affirms the possibility of astrology's significations working as *signs* and not as *causes*. Describing the horoscope, he asks:

> Is this figure not clearly above us? But so are the flight of birds and claps of thunder, nor yet is it usual to expect future things through these phenomena as *causes*, but as *indications* [my italics].

Similarly, heavenly configurations should be read as signs:

> ...no differently than in augury and auspices, when many things are thought to be portended through birds which not at all made by the birds.[14]

The sky, represented in the horoscope, is literally above us, but why should we on that account treat the omens we perceive in it as causative? This distinction between *signs* and *causes*, and the comparison of astrology to augury, is of the greatest importance for astrology, and will come up repeatedly in this study. It reflects a quite fundamental debate in ancient philosophy. It suffices here to remark that Ficino is adopting the Plotinian neo-Platonic compromise position between Plato and Aristotle, which with respect to astrology allows the stars and planets to be to some degree both signs *and* causes. The stars have only a limited scope for direct causation, says Plotinus, but 'their symbolic power extends to the entire realm of sense'.[15]

Following in the footsteps of Plotinus, we can recognise in Ficino the most significant attempt in the late European tradition to treat astrology as an art of the 'sign' (or in our modern terms 'symbol'). It is this above all, I believe, that demarcates astrology as divination from astrology as science. The foundation both of Ficino's own practice, and of his attack on contemporary astrologers, appears to be his magical-philosophical understanding. It is that understanding that divides his natural magic astrology from the deterministic astrology of his day.[16]

PICO

Pico arrived in Florence on the very day in 1484 when Ficino's translations of Plato were being published. It seemed to Ficino that his late patron, Cosimo Medici, was speaking to him from beyond the grave:

> By divine providence... while Plato was as it were being reborn, the hero Pico, who was born under Saturn [in] Aquarius (under which I similarly had been born thirty years earlier), came to Florence on the very day that our Plato was published, and miraculously breathed into me that ancient wish of the hero Cosimo concerning Plotinus, a wish totally hidden from me but breathed into Pico from heaven.[17]

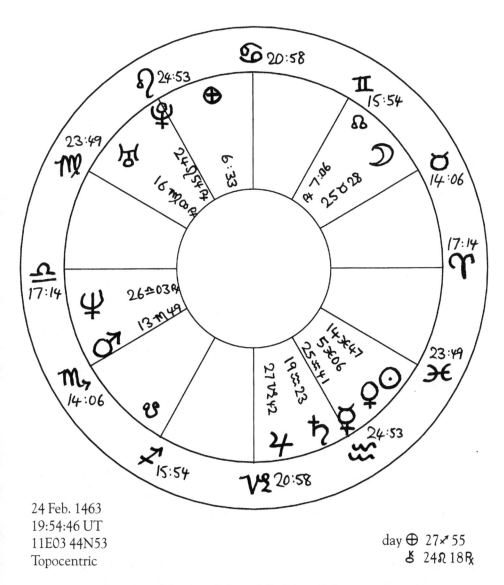

24 Feb. 1463
19:54:46 UT
11E03 44N53
Topocentric

day ⊕ 27♐55
☊ 24♌18℞

FIGURE 2 Pico della Mirandola
recomputed from version given by Luca Guarico

note: version given in Pico's collected works (1965, Umanismo, Florence) gives
asc. 5♌ 04.

This stroke of providence reveals the whole Platonic chain, Plato-Plotinus-Ficino-Pico. Ficino accepted the heavenly prompt and began the translation and commentary on Plotinus which Cosimo had always desired. Pico fulfilled all that might be expected from the omen of their meeting by becoming Ficino's most extraordinary pupil. Ficino called him a 'sublime son of Saturn'.

This Saturn-Aquarius theme draws our attention immediately onto the most striking similarity of all, the close applying Sun-Uranus oppositions in the horoscopes of both men. In their own day Ficino and Pico knew the philosophical Saturn and believed they were restoring the authoritative transmission of antiquity. From our perspective we see also the revolutionary Uranus, and as every astrologer knows it is Uranus who breaks once and for all the mould of the classical Saturnine order of astrology. In the same way, the awakening of the Renaissance points away from the orderly hierarchy of the Middle Ages and forward to the Age of Reason and the Scientific Enlightenment. The medieval mould is cracked in Ficino's neo-Platonism and finally broken open by the genius of Pico, which is why all the questions about astrology, magic, science and religion tumble out together. Only in this vast context can we begin to perceive the scope of the challenge that Pico puts to astrology.

In this light we can discern the Sun-Uranus configuration as a signature for the exalted Renaissance concept of 'Man the Magus'. Human being is recognised as *not determined by nature*, hence the rejection of a fate from the stars. In the act of self-conscious reason, man knows himself as completely separate. This is the first step towards the Cartesian ego of the Age of Reason: *cogito ergo sum*. 'The subject consciously stands opposed to the object'.[18]

Unlike the cautious Ficino, Pico directly manifests everything that might be expected from such an opposition. The charismatic young aristocrat created a rumpus in 1486 when he went to Rome with his 'Nine Hundred Theses', being a series of brief propositions on philosophy, religion and magic. His aim was to demonstrate the compatibility of the Jewish mystical system of Qabalah with Christianity. Pure Qabalah, working above the level of natural magic and directly in the intellectual part of the soul, was for Pico the highest form of magic and attained the realm of the angels. Most provocatively, he stated that magic and Qabalah are capable of proving the divinity of Christ, and this raised an immediate storm. Several of the theses were proclaimed heretical, and after a spirited defence which included his famous 'Oration on the Dignity of Man', Pico was eventually forced to retract them.

In the same period he came increasingly under the sway of the monk Savonarola, and at the time of writing his own *Disputations* on astrology he was living a life of renunciation and asceticism, preparing to enter Holy Orders. It has been suggested that Savonarola had a hand in prompting the *Disputations*, and certainly Savonarola was the first to make Pico's ideas on astrology widely public in 1494, naming him 'prince against the astrologers'.[19]

THE SCOURGE OF ASTROLOGY

Pico's *Disputations against Divinatory Astrology* was written in 1493-4, the year before his death. It was posthumously edited by his nephew, the humanist philosopher Gian Francesco Pico, and published in 1495.[20] By the effectiveness of his attack, and by the status it was later accorded, Pico stands in the first rank of assembled opponents of astrology from all ages, approaching the significance of St. Augustine a millennium before him. His text is rambling and occasionally inconsistent, but it effectively marshalled a range of critics from antiquity to his own times and it became a compendium to be dipped into or copied wholesale by later critics. Few of Pico's successors went beyond the *Disputations* and its direct influence as a model for later attacks can be traced into the seventeenth century.[21]

An extended outline of the main themes of the *Disputations* is given in Appendix 1, but I will summarise them here. Pico sets about undermining the claimed authority of astrology's tradition and its authority as revelation, and he exposes illogicalities in its theories. The signs of the zodiac, which he takes as astrology's primary symbolism, are demonstrated to be imaginative projections. He brings forward anecdotes showing the failure of predictions and in effect discusses the psychology of belief in astrology.

As with Ficino's unpublished attack, the core of his argument is an exposure of the fundamental logical flaw whereby astrologers confuse *universal causes* with *particular effects*, which they then imagine they can exactly judge. Particular differences between individual people or things, such as temperament and profession, arise from countless factors other than the stars. Their differences cannot be caused by the light and motion of the heavenly bodies because these have a quite different order of influence and produce only general and universal effects.

THE RUPTURE BETWEEN MAGIC AND ORTHODOX ASTROLOGY

From all that has been said about the grand context of the Renaissance and the brilliance of Pico, we might have hoped for something more profound. Apart from its Christian references and a few curious 'superstitious' lapses, Pico's argument strikes the modern reader as fiercely rationalistic. It is an effective exposition of Aristotelian logic, but with no role, except as delusion, for poetry and symbolism. The modern astrologer will certainly object that Pico has ignored symbol or forgotten about imagination. But to criticise Pico on these grounds would be to miss the point that these were not the grounds adopted by the astrologers of his time in justifying their subject.

It is a loss for astrology that Ficino's potential neo-Platonic reinterpretation, indicated most strongly in the *Books on Life*, was not carried through into the contemporary debate. He was a symbolist struggling against a deterministic conception, but did not see clearly how to resolve the problem. In the absence of any clear lead from Ficino, Pico limited himself to the more straightforward task of destroying astrology in the form in which its practitioners presented it, as a deterministic pseudo-science that threatened the dignity of man.

Unlike Ficino, there is no evidence that Pico practised astrology. There is no place for it in his high magic, and he therefore has no need to justify any element of its practice. The effect of this is that he can unreservedly employ the most negative or deconstructive features already established in Ficino's critique. But – and this is important to recognise – there is no indication that Pico felt a need to reject Ficino's natural-magical astrology, just as he accepted Ficino's natural magic as a weak and limited form compared with his own super-celestial, Qabalistic variant. Unless it is maintained that Pico had by 1493 totally rejected all of his previous views, his rupture with astrology cannot be plausibly interpreted as a rejection on his part of *magic*. Pico's attack is in a line derived from a neo-Platonic interpretation of Magia, using the weapons of Aristotelian logic. In the *Disputations* he describes his own anti-astrology in the lineage of '...our Marsilius [Ficino] following in the traces of Plotinus.'[22] The petty ogres of astrology commit a different crime altogether, the crime of astral determinism, and it is in this that we find the point of departure for the attacks of both Ficino and Pico.

Precisely because the Ptolemaic schema was fully and unquestionably established as the natural universe open to our ordinary senses, natural magic was necessarily part of that universe. This leads to a characteristic tendency for the astrologer to assume that in some fundamental way astrological influence is primary and 'above' the level of natural magic. It is in much the same spirit that astrologers believed that the rise of religions were dictated by planetary conjunctions, or that Christ's mission was determined by His horoscope. Working against this tendency is the vision of an angelic order of spiritual Being above even the stars. This is the order where neo-Platonism, most powerfully expressed by Pico, locates the true divinity of humanity. Hence the total intolerance by the Renaissance magus of the presumption of the dabbler in horoscopes, with his ignorant and baneful predictions subjugating even the soul to the stars.

The crux of the matter is that although astrological symbolism constituted the language of correspondences, and although certain forms of magic employed astrology and could be classed as astral, *astrology as a practice was not perceived by its practitioners as a branch of magic*. Hence the force of the observation by Angela Voss mentioned earlier, that Ficino's task, although clearly not Pico's, was the assimilation of a free-will astrology into natural magic.

The divergence between Magia and Astrologia long antedated the Renaissance, and it has continued to this day. Where we find astrology and its correspondences discussed by a magician, we enter a different world to that of the textbooks of the orthodox astrological tradition. This is immediately apparent in a work such as Cornelius Agrippa's *Three Books of Occult Philosophy*, published in 1533.[23] Astrology is treated in some depth, although non-horoscop-ically, to be employed in the service of magic rather than as a means of reading Fate. Mainstream astrology does not, however, seek a rationale derived from magic, neither does it see its practice as directly related to magical operations. In my observation, magical thinking does not inform conventional astrology even where the two approaches are found in the same individual. While magic and various forms of hermetism have always fully taken up astrological *symbolism* through the doctrine of correspondences, they have never found much joy in astrology's technical method and *theory*.[24]

I hope that the preceding discussion has made it more obvious why the attack on astrology published by Pico is of such moment for astrology. His polemic has origins in a critique from magical-religious humanism but it has formed the basis of so much of the later modern rationalist and scientific attack on astrology. The astrologers have thus achieved a notable feat of double exclusion for themselves, being excluded from both magic *and* science. The *Disputations* of Ficino and Pico comprise the manifesto of this double exile.

ASTROLOGICAL RESPONSES

How did the astrologers respond? The answer to this question leads us to a story that is quite as interesting as the initial attack, but first it is appropriate to consider the various ways in which astrologers present their subject.

We can discriminate different intentions in the production of either a *text-book* or a *discourse*.[25] The text-book consists of canonical statements about what the symbols of astrology 'mean', often combined with instructions enabling readers to do astrology for themselves. There may be some juxtaposing of different authorities, but this is usually limited to the requirements of establishing a canon.

The discourse has an altogether wider perspective, taking up the pros and cons of astrology's possibilities and setting the subject in a philosophical or cosmological context. It may be primarily directed to the practitioner who is adopting a philosophical approach to their practice, or it may be intended to woo intelligent outside opinion, in which case it may be a polemical response to previous attacks. This is the pattern adopted in the first significant published response to Pico, a lengthy treatise by Luca Bellanti which appeared in 1502.[26] The hallmark of the discourse is that even though it may refer to the specialised perceptions of the astrologer, the text is not in itself astrological, but it is *about* astrology.

The third mode, and much the most fascinating for astrologers, is that of *demonstration*. Here the text is geared primarily to the showing of symbolism as revealed through the craft of astrology. The 'casebook' is a typical example. Such a text is in itself astrological, and on that account it can only properly be read by astrologers.

In practice texts often combine two of these intentions and many text-books set out to excite the reader by 'showing' at the same time, but it is interesting to observe how styles change, reflecting wider cultural expectations. Amongst the Arabic and medieval Latin authorities of whom I have any knowledge, the predominant mode would seem to be that of the text-book. The element of discourse is commonly limited to the practical requirements of astrological cosmology, with only a gesture to philosophical questions as an answer to the critics. What is often striking is the minimal concern for demonstration. As with the influential *Speculum Astronomiae* of Bonatti, there is a dearth of horoscopes; astrology does not have to be proved or demonstrated, but asserted on authority.[27] Later astrologers show a greater awareness of demonstration – William Lilly is the superb example – as well as being forced into a wider discourse by the nature of the attacks being made on them from religion and philosophy.

THE DEATH PREDICTION

When it comes to considering the answers to Pico, then on the whole the discourses cannot be said to have had much effect. As I hope to prove in this study, given the limitations of the theory under which astrology has laboured, there is no satisfactory answer. There was, however, a remarkable astrological *demonstration* by way of an answer. Luca Gaurico's *Tractatus*, published in 1539, gives the version of Pico's horoscope with 17 Libra rising and reports the extraordinary circumstance of the death prediction made against Pico:

> He [Pico] was an Orator, Poet and most celebrated Philosopher, and published many most elegant books, and, very angry, published one volume against the astrologers of his time, since three of them had predicted death to him before the completion of the 33rd year of his life, from the direction of the ascendant to Mars, just as it so fell out. Luca Bellanti of Siena dissolved his arguments and old wives' tales, excusing him as having been ignorant of Astrology, despite being a most excellent philosopher.[28]

...since three of them had predicted death to him, just as it so fell out. Gaurico's report suggests that the *Disputations* were written as a consequence of the prediction. In any case Pico did in fact die before the completion of the thirty-second year of his life (17 November 1494).

Whether or not we take this story as plausible, the astrology is technically perfect. Gaurico doesn't need to describe it for the student – it is self-evident in the way that good symbolism often is. Mars afflicts the Moon by opposition in the house of death. This is wide by modern standards, but well within orb for a major lunar aspect in older conventions of astrology. Even without this opposition Mars would probably have been taken as anaretic (death-bringing), and the direction of the ascendant to Mars is a classic text-book example.[29]

Gaurico's report appears to be the primary published source of this story. I have not seen reference to any earlier version, but it seems significant that Bellanti, despite 'dissolving' Pico's arguments in 1502, does not refer to the prediction or mention Pico's death or nativity. The historical details and inconsistencies become of concern when we see the elaboration of the story that has occurred by the time it reaches its final legendary status in John Gadbury's dramatic text of 1662:

John Picus, Earl of Mirandula

> Few Genitures have had the like Fortune as this great Native hath had; for this hath been under the handling of the most able Astrologers the World was ever acquainted with, if we may believe that renowned Person Henricus Rantrovius in his Treatise of the Certainty of Astrological Predictions... where he mentions the Prediction of Picus's Death by several Astrologers by name, in these Words: ...John Picus, Earl of Mirandula, wrote a Book against Astrologers; and

they... to prove their Art to be true, predicted that the said Picus should not live past the 33 year of his Age, from the Direction of the ascendant to Mars...

Sir Christopher Heydon mentions the same thing, thus: 'Picus being foretold by three Astrologers, that he should not live above 33 years, (as Lucas Gauricus, and others, do witness) yet flattering himself with a false Comfort, as if he could wrangle away Death by writing against Astrologie, while he sought to prove the Art vain, his own Death concurring exactly with the time foretold by the Astrologers, confirmed it to be true; and more actually confuted that which he had written against it, then if all the world beside had conspired to answer him.'[30]

Gadbury throws in a contemporary death prediction for good measure by relating the story of Pierre Gassendi. In an extensive critique of astrology, Gassendi had suggested that even if the astrologers had come close with a prediction of Pico's death, this could be put down to an intelligent conjecture. It would be apparent that Pico was 'no long-lived Man, from his weakly Constitution, continual Labours of Minde, &c.' The French astrologer, Morin de Villefranche (Morinus), decided to answer Gassendi for his pains. Gadbury takes up the story:

...behold the great Justice of the Heavens! Gassendus that quarrelled at Astrologers for so certain and splendid a Demonstration of their Art, had, by an Astrologer, viz. Johannis Baptista Morinus, his own Death predicted from his Nativity, long before it came to pass, to make him amends for his ignorant and credulous Confidence.

Morin foretold that Gassendi would fall ill and die at the end of July or the beginning of August 1650. What is not mentioned by Gadbury is that Gassendi died in 1655, which does not give us confidence in Gadbury's eye for the niceties of historical detail.[31]

THE DILEMMA OF THE ASTROLOGERS

It is possible that a prediction of this sort was actually made to Pico, and this issue deserves research. We would need to locate the origin of this particular version of Pico's horoscope, to establish that it wasn't cooked up after the event, but these questions are not of primary concern here. Let us accept the report given by Gaurico and take both prediction and horoscope as true. In that case no orthodox astrologer of Gadbury's day would deny that *such a prediction is within the potential scope of astrological judgment.* All the details fit an eminently practical astrology, not even claiming too much in the way of exactitude in timing. But are we to rejoice, as Gadbury and others clearly do, that astrology can vindicate itself in the fates of its enemies?

Whether the story is historically true or not, the amplification of this legend reflects the desire of the astrologers.[32] Yet I doubt whether those who make and applaud this type of prediction comprehend the emotional and psychic power that it involves. Death is the undeniable event, the one absolute certainty of the future. This event, the 'ownmost possibility' of every mortal, equals and cancels the mystery of birth. There is an altogether total significance carried by this prediction. The first time I came across the death prediction legend I realised why Pico should be so angry with astrologers in the first place.

Assume for the moment that the astrologers involved consider themselves complete masters at judging the indications in the horoscope. If there is any possibility of a judgment not coming to pass – in that, for example, with care of his health Pico might lengthen his life – then to prove both astrology and their mastery of it, the astrologers have put themselves in the position of *wishing that the possible ill-fortune shall not be averted.* This is not a beneficent thing, but the untimely end of a relatively young man, one of the great intellects of his age. Does this mean that they wish him dead?

But the astrologers may answer that of course they have no personal ill-will to the unfortunate man. What they have done is to report something that, having been shown in the stars, is *immutably pre-ordained.* His death at that time is part of the great scheme of things which it is the purpose of astrology to announce to all.

Yet this is an equally uncomfortable position, and few astrologers who stop to think about it want to stay there. On the whole this thread in the astrological fabric is not supported by the authorities and the texts. It is a fatalistic instinct that appears to have first been fully expressed by the Stoic philosophers, and it has run as a thread through the later astrological imagination. It never gained justification in theory and cannot be supported by the Aristotelian – Ptolemaic definition of classical astrology. It is the unsustainable gap between astrology's theory and the deterministic mode of its practice, that critics such as Ficino and Pico easily see through. Quite apart from horary and other katarchic practices which will be discussed in later chapters, a major part of our tradition entertains *electional astrology,* showing that we can choose at least some part of our fate.[33]

I am not without sympathy for the position of the astrologers who answered Pico. They are blindly playing out roles already defined for them – fated – by the epic of astrology. However, seen against the rupture between Magia and

Astrologia, this legend is bad news for traditional astrology, and it is all the worse if it is historically true. There is a dark secret in this prediction, and it is a secret that goes to the troubled heart of judicial astrology. From the point of view of a magical sensitivity, 'realising' symbolism and seeing it materialised in the world is far from being a neutral and objective act. In their own desires, as Mars, lord of the 7th of open enemies in Pico's horoscope, the astrologers will him dead. Through Mercury, lord of the 9th in opposition to Pluto, they allow astrology to curse – whether they know it or not.

And curses can return. The astrologers predicted against the magus Pico, but it was astrology itself that was to sicken in his shadow.

NOTES

1 Quoted from the first book of his *Disputations against Divinatory Astrology*. See D. C. Allen, *The Star-Crossed Renaissance* (Frank Cass, London, 1966), p.23, and E. Garin, *Astrology in the Renaissance: The Zodiac of Life*, trans. C. Jackson and J. Allen (Routledge & Kegan Paul, London, 1983), p.82.

2 On the decline of astrology, see Patrick Curry, *Prophecy and Power* (1989), especially Part II: 'Life after Death: 1710-1800'; also the Introduction to his *A Confusion of Prophets: Victorian and Edwardian Astrology* (Collins & Brown, London, 1992).

3 The most authoritative translation of the *Corpus Hermeticum* is that of Brian P. Copenhaver, *Hermetica* (Cambridge University Press, 1992). This has supplanted W. Scott, *Hermetica*, 4 vols. (Oxford 1924-36, reprinted Boston, Mass., 1985). The spell of the ancient authority of these texts was broken by the scholarship of Isaac Causabon in 1614, 'a watershed separating the Renaissance world from the modern world': see for instance, Frances Yates, *Giordano Bruno and the Hermetic Tradition* (Routledge & Kegan Paul, 1964). Copehaver discusses the history of debate concerning the ultimate origin of the *Hermetica*; recent scholarship has begun to restore the view that elements of these teachings are of considerable antiquity, and of Egyptian origin.

4 Marsilio Ficino, *Liber De Vita*, trans. C. Kaske and J. Clarke *Three Books on Life* (critical edition with parallel text, State University of New York, Binghampton, New York 1989). An earlier translation by Charles Boer, *The Book of Life* (Spring Publications 1980 (University of Dallas, Irving, Texas, 1980), is of interest to the astrologer because of Boer's archetypal psychology sympathies, but his translation has been criticised.

5 The connection between Western herbal medicine, natural magic, and astrology, has been made explicit by Elisabeth Brooke, *The Woman's Book of Herbs* (Women's Press, London, 1992), and by Graeme Tobyn. *Culpeper's Medicine: A Practice of Western Holistic Medicine,*. (Element Books, Shaftesbury, 1997) It is a significant indication of the same connection that Alan Leo, to whom the 20th century astrological revival is so indebted, should have first learned his astrology from a Manchester herbalist, Dr. Richardson, who prescribed for him a herbal treatment for kidney trouble based on Leo's natal chart: see *The Life and Work of Alan Leo* by Bessie Leo et al. (Modern Astrology Office, London, 1919), pp20-22.

6 For Ficino's Orphic Hymns, see D. P. Walker *Spiritual and Demonic Magic from Ficino to Campanella* (Warburg Institute, London, 1958, reprinted Notre Dame Press, 1975).

7　*Three Books on Life Book*, III, ch.I, p. 247. The reference to the 'location of the individual stars' suggests position with respect to the local horizon, the basis of the astrological houses.

8　ibid., III, ch. 2, p249. The word 'house' here refers to what is usually termed 'sign' in modern astrology.

9　ibid., III, pp.255-81 *passim*.

10　Ficino commends Pico's attack in a letter to Poliziano of 1494 *Opera Omnia* (2 vols. continuous pagination, Basle, 1576, facsimile Turin, 1959, p. 958), contrasting the *poetic and metaphorical* approach of his writings on the Sun and Light, and his use of astrology in the *Books on Life*, with the need to rebut the portents claimed by the astrologers: '...just as... mixing poetry with philosophical matters, I sometimes by chance wander rather liberally, along with Plotinus I act more specifically and severely in order that the future will not be ungrateful to me, astrological portents having been refuted particularly by our Pico Mirandula. For I on no occasion affirm these things, rather I deride them with Plotinus, I rejoice in their having been rejected by Mirandula...' It must be emphasised that this rebuttal of what he elsewhere condemns as a vulgar misinterpretation of astrology cannot be held to be a late change of mind. It is consistent for Ficino certainly from the late 1470's, yet the *Books on Life* are as late as 1489. As Angela Voss points out, it is not enough to call Ficino 'vacillating' in his attitude to astrology. He is struggling to distinguish two different programmes for astrology, one of which he rejects, and one of which he (admittedly cautiously) affirms. Ficino's *Disputation against the Judgment of Astrologers (Disputatio Contra Iudicium Astrologorum)* has not been published in English translation. I have, however, consulted the provisional translation by Angela Voss.

　　For an outline of Ficino's arguments, see A. Voss *Magic, Astrology & Music: The Background to Marsilio Ficino's Music Therapy and his Role as a Renaissance Magus*, Ph.D. thesis (unpublished; Music Dept., City University, London, June 1992); p212-214. Angela Voss has summarised the issues involved in the following illuminating study: 'The Astrology of Marsilio Ficino: Divination or Science?', *Culture and Cosmos* (PO Box 1071, Bristol BS99 1HE) vol.4, no.2, Autumn/Winter 2000. This article and other more recent studies by Angela Voss are available on the internet (*dox reference 'Angela Voss'*).

11　A.Voss, op.cit., p192

12　ibid., p192

13　*Astrologia non est Scientia*. Angela Voss sees Ficino as being quite ironic in his critiques when he claims astrology is not knowledge but metaphor. Given his deep appreciation of metaphor, what looks like a put-down of astrology is actually a potent but disguised affirmation. (A.Voss, op.cit., p213).

14　A.Voss, op.cit. p217

15　Plotinus (c205-270 AD) is considered to be the major philosopher of neo-Platonism. The quotation is from his *Enneads* trans. S. MacKenna (1962), II.3.I.

16　The sundering of magic and astrology: it should be noted that despite writing an accomplished and technically proficient astrological text of wide general influence (Book III of the *Books on Life*), Ficino has been lost sight of as an authority in later astrology. The astrology of the Renaissance magus is entirely outside the orthodox tradition.

17　A.Voss op.cit. p191. There is doubt about the day, and as to whether the story represents poetic licence by Ficino.

18　Ernst Cassirer, *The Individual and the Cosmos in Renaissance Philosophy* (Pennsylvania University Press, paperback edition, 1972), p84.

19　E. Garin, *Astrology in the Renaissance* p.84

20　The *Disputationes adversus Astrologiam Divinatricem* by Giovanni Pico della Mirandola have been translated into Italian by E. Garin (Florence 1946). According to F. Leigh Gardner, *Bibliotheca Astrologica* (1911), the date of publication was 16 July 1495 (p.123). For reference to G. F. Pico see F. Yates op.cit pp. 113-14. G. F. Pico was scathing about Ficino's magic and probably wished to dissociate his uncle from it. As he was a 'humanist' in the modern sense, I believe this has led to Pico's critique of astrology being later interpreted more in the light of modern rational humanism, than in the light of Renaissance magical-religious humanism. A study of Ficino's critique and its relationship to Pico's critique restores the balance.

21 Mary E. Bowden quotes as 'clearly lineal descendants' of Pico's *Disputations* the attacks by Gassendi (1649) and Henry More (1660/1681). (*The Scientific Revolution in Astrology: the English Reformers 1558-1686* Ph.D thesis, Yale 1974, p.52). Bowden also traces Pico's influence on Kepler, which she suggests has been hitherto underestimated pp.110-11.

22 F. Yates, op.cit. p.114.

23 Henry Cornelius Agrippa, *Three Books of Occult Philosophy* (translation published London, 1651, reprinted Cthonios Books, 1986); also edition edited and annotated by Donald Tyson (Llewellyn, St. Paul, MN, 1993).

24 The divide in Western culture between magic and classical astrology is a large topic which I have only been able to lightly touch on, even though it can be glimpsed like a thread running through the whole *Moment of Astrology* thesis. The ability to bridge this chasm is the rare exception rather than the rule. The existence of the divide throws into relief the Aristotelian-Ptolemaic structure of our mainstream tradition, a formation which is incapable on its own of sustaining either a magical-religious or a mystical interpretation of astrology.

25 D. C. Allen in *The Star-Crossed Renaissance* op.cit., stimulated this way of categorising astrological texts (ch.I).

26 Luca Bellanti, *De astrologica veritate, et in disputationes Joannis Pici adversus astrologos responsiones* (Venice 1502).

27 Guido Bonatti, *Speculum Astronomiae* (Basle, 1550).

28 Luca Gaurico (Gauricus), *Tractatus astrologiae iudiciariae de nativitatibus virorum et mulierum* (1539).

29 Here are the positions in Pico's horoscope given by Guarico: MC 20 Cancer 58, Asc 17 Libra 12; XI 26 Leo 55, XII 24 Virgo 02, II 11 Scorpio 20, III 12 Sagittarius 00. Planets are given to the degree: Sun 16 Pisces, Moon 21 Taurus, Mercury 25 Aquarius, Venus 5 Pisces, Mars 12 Scorpio, Jupiter 28 Capricorn, Saturn 20 Aquarius; lunar node 7 Gemini 53. The RAMC is 112°38'. The horoscope has been cast for geographic latitude 45N.

The primary direction of the ascendant to the conjunction of Mars has been computed from the 32° arc of rotation required to bring Mars bodily onto the horizon (the arc is measured by the passage of the equator across the meridian and is equivalent to 2h 08m passage of time after birth). The equation of the arc to time follows the measure of Ptolemy, where 1° of the sky's rotation measures one year of life, hence the direction matures sometime within the 33rd year of life. Using the modern computation for the position of Mars, 13 Scorpio 49, decl. -14°12', the arc of direction is found to be 33°53'.

30 John Gadbury, *Collectio Geniturarum* (London, 1662).

31 P .Gassendi (1592-1655) Professor of Mathematics (=Astronomy) at Paris. For a discussion on Gassendi and Morin's prediction, see Jim Tester, *A History of Western Astrology* (Boydell, Woodbridge, Suffolk and Wolfeboro, New Hampshire, 1987), pp.230ff.

32 On the legendary amplification of the death prediction: by the time of Gadbury the story has been dressed up, when compared with Gaurico's account, until it becomes a perfect model of astrology. It is however important that it is still *plausible*, or else it leaves the realm of effective demonstration and enters into the separate domain of mythology. This may be the reason

why an even more dramatic early account has nevertheless not been taken up amongst astrologers. Pontis de Tyard *Mantice ou discours de la vérité de divination par astrologie* (published at Lyon 20 August 1558; Mercury at the 26th degree of Leo), records that 'Pico della Mirandola's death was foretold to the exact year, month and day, by the astrologers.' (See also D. C. Allen, op.cit., pp.78-81). This rendering has come into modern times, for example in Boll & Bezold *Sternglaube und Sterndeutung* (Leipzig, 1931), and taken up by J. Seznec, *The Survival of the Pagan Gods* (Bollingen/Princeton, 1972), p.61.

33 Even Morin allows electional astrology, despite the apparently absolute nature of some of his judgments.

2

An Anti-Astrology Signature

THERE has been nothing in recent centuries to match the impressive significance of the Renaissance critique – probably because astrology itself is less
intellectually significant than it was then. However, the critical impulse has been
sustained by a motley collection of humanists, astronomers, science-proselytisers
and fundamentalist Christians. If we look for anything to compare with Pico's
critique, we will have to settle for just one moment in modern times when the
impulse against astrology – and hence the question of astrology – came into sharp
focus. This was the attack on astrology published in the September/October
1975 issue of the American journal the *Humanist*.[1]

This was a concerted attempt to marshal the scientific establishment against
astrology, and at its heart was a statement circulated to 'leading scientists',
mainly from the US. One hundred and eighty-six of these signed the document.
We are talking about a hard-science elite, chiefly in the fields of astronomy and
physics, the majority of whom were holders of a professorship or equivalent post.
They included no less than eighteen Nobel Prize-winners.

The 'Objections' were drafted by Bart Bok, a former President of the
American Astronomical Society, Paul Kurtz, professor of philosophy and editor of
the *Humanist*, and Lawrence Jerome, a science writer. Coinciding with its
publication, the statement was circulated world-wide to journals and
newspapers, particularly in the hope of persuading them to curb the growth of
popular astrology through the sun-sign columns. Here is the statement, as it
appeared in the *Humanist*:

OBJECTIONS TO ASTROLOGY

A Statement by 186 Leading Scientists

Scientists in a variety of fields have become concerned about the increased
acceptance of astrology in many parts of the world. We, the undersigned –
astronomers, astrophysicists, and scientists in other fields – wish to caution the
public against the unquestioning acceptance of the predictions and advice given

privately and publicly by astrologers. Those who wish to believe in astrology should realise that there is no scientific foundation for its tenets.

In ancient times people believed in the predictions and advice of astrologers because astrology was part and parcel of their magical world view. They looked upon celestial objects as abodes or omens of the Gods and, thus, intimately connected with events here on earth; they had no conception of the vast distances from the earth to the planets and stars. Now that these distances can and have been calculated, we can see how infinitesimally small are the gravitational and other effects produced by the distant planets and the far more distant stars. It is simply a mistake to imagine that the forces exerted by stars and planets at the moment of birth can in any way shape our futures. Neither is it true that the position of distant heavenly bodies make certain days or periods more favorable to particular kinds of action, or that the sign under which one was born determines one's compatibility or incompatibility with other people.

Why do people believe in astrology? In these uncertain times many long for the comfort of having guidance in making their decisions. They would like to believe in a destiny predetermined by astral forces beyond their control. However, we must all face the world, and we must realise that our futures lie in ourselves, and not in the stars.

One would imagine in this day of widespread enlightenment and education, that it would be unnecessary to debunk beliefs based on magic and superstition. Yet, acceptance of astrology pervades modern society. We are especially disturbed by the continued uncritical dissemination of astrological charts, forecasts, and horoscopes by the media and by otherwise reputable newspapers, magazines, and book publishers. This can only contribute to the growth of irrationalism and obscurantism. We believe that the time has come to challenge directly, and forcefully, the pretentious claims of astrological charlatans.

It should be apparent that those individuals who continue to have faith in astrology do so in spite of the fact that there is no verified scientific basis for their beliefs, and indeed that there is strong evidence to the contrary.

(*Humanist*, September/October 1975)

Five hundred years after Pico, the writings of the astrologers still 'intrude everywhere', and continue to make men, especially scientific men, 'anxious and unquiet'.

The *Humanist* featured supporting articles by Bok and Jerome. Bok takes up the impossibility of a physical foundation for astrology. He rejects the idea of qualitative distinctions between the various planets and questions the idea that minute gravitational, electromagnetic or radiative effects could have special significance for the individual at certain precise moments, such as birth:

> Astrology demands the existence of totally unimaginable mechanisms of force and action.

He concludes with a statement drafted thirty-five years earlier by the psychologist Gordon W. Allport. It had been endorsed at the time by the Society for the Psychological Study of Social Issues, and it attacked astrology and other forms of occultism as 'unwholesome flight from the persistent problems of real life ...our fates rest not in our stars but in ourselves'.

Jerome's article takes up the question of magic. Astrology, he says, has nothing to do with the physical effects of the stars. Such considerations obscure the real issue. People in earlier times believed in astrology because it could not be separated from their magical world view:

> ...very few writers have come to the nub of the matter: astrology is false because it is a system of magic, based on the magical 'principle of correspondences' ... astrology arose as magic and physical arguments and explanations ... were only attempts to associate the ancient 'art' with each important new science that came along.

The attack therefore has two main themes. Firstly, although it cloaks itself in pseudo-science, astrology has no scientific basis or verification. It is therefore an irrational belief. Secondly, it is a system of *magic*. It is taken entirely for granted that no further inquiry is needed once this is established – magic is without question false. From these considerations it follows that believers in astrology are ignorant or deluded, and its practitioners are charlatans. The popular promotion of astrology encourages irrationalism and leads people into an unwholesome attitude in which they do not take responsibility for their own actions.

COMPARISONS WITH THE CRITIQUES OF
FICINO AND PICO

Both the similarities and the differences of this attack on astrology, compared with the one published by Pico, are instructive. Starting from a *magical* and *religious* world-view, Ficino and Pico regard the determinism of classical astrology as:

- *irrational*, having a faulty logic of causes;
- *unethical*, weakening human dignity and spiritual freedom.

Judicial astrology as a whole for Pico, and in part for Ficino, is founded in *bad logic* and a *poor religious understanding*. Starting from a *scientific* and *rationalist* world-view, the modern humanists regard all astrology as:

- *irrational*, incapable of verification by science;
- *unethical*, weakening human dignity and rational freedom.

The whole of astrology is founded in *magic*.

The common concerns with rationality and human dignity give the two attacks a great many arguments in common, and yet these arguments are employed in the service of different intellectual and spiritual ends. The humanism of the fifteenth century Italian Renaissance and the humanism of the twentieth century begin to look very different as we probe beneath the surface. In modern thought *science has taken the place once occupied by philosophy and religion* and is the arbiter of rationality. As ultimate authority Pico appeals to religion and is guided in his attack by the zealous monk Savonarola; as ultimate authority the modern humanists appeal to 186 scientists, and most especially '18 Nobel Prizewinners'. There, in one principal detail, is revealed the profound difference in the spirit of these two attacks.

This brings out all the more painfully the circumstance that astrology finds itself on the losing side on both counts: excluded from a magical world view and equally excluded from science. I believe that Jerome is in his blundering way right, and has indeed got to 'the nub of the matter': astrology is part of an ancient magical-religious world view. Historically, astrology has never properly recognised this and disguises itself from itself in the garb of science.

HOW DO THE ASTROLOGERS RESPOND?

This time round, thankfully, there seem to have been no dire predictions laid against the challengers. As in Pico's day, the main response to attack comes in the form of a *discourse* on astrology, rather than in demonstration – but it is a discourse on the scientific possibility of astrology. There is a strong element of *demonstration* as well, to prove to the sceptic that there 'must be something in astrology', yet this demonstration is no longer in the language and method of symbols but in probabilities and statistics. Modern humanists attack and astrologers defend, in both cases using the language of science. It is in this way that astrology has allowed its domain to come under the arbitration of modern scientific rationalism, at the expense of its philosophical self-awareness. This is a theme that will occupy us in some detail in the following chapters, but now I would like to turn to the more truly symbolic question, of whether astrology itself will aid us in some understanding of these attacks on astrology.

THE HOROSCOPE IN ITS CONTEXT:
AN ANTI-ASTROLOGY SIGNATURE

In the attack in the *Humanist*, a single horoscope is included in Bok's article, alongside a diagram and explanation relating to its construction. The horoscope had originally been used in a previous article by Margaret W. Mayall in 1941 and it is included by Bok merely to illustrate horoscope construction. A diagram showing the celestial sphere to illustrate the relevant astronomy is given along with it. As it happens, the diagram is in error and cannot produce the houses of the horoscope it is supposed to represent. No astrological interpretation is given.[2]

The example horoscope is not the birth map of Mayall, Bok, Kurtz, or Jerome.[3] There appears to be no special reason for the choice of this map. Any other time and place could just as easily have been chosen. Why this horoscope was selected is not known. Someone may have gone to the New York House Table for 0° Leo MC, or chosen 4am as a convenient round time for the purposes of showing the construction of a horoscope. Perhaps it was the birth data of somebody's aunt. Who knows? The details appear to be completely irrelevant. Margaret Mayall, back in 1941, chose this map, and no other.

Astrologers belong to that section of humanity that believes there is usually more going on in life than meets the eye. Could there be some hidden meaningfulness about the horoscope that Mayall unwittingly chose? It was certainly in this spirit, hoping and half expecting that something would show itself, that I first encountered the horoscope published with the attack – 'A Conventional Type of Natal Horoscope'.

This horoscope turned out to exceed all expectations and is charged with significance. My first task here is to demonstrate that this map has a public quality as a *signature* for the attack on astrology. By this I mean that its significance is not something that I simply imagine, but that on any ordinary reading of the symbolism it is 'there' for other astrologers. The word 'signature' refers to some symbolism or astrological identity by which is shown an important truth about the subject matter.

The most obvious symbolism relating to the attack is that of the Moon-Uranus opposition, falling across the 9th-3rd axis. These are houses of philosophy and mind, with the 3rd house emphasis being on literal or rational understanding. Uranus, the first sky god, is a general symbol for the sky-sciences of astrology or

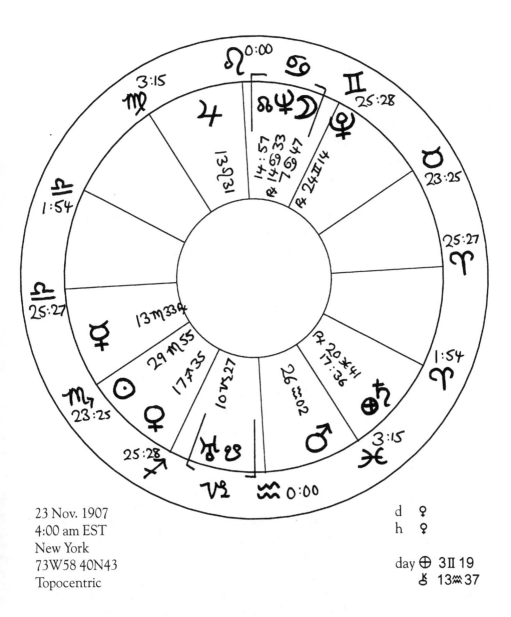

23 Nov. 1907
4:00 am EST
New York
73W58 40N43
Topocentric

d ♀
h ♀

day ⊕ 3Ⅱ19
⚷ 13♒37

FIGURE 3 An Anti-Astrology Signature: the horoscope used in
the *Humanist* attack

astronomy. Its placing in Capricorn in the 3rd suggests a limited and materialistic conception of the subject, more appropriate in this context to the astronomers. The Moon in Cancer in the 9th is swimming in the great sea of popular religions such as astrology, all of which according to their critics offer comfort and security (Cancer) to the gullible masses (Moon-Neptune). The astronomers challenge popular astrology on the opposition of Uranus in Capricorn to the Moon in Cancer.

In addition to this appropriate symbolism describing the attack, there is a close square of Mercury to Jupiter. These planets have a natural affinity with affairs of the 3rd and 9th houses respectively, so the initial approach to interpretation is reinforced. It testifies to conflict between contradictory ways of thought.

A broad natal-astrology style approach is enough to bring this horoscope to life. However, traditional horary offers a more discriminating technique in cases like this, where the subject matter is narrow and well-defined.

We can take the *Humanist* attack as a whole, and the horoscope that signifies it, as 'asking a question of astrology'. Questions concerning any higher branch of learning belong to the 9th House. This allows us to locate horary significators, and decide whether the map is *radical*, i.e. appropriate in its symbolism and therefore readable within the limits of the horary approach.

I will start with the Moon. This is a universal cosignificator in all horary questions, and is most usually given to the one asking the question. In some types of horary, however, the Moon shows the quesited (the thing inquired about), because it is this that has 'made the action' in the situation, which is what the Moon in general signifies. Here, I believe the Moon in the 9th house of astrology is a cosignificator for astrology. This is consistent with our original non-horary approach, observing the big opposition across the 9th-3rd, astrology (Moon) and astronomy (Uranus).

This brings out another detail which the horary eye will not miss. Uranus has cut in ('prohibition') in an attempt to stop the Moon making her way to Neptune in the 9th. The attack is geared to astronomers putting a spanner in the works (Uranus in Capricorn) of the popular media usage of astrology. This dissemination, so we are told, 'can only contribute to the growth of irrationalism and obscurantism' which sounds like the Moon and Neptune. The interception of these planets in the 9th suggests the role of astrology as latent mysticism or closet religious belief. We need only add that popular interest in the subject is usually attributed to women, and the main theme of the Moon becomes complete.

But where are the humanists? Libra rises, a sign of logic and rationality, and Venus in Sagittarius gives them an optimistic image. Venus as ruler of the ascendant is the primary significator for those who ask the 'question'. Their

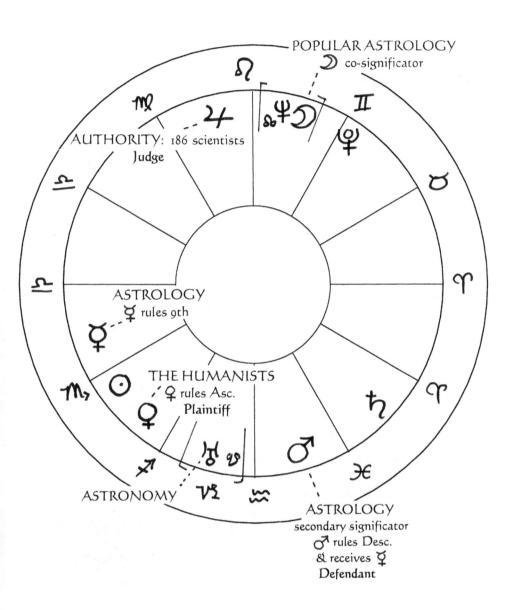

FIGURE 4 Astrology on trial
using Horary method to locate significators in the anti-astrology signature

friends, the astronomers and astrophysicists who form the core group amongst the scientists who brought the attack, are indicated by Uranus. There is a minor testimony to this alliance in the detail of the parallel of declination between Uranus (23 S 23) and Venus (23 S 32). The astronomers find themselves on the same side of the street as the humanists who have initiated the attack.

So how does this Venus show us the conditions of the attack? William Lilly's discussion on matters concerning the 9th house gives indicators which show whether or not an individual might benefit from the pursuit of a branch of knowledge. True knowledge, and benefit from it, are shown where there is a favourable application between the rulers of the ascendant and the 9th, 'the more so if it be with Reception'. In this chart, Venus has no relationship with planets in the 9th, nor with its lord, Mercury. The two significators actually invert the requirement for knowledge and benefit by being out of aspect and in mutual detriment, with Mercury in the sign of Venus's detriment and Venus in the sign of Mercury's detriment. Knowledge is spoiled. Moreover, Venus applies to the square of Saturn. The high hopes of the humanists (Venus) are stultified, since they are unable to comprehend astrology's order of reality. As Lilly remarks:

> If an infortune aspect either the Lord of ninth or first, the man hath wearied himselfe, and will doe, but to no purpose, for he shall never attain the perfection of the knowledge he desires.[4]

Saturn, obscure in Pisces, gives a shadowy indication of the imaginative limitations under which the attack labours. Note also that Saturn disposes Uranus in the 3rd, showing the materialism that clouds the vision of the astronomers.

The initiative is on the road to nowhere, but where does it *come from?* Venus separates the trine of Jupiter, its dispositor. Venus in Sagittarius, showing the humanists, is under the rule of Jupiter, regal and splendid, kingly and noble in Leo – the Nobel Prize-winners. By nature and sign, and by its prominent house location in the 10th, it is symbolic of the learned corporate authority of 186 leading scientists. Jupiter is the universal symbol of religion, and science has become the Church of Light in the modern age, the guardian and administrator of our ways of thought. It has replaced religion as judge in the highest court.[5]

Once we have established a reasonable understanding of Jupiter the whole horoscope begins to take shape. Now we can immediately see the extraordinary significance of the close and angular Mercury-Jupiter square. Astrology is shown by its primary significator: Mercury lord of the 9th rising. Mercury in Scorpio – deceitful and occult. This is the criminal element, the charlatan, the vagrant who professes to tell fortunes, hauled before the Magistrate.

THE MEASURE OF TIME

Tracing the pattern of the symbolism has brought us from the humanists back to the subject they challenge. But before attempting to discern further how astrology itself is shown, I will show how astrological timing substantiates the radicality of this signature beyond all reasonable doubt.

A feature of the 1975 attack that was obvious to all astrologers at the time was its coincidence with the first contact in a series of Saturn-Uranus squares. This fell on *4 October 1975*, with Saturn at 1 Leo 27 and Uranus at 1 Scorpio 27. The *Humanist* magazine which launched the attack was the *September-October* issue. This square seemed a significant comment on a battle amongst the stargazers; modern astrology often takes the sky-god Uranus as a symbol, and Saturn is an indicator of time, fate and determinism. A glance at the anti-astrology horoscope shows the relevance of this configuration as a transit. Uranus passed square the MC on its Scorpio ingress (8 September) and Saturn crossed the MC on its Leo ingress (17 September).

The publication of this horoscope is what brings it to life and the progressions make this explicit. By October 1975 the ascendant had progressed to 18 Sagittarius 00 – conjunct Venus, the ascendant ruler. Note also that Venus herself had progressed to the IC in 1941, the year of the original publication of this map in Bok and Mayall's earlier attack. Hence the chart was in all likelihood conceived in 1941 (Venus progressed conjunct IC), but its real showing was in 1975 (ascendant progressed conjunct Venus).

The second major direction for this period brings out the role of Jupiter, representing the authority invoked by the humanists. By 1975 the Sun and Jupiter had progressed into opposition, and were at the same time brought into potent manifestation by a sextile and trine respectively from the progressed MC.[6]

We therefore find symbolically appropriate directions of the first rank, measuring to the year of the attack. They involve progressed angles and the Sun, together with Venus (the humanists) and Jupiter (the 186 scientists). From these considerations I conclude that the 1907 horoscope, arbitrarily derived decades before its star turn, not only *symbolises* the 1975 attack, it also *times* it.[7]

THE GREAT ESCAPE – MERCURY AND JUPITER

But let us now return to the Mercury-Jupiter square, which is a primary symbolism for the whole issue of astrology and anti-astrology. Jupiter in Leo in

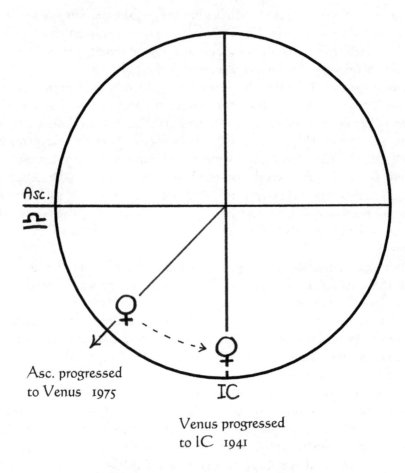

FIGURE 5 Venus, ruler of the horoscope, times its two publications in
1941 and 1975

the 10th is the authority of modern science and Mercury is the charlatan of astrology, an obscure occult art. Charles Carter's description of these two planets in difficult aspect is beautifully appropriate for the struggle that modern thought has with astrology:

> The mind may be sceptical in religious matters, or, on the other hand, there may be superstition; that not uncommon person, the superstitious infidel, seems to come under these configurations. It is often found in maps of those who have 'religious difficulties'... the native tends to exaggerate and scorns the dull formality of facts.[8]

There is no doubt at all that the negative reading of this Mercury-Jupiter square describes astrology's opponents admirably. How easy it is to see these bigots with their naive scientism as 'superstitious infidels'. They have certainly scorned the 'dull formality' of the fact that even within the constraints of their much-lauded modern scientific method there have been positive results for astrology, sufficient to merit discussion and further inquiry. But as many similar instances have warned us, the last thing some of our most vociferous opponents are interested in is the truth of the matter.

However, there is no cause for smugness in the face of ignorant opposition, because we can hardly ignore in this symbolism an equally explicit censure of astrology. The square is *mutually applied* by both planets. Mercury – astrology – is far from being an innocent victim. Mercury retrogrades into the square of Jupiter. Drifting backwards, as if by default and lack of critical self-evaluation, it has brought upon itself the challenge from authority. Using the descriptive categories of traditional horary, Mercury is acting like a thief (by being angular and also peregrine – out of its triplicity, term or face). Mercury is also 'mute' in the water signs, and being retrograde in Scorpio shows that astrology hides a secret – or more plainly does not tell the truth about itself. Perhaps this Mercury is so dumb that it doesn't even know it is telling lies. As if for our benefit here, in his description of Mercury-Jupiter afflictions, Carter adds:

> ...there is a wool-gathering tendency ...judgment is poor and the native is not likely to give good advice, especially in matters coming under either planet. He is a poor prophet, and astrologers with these afflictions are not likely to win credit for themselves or their art so far as predictive work is concerned.

The interpretation of this square is no less appropriate for we astrologers. We are the people who have made wool-gathering into a profession, have manifestly poor judgment about our subject, and despite all our claims, unimpressive powers of prophecy – 'not likely to win credit for themselves or their art'. Even if we let modern astrology off the hook by limiting the symbolism to a description of our opponents' misconceptions, the state of Mercury suggests that our own (non)description of astrology has fuelled those misconceptions. The mute retrograde obscuration of debate within astrology is reflected in the dearth of dialogue with the rest of modern culture.

So what are the prospects for astrology? The horary approach offers a truly decisive answer here. Close though the Mercury-Jupiter aspect is – the two planets apply within 2' of arc – *the exact square never forms*. Nine hours later, with the square just 1' wide, Mercury goes on its station, turning direct. In horary terms, perfection of the square is denied by the 'refranation' of Mercury.[9] Mercury – astrology – tricks his way through by the narrowest of margins, and even Jupiter has to let him slip by. For the square to be broken, Mercury has to turn in his retrograde motion and apply to the trine of Neptune. In the same way it is required of astrology that it should change its current course. I believe we should admit something which our more perceptive critics sometimes hold against us. In our usual description of our subject, its foundation in a magical-religious inspiration has been obscured. The materialism and positivism of our opponents is the complement to a misleading materialism and positivism within astrology itself. If astrology in truth operates according to principles that do *not* belong in present-day science, then astrologers should not present the subject as if it is really a variant of science.

The Moon in the anti-astrology chart gives us an additional image of the turn required in astrology. After her battering from Uranus, the Moon applies trine Mercury before she makes her mysterious conjunction with Neptune. This suggests the need for reform which can free astrology from its historical conceptual bondage (Moon opposite Uranus in Capricorn in the 3rd). We need to find better ways of speaking about its theory (Mercury lord of 9th and 11th).

Mercury and the Moon are primary significators for astrology in this map, but other planets are also directly involved. I suspect that Mars has some affinity for modern scientific astrology, or certainly of an objective and organised approach. Apart from ruling the 7th house (the 'other party' to the humanists who move the attack), Mars is a dispositor of Mercury (astrology). It is a significant detail that Mars is located in the area brought forward by Carter as an 'astrologer's degree', around 27 Leo-Aquarius.[10]

With Mars configured we might expect serious practitioners to come out fighting in response. In fact they did no such thing. The debate that ensued was mostly concerned with a defence of the statistical researches of the Gauquelins, but as I have already suggested, to defend astrology on the grounds of science is really no defence at all. Astrology in the current age can hardly be said to have much sting. The lack of response is possibly suggested by this rather abstracted and objectified Mars, inhibited by its dispositors Saturn and Uranus, and located out of the two primary configurations (Mercury-Jupiter and the lunar aspects).[11]

The other planet elbowing its way into the question is Pluto, on the 9th and in mutual reception with Mercury, lord of the 9th. This is a potent testimony to the radicality of this map along the lines of astrology and anti-astrology. In the Mercury – Pluto reception, there is the possibility of an annihilation of astrology (Pluto wiping out the 9th). Our opponents are not the real problem. The mutual reception with Mercury points back to the theme that I believe comes up over and over again in this signature and in the reality it signifies – astrology's annihilation could be effected only from *within*, if the very condition of its meaningfulness became abnegated even for the astrologers themselves.

Only when Pluto is accepted in all its blind and destructive potential might we have the possibility of the more optimistic reading of transformation. This is yet another play on the turn shown by Mercury. It requires a recognition by astrologers of where their astrology 'comes from'. Astrology, a 9th house affair, is shown here to have an intimate connection with the occult 8th. Pluto is enthroned on on the 9th house cusp. Mercury, in reception to Pluto, is in Scorpio, the 8th sign. If we make the reception by degree, in the manner of modern horary practice, Mercury goes into the 8th.[12] Even the Sun on the cusp of the eighth and ninth Signs discloses the same theme, and opens onto another register of symbolism, beyond what can be reasonably traced out here.[13] We may describe this play of eight and nine in various ways, but whichever form of words is chosen we arrive at a symbolism that suggests astrology is derived from a *magical-religious* world view, although it may equally be referred to as an *occult art*.

Astrology has many masks to disguise itself. Its most successful manoeuvre since the 1930s has been through its contact with depth psychology, and with psychoanalysis, reflected in the relation of Mercury and Pluto ('the talking cure'). In mythical terms, Hermes (Mercury) has found passage in forbidden realms by wearing the cap of invisibility belonging to Hades (Pluto). The very concept of the Unconscious is itself the occult's most sophisticated disguise.

However Mercury twists and turns, the critics of astrology certainly have no trouble sniffing out the odour of occultism. The problem has always been most critical for us, the astrologers. We are the ones who have disguised the question under a surface of rationalism and objectivity, which has left largely unspoken the implications of a discipline founded in mystery.

Some astrologers might not agree with details of my interpretation or certain of the conclusions. Some will not go as far, while others may take the symbolism further than I have so far imagined. However, my main task in this chapter will have been fulfilled if the reader who is an astrologer is convinced that the horoscope really does symbolise various circumstances of the humanist attack on astrology. Paul Kurtz, in an editorial note for the *Humanist*, tells us that

> the American Ethical Union and the American Humanist Association have long been opposed to cults of unreason and irrationalism. What better way to demonstrate this in [the] anniversary issue than by a major critique of astrology.

In the categories of modern scientific thought astrology is entirely unreasonable. Yet it has its own rationale, and survives as a stubborn witness to an alternative vision of reality.[14] What better way to demonstrate this reality than the 'chance' appearance on such a momentous occasion of a horoscope that exactly symbolises the attack – an anti-astrology signature.

ASTROLOGERS OBJECT!

At this point I cannot avoid the fact that the whole project of this interpretation invokes some opposition, not from outsiders, but from astrologers themselves. Moreover this opposition, more convincingly than any particular interpretation I might bring forward, demonstrates the uncomfortable dilemma of astrology's theory and definition – a dilemma that the anti-astrology signature signifies.

Soon after the publication of my original interpretation of the horoscope it received a strong rebuttal from the late Norman de Gournay, an astrologer of many years' experience. While 'agreeing with the necessity to answer our opponents', he stated his opinion that the method I had used was itself 'contrary to the nature of astrology'. This is to say that the very method I have used to interpret the symbolism of anti-astrology is itself anti-astrology. De Gournay's crucial objection was that my interpretation ignores 'one of the two hypotheses on which astrology is founded', namely 'the supreme significance of beginnings':

> ...every astrological chart is cast for the precise time and place of the beginning of that particular person or thing which the map exclusively signifies, and about which the interpretation informs us. Therefore, unless Mr. Cornelius claims that the attack on astrology commenced precisely at 4 am on 23 November, 1907, at New York, the chart he interprets is obviously not 'a symbolic representation of the attack upon astrology'. All that can be claimed is that it symbolises an unspecified birth, or other beginning, which may have occurred at New York at that time.[15]

It should be noted that de Gournay does not even consider the possibility of the map's symbolism being appropriate. As far as he is concerned, on principle it *cannot* be significant in the way I claim.

Let me at this point make clear that these criticisms should not in any way be discounted as insubstantial. De Gournay's rebuttal is logical and consistent, and is fully representative of the mainstream classical tradition of Western astrology that has come down to us from Ptolemy. The relevant tenets of this tradition will be reviewed in detail in Chapter 5.

I had a similar response to that of Norman de Gournay on another occasion, once again from an astrologer whom I had every reason to respect. Indeed it is only an experienced astrologer with a discriminating knowledge of the tradition who would be stirred by the Plutonic threat in the anti-astrology signature. The cotton-wool generalised meaningfulness of some approaches to modern practice would not discern the conceptual issues at stake. An elderly French astrologer admitted to me that my interpretation of the symbolism appeared sound, but that if my demonstration was indeed true this represented a destruction of astrology as he knew it. My answer to this is that the implications demand a transformation of *theory*, but far from being destructive this could deepen our experience of symbol while illuminating certain paradoxes of practice that have hitherto defied analysis. How and why this might be so will, I trust, emerge over the course of this book.

THE PROBLEM OF TIME

The key to this discussion is the astrological treatment of Time. No amount of juggling with the problem of beginnings can get round the classical objection to my demonstration of the anti-astrology signature, because the horoscope I have used is essentially a-temporal with respect to its subject matter. It is a-temporal and a matter of mere contingency because with as much or as little reason Margaret Mayall could have chosen any other time. Other than the brute and non-reasonable fact that she did years ago actually choose this map, it has no logical or material connection with the 1975 attack. Yet although the horoscope is *not the time* of its subject-matter, nevertheless, as has already been shown, it *measures the time* of its subject-matter.

The second hypothesis of astrology, according to Norman de Gournay, is the hermetic aphorism: 'That which is above is like unto that which is below'. De Gournay rightly adds the observation that this likeness is to be read as a *correspondence* of above and below, and should not be materialised into 'cause and effect'. The demonstration of the anti-astrology signature validates the symbolism of astrology – and therefore is a representation of 'as above, so below' – but shows that the working of astrology does not necessarily require same-timeness at a key moment of its history to connect horoscope and subject-matter. Against the taken-for-granted assumption of our classical astrology, I will assert that the ground for the coming-to-pass of astrological effects or showings is *not founded in a coincidence in objective time* of heavens above and event below.

Now if 'same-timeness' of heavens and an event, especially a beginning, is not the real basis of astrology, then what is? An exploration of this issue will concern us in later chapters, but a broad indication of the path I am taking can be given by suggesting that we should look in the direction of *significant presentation of the symbol to consciousness*. Same-timeness is usually part and parcel of significance, but as the current unusual case illustrates, astrology does not finally depend on it.

There is a long way to go in our discussion before such a radical conclusion becomes meaningful, however. At stake here are the conceptual foundations of astrology. The questions raised are difficult ones. Because they defy the conventional rationalisations employed in our tradition, there is a continual temptation to suppress symbolic phenomena – such as the 'impossible' working of the anti-astrology map. A certain courage is needed. Astrology will have to recover the connection with its sources if it is to survive the pressures imposed upon it by alien conceptual structures – especially those of modern rationalism and science. But for now, I would ask only that we return to the map as it presents itself: the single horoscope appearing together with a great attack upon astrology. That this map should astrologically declare its own context and usage is truly the gentle, poetic answer that astrology itself gives to its opponents – and to us.

THE PICO CONNECTION

There remains to be mentioned a further turn of the symbolism, integral to the main argument of this book. Some time after the original debate about the *Humanist* attack, I looked at earlier critiques of astrology and came across the story of Pico della Mirandola and his horoscope in Gadbury. If the reader will now compare the anti-astrology signature with the horoscope for Pico given on page 9, he or she will, I hope, get the same jolt of wonder at the curious manifestations of astrology that I originally experienced. There is a commutation of Mars and Mercury – that is, *Mars and Mercury exchange places between the two maps*. Any close double synastry would have suggested itself as significant, but the planets involved here are the *key significators suggesting astrology or the astrologers in each attack*. Pico is named the 'the scourge of astrology' (Mars-Mercury). The astrologers (enemies – ruler of the 7th) attack Pico through his Mars at 13° Scorpio. His Mercury at 25° Aquarius is ruler of his 9th (religion, philosophy and the question of astrology). In the 1975 *Humanist* attack, astrology is signified by Mercury, lord of the 9th at 13° Scorpio, and in a secondary sense by Mars its dispositor and lord of the 7th at 26° Aquarius. The swopping of those places with Pico is impressive testimony that the *Humanist* attack map has true signature status for astrology and its battles, reaching back in its implications at least to the Renaissance critique.

The trans-Saturnians have a prominent role in the maps I have so far shown, as if we moderns have to reinterpet our history anew. The Renaissance as a whole seems strongly marked by a Sun-Uranus theme, as in the close oppositions of these planets shared by Ficino and Pico; the anti-astrology map appears to mirror this with the Moon opposite Uranus, although I am unsure what this may signify. Pluto configures strikingly with Mercury for both Pico and for the *Humanist* attack. I earlier brought forward as an unresolvable opposition the cursing quality of the death prediction laid against Pico. Now in the anti-astrology signature the same two planets, Mercury and Pluto, are in mutual reception, showing the unbinding of the knot.

Neptune is less immediately apparent but it is already claiming territory in the battle over astrology. Pico's first house Neptune, in mutual reception with his ascendant ruler Venus, is on the ascendant of the anti-astrology signature. This curious connection prefigures an increasing role for this mysterious planet when, later in this text, we unravel some implications of a trans-Saturnian reinterpretation of astrology.

Symbolic connections like these are endlessly suggestive, but I will limit myself to one general line of interpretation here. The two main attacks on astrology in the last thousand years are shown as connected through the relevant horoscopes. The modern attack has brought science to the fore against astrology and astrologers fall into the trap of trying to answer in kind. Yet the enduring and unresolved issue, indicated in the Mercury of the anti-astrology signature, is that our tradition of astrology does not know itself, and does not speak the truth about what it is. Marsilio Ficino's attempt to resolve the divide between astrology and magic shows the way, but the fulfilment of that hope is not possible until the cracking open of the old Ptolemaic cosmos. Some other subtle equation has to be taken into account before we can comprehend the answer that astrology gives to those who question it.

NOTES

1 Jointly published by the American Ethical Union and the American Humanist Association.
2 The map as given shows these variations from the map I have recast: Pluto, Node, Fortuna and declination not given. Retrograde not shown. Mercury 13 Scorpio 38, Venus 17 Sagittarius 36, Uranus 10 Capricorn 28. Sun given to the minute. Placidus Cusps: 11th 3 Virgo 12th 2 Libra Asc. 25 Libra 29 2nd 23 Scorpio 3rd 25 Sagittarius. The rather careless diagram and explanation of the formation of the houses shows trisection of the mundane quadrants by great circles, and would be appropriate for Campanus cusps.
    The only other publication I have been able to trace: an article with the title 'Scientists Look at Astrology' by Dr. Bart Bok and Margaret Mayall in *Scientific Monthly* vol. 52, March 1941. This gave a history of astrology, expressed concern at the growth of 'Lucky Stars' columns in American newspapers and commented on the legal position. It concluded with the statement 'Psychologists State their Views on Astrology', which is given in Bok's 1975 article. The scientific arguments are similar in substance to those used Bok in the 1975 attack.
    Sidney Omarr's autobiography, *My World of Astrology* (Wilshire Book Co., Hollywood, Calif., 1974), gives details of a remarkable encounter of Bok and American astrologers around 1941.
3 Bart Jan Bok: 28 April 1906, Hoorn, Holland. Time given in *2001: The Penfield Collection* (Marc Penfield, 1979) as 15:40, source 'personal', but zone not indicated. Margaret W. Mayall: 27 January 1902, Iron Hill, Maryland, *American Men and Women of Science*, 12th edition (Jacques Cattell Press/R.R.Bouker Co. 1971). Jerome is a generation younger but I have no other data.
4 William Lilly, *Christian Astrology* (London 1659, reprinted Regulus, London, 1985), p429.
5 Another reading of the movement of Venus from Jupiter to Saturn would suggest that humanism, in its attack on astrology, has moved *from* religious authority (Jupiter) at the time of Pico, to scientific authority now (Saturn).
6 Progressions for publication, Sun prog. 8 Aquarius 56, Jupiter prog. 8 Leo 33 for 1 October 1975, configuring with the progressed MC at 9 Libra 01.
7 This map shows its paces in many more ways than the few I have suggested. In my original study in *Astrology Quarterly*, I gave my main emphasis to angular measures in Solar Arc in Right Ascension (SARA), which shows for the 1975 attack MC prog. to 17 Libra 12 (sextile Venus) and Asc. prog. to 24 Sagittarius 33, conjunct 3rd cusp – and marked by the passage of the progressed Moon for the month of publication. Since then I have changed my ordinary working method to SAL (MC by Solar Arc in Longitude) as given in this present study. I must emphasise that although the fine discrimination of technique is important for a healthy craft of astrology, a debate about 'right' and 'wrong' technical methods is usually a misplaced over-simplification. When the symbolism is lively and the astrologer is moving with the material, *any* method will find its way of working. Converse Secondaries, which in my view merit more attention than they are normally granted, are no less illuminating: above all Sun converse conjunct Venus converse, with a precision timing given by Moon converse at 10 Capricorn 30 exactly on Uranus. The converse MC by SARA gives an outstanding direction: MC at 29 Taurus 45 opposite Sun. For the astrologer who favours Solar Returns, these will also be found to be quite rewarding.
8 Charles Carter *Astrological Aspects* (Fowler, 1971), p88.

9 *Perfection* (horary term): this brings to pass the matter asked about. It requires the unhindered joining by aspect of two planets which are significators in a question. They should complete the exact aspect before changing sign. For a good perfection the planets should be well placed and the aspect a favourable one. It is difficult to carry through a satisfactory perfection on a square; however, in this instance the relationship between significators actually fits the square, since Jupiter is about to chastise Mercury as soon as he catches him on the aspect. *Refranation:* by turning on his station just in time Mercury 'refrains' from closing the aspect with Jupiter to exactitude, and therefore denies the unpleasant consequences of a perfection with an outraged Jupiter.

10 Charles Carter, *An Encyclopedia of Psychological Astrology* (Theosophical Publishing House, 1970), pp.38,198.

11 Mercury prog. trine Pluto shows my response (1978). Mercury's progression to Mars (Spring 1979) led only to me being challenged! (see n.15).

12 In this technique, the two planets in mutual reception are permitted to change signs, each planet going to its sign of rulership but holding its original degree. In this case Mercury can be placed at 13 Gemini, Pluto at 24 Scorpio. The changes in aspects, horary perfections etc. signify the possibilities inherent in the original mutual reception. This is an important development in modern horary, originating with Ivy Goldstein-Jacobson and developed to remarkable effect by Derek Appleby. Its effectiveness has been demonstrated on many occasions. It is also a potentially interesting technique in natal astrology.

13 The question of the Part of Fortune: in the first edition of this book I commented on the placing of the Part of Fortune, also in the 8th; I have dropped this reference because I have since this time begun to experiment with varying the Parts by day and night, according to early tradition. The interpretation I gave was, in any case, slight in import. The Part of Fortune by night in the anti-astrology signature is at 17 Pisces 36, conjunct Saturn and in partile square with Venus. This does appear to be illuminating, especially when taken together with the statement from Lilly on 9th house matters mentioned earlier. The complement to the Part of Fortune is the Part of Spirit, which will therefore be at 3 Gemini 19; I am not however at this point seeking any interpretation for this rather obscure significator.

Chiron-spotters will note the remarkable play of the centaur in this map (*see dox reference*).

14 Stubborn witness: Dennis Elwell's apt description, from his *Cosmic Loom* (Unwin/Hyman, 1987, revised edition Urania Trust, London 1999), ch.1.

15 Norman de Gournay, 'What Does the Signature Signify?', *Astrology Quarterly*, vol 53 no.1 Spring 1979.

3

Science and the Symbol 1: Humpty-Dumpty

A GOOD few years ago I got myself something of a bad reputation in the small circle that notices such things when I launched an attack on 'scientism' in astrology. This was at the first Urania Trust Conference, held at Imperial College, London, in February 1986. We were in the immediate aftermath of the devastating publication in *Nature* (December 1985) of Shawn Carlson's 'Double-Blind Test of Astrology'. This is discussed in detail in Appendix 2; it may be briefly characterised as an exercise in which astrologers participated in the annihilation of their astrology.

I wished to make an appeal to the newly invigorated Urania Trust that it should not be party to the funding of destructive exercises of this sort in the name of science. I gave my view that much research in the area of astrology constituted pseudo-science or at least bad science. As speakers in this part of the conference were limited to 20 minute slots, subtleties got left behind. I showed a cartoon with astrologers at the top of several gum-trees, with scientists in white coats standing looking up at them. Chugging by was a gravy-train called 'Urania' with various people hanging on.

I realise that this might have been taken amiss by several scientists and science-oriented astrologers attending the conference and punting around for research grants. It is also probable that most astrologers are puzzled by the science - astrology problem and prefer to get by without thinking about it, and certainly without getting into arguments. But what I said then has to be said repeatedly, and with equal emphasis. In our culture as a whole 'science' has been made a substitute for philosophy, that is, for careful description and reflective analysis of what it is we do. Whenever this attitude is carried over into astrology, we become as if cowed and submissive, and a profound unthoughtfulness results.

ASTROLOGY'S RELATIONSHIP WITH SCIENCE

Astrology finds itself at odds with the orthodox scientific establishment and much of educated thought. It is as if we are inarticulate about our subject, beyond saying to others, 'I don't know why but astrology seems to work - try it and see'. Most astrologers learn to brush the problem aside, especially where they are supported by a community of their colleagues, and get on with their practice relatively unconcerned. But the breach between the world view of astrology and the world view of contemporary thought, however hazy or variously defined these two positions may be, creates a nagging dissonance for many serious practitioners. Few astrologers relish the status of intellectual pariah and the internal dimension of this breach is reflected in the sometimes considerable struggle that goes on for the reflective practitioner to square his or her notions and experience with the contemporary world view.

Even if astrologers are prepared to muddle along with this situation unresolved, we cannot take for granted a live-and-let-live compromise with the rest of society. There is a significant group of sceptics, like the thought-police of CSICOP (The Committee for the Scientific Investigation of Claims of the Paranormal), who see it as their mission to positively attack astrology along with all other manifestations of irrationalism.[1] We face articulate and potentially dangerous critics, both within the academic community and in media. We may choose to scorn the high-profile polemics of individuals such as Richard Dawkins[2], but it is far from clear how effectively we answer him and his friends in the eyes of a wider moderately sceptical intellectual audience. These critics are likely to get noisier and even more virulent as astrology makes small and hard-won advances into the sphere of the universities. The problem of the ambiguous place of astrology in modern culture extends beyond the ideological battleground with scientific sceptics, however. Astrology will continue to encounter dilemmas in areas such as education and counselling. Even fair-minded persons in these professions will feel uneasy about tolerating the explicit practice of astrology or allowing space for its propagation if it cannot offer even a few threads of justification on a rational and scientific basis.

The religious and ethical argument which was so much part of the historical case against astrology is still in place, but it has less authority to the extent that astrology might justify itself scientifically. This is a consequence of the rise of science in place of the authority of religion. It is commonly taken for granted that science has this supreme arbitrating role, so astrologers seek to justify astrology by an appeal to science, rather than to directly engage ethical or religious questions.

However, since astrology repeatedly fails to achieve scientific and rational justification, in reality it takes its chances as another variant of personal or religious belief, whether astrologers like it or not.

The position we imagine ourselves facing is that of the Scientific Sceptic, typified by the *Humanist* attack. Astrology is pseudo-science, 'there's nothing in it'. More research will underscore what existing research has made painfully plain, that the subject is essentially a fiction and in the face of this evidence its continued practice is ignorance or charlatanry. The soft sceptic might add that even if a few of the best results, such as those of Gauquelin, can be replicated – which is far from guaranteed – and we accept the possibility of certain general cosmic influences such as electromagnetic fields, nevertheless these phenomena have nothing to do with astrology as its practitioners conceive it.

Given the weakness of their position, it is understandable when serious astrologers prefer to withdraw from the science-astrology debate altogether. Traditional astrology, which has had something of a revival in recent years, sidesteps the question of science entirely by simply proceeding with its assertions and its practice without regard to verification outside of its own procedures. The problem in this approach lies in its need to isolate its practice from every other cultural concern.

To an impressive degree, the late twentieth century development of psychological astrology isolated itself from the issue and found a mode of practice that offers feasible intellectual and practical solutions to the question, 'What is astrology?'. This mirrors the relationship that the modern psychology of the unconscious has with science, which is one of relative independence.

Yet this position is not finally secure from the challenge of science. The modern rationalist may feel depth psychology is a pseudo-science, but will allow that a rational case can be made for its investigation. Psychological astrology cannot disguise its seemingly absurd and irrational foundation – the hypothesis of a cosmic connection declared to occur at birth and shown in the natal horoscope. I do not believe, therefore, that even this development in astrology can insulate itself from the challenge laid down for us by science.

So what has happened when astrology has moved towards science? We can distinguish two positions here, which may be categorised as 'scientific astrology', and what has been termed 'ideal science' or 'revolutionary-science' astrology. While both positions seek a positive relationship of astrology and science, and employ a full range of scientific methods, the intentions in both approaches tend to diverge.

SCIENTIFIC ASTROLOGY

Even in the nine years since the first edition of this book, there has been a marked decline in enthusiasm for the project of scientific astrology in the European and American astrology community, and it was never much to write home about to start with. Nevertheless, lip-service is paid to the possibility, and the occasional 'research conferences' still soldier on. There survives an identifiable type going by the name of scientific astrologer, and we have to ask what it is that he or she is attempting to achieve.

Scientific astrology seeks a 'hard science' definition for astrology. The orientation is towards physics, and/or empirical psychology, and the favoured methodology is statistics. The main tenet is that more research will reveal a core proto-scientific perception hidden in the rubbish of the astrological tradition. This scientifically verifiable cosmic connection will have dramatic consequences for science. Michel Gauquelin called his project a new 'Copernican Revolution'.[3] The archetypal text for this approach is Geoffrey Dean's vast and comprehensive *Recent Advances in Natal Astrology*, which despite being quite dated now, still looks as if it has just dropped off the bookshelf of a physics laboratory.[4] The scientific astrologer is interested in investigating the 'facts' of astrology, so what are the hard facts which might be acceptable to modern science?

Let us begin with phenomena which are already within the scope of straight science, but which might also have a direct bearing on the astrological hypothesis. There is a fairly impressive list, headed by the well documented fluctuations in the earth's magnetic field, which is in turn responsive to changes in the solar wind. A highly sensitive response of organic life to this field, and to the various geo-cosmic rhythms, such as the diurnal and lunar cycles, has been established. The human body is demonstrably sensitive to such influence, as for instance in the variation in the rate of blood-clotting in response to the lunar phase. At a quite different level of investigation, the new field of cymatics, the study of cycles, has demonstrated apparently orderly rhythms in all manner of phenomena, natural, social and economic. Some of these suggest a tantalising affinity with planetary and other geocosmic cycles, including the sun-spot cycle. All this amounts to a not inconsiderable body of evidence, some of it circumstantial but some of it impressively 'hard', suggesting that things on earth are more sensitive to the cosmos than was suspected even a generation ago.[5]

Moreover, this list does not even contain the most extraordinary of all such findings, those of Michel and Francoise Gauquelin. The demonstration in thousands of European birth-times of statistically highly significant correlations between planets in the diurnal circle at birth, and career and temperament – Saturn and the scientist, Mars and solo athletes and so on – is to date the single most impressive example of rigorous scientific method applied to traditional astrological categories. These results on their own would be sufficient to justify the possibility of a 'scientific astrology'. It is understandable that over the latter decades of the twentieth century serious astrology pinned high hopes on a rapprochement with science through methods such as these.

Because there is an impressive array of hard facts which point to the possibility of a science of astrology, an explicit aim of many modern astrological organisations has been to further 'research'. Now this word does not mean looking up your progressions, pondering the symbolism of Jupiter, or mulling over the writings of Manilius. Most astrologers equate research with its natural science context. It carries the aura of laboratories and white coats, computers and databases. Astrological research is understood as a programme of procedures and tests, dedicated to the elucidation of objective phenomena free of subjective bias and personal desires, and taking as its model the methodology of the natural sciences. The most characteristic of all these methods is that of statistical analysis.

To attempt an entry into the domain of modern science, a mere listing of correlations is not going to be enough. To qualify as a science in its own right, astrology is dependent on a satisfactory physical explanation to bring it into the hypothesis formation model of conventional science. This explains the relevance of the magnetic-field theory offered by Percy Seymour. Hypotheses of this type enable the integration of the Gauquelin findings with existing acceptable scientific theories.[6]

SCIENCE LOOK-ALIKE

When we view the astrological community as a whole, research astrology is notable for its very distinctiveness. It is seen by its proponents as marking a distinct departure from traditional enquiry into astrology, and even the name of the subject has to be qualified. Gauquelin used the term 'neo-astrology' because most of his results give contrary indications to the traditional theses of astrology. There are no signs of the zodiac, for example, and no observable correlations for the Sun's position.

We may wonder whether a similar pressure for research to create distance from traditional astrology underpinned the naming of the National Council for Geocosmic Research (NCGR). This is a leading and prestigious body in

American Astrology, but who would guess from its title that this is an organisation of practising *astrologers*?

The overwhelming power of the scientific paradigm has intruded beyond the level of formal commitment to research. Certain elements of modern astrology have been significantly modified by the need to put on an appearance of science and rationality. This is especially obvious in the distinctively twentieth century European technical development that is best known to the student in the form of 'midpoints'. Dissatisfied with the interpretations available from traditional astrology, from 1913 on, Alfred Witte and Friedrich Sieggruen began the study of planetary and angular relationships ('pictures'). Incorporating no less than eight hypothetical planets stated to be empirically derived, this approach of the Hamburg School was developed into the so-called Uranian System. Reinhold Ebertin rationalised Witte's work into a consistent system of midpoint interpretation, dropping, amongst other things, the hypotheticals. This system has become known as *cosmobiology*. The name reflects a definite attempt to divorce the new discipline from the occultism of the old astrology. Although a non-quantifiable domain is allowed for, there is no doubt about Ebertin's desire for scientific credentials:

> Cosmobiology is a scientific discipline concerned with the possible correlations between cosmos and organic life... cosmobiology utilises modern-day methods of scientific research ... (but does) not overlook the macrocosmic and microcosmic interrelations incapable of measurement.[7]

With its 45 degree dials, graphic ephemerides, vector analyses, distance values and psychocosmograms it all *looks* very scientific, and far indeed from the poetry of the heavens. I have to say that it would not take our notional bogeyman, the scientific sceptic, very long to conclude that this was just as much occult mumbo-jumbo as the medieval superstition it is supposed to replace.

Even today some astrologers cling on to the hope that the project of scientific astrology, or Michel Gauquelin's neo-astrology, is somehow or other going to authenticate their position. It brings the promise of a little respectability, but such hopes have very obscure foundations. Like the physical evidences of a cosmobiological connection, the project of neo-astrology has at best an incidental connection to the way in which astrologers look at horoscopes and understand their practice. Even if all these 'scientific' phenomena are brought into the witness box on behalf of traditional astrology, there is only a rather feeble case that can be made for it. The symbolic or mythological accretions that have grown around the supposed proto-scientific core bear no more than an incidental and arbitrary connection with the real phenomena. Most astrologers realise that this sort of circumstantial evidence will never get us very far in our arguments.

ASTROLOGY AS IDEAL OR REVOLUTIONARY SCIENCE

Even those forms of astrology outside of scientific astrology that hold to their traditional modes have had to compromise with science. The most common form of this compromise accepts a role for research and for hard data, whilst still maintaining that the reasons for astrology's working are inaccessible to modern science. Hence astrology will lead the way to a reformed science, and ultimately to the possibility of an 'ideal' or 'revolutionary science'.[8]

This approach accepts the scientific astrologer's methods but is distinguished by a significant orientation towards metaphysics. Not only will research reveal a core intuition of traditional astrology as true, but this will force a revolution in the *definition of knowledge and science itself*. This goes beyond even Gauquelin's 'Copernican Revolution'. A common theme is that only a completely reformed science can contain the astrological hypothesis, which brings into the scientific equation a living and conscious universe. It is in this sense that Robert Hand calls scientific work with astrology 'revolutionary'.[9] The paradigm which constrains contemporary science is still a mechanical-materialist model, despite all the advances of physics and the philosophy of science. Therefore part of astrology's contribution is to finally remove the last vestiges of this older world-view which is seen as a species of religious belief. Astrology can bring forward 'facts' that destroy the last traces of this inhibiting belief, and demand a spiritual reinterpretation of science itself. Science will become re-integrated into the highest spiritual ideals of humanity, with astrology taking the lead. The revolutionary science position, however it is named, is quite widely adopted amongst the more intellectual and thoughtful of astrologers, and it undoubtedly appeals to ordinary practitioners in a way that the straight science approach never can.

The great astronomer Kepler is the major historical figure inspiring the ideal science quest in astrology. His work was dedicated to the discovery of the harmony of the spheres, and this for him was the far more important aspect of all he was attempting, even while he was laying the foundations of modern knowledge of the planetary orbits.[10] In modern times *harmonics* as developed by John Addey has taken pride of place as the most significant demonstration of this approach. This appeared to offer a reform based on the inner logic of astrology's symbolism which is at the same time able to bring the subject into relationship with science. Addey could with great plausibility claim that many of the most disparate factors of astrology are in fact expressions of the harmonics of circles – signs, aspects, houses, all can be brought under the same unifying concept. Since this can also be carried convincingly across into certain practices of Indian astrology, with their harmonic subdivisions of signs, harmonics appears to offer a key to order and rationalise what had seemed to be a bewildering jumble of disconnected doctrines and symbols. Harmonics suggests a sustainable reinterpretation of Gauquelin's findings, while at the same time spiritualising science.[11]

For the great majority of astrologers who take up the astrology – science debate, even though they characteristically demarcate a dimension of the subject as spiritual ('noumenal') and not amenable to demonstration within the terms of contemporary science, they nevertheless take it for granted that we should demonstrate some component of astrology within the terms of that science. Developing his vision of ideal astrology, Charles Harvey stated:

> Whilst we can be certain that it will indeed require a 'New Science' to accommodate astrology, we cannot evade the need for demonstrable, quantifiable evidence for astrological effects...the future of astrology depends on us facing up to the reality that astrological effects occur in the phemomenal world, even if they are rooted in the noumenal world. Such effects can be measured.[12]

This statement typifies the position of a spiritually rooted astrology which can nevertheless demonstrate certain facts to hard science, even if a complete metaphysical rationale cannot be entertained in the terms of current thought. Not only can we do this, but we *must* do this if our astrology is to be credible. Anything short of this demonstration of verifiable effects is 'evasion'.

The two positions of astrology as revolutionary science and neo-astrology (scientific astrology) therefore come together in the common goal of demonstrating the objective truths of astrology. Revolutionary-science astrology, and Charles Harvey's ideal astrology, may be expected to reinterpret these truths against a concept of the noumenal realm. In many respects this offers a viable loose compromise between astrology and modern culture. Astrologers are not required to abandon any of the exalted spiritual claim of their subject, they can hold on to its core philosophical tradition, and they can at least imagine themselves effecting a relationship with the demands of science. The dissonance between astrology and modern rationality is thereby assuaged. However, there is a price to be paid. Although this position can hold on to ideal forms underlying the phenomenal, it is under steady pressure to reshape astrology's methods to bring them into conformity with both the requirements of demonstration and the expectation of modern science. The danger of this is that instead of really 'doing science', we might try to look as if we are doing science. This is the slide into astrology as a science look-alike.

Against this tendency, there is a possible defensive strategy which does not require a radical remodelling of the forms of astrological practice. This is the position taken by Robert Hand, who has advocated a sharp divide between astrology as *craft* and astrology as *science*. As a craft, astrology works more or less for its practitioners, with little apparent need for abstract theory or hypothesis formation. Its old ways should continue for the foreseeable future, whilst a separate scientific research programme which formulates its own hypotheses could be developed relatively independently. As Hand observes, pure science had little to offer traditional crafts and technologies until recent times, and the craft of astrology may be no different. This in effect brings the schism that currently exists between astrology and science into astrology itself. Mainstream astrology has moved in this direction by appending 'research sections' onto its corporate body. However, this will not save us from an uncomfortable dissonance between the apparently objective assertions made by astrological practitioners and the characteristic inability to find empirical justification for those statements through research. The problem will not go away.

This dissonance is illuminated by the metaphors used by both sorts of pro-science astrologer, straight or revolutionary. Kepler's famous remark was that in abandoning traditional astrology, science should not 'throw the baby out with the bathwater'.[13] Gauquelin likes the metaphor of a 'grain of gold', in amongst the dross of the tradition.[14] An aim of the Astrological Association is (or used to be) to 'sift the wheat from the chaff of the astrological tradition'.[15] It all sounds very exciting, until the practical astrologer starts to ponder the implications, amongst which is the need to throw out virtually everything we have known as astrology. I must say that whenever I come across these images, I have the lingering impression that I would find myself somewhere amongst the dross, the chaff and the bathwater. So what has actually happened when scientific research in astrology has been carried into the heartland of traditional astrology's assertions and practices? The results have been far from happy for astrologers.

THE NEW YORK SUICIDE STUDY

I will give as an exemplary case a study that is generally accepted as the most impressive of its type. This is the New York Suicide Study, begun in 1974 by the New York chapter of the National Council for Geocosmic Research (NCGR), and led by Nona Press.[16] The hypothesis of the study was that there should be some astrological pattern in the birth charts of suicides. Suicide is a good subject for study because of the availability of records and the generally clear-cut and decisive nature of the act. It is also a highly *significant* act, and there are few astrologers, traditional or modern, who would not presuppose the existence of horoscopic indicators of at least a tendency to suicide.

The study was developed in several stages, with increasing data and refinements. It was understood that if horoscopes of suicides could be matched against those of non-suicides comparable in other respects (the 'control group'), then the astrological pattern should be discoverable by noting the differences between the two sets of charts. The researchers gained access to the public records of the 2,250 certified suicides that occurred in New York City during a five-year period, 1969 to 1973 inclusive. The data they were given was that of the date, time, place and manner of the suicide, together with the birth data of the victim. Of this batch of 2,250, the time of birth was available in 311 cases (those born in New York City from 1931 on). This smaller group became the main sample for analysis.

Until comparatively recent times, most astrological research studies were conducted in complete ignorance of the first principles of statistical analysis. However large the sample size, a primary requirement is to establish an appropriate control, otherwise there is no sound basis on which to make comparisons. A second requirement is to ensure that the data is consistent and repeatable ('replicable'). If there is an apparently significant showing in the main sample, such as a particular planet rising more often than in the control batch, is it simply a fluke of that particular sample? In the nature of things every sample has countless such potential flukes to trap the unwary investigator. However, if the main sample is divided into subsets, and each subset shows a similar pattern of that planet rising, then there is a high degree of probability that this isn't a chance fluctuation but an actual factor of astrological significance.

Nona Press and her team were fully conversant with all the techniques of statistical analysis. Using random sampling methods they gathered a carefully-matched control group of 311 non-suicides, each member of the control being born in the same year and borough as one of the suicides. The suicides and their controls were divided into three subsets to eliminate spurious significance arising from random fluctuations in any one batch of the data.

Computer programs were customised and developed to handle the number-crunching, and the data was checked against a vast array of horoscope possibilities. As Nona Press says, they went through 'just about all the traditional investigations and some untraditional ones'. It takes several pages of text just to summarise the factors they eventually analysed, but the following list gives some indication: planets in signs, houses, elements and qualities, signs on house cusps, location of various house rulers in other houses, interceptions, aspects and midpoints using major and minor aspects with various orbs, aspects to angles with various orbs, angular separation between any two factors using various orbs, aspect patterns with various orbs, midpoints and harmonics 1 -12, 16, 24 and 48, for both planets and asteroids, the Gauquelin 12 and 36 sectors, declination and declination midpoints, geocentric nodes, degree areas including Carter's indicators of suicide,[17] Uranian astrology factors, and even biorhythms. In addition the data was analysed for stations and eclipses, for differences in the manner of suicide, and for birth conditions such as number of hours of labour, surgical intervention and other complications. In total something in the order of a *hundred thousand* different possible astrological signatures were examined in each of the 622 charts (311 sample, plus 311 control).

This was a methodologically perfect study. Michel Gauquelin affirmed it to be 'a model experiment', and Geoffrey Dean has called it 'a model of what astrological research should be like... perhaps the most meticulous and comprehensive astrological study yet attempted'.[18]

So what was the result? Of all this immense array of factors that might signify suicide, the number that was reproducible over the three groups was *zero*. This study failed to find anything in the horoscope that suggests the possibility of suicide. This is an entirely negative result for astrology. All that can be redeemed, as Gauquelin observes, is admiration for the courage and integrity of the astrologers in presenting such conclusions.[19]

The authors of the study have indicated further possible analyses of the data, (heliocentric positions, mundane aspects, distance values etc), and there is more work to be done on the Gauquelin planetary temperaments which might show differing dispositions to suicide, and to different methods of suicide. But as far as I can tell an air of gloom soon descended on the whole project. It is clear that these astrologers tried virtually everything they could think of that would reasonably allow astrology to show itself. Nona Press concludes:

The results so far are not significant. And that, I believe, is significant.[20]

THE HOROSCOPE FALLS DOWN

What can we do when faced with results like this? It has to be remembered that this is only one of many similar indications and studies that have obliterated most of our symbolism. All that can be retrieved from the Gauquelin findings are a few fragments of planetary symbolism, excluding the Sun, and a broad indication of the significance of the diurnal circle. *Nothing* of traditional horoscopy survives, and on all the evidence we are unlikely to find any way of rescuing it. As far as Gauquelin is concerned, the major part of our tradition is simply unsustainable – 'the horoscope falls down'.

In the light of these repeated failures, talk of more sophisticated research being required seems increasingly hollow. Some astrologers try a desperate last-ditch defence by an appeal to the subtlety of interpretation and the astrologer's *gestalt* or whole-view. The problem with this defence is that it has to play down the relative simplicity of large parts of horoscopic method, and the communicability of astrological symbolism.[21] Astrological interpretation, especially in its more traditional form, does not usually emerge as a vague or purely subjective intuition which cannot be pinned down to specific symbols. Neither does it present itself as incomprehensibly sophisticated in its basic elements. Astrologers characteristically give quite decisive interpretations based on a few major features of the horoscope. For example, Uranus in the 7th square to Venus might indicate disruptions in relationships, and Saturn transiting the MC could show a crisis at work or a promotion. Despite the limitless possibilities of the poetry of symbolism, there is nothing especially subtle about this sort of practical astrology.

The defence of 'subtlety of interpretation' is no more plausible even with modern psychologically oriented astrology. It offers categories which are just as well defined as the more worldly traditional approach. Even the most sophisticated interpretation of the horoscope utilises the very same simple categories that we find in the Sun-sign columns, even if these are now distributed away from the Sun onto the Moon and the ascendant and one or two other significant locations. As Gauquelin observes, each sign has 'a precise psychological profile... where the zodiac is concerned, astrologers are extremely coherent, even strict, and there is little variation between them.'[22]

There seems little likelihood that research will provide *any* evidence for the zodiac signs, let alone evidence which could support the highly defined profiles regularly used in natal astrology. As far as Gauquelin is concerned the astrologer faces 'an agonising revision of his ideas: a horoscope without the zodiac is surely like a day without the sun'.[23] We are faced with a manifest crisis engendered by the evidence of research because it runs counter not only to our cherished beliefs but to our daily-renewed perception of astrology. On the evidence of the research, our beliefs appear to be folly and our perception an imaginative delusion.

When it comes to scientific verification, we cannot dodge the fact that for modern astrology as a whole, stated expectations do not match reality, which is cruelly shown in the Suicide Study. Rather than plunging thoughtlessly ahead to more of the same, we might be advised to take the mismatch between the evidence of research and the evidence of our experience as a spur to re-examine *what* it is we are seeking to prove. An intelligent re-examination could lead to us asking *different questions*. I will now re-invoke the unhappy Suicide Study and this time ask the wider question of what it indicates to us, not now about objective-empirical horoscopic correlations for suicide, but about the whole of our astrology.

THE SIGNIFICANCE OF THE NEW YORK SUICIDE STUDY

I will therefore start with what we are given. The New York Suicide Study has related all known horoscope factors of conventional modern astrology to the fact of suicide and demonstrated beyond reasonable doubt that:

1. there is no causal (or 'matrix of causes') correlation and
2. there is no *a-causal* correlation either.

The absence of correlation needs to be put in this exact two-part form because of the widely entertained view that Jung's concept of synchronicity – an 'a-causal connecting principle' – could be used to justify the validity of the birth horoscope without invoking causes, or combinations of causes, known to science. If we are going to employ the concept of synchronicity, or anything similar, it cannot be made a simple substitute for causation.

Now let us contrast this negative conclusion with the observations of astrologers. There can be very few astrologers who would not think they could perceive at least some *tendency* to suicide, marking one horoscope off from another. Some astrologers go further, and believe that on occasion they can perceive a signficant likelihood of suicide. But what are the astrologers seeing? The factors they are 'seeing' are certainly not what the New York Suicide Study 'sees' in its comprehensive coverage of conventional astrology's symbolism. Something is adrift here. We are left with the following possibilities:

1. astrologers are deluded
2. astrological perception involves greater subtlety of factor-combination than that revealed by the study
3 some other element is involved in the practice of astrology

Which is it to be? Perhaps we are all deluded. I do not have a rose-tinted view of astrologers and I well recognise the endless possibilities for idle fantasy in everything we do, but delusion does not square with my own experience and careful inquiry, just as it does not square with the experience of others I respect. Since I am not prepared to deny real experience, I want a shot at some other conclusion. The second possibility brings us back to the *gestalt* defence, which as I have already suggested is misleading, and not in accord with the simplicity of much astrological observation and inference. I do not see any other option but the third possibility. If there is anything in astrology at all, we are bound to conclude that *there is some other element involved.*

Usually when this conclusion is reached, a vague mention is made of intuition and the analysis of the phenomenon is taken no further. But as far as I am concerned, far from being the end of discussion this has to be the place where we begin. There is something here at the heart of our practice and it deserves to be understood.

SOME OTHER ELEMENT

If we examine our responses to the negative results of modern research, they will be found to be essentially determined by which side of a great divide we happen to fall. A primary cleavage in astrology concerns the question of SIGNS and CAUSES. This is the rock on which the ship of astrology founders, from classical times to the present day.

The distinction between signs and causes has already been discussed in Chapter 1 in relation to the Renaissance critique (pp. 7–8) and will be developed in later chapters. It is sufficient for our purposes here to distinguish the sign ('symbol') approach by noting that it does not involve explanations in terms of causes, whether these are treated as physical or logical, direct or indirect. From this point of view the heavens and their cycles are absolutely *not* simply one more source of causation placed amongst all the other natural and human contingencies and causes.

A clear instance of this difference in astrological attitude can be seen in different possible approaches to the question of induced births. A *causal* approach to astrology may postulate that a baby is predisposed or genetically determined to be born at a certain time giving its true horoscope at that time. Should medical intervention interfere with that pattern and bring the 'natural' birth-time forward some hours, this would render the actual birth horoscope unreliable. This is a problem for the Gauquelin data, which tends to show its strongest correlations using births prior to recent decades. It has been suggested that the increasing practice of inducing births for the sake of convenience has upset the natural pattern and hence the 'cosmic connection' at birth. In other words, the stars have to compete with the doctor.[24]

The signs approach is of an entirely different order to the level of causes. Here even the medical intervention that changes the natural birth time is already allowed for in the symbolism. The doctor unwittingly fulfils the grand symbolic plan even when he re-schedules his maternity cases to allow a round of golf. No doctor and no mere cause could alter the potential for astrological signification. Put this way, the difference between the two possible orders of astrology is immediately obvious. Our logic of symbolism implies this second position of signs, whatever cause-type words and concepts we use to describe our practice. Astrologers simply don't work as if their astrology is just one more cause to be added on to all the other causes. In Dennis Elwell's pithy phrase, 'astrology is not an add-on'.[25]

It should be clearer now why I earlier divided the negative conclusion from the New York Suicide Study into two parts. The study denies a causal correlation between planets and suicide, and it denies an a-causal correlation at the same time. For a scientific astrology of causes, the lack of correlation for this particular fact of suicide is limiting but not in any sense destructive. Causal connections of planets and other phenomena have been shown in other studies, but may be presumed to have no direct bearing on the psychology of suicide. However, for an astrology of signs, the denial of correlation even in this single case is more radically undermining. It is in the nature of signs that there is nothing humanly experienced which cannot be signified and therefore astrologically symbolised. The whole of experienced reality is open to this symbolising faculty. When faced with a significant reality-at-hand, such as a client with their horoscope, it is the astrologer's practice to find astrological symbolism for all the pertinent details, whatever these might be conceived to be. When a major human act such as suicide is a significant issue, astrologers assume that appropriate symbolism and timing will emerge to suggest and even possibly pre-announce the act and its motive. This will not be a vague intuition or multi-factor synthesis, but a fairly direct and obvious symbolism, communicable with other astrologers in the conventional language of astrology.

Now we can see more clearly the destructive implication of so much research. It is not that a particular detail of symbolism has been questioned (suicides, redheads etc.). Rather, as soon as the astrologer allows objective-empirical research to address astrology's significatory power, then this research threatens to undermine *the whole way of proceeding with symbols*.

On more than one occasion, in meeting astrologers who have put effort into research projects of this sort I have been struck by how crushing it is for their astrology. The sceptic will say, naturally, that their 'belief' has been punctured and now they are deflated. But rather than belief, it is their attitude to symbolism that is punctured because the capacity to symbolise is rendered futile. It is not a question of giving up on a symbolism for suicide, but of giving up on expecting a symbol for almost anything. Like Humpty-Dumpty, astrology has had a big fall. This is not just a matter of a few isolated failures, but the broad conclusion from the whole project of objective-empirical research into astrological correlations. The astrologers who, implicitly or explicitly, make signs (symbols) the basis for their astrology had better put their position more clearly. If they do not, they will find that science has picked up the pieces and arbitrated the whole of their subject for them.

But the question of research is far from exhausted. Perhaps astrology-as-signs might still be verified if we take another line of verification altogether, testing the perception and skill of the *astrologer* rather than supposed objective correlations of *astrology*. For a while, this type of experiment, based on the pioneering tests made by Vernon Clark, promised to be the golden hope of proving astrology. This type of experiment does indeed lead to important conclusions, but not, as I will show in the next chapter, the conclusions that were originally envisaged.

NOTES

1 CSICOP emerged from the same culture as the *Humanist* attack on astrology, with many of the same individuals involved, and in particular Paul Kurtz. Its inception was sometime during the 1976 Annual Convention of the American Humanist Association (30 April – 2 May), and it was initially sponsored by the *Humanist* journal. Its publication is the *Skeptical Inquirer*. See the full discussion by George P. Hansen 'CSICOP and the Skeptics: An Overview' in *Journal of the American Society for Psychical Research* vol.86, January 1992.

2 Richard Dawkins holds the Charles Simonyi Chair of Public Understanding of Science at New College, Oxford. See for example his attack published in *The Independent on Sunday* 31 December 1995 (reprinted slightly emended in *The Astrological Journal* May/June 1996, Vol.38 no.3 pp133-141).

3 Michel Gauquelin, *Neo-Astrology: A Copernican Revolution* (Penguin/Arkana 1991).

4 Geoffrey Dean, *Recent Advances in Natal Astrology* (Analogic, 1977; distributed by Para Research Inc. Rockport, Mass.).

5 For references to scientific evidence for astrology, see Dean, op.cit., and Seymour (note 6).

6 Percy Seymour *Astrology: The Evidence of Science* (Penguin/Arkana, London 1990).

7 Reinhold Ebertin, *The Combination of Stellar Influences*, trans. Roosedale and Kratzsch (Ebertin-Verlag, Aalen, 1972) p.11. My remarks should not be taken as a criticism of midpoints as a method.

8 For the purposes of the current discussion, these two positions may be equated and form a broadly common project. 'Revolutionary science' is the designation given by Robert Hand to indicate a spiritualised science in contradistinction to the mechanist-materialist model that is

an inheritance from nineteenth-century science. Astrology cannot even potentially be a science in the modern meaning of this term. When referring to astrology as 'science', Hand means 'the original sense of scientia or episteme, which is an organized inquiry into truth' (personal communication from Robert Hand to the author). 'Ideal science', as posited by Charles Harvey, has a more explicitly Pythagorean/Platonic goal, and is inspired in particular by the work of John Addey.

 9 Robert Hand 'Astrology as a Revolutionary Science', in *The Future of Astrology*, ed. A.T.Mann (Unwin/Hyman, London, 1987).

10 For Kepler: see the discussion in M. Gauquelin, *Neo-Astrology*, op.cit., pp.87ff.

11 John Addey, *Harmonics in Astrology* (Eyebright, Frome, 2002); see also his 'Astrology Reborn' in *The Future of Astrology*, ed. A.T.Mann, op.cit.

12 Charles Harvey, 'Ideal Astrology', in *The Future of Astrology*, ed. A.T.Mann, op.cit.

13 M. Gauquelin, *The Truth about Astrology*, op.cit., p8.

14 M. Gauquelin, *Neo-Astrology*, op.cit., ch.5.

15 Astrological Association literature *c.* 1980 states certain aims (although not the Association's constitutional objectives): 'To sift the wheat from the chaff of the astrological tradition; to examine new ideas, to encourage research, and to collaborate with people in other fields of study; to tell the world about astrology, especially these newer developments, and to get rid of the popular notion that astrology is concerned with "Your Lucky Stars" columns...', etc. I am quite interested in 'Lucky Stars' columns, as well.

16 Nona Press, 'The New York Suicide Study', *Journal of Geocosmic Research (NCGR)*, vol. 2, no.2. Press states that the study started on 11 March 1974. See also note 20 below. The study is reported by Geoffrey Dean in *Recent Advances in Natal Astrology*, op.cit., pp. 548, 558ff.

17 Charles Carter, *Encyclopaedia of Psychological Astrology* (Theosophical Publishing House, 1970); see entry 'Suicidal Tendency'.

18 G.Dean, *Recent Advances in Natal Astrology*, op.cit., p560.

19 M. Gauquelin, *The Truth about Astrology*, op.cit., p133.

20 Nona Press has reproduced her original article in *New Insights into Astrology* (ACS, San Diego, 1993), ch. 6. Her review of the material indicates a hard struggle to justify a continued love of astrology in the light of the zero results of research. Her solution appears to lie in the direction of an ever more complex technical astrology with a massive super-abundance of factors – a forty-page appendix in this book lists the heliocentric nodes of well over 3,500 asteroids. Press believes we should continue with research: 'maybe if we had a large enough computer to put in all the data, we could see the patterns. Surely, in the "great computer in the sky", everything is significant. If only we had access to so much data and to such a marvellous computer!' (p327).

21 M. Gauquelin *The Truth About Astrology*, op.cit., ch.7.

22 ibid., pp. 128-9.

23 ibid., p.131.

24 See the extensive discussion by M.Gauquelin on the increasing tendency to induce births in recent decades in *The Truth About Astrology*, op.cit., pp. 162-77. Gauquelin comments that 'the Mars effect in sports champions born after 1950 tends to disappear, just as I had suspected'.

25 Dennis Elwell, *Cosmic Loom* (Unwin/Hyman, 1987), p.25.; revised edn. (Urania Trust, London 1999), p.42.

4

Science and the Symbol 2: Two Orders of Significance

I N this chapter we take up the saga of tests on the abilities of astrologers. In the first phase of modern research, trials based on the Vernon Clark model for testing astrologers' judgments produced some remarkable but erratic results. Taken together with the Gauquelin data, the overall pattern suggests a double conception of astrology. However, to secure such a conclusion we must address the issue of how half a century of test results have up to now been interpreted – or misinterpreted.

VERNON CLARK TRIALS: THE FIRST PHASE OF RESEARCH

Clark was a US psychologist who became intrigued by astrology; he obtained the Diploma of the Faculty of Astrological Studies, which puts him in a quite different category to most scientists approaching the subject. He decided to test directly the capacity of astrologers to discern biographical details from the horoscope, using the blind trial approach. The meaning of this terminology is that the astrologer is forced to 'see' only through the horoscope and is 'blind' to all other clues about the person. In most real situations in life we cannot be sure whether the astrologer's deductions are based not purely on the astrology but on clues being picked up from clients just by talking to them or seeing them.

The trials, conducted by post, were made between 1959 and 1961 and involved a total of fifty astrologers from various nations. Each astrologer had more than four years' experience. Following the blind-trial method, test biographies were carefully chosen against criteria designed to avoid extraneous clues, and only persons with fairly accurate birth data were selected. There were three separate tests, with a control group of non-astrologers being set the same tasks.

The first test required the astrologer to match five male charts with five biographical descriptions (occupation, marital status, hobbies and health), and five sets of female charts with biographical descriptions; the astrologer had to list each of the five charts in most likely order of fit with the five descriptions.

The second test required the study of ten pairs of charts against ten case histories, with the astrologer being asked to choose one of the two charts from each pair as the correct match. The astrologers were not told that one of the charts in each pair was spurious, generated for a random time and place near the time and place of the genuine chart.

The third test involved ten pairs of charts without case histories, one of the pair being for a person with an IQ of 140+, and the other being for a victim of cerebral palsy. The astrologers were required to correctly match each of the two charts to the right subject. This last test was conducted 'double-blind', which means that nobody, including Vernon Clark, knew the correct answers. The double-blind represents a meticulous standard of testing, since it eliminates the possibility of subliminal collusion, such as a loaded comment from the researcher indicating the right answer to the astrologer.

The results were extraordinarily good for astrology. In all three tests the astrologers scored above chance at very high levels of significance. In the second test, for example (genuine *vs.* spurious case histories) the significance was at the .00001 level, meaning that there was only a 1 in 100,000 possibility of this being merely chance. The first test scored at the .0001 level, and the third at the .002 level (1 in 500 possibility of chance). Astrologers therefore showed a definite capacity to match biographies, discriminate spurious from true charts, and distinguish gifted individuals from those with cerebral palsy. Vernon Clark had no doubt of the significance of these results:

> Never again will it be possible to dismiss the astrological technique as a vague, spooky, and mystical business – or as the plaything of undisciplined psychics – or as merely the profitable device of unscrupulous quacks. Those who, out of prejudice, wish to do so will have to remain silent, or repeat these experiments for themselves.[1]

We should not be surprised that these results received no scientific coverage whatsoever. It is simply a fact of life that research astrologers long ago learned to accept: that it is virtually impossible to find a reputable science publication prepared to carry material, however convincing and from whatever source, that might be considered to lend credence to the astrological hypothesis.

These extraordinary results encouraged numerous attempts at replication, but unfortunately for the astrologers, no later tests got near the success achieved by Vernon Clark. The cumulative trend of the results has been towards a zero result, with no consistent capacity being shown in the attempt to discriminate charts and biographies under test conditions.[2]

But before we abandon ourselves to despondency, it must be observed that there is an inexplicable phenomenon at work, in the very fact that these carefully constructed trials produce such *erratic* results. This became obvious from the very first follow-on trials. Some tests are out-and-out failures, despite following Vernon Clark's approach. In 1975 Tony Joseph ran a version of the third of Clark's tests, this time using charts of gifted children paired with charts of severely retarded children who required care. Cases were selected by a paediatrician. The twenty-three astrologers were selected as competent from three reputable U.S. astrology bodies. The result was negative – the astrologers showed no ability to discriminate horoscopes of gifted from retarded children. Then in 1976 Nona Press, using data from the New York Suicide Study, ran a trial on suicide along the lines of Clark's second test. In each pair of charts one was of a suicide and the other was a spurious chart. The test was in effect run twice, once where no death data was provided and the second time with different charts, where the data for the death was provided. Sixteen astrologers took part in the first test, thirteen in the second. The astrologers showed no capacity to discriminate suicides except for one astrologer in the second test, whose answers were significantly above chance. This astrologer was not able to offer any testable factors or combination of factors to explain the good result.[3] The result could therefore be put down to chance or to intuition.

However, in 1976 the magazine *Astrology Now* repeated Clark's second test (spurious *vs.* genuine case histories) with ten new pairs of horoscopes. Forty-nine astrologers participated, of whom twenty-three had over five years' experience. About a third of the whole group were professional astrologers. This group showed an ability to distinguish the horoscopes, although at a lower level of significance than in Clark's test. A curiosity of the result is that the less experienced astrologers did just as well as their more experienced colleagues.

Geoffrey Dean and R.A.Edwards followed up by applying the Vernon Clark method to astrologers' judgments in matching horoscopes with personality inventories as used in psychological testing. This appears to have been a thoroughly designed test. A point of particular importance for this type of psychological test approach was that the chosen subjects were those whose own self-evaluation of their personality was a good match for the results of the administered personality inventory. In the test a group of eight astrologers were required to discriminate between certain traits, including introversion-extraversion, from the horoscopes alone. The astrologers showed a significant ability to make these discriminations.

The earliest phase of follow-on tests therefore produced results that were erratic but which were nevertheless sufficient to cautiously vindicate Vernon Clark's original enthusiasm. However, the research – or perhaps one should say the researchers – took a peculiar turn at this point. Gauquelin was dismissive of the usefulness of such trials and Geoffrey Dean, who we must remember produced a successful result, offered a verdict which is a revealing expression of what passes as scientific inference in our field:

> It is clear that the significant blind trials have not demonstrated that astrology works but only that astrologers work. Hence to adequately test astrology *the participation of the astrologer must be eliminated.*[4] [my italics]

I imagine that most astrologers reading this extraordinary statement will switch off from the whole project of research if this is what science is supposed to mean for astrology. They would be right. This position is thoughtless, because it begs the question of the definition of the very phenomena it sets out to research. There is something deeper at work here, something about the participation of the astrologer that must have rung a warning bell for Geoffrey Dean, because it might lead him in a different direction to the preconceptions on which he has founded a lifetime of research.

Digging below the surface of the early Vernon Clark trials there are curious inconsistencies, several of which, on their own, might be easily enough accounted for; taken together, they raise puzzling issues. In the 'suicide' blind trial which was a failure overall, one astrologer did achieve a significant result, although this might be put down to chance, especially in view of the total null result of the New York Suicide Project. The failure of Tony Joseph's gifted *vs.* retarded as opposed to Clark's gifted *vs.* palsied trial, though not unaccountable, is odd. Does palsy show where retardedness does not? More strikingly, experience in astrology did not make any difference to the level of achievement in the successful *Astrology Now* test. Similarly in the Dean and Edwards test the different techniques employed by the astrologers *made no difference* to the success rate, and yet the astrologers showed a disconcerting tendency to be either *all in agreement right* or *all in agreement wrong* in their selections. Taken together, this is a combination of factors which is difficult to account for, and has never been adequately acknowledged.

Even more alarming was the Gallic passion stirred up in the original Vernon Clark trial. As Gauquelin records,

> the French astrologers who tried Clark's test – all serious professionals – failed it completely... the failure... remains inexplicable: there is nothing to show that

their qualities as practitioners were in any way inferior to those of Vernon Clark's colleagues.[5]

We begin to form a picture of erratic and unpredictable behaviour here, as if astrology is mediocre and perversely brilliant in patches. But the most damning feature of all, as far as 'hard science' is concerned, is the open admission of intuition as a significant element. The two highest scoring astrologers in the *Astrology Now* trial both indicated that intuition entered into their judgment – and neither had been in astrology for longer than two years!

I suspect it was the comment by Dal Lee, an experienced investigator of ESP in astrology, which put the tin hat on everything. In one of the tests involving ten pairs of charts he scored the first seven correct and the last three wrong. This was an above chance result and therefore contributory to the success of astrology in the trial. However, he had completed the test in a last minute rush on the day the papers were due to sent back:

> It should have taken an astrologist at least half an hour to evaluate each theme, that is to say, ten hours in all. I decided to give each horoscope precisely one minute, thus twenty minutes overall, and I sent off my answers to Mr. Clark... but I could not consider it as purely astrological because I only gave a minute to each theme. I believe rather that it was a case of 'extra-sensory perception', and that would also explain why, as I grew tireder, my 'extra-sensory perception' did not allow me to find the right date for the last three pairs of horoscopes.[6]

Dal Lee's explanation is a reference to the well-known parapsychology effect whereby ESP phenomena tail off as the subject's interest in the experiment declines. On its own, Lee's anecdote proves nothing, but it is illuminating in posing the question of ESP explicitly, and it is consistent with Lee's thesis that many surprising results that are claimed for astrology are properly a function of ESP.[7] The rigid separation of ESP and conventional astrological practice is perhaps understandable but it is unhelpful. It comes from unreflective preconceptions about both astrology and ESP, and it stops us exploring the phenomena that are before us. However, as far as Dal Lee, Geoffrey Dean and the hard scientists are concerned, if it's ESP then it can't be astrology.

TWO PHASES OF RESEARCH

The problematic issue of ESP brings us to the question of how we are to understand these various results. How has the overall *interpretation* of these results proceeded? What conclusions have been drawn in the past, and should be drawn now? Viewed from this perspective the course of research after 1950, and the corresponding attitude of astrologers and researchers, divides broadly into two quarter-century phases, appropriately demarcated by the 1977 publication of the most significant single text in the field, Geoffrey Dean's *Recent Advances in Natal Astrology*. This work is definitive not only for the sheer depth and breadth of its coverage, but also for Dean's claim to authority as an expert in the field of statistical research. It also marks the point at which many practising astrologers finally lost heart in the scientific enterprise.

After *Recent Advances* the landscape began to change for even the most optimistic researchers. In the same year, and with the results already reported in Dean's text, the sterile results of the New York Suicide Study were published. They were an unambiguous pointer to where all such endeavours must lead. The darkening gloom was poisonously distilled in the NCGR-Berkeley 'Double-Blind Test of Astrology' conducted in 1981-2 and published in 1985. The astrologers involved went like lambs to the slaughter, and at the time this test damaged the already slight repute of serious astrology in the eyes of educated opinion, quite apart from confounding astrologers. It ranks as an unrivalled illustration of all that goes wrong when bad science meets naive astrology, and any research astrologer tempted to go down the path of large-scale double-blind tests in the future would be advised to learn its lessons with care. It is given detailed treatment in Appendix 2.

Further erratic results continued to manifest in Vernon Clark trials, but they appear to have been on a downward path ever since. On the other major track of research, Michel Gauquelin's suicide in 1991 underscored the depressing failure of his earlier work to gain scientific status, and both literally and metaphorically the genius of this project had now departed.

For the practising astrologer, scientific research as currently understood is all pain and no gain, but it did not always look like this. When I first came into astrology there were, amongst the small band of research-oriented astrologers, high hopes for the prospects offered by Vernon Clark trials. Taken together with Gauquelin's impressive results, it seemed that we were at the dawn of a new epoch of scientific exploration of astrology. From our present-day perspective these are tattered dreams, but the enthusiasm of an earlier era can be appreciated as a positive attempt to bring astrology into the modern world.

Throughout the 1970's and 1980's, like other astrologers actively involved in the community, I had my chance to take part in one or other of the Vernon Clark replications, but I stayed well clear. I have to admit to an element of Cancerian timidity here; I might undertake a trial that was relatively simple from the point of view of horoscope interpretation and embarrassingly fail. How humiliating – what would I make of my much-vaunted horoscopy then? But the more important factor in my own response to these trials was a sure instinct that not only would I very probably fail, but that intrinsically the experiments as a whole *must* fail, for all of us. I was sure they would fail not because I doubted that astrology is a true thing, but *even though* astrology is a true thing. I had arrived, without philosophical clarity but with intuitive certainty, at the recognition that the premiss on which tests such as those of Vernon Clark have been consistently interpreted, either in success or in failure, is conceptually inadequate to describe and reveal the phenomena with which we are concerned. Part of the project of this book is to construct a conceptual framework which might articulate this intuition.

I have no doubt that many astrologers have a similar gut instinct, which may in part account for the low response to appeals for involvement in experiments. However, this instinct has found little intellectual development in the mainstream literature of astrology, and with a few notable exceptions, most authors leave its ramifications unexamined. The community as a whole has been left bereft and uncomprehending in the face of the generally poor showing of research, and retreats into mute ignorance and non-cooperation.

We face a seemingly unbridgeable chasm between expectation and reality; the expectation of astrologers, following their beliefs, their tradition, and their books, as against the reality – the seemingly feeble results they actually obtain when put to the trial. The obvious and prima facie interpretation of this mismatch is the knock-down: there is 'nothing in astrology', and therefore astrologers' expectations are founded in illusion. Any apparent results are either sampling errors or artifacts, the product of astrologically-induced bias, wish-fulfilment, and stereotyping. There is a less obvious but equally logical possibility: that although there is 'something' in astrology, both researchers and astrologers have a wrong understanding of that something, and therefore a wrong expectation about the sort of results a Vernon Clark trial ought to show. The evidence is more consistent with this view than it is with the knock-down interpretation.

WHAT DOES THE RESEARCH TELL US?

There has been a recent and laudable attempt to provide an overview of the current state of research in Garry Phillipson's *Astrology in the Year Zero*.[8] The discussion is, unfortunately, likely to leave the practising astrologer in a mood of ennui, with a weary shrug of the shoulders as the only sane response. As

Phillipson's book makes clear, almost every facet of earlier research seems to be in question, its conclusions largely discounted, and the only consistency we find is in the general direction of a thumbs-down verdict. The more research that is done, the less we discover astrology. Even Gauquelin's work has needed an extensive rearguard defence to avoid being pulled down, and the termites will remain forever busy, not content until they have undermined the edifice of his results.

In the area of tests on astrologers, Geoffrey Dean has arrived at a tough-minded rejection of all the early Vernon Clark type trials. He has shifted from his 1977 ESP-influenced stance that 'astrologers work' even if their astrology doesn't, towards a total scepticism that sees previous results as entirely the product of artifacts and statistical errors; we will be examining the reasons for this change shortly. However, if we can bracket off the extremes of ideological scepticism for a moment, then the evidence of many decades of research does reasonably suggest the following conclusions:

Results from Research

    (i)   There is a well-established domain of physical relationship (gravitational, electromagnetic etc) between celestial phenomena and terrestrial events, some of which relationships directly affect human behaviour (primary source: various sciences outside of astrology).

   (ii)   There is an objectively verifiable domain of correlation of planets at birth, and temperament and career (primary source: the Gauquelin research).

 (iii)   Neither of the above two categories is likely to validate the great majority of horoscope factors utilised in astrological practice (primary source: New York Suicide Study and many other studies including those of the Gauquelins).

 (iv)   Despite the reservation of (iii) above, conventional astrological interpretation, which may involve intuition or ESP, is shown to be significantly but erratically effective (source: blind trials on the Vernon Clark model).

'Significant but erratic' would, I am sure, sum up the experience of most of us about our astrology, so the above conclusions are unlikely to be a surprise to most astrologers *except* for the hiatus represented in (iii). Before the modern period of research, most astrologers took it for granted as a simple fact that such correlations at the root of their ordinary practice would be capable of a straightforward objective demonstration, and they frequently made vague invitations for the scientists to discover this. When the scientists duly got round to this examination, these hopes were shown to be in vain.

Yet this apparent failure turns to our great advantage. These research conclusions point to a fairly unambiguous distinction between the physical realm of astrology, with its possibility of objective correlations, and some other realm which is experienced when we make practical interpretations from astrological symbolism. Making this distinction allows us to take on board the following conclusions from the results of research. I have appended some important inferences drawn from these conclusions, in brackets:

Conclusions from Results of Research

(v)   Conventional astrological interpretation is not dependent on objective correlations.

(vi) Some unknown 'other element' is involved in the astrological interpretation. This element is not correctly posited by the description of astrology implicit or explicit in the framing of the various studies.

(This in turn suggests that the theoretical framework of traditional astrology is likewise inadequate to describe the phenomena.)

(vii) This 'other element' is broadly but frequently characterised, by astrologers and researchers alike, as either ESP or intuition.

(viii) The perception of astrology is founded in *no special technique* – experience does not improve it.

(The correctness or otherwise of astrological interpretation is therefore not a technical problem. Alternatively, the nature and function of 'technique' have been completely misunderstood in astrological theory.)

(ix) The perception in astrology is not regular but unpredictable and non-regular.

(It is not open to a rule and it appears to be a function of the situation and the participants. If it is a function of the situation, then it is also context-specific rather than universal.)

We should not be put off by talk of ESP and intuition, as if they in some way annul astrology.[9] If astrology is itself a structure or vessel of this mysterious intuition then our prime task must be to study how astrological interpretation can be said to be informed by it, and therein we might find our definition of astrology. Obviously, this position will not suit the scientist who wishes to redefine phenomena into a quantifiable and objective form and then disallow any other definition, which is the danger for astrology in much that passes for research.

FLAWED RESEARCH, FLAWED CONCLUSIONS

The conclusions suggested above are a reasonable interpretation of the results to date, and serve as a stimulus to a more philosophical concern. There is however nothing secure or convincingly reliable in any of this material. The attempt to arrive at inferences about the judgments of astrologers through statistics – or properly speaking, statistical analysis founded on the theory of probability sampling – has been seriously flawed, leading to erroneously negative conclusions. As the long-running debates in *Correlation* have shown[10], many experienced astrologers feel as passionately as I do that this whole scientific approach misses the unique nature of astrology. They are right in the broader philosophical spirit, but they have not managed to halt the monstrous contraption in its tracks because they grant the sceptical researcher an undeserved credibility in the very statistical methods he or she employs. We tend to think that the number-crunching, with its impressive apparatus of standard deviations, chi-squared, Pearson coefficients and the like, must surely within its own little world be 'scientific' and therefore correct. But this is something of an illusion, and conceding it gives far too much away. At this point we fall prey to the same bedazzlement in the face of technique that is such a bane within astrology itself.

However, to back up this critical stance on statistical research, we need to explore in more detail just how clumsy and meaningless are the inferences that have in recent times been drawn from it. We do not have to look far to find glaring inadequacies and failures of logic.

Our point of departure for the current verdict of the researchers remains the work of Geoffrey Dean, and in particular his overview of the Vernon Clark trials. While Dean does not speak for all research, he has been for many years its dominant voice; he has also published his results in cooperation with various independently acknowledged researchers, including Mather, Ivan Kelly, and Nias, who along with Suitbert Ertel appear to endorse his Vernon Clark conclusions.[11] Dean's method has been to create a 'meta-analysis', lumping together all known Vernon Clark trials by plotting a distribution of effect sizes. In other words, the statistical significance attained in each separate trial has been entered on a graph. The results have been tabulated according to the year of the trial, in order to observe possible trends over time, and according to sample size, i.e. the number of horoscopes (or horoscope pairs where relevant) used in each trial. The original Vernon Clark trial yields three separate plots, because three separate tests were conducted. The resulting diagrams have been reproduced several times, including *Correlation*, and *Astrology in the Year Zero*[12].

The main quantitative conclusion computed from the meta-analysis is that when the studies are combined there is only a small overall apparent effect size, or plus result for astrology. From the 40 studies up to 1994, astrologers' judgments showed an accuracy of around 52.5% compared with a chance level of 50% (correlation .05). Seventeen studies where subjects were asked to pick out their own chart interpretation, prepared blind by the astrologer, showed a slightly more promising outcome at 56.5% (correlation .13). It must be stressed that compared with the expectations of many astrologers these are low and uninspiring correlations; but they are nonetheless statistically significant non-zero results.

These tiny correlations are not however the most interesting feature. A striking phenomenon which emerges even at first sight is the *wide scatter of results*, ranging from highly positive to very negative effects, and a feature of both the earliest and the most recent studies. This means that Vernon Clark trials appear to give more often than would be expected by chance surprisingly good or alternatively surprisingly poor results.

META-STATISTICS AND THE FARTHING ADRIFT

In his young days my father, a Virgo who was smart with figures, worked as a clerk for a stock exchange broker. Every day at the close of trade the books had to be tallied. One detail fascinated me when he recounted it, just as it fascinated him; there might be thousands of pounds traded and dozens of trades, but if there was just one farthing error, the whole lot would have to be painstakingly checked and rechecked. It could not just be left alone as inconsequential; for one farthing might be the sum of two huge mistakes, a thousand pounds wrongly accounted in and a thousand pounds plus a farthing wrongly out. The specifity of accounting is a world away from the generalisations of statistics, but the analogy holds in one important respect. Adopting the statistician's golden rule of the null hypothesis, which starts on the assumption that there is 'nothing there', then however tiny a thing, any non-random result beyond our conventional limits of significance must suggest to us that, on the contrary, there may be 'something there'. The farthing cannot be allowed to drift.

But the more important potential message of the accountant's farthing is that the slight overall positive result in the trials could easily disguise a much more significant circumstance: two or more overlapping, mutually exclusive and highly non-random profiles of success and failure amongst the astrologers. We have already referred to several instances of curious phenomena occurring in the early experiments, including the inexplicable failure of all the French participants in the first Vernon Clark trials. From these considerations follows the possible significance of the strongly-marked scatter over the whole range of tests. Sadly, far from being taken up as a challenge to think again and rework the parameters of research, this phenomenon has been consigned to the dustbin, in a move that can only be described as numerical sleight-of-hand.

THE RED-AND-BLACK FALLACY

From the outset Geoffrey Dean has shown little enthusiasm for the results in the Vernon Clark trials; by the time of *Recent Advances in Natal Astrology* he was eager to discount them as ESP or intuition, and therefore nothing to do with astrology. That is, however, an uncomfortable move, begging awkard questions. Sometime after 1977, courtesy of Hans Eysenck, he discovered the daisy-cutter with which to obliterate all trace of these embarrassments. Here is how Geoffrey Dean deals with the otherwise inexplicable distribution of effect-sizes in over 40 experiments:

> Imagine a hand of 10 playing cards picked at random. Even though there are equal numbers of red and black in the pack, we seldom end up with equal proportions in our hand... The same with birth charts... charts will tend to be of two kinds, those that fit their owners (call these red) and those that don't (call these black). Suppose like Vernon Clark we want to know the proportion of owners with red charts. We collect ten owners and send them to astrologers. If the astrologers know their stuff they will quickly discover which charts are red and which are black. But the reds in such a small sample will be determined much more by sampling variations than by the proportion in the population (which is what we want to know)... Yes, we may have three or seven reds instead of the five predicted, but so what?[13]

The identical red-and-black playing card example appears in the *Encyclopedia of the Paranormal* article on astrology, where sampling errors are described as being 'like magic – out of nothing they can produce results that are interesting, exciting, and totally spurious.'[14] Hans Eysenck is credited with the original observation. Here is how he described this 'statistical point of some subtlety' in 1982:

Clearly the life patterns of some subjects will agree with astrological prediction, while those of others will disagree. If we now pick 5 or 10 people to provide birth times and details about their profession or personality, then we will pick some who are astrological confirmers, and others who are astrological disconfirmers, that is, some for whom it would be judged incorrect in terms of agreement between their birth chart and their personality or occupation.. If we take more confirmers than disconfirmers, then the outcome will be positive (provided the astrologers know their business).. with small numbers chance.. may entirely determine the outcome.[15]

Let us think through several possible scenarios. Firstly, follow the original Vernon Clark model, but with only a single astrologer who is asked to judge ten cases, comparing ten pairs of charts (one correct, one fictitious) against ten life histories; the test equally could be that of a comparison between charts of people with high IQ and cerebral palsy. We must play the statistics game and assume the null hypothesis, that there is in reality no true connection between horoscopes and lives; it is this null assumption that the astrologer hopes to render implausible. In this situation the logic of confirmers/disconfirmers, red/black, holds. Taken out of context a success rate of 6 to 4, or 60%, sounds convincing, yet it has been produced by a single variation, equivalent to picking 6 red cards to 4 black. However many factors the astrologer is bringing into account, whether it is just one or dozens, by chance alone there will be six or more cases of a lucky hit out of ten tries on 38% of occasions; and a promising showing of seven or more hits on one occasion in six. Equally, by chance, the astrologer will get the disappointing result of three or less on a similar number of occasions. If we repeat this test of our single astrologer a number of times, we expect to see a mean of five out of ten, but with a wide variability or scatter of results mainly between two and eight hits out of ten.

We can hardly fail to see the problem of a wide variation of results if we conduct repeated ten-horoscope tests on just one astrologer. However, Eysenck's observation comes into its own if, instead of a single astrologer, we test ten astrologers who each have to go through the discrimination of the same ten pairs of charts and ten life histories. It may not be obvious on first consideration, but provided the astrologers use similar methods of interpretation, then the very same sampling error applies to them in equal measure as in the case of the single astrologer. The sampling error does not reduce because there are ten astrologers instead of one, since the result depends on a random initial choice of reds/blacks, confirmers/disconfirmers in the sample. Under these conditions Eysenck's statement is vindicated – chance may entirely determine the outcome of apparent success or failure in any trial.

It is however necessary to add a crucial qualifier to the original formulation; *Eysenck's observation has force only to the extent that the astrologers are using similar methods of interpretation.* For the observation to hold, all ten astrologers must behave as if they were in effect one. The observation breaks down where the astrologers use different methods of interpretation, as becomes apparent in our next example.

Take the situation of ten pairs of charts being matched for indications of being married or staying single. Astrologer A gives priority to Venus and the Moon in a male chart and Mars and the Sun in a female chart. These choices, and the way in which they are handled by the astrologer, constitute his or her *profile of interpretation* with respect to the matter under scrutiny, marriage. Let us allow that the random sample presented to astrologer A happens by chance to give a correct match for that astrologer's interpretation profile in seven of the ten pairs, creating a good score. Astrologer B, more traditional in approach, employs a quite different profile and makes an assessment on the descending sign and its ruler, together with its relationship to the ruler of the ascendant. The random sample that gave seven matches out of a group of horoscopes to astrologer A may equally 'by chance' give four matches to astrologer B, in the very same group of horoscopes. The choices for astrologers A and B are likely to overlap, agreeing in several cases and disagreeing in others; the usual tendency will be for the sampling error in the second profile to neutralise or cancel out the effect on the overall result produced by the sampling error in the first profile. Now add astrologer C who is more interested in a broad sign-based approach and believes that Librans can't bear to be alone, and astrologer D who combines bits of the approach of A and B plus a neat line of interpretation on Uranus in the 7th, and we can see that the existence of distinct profiles amongst the interpreting astrologers has an effect equivalent to multiplying the sample size, thereby reducing the overall result of sampling error.

We can expect the degree of variation between interpretation profiles to depend on the particular test; for example, a simple discrimination of the psycho-logical characteristics of extraversion and introversion is likely to be handled quite similarly by most astrologers, on the basis of the preponderance of positive and negative zodiac sign placings. Even so, astrologer A could emphasise Sun and Moon signs while astrologer B gives more weight to the ascendant, and so on, so that in this simplest case we could find three or more profiles in a group of ten astrologers. Where there are a number of factors compounded together, as in Vernon Clark's first trial which involved occupation, marital status, hobbies and health, and especially where the tradition of astrology allows several possible significations for each of these biographical categories, then we would not be surprised to find at least six or seven relatively distinct interpretation profiles amongst ten competent astrologers, with additional subtle variations even between closely similar profiles.

From the point of view of theory, it is a complicated matter to predict the probable impact of interpretation profiles on overall sampling error, because much will depend on whether the profiles are wholly distinct (independent variables) or partial subsets of each other (dependent variables). However, it can immediately be grasped that the simplistic single-choice red-and-black analogy proposed by Eysenck and Dean has by several orders over-estimated the extent of sampling error in Vernon Clark test results, and is therefore unlikely to account for their wide variation of effect-sizes.[16]

How did Eysenck fall into this error? The clue is in the statement he puts in parenthesis, 'provided the astrologers know their business'. Dean repeats this as astrologers 'knowing their stuff'. The implicit and unthought-through assumption is that competent astrology involves one main route or profile of interpretation in order to arrive at its result. I am sure that few experienced astrologers would regard this assumption as correct, and the diversity we see in astrological practice and literature certainly contradicts it. Dean himself contradicts it, apparently without being aware that he thereby undermines his red-and-black argument. He quotes a correlation of just .10 between the test results for different astrologers, which 'shows that there is almost no agreement between astrologers on what a birth chart means'.[17] He goes further into the process of interpretation, explaining that astrologers 'focus on whatever tiny subset of factors their experience or their teacher's experience has shown to "work". But the subset that "works" is rarely the same from one astrologer to another'.[18] Dean's subsets are none other than the interpretation profiles discussed above.

In fairness to Eysenck, it should be observed that his original observation arose in the context of a balanced and open-minded analysis of astrological research up to 1982, treated within the limits of contemporary science. We cannot expect Eysenck as a psychologist to be well acquainted with either the detailed methods of astrologers, or with the wide variations in those methods. Even though his overall conclusion is wrong, his observation rightly places small-sample Vernon Clark trials under notice that the question of sampling error should be explicitly addressed.

TWO ORDERS IN ASTROLOGY

It is disappointing if the efforts with statistical trials over so many years are discounted simply for lack of clear thinking about what they may or may not show. If they are to be bothered with at all, these experiments need to be worked in an exploratory spirit, and not in the negating, gainsaying mood that seems to dominate present research. We must remember that the original Vernon Clark experiments, and their replications, really do show undeniable results of 'astrologers working', and the weakness of further replications remains just that – a weakness of replication. Perhaps astrologers doing these tests don't believe in them any more, and that is why they will decline over time, especially in a withering research environment. There is no point doing more tests if any positive result whatever will eventually be washed away and declared void.

A confusion that we should particularly guard against is that of allowing negative or weak test results to be used as a basis for the negation of astrology as a whole. Astrology is not the same in test conditions as it is in life, and a non-showing or a weak showing in a test does not disprove anything except the capacity of astrology to show in that particular test, and tests of a similar nature. On the other hand this observation does not spare us from the obvious and commonsense conclusion that we astrologers seem to entertain unsustainable notions about how we expect our astrology to show, and that must throw into doubt the credibility of our own definitions and descriptions of what we do. Vernon Clark, like the Gauquelins, represents a true if limited spirit of inquiry, but in the worst cases our own weakness allows a false definition and understanding to breed. This joins with a sterile vision of science to produce a marriage of scientism and naive astrology.

Despite all the frustration and disappointment of astrology's flirtation with science, there is an extraordinary amount to learn from the experience. Looking back on the itemised conclusions from research, two relatively independent orders have emerged, the first in the objective correlations established in particular by Gauquelin, and the second in the evidence of the blind trials. All the evidence, both from experience and from research, points to a primary conceptual division in the field of astrology along these lines. This immediately falls into place with the ancient distinction between an astrology of *causes*, objective, universal, regular and astrologer-independent, and an astrology of *signs* which is participatory, context-specific and irregular. This is, I believe, the very same distinction found since medieval times between *natural astrology* and *judicial astrology*. Judicial astrology is what we all do in regular astrology, the work of *interpretations* in particular situations, most usually but not necessarily from horoscopes. It is based on a symbolic approach.

Natural astrology refers to a universal domain of planetary and celestial influence. Although, as with Gauquelin's findings, there is a distinct level of influence on the individual, this does not allow definite judgment and interpretation or even a strongly probabilistic assertion, such as, for example, 'with Uranus in the 7th you are likely to have an unconventional partner'. Such interpretations are the hallmark of a judicial astrology approach. I would argue that natural astrology is appropriate to the domain of science while judicial astrology relates to divination. The subject that we regularly practise, setting up and interpreting horoscopes, and talking about each other's Sun-Signs, is a practice of astrological divination. Because of this, and to avoid confusions with older uses of the term 'judicial', whenever I need to make a specific contrast with natural (scientific) astrology I will term the primary division of the subject *divinatory astrology*.

Once this division is accepted many problems about research become clarified, as the method of testing or discrimination appropriate to one order are seen as inappropriate to the other. We do not have to reduce one to the other, nor do we have to abandon one viewpoint just to hold on to the other. Both have their relative validity, as all the evidence indicates. Further, this division is a practical and realistic reflection of the state of astrology and it does not preclude the ultimate philosophical goal for those who wish to seek it. The dream of Kepler and John Addey is of an 'equation of the orders', whereby we can find a way of relating both in a cosmic whole. Such a possibility is an issue of considerable philosophical importance, but it goes far beyond the requirements of this current thesis. My main concern is that practising astrologers should develop for themselves a way of understanding their practice in the light of divination. This is not a simple task, and there are many puzzles on the way. Until that task is adequately achieved, any idea of synthesising these great orders of science and divination is to my mind premature. In any case, our era may not be quite ready for it.

PSI – NEPTUNE

At this point I would like to take a step back to symbolism. On the basis of my own experience over many years, supported by the overall picture given to us from scientific research, I suggest that this 'other element' mentioned in the itemised conclusions above has the following properties: it is non-regulated and mysterious, difficult to disentangle from illusion and delusion, not capable of being grasped and controlled, not separated from the situation in which it occurs, and – a significant clue – characterised as paranormal. In various ways I have arrived at the understanding that a primary symbol here is Neptune. Neptune is a mysterious signifier for astrology, hidden and ignored by astrologers but there in everything they do. It will be found frequently associated with the more obvious modern symbol for astrology, Uranus, and the two between them show the extreme polarities of the subject, but that would take us into another discussion.

A remarkable facet of Neptune's symbolism is the association of the glyph with the Greek letter psi, which is used as an indicator of both the paranormal unknown element in parapsychology *and* as an abbreviation for psychoanalysis. Taking a hint from these clues, I treat Psi-Neptune as a symbol for a mysterious agency at work in our astrology behind our everyday consciousness.

As will become more obvious in later chapters, there is great value in keeping this symbol open and not over-defined. Psi-Neptune may refer to ESP and intuition, personal or collective, or simply to the strange context-specific and unpredictable working of astrology. In the absence of definite knowledge, and in the face of a mystery, we are wise to keep our definitions open and fluid.

This is an appropriate juncture to bring forward a piece of evidence from the horse's mouth, so to speak. Vernon Clark came to a definite conclusion about what his famous trial demonstrated. In retrospect we can see that his implicit premiss about the objective and demonstrable nature of horoscopic interpretation could not be sustained. What he thought he had dispelled forever was a distorted image of the very truth that his genius had revealed:

> Never again will it be possible to dismiss the astrological technique as a vague, spooky, and mystical business – or as the plaything of undisciplined psychics – or as merely the profitable device of unscrupulous quacks...

Vague, spooky, mystical, psychic, undisciplined, quakery. Which planet might Vernon Clark be referring to, I wonder?

CONTEXT-PSI IN ASTROLOGY: A JUNGIAN VERSION

It is worth mentioning that the suggestions I have brought forward concerning the 'mysterious other factor' have been well-known to astrologers for many years through the work of Carl Jung on synchronicity. It has only been with the pioneering studies of Maggie Hyde, however, that the implications of Jung's work have been explored.[19] In his astrological marriage experiment, published in 1952,

Jung gave the results of a statistical study of the horoscopes of married couples, which had been analysed in respect of classical synastry indicators he was looking for – Sun conjunct Moon, Moon conjunct Moon, ascendant conjunct Moon.

The data was analysed in three batches, checking results of one batch by replication in the other batches. The first batch, impatiently analysed ahead of the others by Jung, showed an extraordinary promise for astrology. The greatest of the classical indicators, Sun conjunct Moon, topped the distribution of synastry contacts amongst the married pairs. Was astrology going to be validated?

But then, as Jung observed, Mercurius, the synchronicity trickster, was playing his old game.[20] The second batch no longer gave a significant showing to Sun conjunct Moon – instead it came up with *another* of the three contacts as significant: Moon conjunct Moon. And the reader can no doubt guess the punch line of this joke: the third batch gave as most significant the ascendant conjunct Moon. Taken overall, in the terms of statistical analysis, there was a failure to confirm the astrological hypothesis and each of the three separate apparently significant results washed out the statistical significance of the others when they were taken together.

Jung realised that a quite different order of significance appeared to be in play here. He was finding the three results which he was looking for, so his own subjective state as an observer seemed to be implicated in the results. In order to test this observation, Jung then played a little game with the material. He wondered what would happen if the material was handled by different observers. He selected three individuals whose psychological states were well known to him and asked them to draw by lot the horoscopes for twenty married pairs from the collection of data. The first selection, by a woman in 'an intense state of emotional excitement' produced a preponderance of Mars aspects, which Jung considered to be fully descriptive of her psychic state. The second participant was a self-suppressive woman 'unable to assert her personality'. Appropriately to her problems, she chose a preponderance of ascendant-descendant plus Moon contacts. The third subject was a woman with 'strong inner oppositions' where union and reconciliation were major issues. She came up with Sun-Moon conjunctions in her batch, reflecting her own desire for the 'union of opposites'.

As Maggie Hyde observes, 'the whole conduct of this "scientific experiment" has by now broken down into divination'. In response to this peculiar experience, Jung began to talk of the 'secret mutual connivance' which he considered to be at work in astrology, implicating the astrologer in his or her material. Now consider what Jung has done. He started his synchronicity experiment using statistical method to detect an a-causal correspondence at work in astrology. But then when the experiment took a funny turn, he realised that the a-causal correspondence he had found in some mysterious way implicated *him*. In her analysis of Jung's development of the synchronicity concept, Maggie Hyde has named this as 'Synchronicity II', distinguishing it from the more objective and universal working of 'Synchronicity I' that Jung hoped he might demonstrate in astrology. If we compare this discovery of Synchronicity II with what has been said earlier about the peculiar and erratic behaviour of statistics in other astrology experiments, it can be seen that Jung has taken the step implicit in context-psi and interpreted *an order of significance at work beyond the significance statistically established within the data*. He has, in other words, interpreted the context which has apparently produced the psi.

I can therefore re-emphasise a theme that has already been brought forward. The erratic and unregulated behaviour of astrological experiments, especially but not exclusively those on the Vernon Clark model, may be a manifestation of context-psi, responding to the attitudes and desires of the participants. By implication therefore, each statistical experiment in the field of astrology should be examined for the possibility of a further order of contextual interpretation, and I have the strong suspicion that it is this that will turn out to be the really significant interpretation.

But I am not so naive as to imagine that statisticians will take this possibility seriously. Indeed, how can they? It would be an example of Neptune sinking the whole ship of modern statistical practice were this to be taken on board. Yet we astrologers should remember that the last word of interpretation must never be given to the arbitration of the merely mechanical application of 'statistics'. Each result must be interpreted in its own context, on its merits, and wherever possible in the light of the symbolism that is being revealed.

* * * * * * *

On all the accumulated evidence we have before us, the results of science-research in astrology fall into two broad categories. When they are in the realm of purely objective correlations, then they apply to natural astrology. In this case they are of a *different order* to the interpretations of symbol made by astrologers, and it would be disingenuous of us to pretend otherwise. On the other hand, when science research attempts to grasp the interpretive domain of divinatory astrology, then the results become unstable and contradictory.

Earlier, in giving an overview of the conclusions from research, I suggested that our inability to contemplate the mysterious other element at work in our practical astrology reflects an inadequacy in the theoretical framework of traditional astrology. Despite the fact that the distinction between 'signs' and 'causes' has been well understood since ancient times, our mainstream tradition has never successfully differentiated the two orders of significance. Instead, it has continually forced the phenomena of divinatory astrology into a natural astrology mould. This brings us to the consideration of the roots of our dilemmas of science and the symbol, in the taken-for-granted treatment of time, and the Ptolemaic construction of astrological theory.

NOTES

1 Vernon Clark, quoted in J. A. West *The Case for Astrology* (Penguin Viking/Arkana 1991), p358.
2 For the studies up to 1976, my main source is Geoffrey Dean's Recent Advances in Natal Astrology (Analogic, 1977; distributed by Para Research Inc., Rockport, Mass). In my original discussion in the first edition of *Moment of Astrology*, I suggested that enthusiasm for Vernon Clark-type trials had declined after 1985, but this was a wrong assumption since in fact a cluster of trials have been made since then. These are indicated by Geoffrey Dean in *Correlation* Northern Winter 1998 p75, and reproduced in *Astrology in the Year Zero* p147. In my brief review I erroneously missed out five experiments prior to 1985 which at the time of writing had been reported in *Correlation*. See correspondence on this matter in Letters, Astrological Journal vol. 37 no. 2 March/April 1995 (letter from Geoffrey Dean, to which I reply). As I observed at the time, these additional experiments up to 1985 confirmed the general thesis I advanced in the first edition, since they "display a similar pattern to those I reviewed, namely a curious patchwork of erratic and unpredictable success and failure".
3 'The New York Suicide Study', *Journal of Geocosmic Research (NCGR)*, vol. 2, no. 2.
4 G.Dean, op.cit., p.554.
5 Michel Gauquelin *The Truth about Astrology* (Basil Blackwell, Oxford, 1983), pp.138-9.
6 ibid., p.138; quoted from Jacques Soudel.
7 Over 25 years Lee made a special study of ESP and astrology. He makes the following points:
   1. Astrological meanings are so broad that specific indications are impossible to obtain blind unless some ESP faculty is used.
   2. Some astrologers have ESP at least some of the time. They often get a perfect answer but hardly know where it comes from.
   3. The role of ESP is rarely mentioned in textbooks. Instead they tend to list unusual ESP-derived feats, implying that astrology can do this all the time. This is unfair to astrology, to ESP, and especially to unsuspecting students. (Summary from G.Dean, op.cit., p.18).
8 Phillipson, G. *Astrology in the Year Zero* (Flare, London, 2000).
9 The words 'ESP' and 'intuition' are used as tokens in the face of some mysterious essence of judgment or inspiration, not just in astrology but in art, music, literature – and science. But to say, for example, that we should ignore music as a study because at the heart of it is some 'intuitive' knowing of music which is more fundamental would be immediately recognised as absurd. What has happened with terms like 'intuition' is that they have become hypostatised and made substantial, and then hived off as if in a separate category from the activity they are being used to describe.
10 *Correlation* debates: see especially series of *Key Topics* organised by Geoffrey Dean et al. and

ensuing correspondence. *Key Topic 1* 'Is the Scientific Approach Relevant to Astrology?' appeared in issue 13:1 1994.

11 Phillipson op.cit p166.

12 Meta-analysis of Vernon Clark trials: see Smit, R. H. (1998/9). 'Results of the Knegt Follow-up Test.' Correlation 17(2): 75.; and Phillipson, G. *Astrology in the Year Zero.* (Flare, London, 2000) p147.

   An earlier version with results up to 1994 appeared in a major study on astrology, highly sceptical in tone, by Dean, Mather and Kelly, 'Astrology' in the *Encyclopedia of the Paranormal* ed G.Stein. (Prometheus, New York, 1996) p76.; and in Dean, G. A., D. K. B. Nias, et al. *Graphology, astrology, and parapsychology. The Scientific Study of Human Nature: tribute to Hans J. Eysenck at Eighty.* (H. Nyborg, 1996), p517.

13 Phillipson op.cit p145.

14 op.cit. Dean et al. *Encyclopedia of the Paranormal* p76.

15 Eysenck, H. J. and D. K. B. Nias *Astrology: science or superstition?* (Maurice Temple Smith, London, 1982) p86-7.

16 The extent of the over-estimation can be indicated if we look more closely at the example where the astrologer scores seven or more hits out of ten. This result, seeming to show that 'astrology works', will actually turn up by chance once every six times (p=.172). However, if we find that amongst the astrologers tested are just two distinct interpretation profiles, then the probability of a mean hit rate of seven out of ten or better coming out by chance is cut by two thirds to p=.056, or once in 17 times. With three distinct profiles the probability of sampling error producing a mean rate of seven or more hits declines to one in 50 (p = .021). Four distinct profiles is probably a conservative estimate wherever astrologers are judging a range of biographical factors, and at this level the expected mean of seven or more hits in ten falls to one in 120 (p=.0083), while even the modest mean of six or more hits out of ten drops to less than one in seven trials (p=.134).

17 Dean, G., A. Mather, et al. op. cit 'Astrology'. *Encyclopedia of the Paranormal..* p74. See also Phillipson op.cit. p157.

18 Phillipson op.cit. p161.

19 Maggie Hyde, *Jung & Astrology* (Aquarian, London, 1992), ch.7.

20 The reader may be wondering about my attitude to symbolism here since I have Psi-Neptune and Mercurius weaving around the same material. In brief, Mercury is directly concerned with the step that crosses from light to dark, dark to light and *makes conscious* in interpretation. Mercury has a gift of language and writing. Neptune 'inspires' our interpretation and may secretly move us but is strictly unconscious for us, although occasionally flooding through into consciousness.

5

Ptolemy's Broad Shoulders: The Moment of Astrology in the Western Tradition

TIME is of the essence for astrology, yet it is commonly taken for granted. It is treated as the background *in which* astrology occurs, although unlike the time of science and everyday common-sense, it is modulated and qualitative. How do the phenomena of astrology relate to time? Carl Jung's 1930 formulation succinctly states a position that is often taken by astrologers as definitive:

Whatever is born or done in this moment of time has the quality of this moment of time.[1]

It is usually forgotten that Jung himself eventually retracted the statement and criticised its tautology, and it is incompatible with the later development of his description of 'synchronicity'.[2] Be that as it may, it well represents the understanding of most astrologers, and serves as a useful starting point for the description of viewpoints. What is this mysterious quality of the time-moment? There are two approaches found in traditional astrology, often woven together - or muddled - in the attitudes of the same author. The orthodox classical position has an Aristotelian foundation, and is a species of *celestial causation*. The quality of the time moment is determined by the disposition of the influencing heavens 'at that moment'. The second approach is Platonic in its inspiration. It may be characterised as *cosmic sympathy*: the planets and their positions *mirror* the occult quality of the totality of the macrocosm-microcosm 'at that moment'. This sympathy is also mirrored in the knowing that belongs to the soul. The distinction of these two positions tends on the one hand to an astrology of *causes*, and on the other to an astrology of *signs*, thus giving two different orientations to astrology right down to the present day.

In describing the two positions I have in each case added the phrase 'at that moment' because this reveals a point of complete agreement between them. The phenomenon of astrology is taken to be at root *contemporaneous*. An effect or a sign produced in a distinct moment of objective time relates the situation on earth and the state of the heavens *at that moment* and therefore allows an astrological interpretation for the thing born or done *at that moment*. For much of practical astrology, therefore, it does not matter which of the two perspectives we take, because in either case the question of time leads to the same outcome. A horoscope for the objective time of a thing, especially in its origin, is astrologically imprinted at that time, and the imprinting is a fact of objective and historical reality independent of any interpretation of that reality that may take place. Therefore, we say, the astrological imprinting or significance 'really is there', quite independent of any later act of interpretation. The heavens become like a clock ticking out the changes and the horoscope is seen as a factual record of astrological imprinting. We may be unaware of the true astrological significance, we may misinterpret it, we may have inadequate techniques to bring it to light, but we suppose this real significance to continue as an objective and empirical reality regardless of consciousness.

The mystery of time is really no mystery at all for this 'same-timeness' premiss, which adopts a completely taken-for-granted notion of objective time. Further, the astrological character is treated as a fixed feature, as if once imprinted it is a stable property of the thing 'born or done', wholly independent of the context within which it is taken up as significant by and for the one interpreting. This view of an enduring real significance, posited as existing independent of all interpretations, is equally part of the attitude of modern scientific rationalism.

I have had to labour this description of the traditional treatment of the moment in astrology because the issues involved so easily slip away from our grasp. The nature of time is, after all, one of the most elusive and intractable of all philosophical problems.

Saturn is the symbol for time, and traditional astrology has fallen to the maleficity of that signification. In taking the question of time entirely for granted, and in securing a wholly 'objective' demonstration through the objectivity of the time moment, astrology has set a fateful and binding limit to its expression, and represses a whole domain of its experience. This rather strong claim against the classical tradition can be made on several counts. Quite apart from the instability and elusiveness of its results, especially in horoscope interpretation, all the evidence from disciplines with some relevance to astrology point to relativity in time, rather than a fixed order of objective time. This is not simply a cliché borrowed from physics. The psychology of the unconscious has revealed the psychic relativity of time and space and parapsychology has revealed their psi-relativity. And which student of Magia and the imagination, ancient and modern, could there be who did not know of the capacity of the Soul to draw the object of its desire towards it across time and space?

But the most convincing evidence of all must emerge from within astrology itself. The experience of our astrology, when closely examined, should convince us that its working cannot be contained in the traditional approach to its moment. The need for a convincing formal demonstration of this dilemma was a primary goal in establishing the 'anti-astrology signature'. The working of this horoscope, remember, demonstrates as conclusively as can be established within the limits of astrology's own method, that in divinatory (judicial) astrology,

The same-time coming together of OBJECTIVE EVENT and OBJECTIVE HEAVENS is not a *necessary* condition for the astrological effect to come to pass.

To reiterate, this was established by showing that the horoscope for a moment in 1907 showed proper astrological significations for an event in 1975, without in any sense being an origination (birth) or otherwise significant moment for that event. The meaningful connection between 1907 and 1975 originated in the random choice made by the participants and in our interpretation of that meaning.

Further, I went on to offer a second suggestion which of its nature is not reducible to a single demonstration but which, as experience will affirm, is frequently encountered in the practice of divinatory astrology:

The same-time coming together of OBJECTIVE EVENT and OBJECTIVE HEAVENS is not a *sufficient* condition for the astrological effect to come to pass.

In other words, not every horoscope supposedly 'of' something is astrologically significant for that thing. Without going into further detail on this second statement at this point, I would only remind the horary and inceptional astrologer of the phenomenon of lack of radicality - i.e. completely irrelevant symbolism - in some charts. In any case, the classical tradition only fully admits the same-time as a sufficient condition to produce astrology in a very limited category, that is the 'causal-temporal origin' of the thing or person, but this is fully taken up in the discussion on Ptolemy that follows.

It is evident that if same-timeness is neither necessary nor sufficient for the phenomenon of astrology, we will have logically removed the first condition of the classical statement of the 'moment of astrology' as far as horoscopy is concerned.

As I have already indicated, classical Greco-Roman astrology's statement of temporal objectivity is at one and the same time a statement of the empirical objectivity of the astrological effect - each premiss entails the other. Thus at one stroke the challenge to the classical 'moment' appears to destroy the foundation of traditional astrology's secure claim to truth. The student could be forgiven for thinking that this points to a ruinous state of affairs, and that one might as well abandon astrology as a fiction. It is my purpose to suggest that by loosening some of its old bonds astrology will begin to discover another and greater order of its revelation, which has in any case always informed it, despite the constraints of its classical theory.

Before that task can be attempted, it is important to gain a clear picture of just how our tradition has answered the question 'at what moment does the astrological effect come-to-pass?'. The theoretical answer to this question from late Hellenistic astrology has laid down the foundations of astrology's theory. These foundations have endured essentially unchanged to the present day.

THE PTOLEMAIC CONSTRUCTION OF CLASSICAL ASTROLOGY

It was the gift of Ptolemy to formulate the fundamental lines along which has developed the greater part of our astrology. A return to his formulation will reveal the cardinal point of reference for later treatments of the moment of astrology.

For Ptolemy, and for the tradition that has been his heir, the description of the moment of astrology is compounded with the explanation of *how* astrological effects come to pass. In order to discern his treatment of the moment of astrology, we need to follow the explanation he offers as to how astrology works.

Ptolemy postulates an 'ambient', or ether, suffused through the heavens and nature. Changes in the ambient affect the elements, fire and air first, then earth and water. The Sun's influence prevails in producing the general quality of the ambient, through both the seasonal and diurnal cycles. The solar influence is modified by the separate influences of the Moon, other planets, and the fixed stars. Through the mediating ambient, all things under the sky are affected by the heavenly bodies.

Two orders of effect upon the world are carefully distinguished. The more powerful order is the universal, or general, acting upon 'whole races, countries, and cities', and upon 'periodic conditions, such as wars, famines, pestilences, earthquakes, deluges'. A further subdivision of this universal effect concerns occasional conditions such as 'variations of the intensity of storms, heat, and winds, or of good and bad crops, and so on'.[3] What is the moment of astrology for this order of universal influence?

> In the case of universals we have to take many starting-points, since we have no
> single one for the universe...[4]

It is clear that by the term translated as 'starting point', Ptolemy also intends the
meaning of 'causal origin'. Such starting points of the astrological effect are
various celestial configurations, but especially 'the more complete eclipses and
the significant passages of the planets'.

Knowledge of the working of this universal order of astrological influence
allows the possibility of predictions on a wide scale, but does not lead to
prediction at the individual level. Different individuals will suffer widely different
circumstances, whatever fate may befall the whole species or community of
which they are part. Specific prediction at the level of the individual is, however,
possible from a knowledge of the second order of astrological effect, the
particular. The heavens, while continually and universally affecting all things,
carry especial power to stamp their impression on the critical and initial
formation of planets, animals, or man. Ptolemy states:

> ... not only must things already compounded be affected in some way by the
> motions of these heavenly bodies, but likewise the germination and fruition of
> the seed must be moulded and conformed to the quality proper to the heavens at
> the time.[5]

In this way the heavenly configuration has a powerful effect at the seed's
uniquely impressionable moment, the instant of fertilisation. This effect is
entirely modified by the local aspect of the sky, that is by the place on the earth's
surface. The heavenly configuration moulds and conforms the seed and thus
determines particular individual characteristics of the entity into which the seed
will grow, within the limits of the genetic and environmental possibilities for that
entity.

The instant of fertilisation is taken as the *origin*, causal and temporal, of the
entity. This moment is so decisive in forming the astrological character that all
further changes in the ambient following the instant of origin can have only an
indirect influence on individual characteristics, working on the astrological
imprint established at fertilisation. Therefore, at the individual level of the
astrological effect, *all other moments are mediated by the moment of origin, and all
other horoscopes are mediated by the horoscope of origin.*

Ptolemy, and the tradition of horoscopic astrology that follows him, gives
absolute primacy to the temporal beginning, the moment of origin:

> For to the seed is given once and for all at the beginning such and such qualities
> by the endowment of the ambient; and even though it may change as the body

subsequently grows, since by natural process it mingles with itself in the process of growth matter which is akin to itself, thus it resembles even more closely the type of its initial quality.[6]

The pattern given to the seed is seen as the type to which the individual grows, and towards which all later changes tend. This is an idea which, when applied to the natal horoscope, is encountered even in the most modern humanistic astrology.

Through his second order of the astrological influence Ptolemy has established this instant of origin as a moment of astrology. In this way he can justify the interpretation of a conception horoscope as yielding meaningful predictions concerning the fate of the entity. For man, as for other living creatures, the prime origin is the instant of fertilisation of the seed, at conception:

> in cases in which the very time of conception is known either by chance or by observation, it is more fitting that we should follow it in determining the special nature of body and soul.[7]

However, Ptolemy's great concern, the whole project of the third and fourth books of the *Tetrabiblos*, is the horoscope of birth, and not the horoscope of conception. This is so even though when birth is compared with conception 'its importance in time is secondary', and it is 'not...causative in the full sense'.[8]

His justification of the natal horoscope builds on the foundations already established for the horoscope of conception. He makes this justification by combining two logically distinct arguments. In his first argument, Ptolemy suggests that birth is 'even more perfect in potentiality' than conception:

> For the child at birth and his bodily form take on many additional attributes which he did not have before, when he was in the womb, those very ones indeed which belong to human nature alone.[9]

This pivotal assertion, on which so much is made to depend, is not illustrated or amplified. It is implied that birth is the origin of truly human existence, as contrasted with the merely biological existence of the foetus. Further, it is the very instant of birth that is referred to, and Ptolemy will go on to demonstrate the reading of the horoscope of that instant, the natus. The assertion of birth as an 'origin' of human nature is juxtaposed with the earlier discussion of the impact of the heavens at the instant of fertilisation of a seed. In this way, Ptolemy induces his reader to make an analogy between the instant of fertilisation and the instant of birth. Birth is then the 'seed' of independent human existence. But this analogy is highly problematic. It may be easy to envisage Ptolemy's second, particular order of the astrological influence physically impressed upon a little seed, but a baby at birth is a complex creature 'already compounded'. It is difficult to imagine an actual seed of 'human nature alone' except as a poetic metaphor. The analogy carries over a physical and literal statement about seeds, appropriate to farming and husbandry, to a beginning of a quite different order. This entails a considerable logical jump.

Many astrologers recognise poetic metaphor as the very substance of their art. They will not be discomfited by such an imaginative leap, indeed they will welcome it. Yet the scientist in Ptolemy, the demonstrator of cause and effect, appears embarrassed by this logical hiatus. Before he allows this first line of reasoning to develop he immediately supports it with a different argument. The second justification for the natal horoscope is that, whatever may be its separate status as a moment of origin, in any case the moment of birth will show astrological correspondence with the moment of conception,

> since nature, after the child is perfectly formed, gives the impulse to its birth under a configuration of similar type to that which governed the child's formation in detail in the first place.[10]

Although Ptolemy says nothing further to illustrate this second assertion, he may have in mind the 'pre-natal epoch' (Trutine of Hermes). This doctrine, attributed to the Egyptians, postulates an interchange of Moon and ascendant positions between the horoscopes of conception and birth. The fact that such a connection is crucial to one part of the Ptolemaic justification for natal astrology has lent weight to this doctrine over the centuries.

DOCTRINE OF ORIGIN AND HYPOTHESIS OF SEEDS

Having followed Ptolemy's carefully woven arguments to a conclusion, it will be possible to separate his explanation of how astrological effects are impressed at the individual level from his description of the moment of astrology. He posits the instant of the fertilisation of the seed as a moment of astrology. Hence, from the horoscope of that instant, astrological inferences can be drawn for the fate of the entity into which the seed will grow. Both conception and birth are given pre-eminence as beginnings in time, or moments of causal origin.

Ptolemy's position may be defined as the *doctrine of origin*. This is the positing of the instant of origin of an entity as a moment of astrology, for which a horoscope may validly be delineated with respect to that entity.

Ptolemy also seeks to explain *how* the astrological effect operates at the moment of origin. To do this he establishes a causal explanation in line with the Aristotelian physics of his day. In an argument that is part literal statement and part metaphor, he founds the possibility of an astrological effect on the receptivity of the seed to celestial influences at the critical instant of germination. This explanation, of 'how' the astrological effect comes to pass, I will term the '*hypothesis of seeds*'. Ptolemy uses this hypothesis to support the doctrine of origin, since it offers a rational and causal justification for it.

The hypothesis of seeds, supported in the case of nativities by a secondary argument of similarities between conception and birth, is in turn inseparable from a total structure of astrological causation at the universal level. The astrological influence is necessarily understood to be impressing all seeds without exception, by the continuous and universal power of the heavens.

I believe that the careful discrimination of the parts of the Ptolemaic model, and especially the distinction between the doctrine of origin and the hypothesis or metaphor of seeds, is essential to an adequate study of the later development of horoscopy. Our tradition is embedded in the Ptolemaic attitude.

CONTINUOUS CORRESPONDENCE

It is worth asking to what extent the classical model permits the extension of the moment of astrology into some sort of continuous influence. Returning to Ptolemy, it is seen that he conceives of a continuous process of celestial influence, playing at all instants upon terrestrial affairs. As we have seen, the influence is especially effective at a moment of origin, which provides the foundation for the individual effects manifested through the doctrine of origin. However, later astrology has never forgotten its founding in the idea of a universal and continuous relationship of macrocosm and microcosm – heavens above, earth and man below. Several applications of astrology work directly from a *continuous correspondence*, without the mediation of a moment of origin, and in this follow Ptolemy's approach as discussed in the second book of the *Tetrabiblos*.

Continuous correspondence implies a continuous moment of astrology. A pure illustration of this can be found in astro-meteorology, which interprets current change in the ambient directly for current weather conditions. Mundane astrology also embodies a 'continuous moment' with a potentially continuous interpretation, such as, for example, the broad cultural effects of the planetary cycles and the precessional ages. Such interpretations do not require a moment of origin, or its horoscope, as the fulcrum of method.[11]

From all that has been said it should be clear that continuous correspondence does not explain the working of transits as ordinarily employed. Although these suggest to us a continuous influence from the heavens, we only have an interpretation by referring to a particular horoscope which a planet may be currently transiting. In this case the working of transits is really an extension of the doctrine of origin.

INTERPRETATION DOES NOT DEPEND ON THEORY

Ptolemy's explanatory theory has had a tremendous affect on how we justify and rationalise our astrology. It has also laid down clear parameters by which we could decide what might and might not be valid applications of astrology, but it is important not to imagine that this theory underpins or could explain the majority of particular symbolisms or rules of interpretation in traditional astrology. Rules of interpretation can and do exist without any rational explanation to support them. This is as true for the *Tetrabiblos* as for any other astrological textbook. In fact Ptolemy's detailed justifications for elements of symbolism are far less convincing than the overall power of his model, as when he tries to found the meanings of the Signs of the Zodiac in hot, cold, moist and dry.[12]

Consider the 'doctrine of nativities' as traditionally understood. It is essentially the 'doctrine of origin' defined above, applied to birth, together with all the particular and continually changing rules of interpretation which allow meaningful inferences with respect to the life of the native. These rules are articulations or expressions of the doctrine of origin – but they do not *explain* it. An astrologer can follow the method whether or not he or she can give a rational justification for its working, and whether or not he or she accepts some metaphorical approximation to Ptolemys hypothesis of seeds.

We should be careful not to overestimate the value of the explanatory models in astrology. I doubt whether Ptolemy started with his speculations about influences and seeds and then worked up to formulate a practice of horoscopy, just as I doubt whether he satisfied himself first with the validity of the conception horoscope and then proceeded to nativities. As a matter of speculation I would imagine that like most astrologers he first encountered astrological symbolism and came to 'believe in' natal horoscopy. Only then would the intellectual process of rationalisation and justification be taken up in terms of Aristotle's logic and metaphysics, which were gaining ascendancy in his era. Even if Ptolemy did not personally proceed in this way, that has been the effect and contribution of his work: to sustain and justify an existing belief and an existing practice. Until very recent times, astrologers have been mostly content to allow his rationalisation to stand, more or less intact, since it secured the position of horoscopic astrology amongst the medieval sciences. So if Ptolemy is challenged and the classical moment of astrology falls, that in no way threatens horoscopy, or the major part of its practices and symbolism. What does change, however, is our rationalisation of those practices, and what we think they imply for the nature of reality and the nature of humanity.

THE *TETRABIBLOS* AS THE FOUNDATION OF
WESTERN ASTROLOGY

It is not surprising that the *Tetrabiblos* has often been called the Bible of astrology. Whatever difficulties may exist in its schema, its author's views both on the doctrine of origin and on the nature of astrological causation became accepted as basic tenets. The broad theme of his argument has become so deeply rooted that it is hard to imagine any radically different description or explanation of the moment of astrology. Few astrologers have reworked his ground with any degree of thoroughness. His views are generally imbibed at an unthinking level, implicit and unstated, the supposed stock-in-trade of astrology.

Under the pressure of differing philosophies, revisions have been made to the explanatory part of the structure, the hypothesis of seeds. However, viewed in the context of the original question concerning the moment of astrology, most of the amendments are entirely inessential. They are inessential because they accept without question the injunction of the doctrine of origin, which is to treat the moment of origin as the moment of astrology. This great doctrine, protected throughout the later tradition by the explanatory hypothesis of seeds, or a related metaphor evoking that hypothesis, has sustained and protected astrological practice. Astrological interpretation based on the moment of origin has been an unbroken stream, the central current of horoscopic practice.

PTOLEMAIC ASTROLOGY IN MODERN GUISE

With the revival of Western astrology over the last century has come the growth of forms which appear to have left old Ptolemy far behind. Beyond all the new discoveries and techniques, the computers and the research programmes, and deeper even than the exotic depths of psychological astrology, this appearance is entirely illusory. Apart from the isolated outbreak of horary, mainstream astrology today is as thoroughly Ptolemaic as at any time in the last two millennia. In order to demonstrate this, the treatment of the question of the moment of astrology will be briefly reviewed in several representative modern formulations, some of which have overturned large elements of traditional astrology.

In the light of so many changes in modern astrology, my remarks concerning the staying power of Ptolemy's ideas may seem surprising, but some modern developments seem set to strengthen those ideas rather than weaken them. The remarkable work of the Gauquelins has established a secure possibility for what may be termed natural astrology, but at the same time that is likely to strengthen the hold of the 'objective' Ptolemaic approach over all other parts of astrology, especially if the separation of the 'two orders' discussed in Chapter 4 is not undertaken.

Within the limited terms of their method, the Gauquelins have established an astrological effect at the moment of birth. Their speculative explanation is an inversion of the Ptolemaic hypothesis. They have suggested that the unborn child may 'select' the appropriate hour of birth:

> The child might have a predisposition to come into the world under certain cosmic conditions which corresponded to his biological constitution.[13]

Michel Gauquelin referred to this as the 'theory of mid-wife planets'.[14] The exact mechanism of this midwifery is the 'trigger effect', a planetary position in the diurnal circle which might contribute significantly to the conditions which trigger the foetus into being born. The effect appears to be obliterated by methods of inducing birth artificially.

The biological constitution is to some extent hereditary, hence the importance attached to the attempt to demonstrate 'planetary heredity', the correspondence between planetary positions in the horoscopes of parents and children.

As it is, the tradition that the Gauquelins have tested has taken the doctrine of origin for granted. Since they have demonstrated correlations consistent with this doctrine, scientific astrology has no reason to question it. The problem of the mechanism of the effect becomes the critical focus of its theory and speculation. In the face of such results, research in natural astrology can hardly be expected to take up as problematic the question of the moment of astrology, which is in any case an issue of philosophy rather than one of science. It therefore seems most unlikely that any future research programmes developed along these lines will have cause to reveal the separate identity of the question of the moment in divinatory astrology. Ptolemy's position remains assured.

Other modern developments have furthered discussion on *how* astrology might work, without revealing as a distinct question the moment of that supposed working. In discussing the theory of harmonics, John Addey offers the following unusual metaphor to suggest how the astrological effect comes to pass at birth:

> The major harmonic patterns, being relatively slow-forming, determine the approximate time of birth; the higher frequency harmonics indicate possible appropriate moments of birth of shorter duration but which occur more often... Thus one after another the wards of a complex combination lock can engage, as it were, to yield a moment of birth which corresponds symbolically with the pattern of life to be born.[15]

This differs markedly from the model of Ptolemy in that it dissolves the divide between universal and particular orders of astrological effect. Instead, there is a continuous spectrum of harmonic patterns from low to high frequency. However, in line with the Platonic and neo-Platonic strand in traditional astrology, an all-embracing universal harmony is invoked, the ancient conception of Cosmos. Addey's astrology is invoking *signs* rather than *causes*, but this Platonic conception is reined in by the objectification of the moment of astrology. The heavens above and the human being below move into concordance at the moment of birth, answering some non-material and *absolute necessity*. One by one the wards fall until the door is locked – or unlocked – at the instant of birth. Despite the Platonic inspiration, therefore, the core Ptolemaic doctrine has been left intact. Completely in line with the classical formulation, the invariable validity of the moment of birth as a moment for the imprinting of the astrological signature has been treated as obvious and unproblematic.

If any trend in astrology should have broken free from the trammels of an outworn tradition, then the major movement broadly termed 'humanistic' ought to have achieved this. Because it is such a significant development in shaping the attitude of many modern astrologers, and because it is so set against determinism and 'influence' from the stars, this is a fascinating test of the survival of the Ptolemaic structure.

Humanistic astrology is particularly associated with the pioneering work of Dane Rudhyar, from the 1930s on. It builds on the earlier work of Alan Leo in moving natal astrology towards a richer description of character, in line with the 20th century's interest in psychology, and it taps an occult philosophy derived from a fusion of Renaissance hermetism and modern Theosophy. As with John Addey's harmonics, there is a strong Platonic undertow.

Drawing on a parallel movement in psychology, humanistic astrology seeks to lift the study of man beyond the bounds of materialistic reductionism. Astrologers in this vein turn away from a tradition which they see as limiting consideration of destiny to tangible evidence of events. They seek instead a celestial symbol of the inner, psychic, life. The natal horoscope becomes an inexhaustible matrix of potentials awaiting the awakening of the human creativity which may fully realise them. The great goal of natal astrology is to assist the individual on the path towards this awakening. These aspirations give voice to astrology's most noble possibilities.

Rudhyar's first book, *The Astrology of Personality*, lays out the groundplan for this new approach. He rejects the notion that we can develop a meaningful astrology by using scientific methodology to search out 'rays' or 'waves' of celestial influence. He sees astrology as a formal or symbolic system, an 'algebra of life':

> The revolutions of celestial bodies constitute in their totality a vast and complex symbol which, of itself, is made up solely of cyclically changing patterns of relationship.[16]

Just as a measuring rod does not influence that which it measures, so the symbol is without substance, yet it will serve to correlate, order and illumine any living experience onto which it is mapped. The entity measured by the natal horoscope is nothing less than the total, potential individual life-meaning. Our measurement begins with 'the first point of independent existence; in the case of human destiny, the first breath'.[17]

The idea of the horoscope as a blueprint of possibilities, presented at the moment of birth, has remained central to Rudhyar's thought. In 1975 he states:

> [the human being] is born at a particular time and in a particular location because the all-encompassing Harmony of the universe dictated that such an archetypal solution to a particular need in the three-dimensional world of physical existence should take form as a human organism. This archetypal solution is 'coded' in the language of the sky as the birth-chart of a particular person.[18]

If we can penetrate Rudhyar's somewhat abstract expression, we will discover an essential consistency with Ptolemy's formulation. Where Ptolemy sees a universal order of the astrological effect working continuously, Rudhyar sees an 'all-encompassing Harmony of the universe', equally ceaseless and absolute. Ptolemy brings the astrological influence down to the order of effects specific to the individual through the impression of the heavens moulded upon the seed at the instant of conception, and secondarily at birth. Rudhyar translates the universal harmony down to the level of the individual by allowing it to 'dictate' an 'archetypal solution', shown in the astrological code at the instant of birth. In both formulations the process is a matter of inevitable cosmic law, working without exception at the origin of all individual organisms, and *independent of the act of interpretation*.

I stress this latter point in particular because it is one of the most characteristic features of humanistic astrology and its derivatives that the significance of symbolism operates primarily in consciousness and the psyche, rather than in the forces of nature. As Dennis Elwell proclaims, 'Consciousness is the currency', and he even evokes the concept of 'participatory consciousness' from the leading edge of modern physics.[19] Yet like Rudhyar he still presents the original signature of birth as a given. It remains given by nature in objective time, not assigned by consciousness. I conclude, therefore, that despite the appearance of turning away from tradition, Rudhyar and the many astrologers who have been influenced by him adhere closely to the Ptolemaic foundation of that tradition in its most significant tenets, that is, the core description of the causal-temporal origins and the relationship of those origins to the realm of the universal.

Although the Ptolemaic foundation has been left untouched, humanistic astrology has taken Rudhyar's lead in transforming the whole superstructure of astrology, especially the interpretive part of the doctrine of nativities. Modern 'person-centred astrology' has realigned interpretation onto the subjective, the experiential and the spiritual, taking it away from the prediction of 'external' events. Through this, humanistic astrology slips past the hoary old problems of fate and free-will, since the blue-print at birth shows a potential for experience, but does not delimit the manifestation of that experience. However, the thread of the Ptolemaic treatment of the moment of astrology is undeniable, since the individual has still been 'fated' with a particular pattern of these potentials at the instant of birth.

Since humanistic astrology is not under pressure to provide a literal explanation for the astrological effect, it is free to choose various metaphors. It does not have to convince us about the impressionability of little seeds, which is a necessary step for Ptolemy. Even so, the hypothesis of seeds lives on amongst the favoured metaphors, quietly fulfilling its role of justifying the doctrine of origin. As a brief but characteristic illustration, it is worth noting its association with the philosophy of cyclic time, developed in *The Astrology of Personality*. A particular life, from first to last breath, is one such temporal cycle. Rudhyar describes the points of commencement of cycles as 'seed moments'.[20] He goes on to describe the divisions of the cycle, and describes the 'beginning' in the following terms:

The beginning of every cycle is a One: a monad...it is the germinating seed, or that point within the seed whence rise root and stem...[21]

We come full circle, therefore, back to Ptolemy's hypothesis of seeds as the justification for the doctrine of origin.

I have given a lot of attention to Dane Rudhyar because he is truly representative of the most significant shift in astrological attitude in modern times. As I hope I have illustrated, considerable though that shift is, it has occurred *within* the broad limits set for us by Ptolemy, and not beyond them. The same seems to be true wherever we look at modern astrological theorists. So, despite its influential remodelling of the interpretive part of astrology, 'psychological astrology' cannot be said to have broken free of the Ptolemaic structure with its implicit determinism.[22] Other recent theories, despite varying degrees of sophistication in weaving astrology together with modern psychology and philosophy, are in no different a position. Michael Harding's proposition of a 'primal zodiac', impressed with a collectivity of experiences, still works like Ptolemy's ambient. The astrological effect is produced at the objective moment of birth by an *inevitable* process:

> ...the infant locks into the energies of the outer planets during the process of birth, because it is genetically programmed to use these energies... in doing so it inevitably 'absorbs' those experiences which all others have previously impressed upon the primal zodiac.[23]

This is the language of energy and natural laws, transposed into human experience but completely objective. Like much of modern astrology, this formulation has abandoned physiological seeds in favour of origin-moments in consciousness, but Ptolemy's temporal structure has been left intact.

THE DEEP FORM OF PTOLEMY'S CONCEPTUAL STRUCTURE

Few authorities nowadays bother to quote Ptolemy. Some have never even read him, but every one of them depends on him. The list of authors I have made could be vastly extended without any great gain in insight. What is so remarkable about this is the complete hegemony of Ptolemy's stance over the whole of astrology's theory. Now of course, Ptolemy may indeed be 'right', but even if he had at one stroke established the essential foundation of our subject, is it not remarkable that there seems to be no other way of thinking about astrology?

This extraordinary transmission is all the more powerful by being disguised beneath the surface of Ptolemy's dry text. It takes effort of thought and imagination and some depth of experience in astrology before the full power of his conceptual structure is recognised. The two doctrines of origin and continuous moment, together with the explanatory hypothesis of seeds, form an exquisitely integrated model, since the moment of origin is a special instant drawn out of a continuous series of potentially significant moments. The integrity of this structure can be discerned in the durability of its principal components, and in the fact that astrologers of all philosophical complexions use it naturally and easily to justify natal astrology. The structure is also integral with Ptolemy's perfection of a cosmology derived from Eudoxus and Aristotle and which clothed the heavens for fourteen centuries. Through this, astrology was indivisible from what we now know as astronomy, and was assured an abode in the scheme of rational knowledge. Perhaps it is in these wider questions of the cultural and scientific context that we will find the clues to the Ptolemaic hegemony within astrology.[24]

The rational formulation of horoscopy achieved by the Greek astrologers secured its firm foundations through Ptolemy. It provides the deep form for our experience of natal astrology. It goes so deep that it is acquired by each succeeding generation as a habit, hardly worth a moment's reflection. The modern schools that imagine themselves so far from the old astrologers are perched on Ptolemy's broad shoulders.

Through the whole range of later horoscopy, development has been limited to re-expression of symbolism and the changing fashions of interpretation. What little philosophical enquiry there has been has tinkered with the lesser part of the Ptolemaic structure, the explanatory hypothesis. It has not further revealed the fundamental description, the *what* of the phenomena which this hypothesis seeks to explain. As we will see, however, there are many mysteries of the moment of astrology which Ptolemy's structure cannot contain.

NOTES

1 C.G.Jung, 'In Memory of Richard Wilhelm', memorial address delivered in Munich, 10 May 1930.
2 Maggie Hyde, *Jung and Astrology* (Aquarian, London, 1992), p.127.
3 Ptolemy, *Tetrabiblos*, trans. F.E.Robbins (Loeb Classical Library, 1980). Robbins's translation has been followed throughout.
4 ibid., I.2.9
5 ibid., I.2.9
6 ibid., III.1.225.
7 ibid., III.1.224-5.
8 ibid., III.1.225 and 227.
9 ibid., III.1.225.

10 ibid., III.1.227.

11 Although mundane work does also extend to the study of horoscopes of nations and of leaders – Ptolemy tells us to consider the founding horoscope of a city (II.5.163).

12 There is a discussion on Ptolemy's symbolism in the light of his theory in Nicholas De Vore's *Encyclopedia of Astrology* (Philosophical Library, New York, 1947): section on 'Ptolemaic Astrology'.

13 Michel Gauquelin, *Astrology and Science* (Mayflower, 1972), p156.

14 Michel Gauquelin, *The Truth About Astrology* (Basil Blackwell, Oxford, 1983). See ch.8, p146.

15 John Addey, *Harmonics in Astrology* (Fowler, 1976). See p234.

16 Dane Rudhyar, *The Astrology of Personality*. ch.1, p.51. The page numbers given here are from the first edition (Lucis Publishing Co. New York, 1936).

17 ibid., ch.1, p.53.

18 Dane Rudhyar, *From Humanistic to Transpersonal Astrology* (The Seed Center, Palo Alto, Calif., 1975).

19 Dennis Elwell, *Cosmic Loom* (Unwin Hyman, 1987), especially ch. 5 and p.96; revised edn (Urania Trust, London, 1999), ch. 5 and p.126.

20 ibid., ch.3, p.123.

21 ibid., ch.3, p.125.

22 Concerning psychological astrology, theoretical statements are few and far between, but see for instance Howard Sasportas's comments on 'Your Inborn Images' in *The Development of the Personality* (Routledge & Kegan Paul, 1987), pp.4-6. *The Astrology of Fate* (Allen & Unwin, 1984) shows Liz Greene in a deterministic vein, as in her suggestion of a pattern of fate in horoscope transits: 'such timing is inherent from the birth of the organism, just as the timing for a tomato plant to flower and produce a fruit is inherent in its nature' (p.277). For a detailed critique of psychological astrology in the light of a divinatory reformulation of astrology, see Maggie Hyde, *Jung and Astrology*, op.cit.

23 M. Harding, *Hymns to the Ancient Gods* (Penguin/Arkana, 1992), p.117.

24 The wider context of Ptolemy involves interesting questions for astrology which, I regret, go beyond the scope of this current study. The spell in which the Ptolemaic conception holds astrology is in itself a subset of the spell in which it held medieval cosmology and physics. A remarkable dimension of this is the strong possibility that Ptolemy as a scientist was a *fraud*, falsifying his sources, cooking his famous star catalogue, and most terrible of all, destroying in the process ancient records of eclipses, etc. This set the development of scientific astronomy and various related historical studies back for centuries and made inordinately difficult the task of later scientists up to the time of Copernicus. On this, see Robert R. Newton, *The Crime of Claudius Ptolemy* (Johns Hopkins University Press, Baltimore/London, 1977). As astrologers, we have every right to ask how far Ptolemy cooked the picture of astrology to fit his scientific schema. Newton's arguments, which on my limited appraisal of them seem well-founded, threaten to overturn all established scholarly interpretations of the history of science and astronomy. Newton has not developed the argument to the wider context, where we would have to ask the question: *How come* such a construction of physical reality made such a deep appeal? Falsification of the data is not a sufficient explanation for the enduring nature of the Ptolemaic cosmos; there is genius in it. Astrology's hook, line and sinker dependence on this construction illustrates the same philosophical problem. I believe the issues lead back to the even greater question of the hold on the European mind of the Aristotelian conception of reality. This is one of the most important questions for a fundamental review of the philosophy of astrology.

6

The Question of Horary

MANY parts and practices of astrology are ill at ease in the Ptolemaic framework, yet do not contrast with it sufficiently to be recognisably distinct. However, one major dimension of horoscopy has manifestly no place in the scheme. This is the tradition of horary astrology, the art of judgment of a horoscope for the moment a question is posed to or by an astrologer. The contrast between horary and the usual description of natal astrology allows a more exact understanding of the limitations of the Ptolemaic attitude, since horary places in critical focus the whole problem of the moment of astrology.

The master of horary astrology was William Lilly, and one of his well-known horary charts concerns some stolen fish. In February 1638 Lilly was living in Walton-on-Thames, and he cast a horary when he heard that the fish he awaited by barge from London had been stolen: 'I took the exact time when I first heard the report, and erected the figure accordingly, endeavouring to give myself satisfaction what became of my goods, and, if possible, to recover part or all of them.'[1]

According to traditional methods for the judgment of theft, the thief may be shown by a peregrine planet in an angle, especially the descendant. Lilly finds Jupiter in Scorpio on the descendant and Jupiter is peregrine, having no dignity by its zodiacal placing. Its dispositor Mars, lord of the 7th, is in Scorpio in the 7th, and from this Lilly finds the description of the thief, 'of Mars and Jupiter his nature'. The preponderance of water signs, together with common sense, informs Lilly that his man has close association with water. By an exquisite movement of symbolism, he sees that Mars, about to change sign and move into Sagittarius, shows someone about to move house. Lilly makes local inquiries, and 'such a one I discovered', fitting the description given: 'much suspected of theevery... a Fisherman, of good stature, thick and full-bodied, faire of complexion, a red or yellowish haire'. Further, Lilly can describe from the horary chart the condition of the fish in a moist place or low room. He also sees that he will certainly gain news of the fish because the Moon applies sextile to Mercury, lord of the 2nd – his goods – in the sign of Pisces, the Fishes. The likelihood that Lilly will obtain at

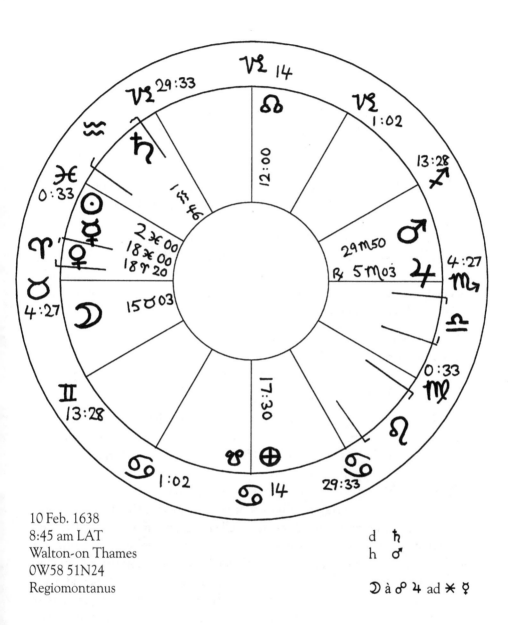

10 Feb. 1638
8:45 am LAT
Walton-on Thames
0W58 51N24
Regiomontanus

d ♄
h ♂

☽ à ☍ ♃ ad ⚹ ☿

FIGURE 6 Fish Stolen
figure given by Lilly, *Christian Astrology* p397

least some news of his fish is obvious from this symbolism to astrologers with only the briefest acquaintance with horary method. On the strength of this symbolism, Lilly procured a warrant from a Justice of the Peace. On the Sunday of the following week, accompanied by a constable and a barge-man, he went straight to the culprit and discovered his fish, 'part eaten, part not consumed, all confessed'.

Lilly's judgment carries the mark of his mastery, yet the circumstances are not more remarkable than countless similar experiences recorded by horary astrologers. To arrive at such a judgment requires only the horoscope of the moment of the question, without reference to a nativity. Where a natal chart, or any other horoscope of origin, is occasionally brought into consideration, its role is commonly limited to providing secondary testimony to the indications of the horary map.

If horary is not a method applied to some other moment of origin, it is reasonable to ask whether the horary moment is *in itself* such an origin. By some authors the horary moment is spoken of as the birth of an idea, or of a question. Ivy Goldstein-Jacobson follows the maternal instinct through from natal practice to provide this description:

> Sometimes a problem is mulled over for weeks and needs time to develop, like a gestation-period, before the planetary positions are in line to answer: circumstances will unerringly take care of that, and the question will be born at the right time for it to be given its answer.[2]

This metaphor dissolves the sharp distinction between horary and the conventional description of natal astrology. In this way horary might seem to take on a little of the plausibility so carefully established in the Ptolemaic tradition on the foundation of the hypothesis of seeds.

However, the metaphor of the birth of a question is open to doubt, since it obscures the distinctive nature of horary. It is certainly true that the moment an idea pops into mind for the first time may well yield a potent map, but this is only one of horary's possibilities. A question will frequently arise in full significance long before it is formally posed to an astrologer. Further, the horary moment most characteristically occurs in the middle of the action to which it refers, and not at the beginning of that action. In the case of Lilly's missing fish, the horary cannot be considered a significant origin of the affair: such status should be reserved for the instant of the theft, and not the instant of its reportage.

What other sort of origin could the horary moment be? Perhaps we could see it as originating the astrologer's *involvement* in the affair. Thus the outcome of a matter may be decisively influenced by the astrological judgment, as in Lilly's astute detective work. However, quite apart from the fact that horary astrologers have not to my knowledge ever entertained this view of horary origins, it is clear that a description involving the participation of the astrologer would step right outside the Ptolemaic frame. This is a line I shall be taking up later. However, the common description of astrological origins treats these as occurring as a fact of nature, independent of the astrologer. From Ptolemy's point of view, and for the tradition that follows him, the significance of a horoscope is not dependent on whether or not an astrologer bothers to cast it.

The question of the natural origin of the horary question has always given astrologers trouble. One line of resolving the dilemma, rather more subtle than simply asserting the horary moment itself as an independent 'origin', is to give it a parallel originating power with the moment of birth. Albertus Magnus suggests that if births are 'natural things' then horaries and elections are 'like natural things'. Further the moment of horary can substitute for birth because its significations are related to those of birth:

> Take the interrogation itself in place of birth as a foundation... if the birth is unknown, take his most certain interrogation, since when a man interrogates, he comes then from his birth to the good or evil which his birth indicates.[3]

Horaries are like natural things, says Albertus - but what exactly is covered over by this word 'like'(*similes*)? And when a man comes from his birth, given by nature, to a horary interrogation freely chosen, is that 'coming' really 'like birth'?

Horary ignores the limit established by Ptolemy as inherent in the structure of astrology. It works with moments that are not natural origins in any ordinary sense of this phrase, yet it interprets the heavens in a point-for-point correspondence with exact and particular details of a transitory situation. It is not uncommon for horary astrologers to abandon the classical construction and in effect revert to a pre-Ptolemaic and tough-minded Stoic conception of fate. When Ivy Goldstein-Jacobson says 'circumstances will unerringly take care of' the exact alignment of planetary positions required to allow an answer at the moment of a horary, the idea is suggested of a grand design penetrating the tiniest details of human behaviour and the natural world, to hold these moment by moment in perfect concordance with the celestial pattern. The concordance is Fate, a matter of inevitable necessity: 'it could not have been other than this'. In the last analysis, nothing of any human significance is seen as a matter of contingency or mere chance, since a pre-ordained universal pattern or divine Providence is ceaselessly at work. This certainly moves in the direction of astrology as absolute knowledge.

To refer back to the distinctions already established in the analysis of the

Ptolemaic model (chapter 5), this interpretation of horary might seem to imply a *continuous moment* of astrology capable of interpretation in the realm of the particular, where Ptolemy's continuous moment is in principle limited to the realm of universals. I believe it is one of the archetypal images of astrology itself that is to be found in this vision of a continuous correspondence, ceaseless, absolute, and particular to the tiniest details of 'God's plan'.

However, it takes only a little reflection on the phenomena actually encountered in our practice to dispel the hazy notion of continuous correspondence as the basis of horary. To state a very obvious point, there has never yet developed a craft of horoscopy that goes anywhere near indicating that the movement of the heavens continuously matches point for point the myriad diverse circumstances below, at the level of detail found in the usual horary. We should take heed of the careful logic of Ptolemy's construction and let it guide us to asking the question of horary. All the evidence suggests there is something special about the horary moment which enables an interpretation for particulars, just as for the Ptolemaic tradition there is something special about the moments of conception and birth. And it is this 'something special' that we need to uncover if we are to have any understanding of the horary moment.

Horary stretches to breaking-point the reasonable attempt to 'explain' horoscopy adopted by the Ptolemaic tradition. It was earlier suggested that there is a logical hiatus in the way Ptolemy carries over to the moment of birth the same way of talking about influences that seems so plausible for conception. This is but a small matter compared with the chasm of belief that opens when the literal talk appropriate to the hypothesis of seeds is stretched to cover the horary moment. How can the particular detail to which horary refers be so exactly determined by the heavens, simply in a transient horary moment? This would no longer be a celestial patterning of the seed, or 'seed-moment', which may determine or signify lines of development of an entity. The horary astrologer works with a detailed celestial correspondence with the particular forms of fully-developed entities, *at the instant* of asking a question. The mechanism implied in the hypothesis of seeds, however artfully described, becomes inconceivable and absurd.

The fact that there exists another class of astrological moment, not itself obviously reducible to causal-temporal origins, yet capable of interpretation for particulars, throws the Ptolemaic model into disarray. At the very least, that model is dethroned from supremacy as a complete description of astrological reality. Beyond this lies the possibility that in seeking a description of the moment of horary, a more fundamental treatment of all of astrology, including the horoscope of birth, will be required.

For these reasons it is not surprising that throughout our tradition horary has encountered stiff resistance. Ptolemy himself does not allow horary, or anything like it, into the *Tetrabiblos*. 'Ptolemy conceded revolutions and nativities... but he did not find that interrogations were true', notes Ibn Ezra.[4] Since Ptolemy does not once refer to horary by name, his rejection has to be inferred from a study of his model of astrology. The situation was obscured for earlier authors by the influential *Centiloquy*, or 'Fruits of the Four Books', commonly ascribed to Ptolemy but in fact originating sometime between the seventh and tenth centuries AD.[5] Horary aphorisms are included amongst other diverse material, and the work as a whole is inconsistent with the fundamental theory of the *Tetrabiblos*.

There is an intriguing passage in the *Tetrabiblos* in which Ptolemy rounds on the majority of his contemporaries calling themselves astrologers. They are censured for adopting divinatory practices which cannot properly take the name of 'astrology':

> Most, for the sake of gain, claim credence for another art in the name of this (astrology), and deceive the vulgar, because they are reputed to foretell many things, even those that cannot naturally be known beforehand.[6]

Ptolemy adds that the effect of this deception is to make thoughtful observers reject even 'the natural subjects of prophecy'. It is probable that horary astrology was the major horoscopic practice of the day to offend Ptolemy as unnatural.

The insistence upon what is 'naturally' possible is crucial, and recurs throughout the tradition. From the seventeenth century, Placidus, one of Ptolemy's most loyal advocates, makes clear the logical ground on which his rejection of horary 'interrogations' resides:

> The stars cannot be the signs of effects, unless they are also the causes; wherefore interrogations, in the manner of the ancients, have no place in nature.[7]

For the Ptolemaic astrologer specific significations, such as the description of the thief derived by Lilly from Jupiter in his 'Fish Stolen', could be attributed only to a planet acting at the time of the horary by transit upon an appropriate promissor in the natus. This possibility is taken to include action upon some directed or progressed position produced within the natus. Unless the mediation of a horoscope of origin can be shown, the interpretation of Jupiter's momentary effect is valid only at the universal level, and not at the level of the particular. In practice, if we were to limit the validity of horary to universals, we could interpret only situations in which the stars are supposed to be influencing the 'approximate cause' of some natural phenomenon. Placidus cites the example of the universal natural effect produced by the Sun, which indiscriminately 'melts wax, dries up the mud, whitens it, blackens the human skin'. But in no such way can Jupiter, coincidentally setting at the hour of Lilly's question, approximately cause the physical appearance and moral nature of a fisherman in Walton.

When the Ptolemaic attitude is most clearly adopted, then the repression of horary follows, not from experience, but as a matter of logical necessity. This does not appear to relate to the skill of the astrologer: an array of talents can be found to accompany Placidus. It is sufficient to cite the rejection by practitioners of the calibre of Al-Biruni, often acknowledged as the most outstanding of the Arab astrologers, and Morin de Villefranche, Lilly's illustrious contemporary.

It is but a short step from the designation of what is natural to the imputation that success in horary is attributable to supernatural agency, probably beyond the lawful bounds of Islam or Christianity. So Al-Biruni, categorising the divisions of astrology, finds that beyond those which are acceptable lies a further category where particular 'beginnings or origins' are unrecognised:

> ...here astrology threatens to transgress its proper limits, where problems are submitted which it is impossible to solve for the most part, and where the matter leaves the solid basis of universals for one of particulars. When this boundary is passed, where the astrologer is on one side and the sorcerer on the other, you enter a field of omens and divinations which has nothing to do with astrology although the stars may be referred to in connection with them.[8]

It is a task of this study to disagree with this great scholar, by turning his categorisation on its head. I believe that our astrology of judgments, in all its parts, has everything to do with 'a field of omens and divinations'.

Echoes of Al-Biruni's assertion will be found at all epochs. A modern reflection on the same theme would put success in horary down to psychic gifts or intuition. In this present study I have brought forward the possibility of a psi-function in astrology, but my argument is not in the same category because I see this as *allied with* or functionally related to rational interpretation. Most authors who talk of psychic gifts attached to astrology have in mind an 'anything goes' process whereby the rational employment of astrology's established conventions of interpretation is incidental or even wholly absent. Al-Biruni likewise is giving the impression that 'sorcery' can have nothing to do with astrology.

The repression of horary by astrologers with some claim to authority continues into the present. Jeff Mayo does not require the precision of Placidus or the breadth of learning of Al-Biruni to rally the modern assault. Simple gusto will suffice:

> In my opinion this is not astrology. Each moment in time may possess a distinct quality and be the link between past and present, but this is sheer nonsense... Horary astrology makes a mockery of a serious subject.[9]

Astrologers in general are a tolerant lot. Modern exponents of the Ptolemaic attitude, whether knowingly or unknowingly, rarely pronounce against horary in such an uncompromising or provocative manner. However, it is not difficult to discern their discomfort in the presence of horary. It cannot be taken seriously, it has no real ground, no rational justification. Horary appears arbitrary, subjective, and lacking clear boundaries. Further, few horary astrologers are likely to offer any intellectually satisfactory way of describing their practice – the current philosophy of astrology does not provide even the rudiments of such a description. Horary has to be left a matter of faith, experience and cunning. Horary astrologers thus find themselves in a different and discreditable position to their colleagues in natal astrology, who have at least the beginnings of a reasonable explanation behind them – such is the gift of Ptolemy. It is oddly fitting, therefore, that horary rises up like a shadow to embody the worst fears of rational astrology. We often find ordinary horary practice defiantly demonstrating the absurd and the trivial, as if to pull down the façade of a 'serious subject'.

It is apparent with horary, more immediately than with other branches of horoscopy, that the *a priori* philosophical conception dictates experience. For many centuries the whole of our tradition has depended implicitly on the explanation offered by Ptolemy to justify natal astrology. This makes astrology plausible, and has thus contributed substantially to its widespread continuance. But there has been a price: the repression of experience that does not fit. Such experience, if acknowledged at all, becomes inexplicable, non-sense.

This comes back to a central theme of this study: the *how* of astrology is by no means the same question as that of the moment of astrology. Attempts at explanation are in danger of confusing our description of the phenomena which we face – the ambivalent and illuminating experience of astrology. Astrology is better left inexplicable if in explaining we lose it.

THE HORARY MOMENT IN PRACTICE

What can be inferred from horary practice about its moment of astrology? Once the distractions of the Ptolemaic schema have been pulled aside, a realm of uncertainty is entered. The bringing to light of implicit notions is an uncertain project since nothing of the nature of explicit philosophical discussion has passed down the horary tradition. Horary has had mighty craftsmen, but no Ptolemy to provide it with theory.

A detailed study of horary practice will finally dispel any lingering notion of Ptolemaic origins. A possibility sometimes adopted in modern practice casts the horary question for the place of the querent, but at the time of its receipt by the astrologer. If a letter comes from Australia, an astrologer in London may choose to use the geographical co-ordinates for the place in Australia, but will take as the time of the horary the moment in London when he or she reads the letter. The horoscope is therefore not now for a unique spatial-temporal origin. The decision on this convention is made by the astrologer and the test is what makes sense in the symbolism, not a criterion drawn from geography. Now this is a small instance, and some traditional horary astrologers will not make this move, but it serves to demonstrate the possibility that the final form of horary, far from being simply a 'gift of nature', involves an element of creative choice by the astrologer.

But the tradition offers more substantial indications of the moment of horary. The transmission from Arabic astrology undertaken by Guido Bonatus in the twelfth century is a primary source for later European horary. His 'First Consideration before judgment' leaves us in no doubt that *the moment of horary is a function of human decision*:

> Observe what it is that moves a person to propose or ask a question of an Astrologer; where we must take notice of three motions: the First, of the mind, when a man is stirred up in his thoughts and hath an intent to inquire; a Second, of the superior and celestial bodies; so that they at that time imprint on the thing enquired after, what shall become of it; the Third, of the free will which disposes him to the very act of enquiring; for although the mind be moved to inquire, 'tis not enough, unless the superior bodies sympathise therewith; nor is such motion of the stars enough, unless by the election of his will the person does actually enquire.[10]

Of these three defining motions of horary it would be possible to equate only the first with the Ptolemaic model. From the perspective of the natal horoscope one may indeed be 'stirred up' by the current state of the heavens, and on this count fruitful interpretations of horary moments can occasionally be made simply on the basis of natal transits.

The remaining two motions break with Ptolemy. The second shows the characteristic horary transgression of the divide between universals and particulars - a heavenly 'imprint on the thing inquired after', without reference to any horoscope of causal-temporal origin. But it is the third motion, that of free will, which is the most interesting of all. We have no horary moment *unless by the election of will the person does actually enquire.*

It is this 'election of the will' that marks out the astrology of human initiatives, which will be taken up in the next chapter in the form of the katarche. Here it is sufficient to note that the intentionality of the one inquiring is given by Bonatus as part of the *definition* of horary. The *what* of the horary moment is not simply the posing of a significant question. It is the posing of a significant question *to an astrologer*, with the explicit intention that this question shall be subject to astrological judgment.

The founding of horary in the will-to-inquire shows us why we need to ask for seriousness of motive to guarantee 'radical intention' and thus 'radicality' in the symbolism and the judgment. This is an idea that we find insisted on by the early astrologers. Masha'allah (eighth century) warns the artist to make no response

> except to honest and serious questions, or to a person who, with much concern and solicitude for himself or for another with whom he is closely involved comes as an anxious inquirer himself or through a messenger.[11]

In his 'Second Consideration before judgment', Bonatus advises that the inquirer should first pray, and then

> ...let him apply himself to the astrologer with a serious intent of being satisfied in some certain and particular doubt, and this not on trifling occasions, or light sudden emotions, much less in matters base or unlawful.[12]

– a statement that William Lilly commends to the student by an insertion in Coley's translation.

Although the seriousness of intention of the *astrologer* is taken for granted by these authors, there is little doubt that a reciprocal radical intention to answer truthfully is equally required. I would suggest that this too enters into the definition of the horary moment, since the astrologer has to make the final decision, by a free act of will, to take up the question as a horary.

One of the most powerful features of horary method, which can be a revelation to the natal astrologer coming across this possibility for the first time, is the signification of the astrologer giving judgment in the symbolism of the horoscope. This is not simply a peripheral possibility or additional colour, but rather, it is integral to the method. The traditional set of considerations that in modern horary are known as 'Strictures against Judgment' are significations warning the astrologer not to offer an interpretation. One of these, relating to Saturn and the 7th house, is explicitly about the role of the astrologer. The fact that the astrologer giving the answer is signified 'in' the horoscope underscores the fact that horary depends upon an astrologer being there to make a judgment.

Because of this, the description of horary must move further still towards acknowledgement of the active participation of the astrologer. The horary moment is the posing of a question that will be taken up by the astrologer. *It does not 'exist' as a horary until it is so taken up.*[13] Whether or not the whole exercise is finally going to work is then the function of an intangible – the state of the astrologer, and whether he or she is at that juncture capable of the creative expression of traditional craft.

A horary is not like a natural creature, born at a particular time and place. Neither is it a 'significant question' floating around without an astrologer to answer it. The whole project depends upon the participation and mutual intentions of astrologer and client. It therefore constitutes a special and uncommon form of inquiry, strongly reminiscent of divination. In divination as this is commonly recognised, a diviner puts a specific question to an oracle-system, such as that of the Tarot cards, or the *I Ching*. Sometimes the diviner puts the question on behalf of an inquirer and interprets the oracle's response. In horary, the oracle may be seen as the heavens themselves, the astrologer interpreting their response on behalf of the querent. It is therefore not surprising that horary has earned the appellation 'divinatory astrology'.

For horary it is manifest that the creative intervention of the astrologer is decisive in determining the moment of astrology. The whole story cannot be given over to the influence of the heavens. However, to have established the active participation of both astrologer and inquirer as definitive in even one branch of the art opens up questions for every other part of astrology and this is yet another reason for the uncomfortable reception sometimes given to horary. The desire to treat it as a distinct beast disguises the unease of many astrologers at the dilemmas it raises. To define horary as having a distinct status would also be the prelude to excising it altogether from the canon of astrological practice, if it became embarrassing to our aspirations for respectability. Out of these considerations I do not follow the many modern authorities who call horary 'divinatory astrology', even though this phrase puts us in the right way of approaching it, because this implies that the rest of horoscopic astrology is *not* divinatory.

Rather than treat horary as something quite distinct, I will adopt the alternative strategy. This is to suggest that the doctrine of horary reveals phenomena inherent in all astrological practice, which are nevertheless not articulated by the rational model given by our tradition. This model is then recognised to be inadequate to describe and define the whole project of horoscopic astrology. The question raised by horary challenges the theoretical framework of astrology at its philosophical roots.

We still have a long way to go, however, before we can bring out some of the most important implications of horary. With this goal in mind, I will now turn to one of the most fruitful discussions on horary in modern times.

THOUGHTS FROM CHARLES CARTER

In 1962, towards the end of a long life in astrology, Charles Carter published an article entitled 'Some Thoughts on Horary Astrology'. This includes a horary question: '*Is there anything in Horary Astrology?*'. The article has been reproduced complete as Appendix 3. This truly remarkable horoscope and discussion, both a manifestaton of Carter's rich and deep astrological experience, combine to illuminate the nature of horary. I will here summarise his discussion, comment on his arguments, and then consider the horoscope.

Carter prefaces the debate by noting the reduced status of horary in modern astrology. Not only was it a rare item on astrology lecture programmes at the time of writing[14] but it was often treated with scepticism by other astrologers. Nor had contact with devotees impressed him:

> My own experience with figures cast for me by horarists has been unfortunate. In fact, they have usually been downright wrong and never strikingly right.

He returns to this sceptical theme later, when he puts forward the common-sense argument that if horary's claims were true, those employing it 'would have the world almost at their feet; at least financially speaking'. We may feel this is less than a fair comment, since the same common sense can be employed just as effectively against most practices of astrology. However, Carter's observation reflects the fact that horary more than most other parts of astrology has got itself stuck with an image of simplistic materialism. If so, its claims are badly in need of an overhaul. Nonetheless, despite his catalogue of doubts, Carter finds it 'difficult to believe there is *nothing* in horary astrology'. So with this dilemma before him, he sets out to address the problematic nature of the practice.

Horary suggests itself as an alternative choice for horoscopy where there is no reliably recorded birthtime, which was more of a problem for astrologers in past centuries than it is today. However, this is a secondary consideration in assessing the decline of the practice. The issue for him resides in the 'obscure' nature of the *theory* of horary. It is its whole rationale that is at stake. For the rest of his discussion Carter addresses that rationale and suggests a theory.

His starting point is the issue of whether horary is about the 'birth of an idea'. This might be the case where a map is cast for the very first occasion that a question comes to anyone's consciousness. If, for instance, nobody has ever wondered whether a particular couple might marry, then Carter seems sure that the question 'Will Edwin marry Angela?', emerging for the first time in Edwin's mind, should lead to a valid chart with a clear answer.

He is much less certain of the validity of questions which are in the public domain. When someone asks, 'Will the favourite win the Derby?', Carter suggests that 'thousands of other people, at all sorts of times, have asked themselves the same question.' The telling phrase is 'at all sorts of times'. The reader who has followed the earlier chapters of this book will have no difficulty locating Carter's dilemma. He has reverted at this point to the *doctrine of origin* and assumed it to be a foundation for horary. He resists acknowledging a horoscope that is not the objective time of a distinct causal-temporal origin of the matter under question. In this particular case the subject-matter is not any material thing, person or horse, it is a *thought* about those things, but Carter is working on the assumption that thoughts have causal-temporal origins, too.

Carter's own practical horary approach makes his dependence on a theory of the causal-temporal origin completely explicit:

> I have cast numbers of horary figures for myself, when it was possible to assert fairly confidently that the time of the 'birth of the idea' was ascertainable.

In effect this turns horary questions into a form of inception. By defining horary as the inception of an idea, some sort of compromise can be cobbled with the 'origins' of mainstream natal astrology. But before the modern horary astrologer berates our author for his lack of education in these traditional forms of practice, we should remind ourselves that when it comes to providing any serious discussion of theory, horarists commonly do a lot worse than Carter. As he develops his theme, he raises and sustains considerations that are hardly ever made explicit. I have found nothing comparable in the modern literature.

The ambiguity over the causal-temporal origin is only the beginning of the issue as far as Carter is concerned. There is a puzzle at the heart of horary, and he will not let it go. He suggests that if we suppose horary is about ideas that come to us, then where do these thoughts come from? Many of our ideas can be put down to responses to things we see or hear around us in our day-to-day concerns, but it is implicit in Carter's argument that such external promptings are not a sufficient foundation for valid horary questions. There is another class of thoughts which cannot so easily be explained, and which seem 'just to float into our minds'. Carter quotes Socrates and his Daemon, and puts forward the suggestion that we telepathically pick up an idea from this being. Whether we think of it as the transcendental self, the genius, or the guardian angel, this entity knows far more about our future than the lesser self could foresee. This being uses various means to prompt us, either by direct voice, or through oracles, augury and divination, and is able to prompt the astrologer at the moment of inspiring a horary question.

At this point it is worth pausing to take stock of just how radical a step has been taken here. By invoking the ancient concept of prompting by intelligences or daemones, Carter has moved entirely away from the conventional understanding of astrology as a pattern of celestial causes or harmonies. As will become apparent in later chapters, far from being an incidental outcrop of the astrological imagination, it will be found to lie at the foundations of astrology-as-divination. But for the moment let us see where Carter's treatment of the topic takes us.

The hypothesis of the daemon brings with it a further important and rather uncomfortable consideration. Carter adopts the characteristic stance of traditional occult philosophy. He believes that, amongst the many 'immaterial or semi-material beings of varying grades of intelligence', some will intrude upon our mental integrity with silly or even mischievous promptings. There is no doubt some horary practitioners are able to contact trustworthy entities, but other astrologers may be less fortunate or gifted. In short, the validity of particular instances of horary will depend on the character and quality of the prompting daemon.

Even at this point, with his theory diverging markedly from the orthodox astrological view, Carter's attitude is nonetheless constrained by the conventional interpretation of the doctrine of origin, daemones or no daemones. How, he asks, can horary astrologers imagine that a 'valid figure can be cast for the moment *they* receive the idea, which is not their own, but the querent's?' Surely, the astrologer should find the moment that the thought first came to the *querent*.

I take it that Carter has in mind the querent's daemon prompting the question, but given the unreliability of daemones, it would seem wise to invoke the *astrologer's* daemon here, all the more so if we accept that over the course of practice the astrologer will build up an attunement to a credible source. This makes immediate sense of horary method in that the chart is cast for the moment the *astrologer* receives the idea. The astrologer's daemon is enabled to intervene, especially through the marvellous symbolism of the strictures, to protect both parties from foolish questions.

The uncertainty of Carter's argument is exposed when he returns to the practical experience of astrologers. He permits an exception to the rule of origins, namely in 'very serious cases when the astrologer is literally inspired by entities of a high order'. He quotes a famous case of William Frankland, which I shall be discussing more fully further on. Frankland was able to assist the police to find a dead body, from a horary cast for the moment a relative put the question to him. Why should Frankland's case be the exception, when the whole tradition of horary points the same way? It is only an exception if we are stuck on origins. Carter allows the hypothesis of daemones to be distorted by the inappropriate overlay of the doctrine of origin.

Putting to one side the problem of origins, the hypothesis of the daemon leaves us with a critical decision in practice. How do we discern valid from invalid, the promptings of an 'entity of a high order' from those of a mischievous imp or of our own uninspired thoughts? For most astrologers, genuine horaries are quite rare. Carter declares his 'firm conviction' that:

> for some reason or other which I cannot discover and perhaps am not meant to discover, many figures are not meant to be judged; they must be thrown aside, discarded.
>
> *But* on the other hand, where the answer appears plain, that answer is trustworthy.

The 'bloomers' which are often committed in the name of horary arise where astrologers *fear to discard*, and worry at the map to make it yield an answer. On the other hand, where the symbolism is straightforward and appropriate, Carter believes the chart will then speak to us.

I completely endorse this observation. It is the simplest and most practical piece of advice that could be given to the student and is a foundation for successful practice. Yet it is surprising how often it seems to be ignored by practitioners. Carter is also right about the obscurity of the process. It is difficult indeed to work out why some situations should produce a radical horary where other situations simply lead to dumb maps, but unless we learn to discriminate and to discard non-radical charts, weak judgments level out the impact of those uncommon gifts of symbolism when a powerful horary does come our way.

Carter's views are of great interest and importance, but I cannot go further without taking head on the issues raised by his cavalier treatment of traditional horary method. What are we to make of the following assertion?

> ...there is no need to bother much about house division or house rulerships; the oracle will speak clearly.

Lilly would turn in his grave. Signification through house rulership and placing forms the solid foundation of horary symbolism, just as it has done since the time of the earliest horaries we have on record. If Carter abandons this, how can he locate his querent and quesited? Further, there is no indication that he is at all interested in the dynamic astrology of perfection and denial, which is another major strand in our tradition. How can he therefore reliably discern whether matters will or will not come to pass, even in a radical chart?

We have here an example of a 'method-switch' which occurs where the conventional method developed in one area of astrology is brought over to another branch where it is not usually employed[15]. Horary had declined so far in significance by the time of Carter's generation that its claim to a distinctive technical method could go unmentioned. Carter hardly seems to realise that he is using the methods of modern natal astrology in his approach to horary. In the wider perspective of my argument, the dominance of natal astrology has been such that all other branches of horoscopy have tended to undergo a similar reversion to natal technique.

However, the horary practitioner would be unwise to ignore Carter's observations simply on these grounds. I am not convinced that emphasis on traditional method is by itself going to guarantee convincing horary results. The partial recovery of horary in recent years has not fulfilled the expectations of the initiators of that revival. The very few fine illustrations of the capacity of traditional horary which have appeared in print or on lecture platforms have been entirely eclipsed by the upsurge of weak and strained horary judgments dressed up in traditional guise. I am not surprised that mainstream astrologers remain largely unimpressed.

The problem of horary, as of all astrology, goes beyond technique. Technique counts for very little if the astrologer lacks a symbolic sense. Technical form is the 6th house servant of symbolism, not its master, but Carter knew symbolism in great measure, and that is why he would be able to make a sound judgment in those cases which impressed him: 'the oracle will speak clearly'. If Carter is right to suggest that radical horaries are uncommon rather than common, an ability to see symbolic fittingness is far more a guide to sound judgment than the mechanical application of strict horary rules. These will actually *mislead* the astrologer who lets them supplant symbolic sense.

We should now turn to the horary question which forms the intriguing and provocative conclusion to Carter's comments. It must be assumed from the context of the whole article that Carter regards this question and the horary figure to be one of those rare genuine promptings by the genius or daemon.[16] He asks, 'Is there anything in horary astrology?' The interpretation is brief:

> Sure enough, it looks radical. The prophetic Sagittarius rises; Mercury is exactly setting in its own sign but it is also square Jupiter, also in its own sign, and in the 3rd. Also Mercury has a nice couple of trines to Moon and Saturn.
>
> I think horary astrology has given a pretty clear verdict in its own favour; but that square to Jupiter does contain a certain warning.

Consistent with what he has already said, Carter finds no need to employ traditional horary rules and reverts to a broadly natal style in reading this symbolism. There is no indication of a perfection approach even in the treatment of the Mercury-Jupiter square, and the 'nice couple of trines' he mentions for Mercury are both *separating*. It looks as if he sees the theme indicated as

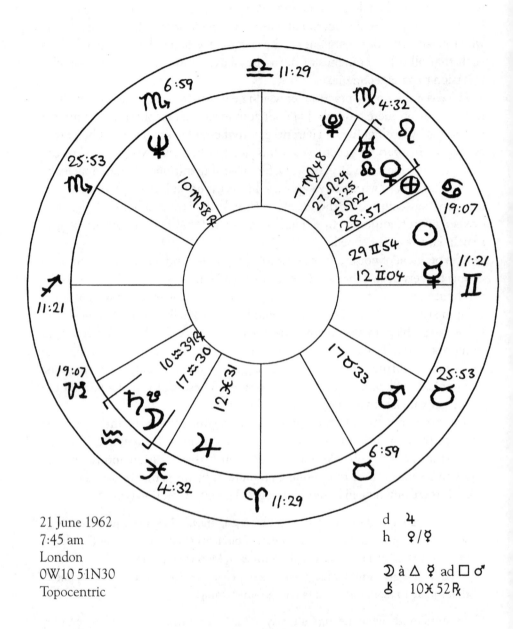

21 June 1962
7:45 am
London
0W10 51N30
Topocentric

d   ♃
h   ♀/☿

☽ à △ ☿ ad □ ♂
⚷   10♓52℞

FIGURE 7
'Is there anything in horary astrology?'

'prophecy' (Sagittarius ascendant) and 'horary questions' (Mercury by its nature), which is backed up by Jupiter, ruler of Sagittarius, being in the 3rd house of questions. Carter sees horary as strengthened by the dignities of the zodiacal placings of Mercury and Jupiter, as well as by Mercury's trines.

The warning of Mercury square Jupiter is developed on the basis of their universal symbolism. It points to a conflict of reason and faith which may result in bad answers when faith in horary overrides both sense and symbolism. I have already quoted Carter's eloquent description of the difficult aspects of Mercury and Jupiter in Chapter 2, concerning the anti-astrology signature:

> He is a poor prophet, and astrologers with these afflictions are not likely to win credit for themselves or their art so far as predictive work is concerned.[17]

With his last words Carter addresses each of us directly: 'What do *you* think, dear reader?' I cannot help thinking that he plays this rhetorical trick with an eye on Mercury on the descendant, literally passing a question on to another.

As one of Carter's dear readers, I would like to take up this invitation and give a further reading of the figure, based on traditional horary method. As ruler of the Sagittarian ascendant, Jupiter signifies the querent. It is in dignity in the last sign of the zodiac. What a superb symbol for Charles Carter, the big man of English astrology at the full and final maturing of his reputation. Here he is in the 3rd, the house of questions, asking the question of questions, and, like Jupiter, assuming for himself the mandate to be judge in the matter.

This is a 9th house question, concerning a branch of higher learning. Mercury as lord of the 9th is therefore the significator for horary astrology and of his essential nature, and here in Gemini, he is a perfect representative for 'interrogations', or the Art of Questions. We note that the almost exact Mercury-Jupiter square is applying. Mercury is in dignity, powerful on an angle, signifier of horary astrology, set against Carter, Jupiter in Pisces. The very closeness of the application throws them both into extreme contrast. The wise old man of astrology has thrown down the gauntlet and made a challenge to horary to answer him, just as he has challenged his reader for an opinion.

The truly extraordinary thing about this map is that it does indeed give an answer, and it is simply the fact that it gives an answer that *is* the answer. For once Mercury has been trapped in his wiles by Jupiter - how could he 'answer' no? This transcends the technical concern of whether there is or is not horary perfection in the matter.[18] The moment that there is a radical chart, then there *is* 'something' in horary astrology. Since this is a map of quite uncommon radicality, 'jumping' with it as Lilly would say, then horary astrology has given a manifestly unequivocal affirmation of its reality.

There is a most special and unusual understanding to be derived from the curious circle that is in play here. This situation which is apparently a question about the Art of Questions is itself *one of those questions* about which it is a question. It is therefore strictly self-referential. It follows that for Carter to ask and receive an answer to the question 'Is there anything in horary astrology?' is at the same time *what* there is in horary astrology.[19]

Whenever astrology appears and works, the inexplicable issue of 'How come astrology works?' is always there, sometimes in the background of attention and sometimes in the foreground. However, the more important problem is the issue to which the symbolism refers, since astrology even when employed playfully or for aesthetic appreciation, is being turned towards other human concerns. If we apply this to horary, all possible horaries *bar one* show the way horary works compounded with the way the world works in the symbolism of a particular worldly situation. In the unique category represented by Carter's question all other circumstances outside the magic circle of astrology drop away.

But as any astrologer might suspect, this initial declaration of significance can only be the starting point. If we have genuine radicality, it should be capable of a fruitful working-out. This is the case here, for the chart's symbolism is found to reflect accurately the themes of Carter's own discussion. This becomes plain when we treat the major symbolism of the map along the lines of the conventional horary methods which Carter himself pushes aside.

Let us first recapitulate Carter's argument in its simplest outline. He suggests that horary theory is obscure with respect to *origins*, as its method does not generally square with the concept of the birth of a question. He moves from this observation to offer a daemonic theory of horary. The daemon or genius communicates to us, or to the lower mind, at certain moments, and prompts the querent to put a horary question. However, reliability is a problem, as evidenced in the poor results of horarists. Plain symbolism is required, and the astrologer should discard ambiguous maps.

How are these views shown in the horoscope? Taking as a starting point Carter's original interpretation, we have already affirmed the crucial significance of the applying Mercury-Jupiter square. Mercury is also closely trine Saturn, and on first glance might appear to be lately separating that aspect. That is an illusion, because Mercury is just beyond its station, and in its recent retrograde arc never got back to the exact trine before turning direct at 11 Gemini 50. This is horary (Mercury, lord of the 9th), placed at the moment of a question *as if* originating from a temporal origin (Saturn), but more truly originating in the querent, shown by Jupiter. Mercury has already retrograded past the square of Jupiter, before its station.

Carter says that the theory of horary astrology is obscure. Like the air trines and the objectified 7th house placing of Mercury, he wants to frame horary as an objective showing derived from the time-moment. Saturn in Aquarius looks like this theory, the doctrine of origin in objective time. Saturn is dignified in Aquarius but despite this it is spoiled by the South Node. Carter complains that horary astrologers do not observe temporal origins. But why should they if, despite surface appearances, Mercury does not in fact come from Saturn (time) but from Jupiter (the one who seeks)?

Jupiter, showing the one asking, is separating the trine of Neptune. That, says Carter, is where questions get their initial impetus, in the prompting of the guardian angel, the genius, the daemon. The old meaning of the 11th house, from early Greek astrology, was the 'good daemon'. In this horary, Neptune is the spirit guide who prompts, and it is from Neptune that Jupiter draws its own inspiration to ask. Jupiter is in Pisces, his own sign, and Neptune is the co-ruler. Neptune cannot dispose of Jupiter in its own sign, but since they share the sign, they combine in a mysterious union when the question (3rd) is asked.

We have already established that Carter has difficulty 'squaring' his view of the birth of an idea, based on the theory of the temporal origin, with the notion of the prompting daemon. This is no surprise from the horoscope when we observe Neptune closely square to Saturn. In fact the two concepts do not really tie together at all, because despite appearances the square has not been made in the recent past nor will it be made in the immediate future.[20] It emerges more and more obviously that Saturn, despite the closeness of his aspects, has little determining power in this map. Saturn has not succeeded in closing on Neptune, just as Time does not bind the Daemon.

With the daemon located, a configuration that is second only to Mercury-Jupiter in significance falls into place, that of the almost exact applying square of the Moon to Mars. Carter's final thesis is that our promptings may be uninspired, or worse, we may have a low-grade daemon. Horary astrologers sometimes trip over the Mercury-Jupiter and give wrong judgments, but a prime source of bloomers is the *fear to discard*. Look at that brutal square with the Moon in the second, ruler of the 8th. This is a possession of no value, something to be cut out and got rid of immediately, Moon square Mars. Mars also has power over the daemon by disposing of Neptune in Scorpio.

On the other hand, if we are not afraid to discard, this allows the few trustworthy horaries to stand out, 'where the answer appears plain'. There is nothing less adorned and plainer than Mars in Taurus with the Moon in Aquarius. It is, to quote the old saying, as plain as a pikestaff.

TESTIMONIES OF THE DAEMON

There is no indication at all that Carter has taken the signification of Neptune as his theory of the daemon, yet once it is pointed out it seems obvious. Because of the relevance of this theory for the main argument of this book, I will include here two demonstrations in the way of testimony to this symbolism.

The first testimony affirming the signification of the daemon in Carter's horary is the horoscope for the perfection of the Mercury-Jupiter square. If there *is* anything in horary astrology, according to Carter's question, then it is signified when the applying significators complete their aspect, which is the technical definition for the horary term 'perfection'. A chart of a perfection is necessarily of entirely secondary status to the horary of which it is an expression, but this class of figure does offer a rich source of testimony where it is desired to expand the original symbolism.

In the chart for the Mercury-Jupiter perfection by square, we note that the Moon is separating from Jupiter, the original significator for the querent, and passing its light by translation to Mars. The Moon-Mars square has transmuted into a benefic sextile when horary is perfected, which is consistent with Carter's interpretation of what happens in a good horary (as against the bloomer of the square in a bad horary). But look at Neptune, exactly rising as this perfection is made - *the perfection of horary is identified with the daemon.*

At the same time, Uranus has sprung into great prominence, conjunct the MC. Uranus culminates as Neptune rises. Without going into an extended discussion that would take us beyond the bounds of what is required for the present, I suggest that we have here an image of how the mysterious working of astrology is revealed to us in the trans-Saturnians. Most modern astrologers take Uranus as a universal symbol for astrology itself, supplanting the Saturnine image of tradition. Neptune has so far not been considered in any similar role. The theories advanced here bring in an order of the working of the astrological that would join its phenomena with parapsychology, spiritualism, psychoanalysis, the unconscious and all the other manifestations that go under the epithet 'psi'. For we moderns, these two tran-Saturnians have to be seen working in concert. Whenever we can say 'astrology has shown itself' (Uranus conjunct MC), we should add, 'and has come into being as psi' (Neptune conjunct ascendant).

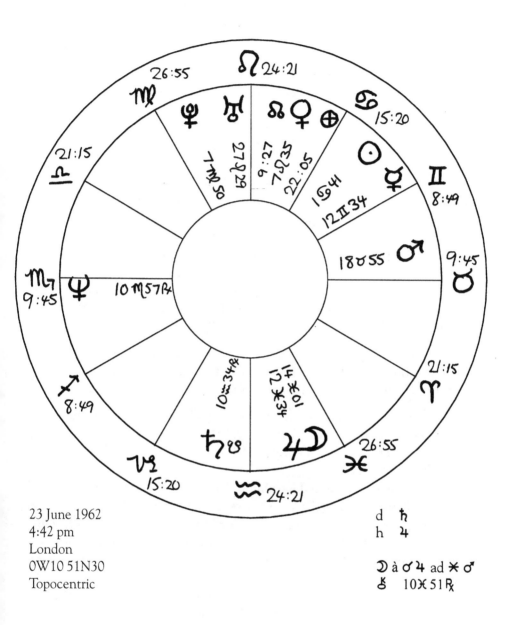

23 June 1962
4:42 pm
London
0W10 51N30
Topocentric

d ♄
h ♃

☽ à ♂ ♃ ad ✶ ♂
⚷ 10 ♓ 51 ℞

FIGURE 8 Carter's Horary
Neptune rises at the Mercury-Jupiter perfection

WILLIAM FRANKLAND'S HORARY

Now I come to a case that seems to bear out Carter's daemon hypothesis. This is the 'Missing Father' horary of William Frankland, quoted by Carter. The curious circumstances of the case are detailed in Appendix 4, but I will give the main elements and the horoscope interpretation here.

Frankland's work deserves to be better recognised. He was known to an earlier generation of English astrologers for his pioneering development of 'symbolic directions' which much influenced Carter in the late 1920's.[21] He was a full-time consultant astrologer with an office in the West End of London and a thriving practice in the period between the wars. He was also one of the very few gifted horary astrologers of his period.

Frankland briefly achieved public prominence in 1926 when a detailed account of one of his horary judgments appeared in the London *Evening News*. It is this that Carter has in mind when he is writing his article in 1962. The daughter of a Burnley man who had been missing for two days phoned Frankland for advice. He took the call as a horary, and after confirming its consistency with afflicting natal directions, gave the following judgment:

> There was probably death by water, in a stream or canal; South and a little West; not exactly near the home but at no great distance; in a place where there are sheds, tools and boats, at a rather barren place.

The daughter's husband was able to locate the place from these instructions, dragged the canal around that spot and caught hold of the body. He was reported as saying 'It was a marvellous thing'. The Coroner observed that it was 'a remarkable coincidence'.

There are some curious and uncomfortable details about how the astrology has worked in this case, and the interested reader is referred to the Appendix. For my current purposes it is sufficient to observe Frankland's choice of the 4th house for the father: 'the planet Saturn therein, square to Neptune, a very depressing influence, and which also marked the Figure as a true one'. Saturn square Neptune, the drowned father.

Now there are several significant associations with Carter's horary. Notice the repeat of the Saturn-Neptune square, and here, in Frankland's horary, Neptune is *conjunct the ascendant*. It is also in mutual reception with the Sun, significator for the daughter asking the question. We should not leave out of the account the fact that the ascendant is conjunct within a degree the Uranus of Carter's horary – an association that turns out to be suggestive in the light of the play of Uranus

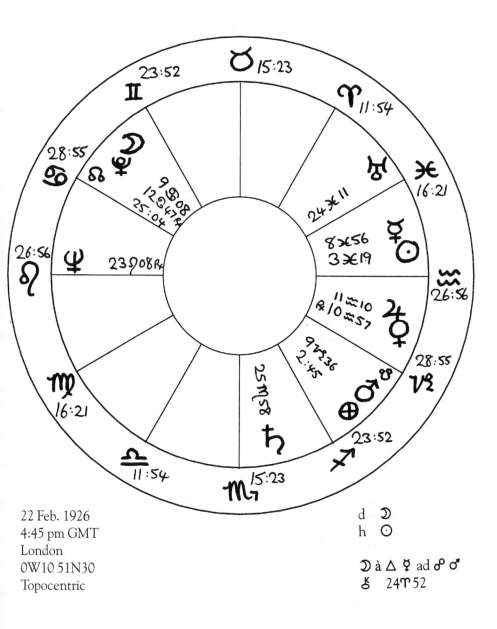

22 Feb. 1926
4:45 pm GMT
London
0W10 51N30
Topocentric

d ☽
h ☉

☽ à △ ☿ ad ☍ ♂
⚷ 24♈52

FIGURE 9
'Missing father'

in the Carter horary perfection horoscope, mentioned earlier.

In Carter's horary, the placing of Neptune in Scorpio is entirely apt for *suicide by drowning*, but equally for assisting the police discover a dead body through paranormal means. Since the Frankland horary is Carter's illustration of daemones, *here* is the daemon arising, *showing himself as a guide to the querent* – exactly as Carter's theory has suggested!

* * * * *

I hope the reader is now fully convinced of both the potent radicality of the horoscope left to us by Carter, and the great relevance of his discussion for our understanding of the question of horary. I believe it is difficult to deny that all the evidence confirms his daemonic theory of horary. What do *you* think, dear reader?

NOTES

1 William Lilly, *Christian Astrology* (1659, reprinted Regulus, London, 1985), p.397.

2 Ivy Goldstein-Jacobson, *Simplified Horary Astrology* (Pasadena Lithographers, Pasadena, Calif., 1960), p.1.

3 Quoted in E. Garin, *Astrology in the Renaissance – The Zodiac of Life*, trans. C. Jackson and J. Allen (Routledge & Kegan Paul, 1983). Garin discusses the 'notable variations in the way of understanding birth' that are required to accommodate horary and electional astrology (pp.38-9).

4 E. Garin, op.cit., p.39.

5 Richard Lemay, 'The True Place of Astrology in Medieval Science and Philosophy', in *Astrology, Science and Society*, ed. Patrick Curry (Boydell, Woodbridge, Suffolk, 1987), p.70: 'The most important spurious work of astrology ascribed to Ptolemy which had an influence far outstripping all others was the "Kitab at-Tamara" or Liber Fructus/Centiloquium put up by the Egyptian astrologer and mathematician Ahmad ibn Yusuf (*ca.* 920 AD). Another dating puts them in the 8th century AD. see ch. 16 n27.

6 Ptolemy, *Tetrabiblos*, op.cit., I.2.13f.

7 Placidus de Titis, *Primum Mobile*, trans. John Cooper (1814), Thesis 6, p.3. (Republished by ISCWA, Bromley, Kent, 1983).

8 Al-Biruni, *Elements of Astrology*, trans. R. Ramsay Wright (Luzac & Co., London, 1934), pp.317-19, quoted extensively in *An Introduction to Islamic Cosmological Doctrines* by Seyyed Hosein Nasr (Thames & Hudson, 1978), p.164. Al-Biruni lived from 973–1051 AD.

9 Jeff Mayo, *Teach Yourself Astrology* (English Universities Press, London, 1964), ch.15, p.184.

10 Guido Bonatus, *The Astrologer's Guide* or *Anima Astrologiae*, Coley's 1675 translation republished by W.C.E.Serjeant (1886), and this latter edition reprinted by Regulus, London (1986), p.1.

11 Masha'allah (Mesehella), 'On the Rationale of Inquiry and its Method' from the *Book of the Nine Judges* (1509) - trans. Graeme Tobyn (unpublished; Company of Astrologers Latin Translation Group, 1993).

12 Guido Bonatus, op.cit., pp.1-2.

13 It can be demonstrated from practical experience that valid horary is possible even where the querent has not intended that the question be put in this way: it is sufficient for the astrologer to 'take it up' as a horary. He or she will soon find from the pertinence or otherwise of the symbolism whether a fruitful decision has been made.

14 I can affirm this. In my early days in astrology, attending Astrological Association and Astrological Lodge meetings in London in the 1970s, it was common to go a year without horary being on the programme. Very few of the experienced astrologers had more than a smattering of the horary method.

15 I am not suggesting that method-switching is 'wrong', although it does raise many problems, especially between horary and natal astrology. It is a useful concept for describing modifications in various practices of astrology. It tends to reverse the counter-movement of technical differentiation which sophisticated astrology develops over the course of time.

16 On the face of it, Carter hasn't even followed his preferred rule of the birth of a question. The article leads us to imagine that his ideas about horary preceded his decision to take a horary on those ideas, but it is quite possible that the horary came first.

17 Charles Carter, *Astrological Aspects* (Fowler 1971), p.88.

18 *Perfection*: See note 9 to chapter 2.

19 Self-referencing and the wiles of Mercury: The matter was well put by David Porter when I showed this judgment at an Astrological Lodge lecture many years ago. He pointed out that Carter's position was rather like a man going to a door, knocking, and calling 'Is anyone there?'. What are we to infer when a voice inside calls out 'No'?

20 Prior to this horary Saturn reached 11 Aquarius 24 on 22 May and turned on its station retrograde. At that moment Neptune was retrograding at 11 Scorpio 37 so Saturn was 13' short of the square. It is January the following year before Saturn finally catches up and makes the square.

21 William Frankland, *Astrological Investigations*, 1927; *New Measures in Astrology*, 1929 (?); *Keys to Symbolic Directing*, 1930. All three published by L.N.Fowler, London; publication dates are not given in books. Frankland never published his findings in horary astrology, although on the evidence of papers kindly made available by his son he was working towards a book on the subject. It is hoped to make extracts from Frankland's work available in due course.

7

Katarche: The Line of Descent from Augury

Great ones, gods of the night,
Bright one, Gibil, warrior Irra,
Bow star and yoke star,
Pleiades, Orion and the Dragon,
Great Bear, Goat and Bison,
Stand by, and then
 In the divination which I am making,
In the lamb which I am offering,
Put truth for me.

Prayer for Haruspicy at Night[1]

THERE is something in horary astrology that does not match the pure rational model bequeathed to us by the Greeks. The mismatch is obvious and does not require much teasing out. This prompts us to ask what else in the experience of astrology has become inarticulate because it has no place in the classical system. By taking horary seriously other things we thought were secure are brought into question. However, to track the 'something special' in horary requires a longer historical perspective than it has been given up to now. As we dig far back into the origins of our subject, we begin to recover a substratum of the astrological phenomenon that has for long been completely obscured by the classical form.

Prior to Ptolemy, horary can be traced in the work of Serapio of Alexandria and Dorotheus of Sidon (*fl. c.*50 AD). Although many details of early horoscopy bear little relationship to modern practice, there are nonetheless some remarkable consistencies of major principles of interpretation. Predating by one and a half millennia the identical method employed by Lilly in his 'Fish Stolen', Dorotheus describes the planet in the descendant as determining the character of the thief in judgments on stolen articles.[2]

In the early authors, an astrological forecast of the horary type was named by the Greek term *katarche*. A literal translation of this word is 'beginning', which seems to present another facet of the all-pervasive doctrine of origin. A rendering that is more faithful to the astrological usage is 'initiative'. This accurately conveys the idea of human action and purpose, as contrasted with a natural origin.

The term was in use as late as the fifth century AD, from the evidence of the collection attributed to Palchus.[3] In this collection are such typical horaries as 'Concerning the lost linen of a slave girl' (Taurus ascendant with Venus in Virgo), and 'A Little Lion: whether he will be tamed' (2 Leo rises). This latter is not termed a katarche, but the question on the linen is so described: 'Katarche, concerning the lost linen of a slave girl'. This is also mentioned as an 'inquiry' in the text. Another katarche is taken for the moment of receipt of distressing letters, a method that is used by horary astrologers. Yet another judgment which we would certainly treat as a horary juxtaposes the terms katarche and inquiry: 'Inquiry about a katarche concerning fear for a journey to Athens'.

Apart from its usage to describe horaries, the term 'katarche' is distinctively applied to the moment of the beginning of some enterprise. Palchus gives a judgment on the moment when Theodoros, Prefect of Egypt, entered Alexandria (17 March 486 AD, about 7.30 am). The signification for Theodoros's rapid disgrace is demonstrated from the horoscope. The katarche thus includes what we now term 'inceptional' astrology. The extension of this method to the 'election' of a favourable moment follows naturally, and indeed, in this collection is the horoscope of the moment elected for the crowning of Leontius at Antioch. Leontius attempted to establish himself as Eastern Emperor of the Roman Empire: 'this person taking a katarche from two astrologers was crowned and immediately expelled from kingship and fortune'. The term 'katarche' is used to describe the moment elected for the coronation (18 July 484, at 6 am).

If we consider the term katarche principally as indicating a *beginning*, or a forecast based on a beginning, then there is something of a puzzle about its usage for these various cases. It seems odd that inceptional and electional methods, which fit well enough the notion of beginnings, should be joined by horary inquiries, which usually do not suggest themselves as beginnings. In describing modern horary practice, it has already been shown in the previous chapter that the horary moment is commonly not a beginning. We have the same problem with the inquiry about the slave girl's linen. Perhaps the horary leads to a beginning in the sense of the initiating of action, but this interpretation is no more obvious in Palchus than it is in the discussion of modern authors.

Whatever may be inferred from Palchus, there is some indication that the katarche was becoming redundant as a concept. This view is reinforced by the evidence that Arabic astrology does not translate 'katarche' as a generic term for the individual practices previously gathered under its wing. Instead we find separate Arabic words for horary inquiries, elections, and inceptions. The generic relationship of these practices is thereby erased.[4] Since this loosening of the katarche, inceptional and electional astrology, readily subsumed within the Ptolemaic attitude, have gone their own way. They are frequently treated independently of horary, which cannot be so easily rationalised. The practices that were once seen as close in spirit thereby lose all family identity. They are seen as having different logical foundations. Morin is typical of this tendency in late European astrology – he rejected horary yet wrote on the doctrine of elections.

In this ambiguity lies the clue that the term 'katarche' had already effectively decayed by late Hellenistic astrology in the fifth century at the time of Palchus, and had become the husk of an earlier understanding. Perhaps there is more to this than the gathering of disparate non-natal applications. We need to trace the katarche back through the origins of horary. This attempt takes us on a circuitous path through little marked territory, to the ancient practice of divination. It is this which forms the substratum out of which has issued the whole project of astrology.

The early development of western astrology cannot be understood in isolation from the immense movement in thought and attitude which provides its cultural context. Horoscopy developed in an era in which the perceptions of antiquity were undergoing great change. Even before the ascendancy of Christianity, which successfully assimilated Greek thought into its system, the old gods had been rendered absurd. It would be surprising indeed if the pressure of these changes had not affected the practice of astrology, and the descriptions offered by its practitioners.

It is the intention here to indicate something of the essential character of an archaic divinatory attitude which was eventually undermined and superseded in the evolution of Greek thought. The earliest astrology arose in conformity with this archaic attitude, and is an expression of it. Further, there is good reason to suppose that this attitude continued to be at least a partial influence in the perception and description of astrology late into the Hellenistic development. The vehicles of its overt expression were destined to atrophy under the pressure of change towards a rational model. Yet its trace lingered on in those branches of astrology, notably horary, which gathered together under the name of 'katarche'.

The aim of this historical examination is to support the following thesis: that the 'katarchic attitude' discloses a ground of all astrological practice, ancient and modern. An understanding of its historical obscuration will assist in the difficult task of recovering that same ground in modern astrology.

It is common for words of wide currency to take on a specific technical meaning within a particular discipline. The specific meaning frequently has a close semantic relationship with other non-technical uses. In astrology, such words as 'election' and 'rulership' are typical instances. The same is true of the word 'katarche' when employed as a technical term in early Greek astrology.

Let us look at the non-astrological meanings of the term. The word carries several meanings depending on context. The most general of these is 'beginning'. It may also refer to 'primacy, sovereignty, and basis'; 'the part of the sacrificial victim first offered'; and 'to begin the rites of sacrifice'. This last usage appears to be the most ancient, dating back to Homer.[5]

The word 'katarche' thus carries a semantic thread of sacred primacy and authority. Does this have any bearing on the astrological katarche? What possible relationship is there between astrological beginnings and ritual? It might appear that any connection is little more than an inconsequential play of language. However, the semantic pattern of two Latin words of related meaning suggests that the connection discussed is essential. The Latin words are more accessible to us, since they have passed into English as 'auspice' and 'augury'. The parallel quality of all three terms is illustrated in the abstract of principal meanings set out on page 128.

It remains to be added that *auspicium* is, by the usage of at least one modern authority, a valid translation for the astrological 'katarche'.[6]

For the Latin terms, 'beginning' is a metaphorical derivative rather than a primary sense (hence the brackets in the table). However, this derived usage was quite common, especially in the later period of the Roman Empire. Whatever distinctions might be made between primary and metaphorical meanings, all three words state an overall semantic pattern, *linking ritual observance and human initiative*.

For the cultures of the ancient near East, few matters of great consequence would be begun without invocation of the gods and the consultation of auspices. The use of divination 'authorised' a course of action at its inception, by giving it the sanction of the gods. To take an auspice, or to determine an omen of good or bad fortune, was at one and the same time to undertake human initiative under the guidance of the gods. As the necessity for sacred dialogue declined with changed perception and the erosion of belief, the words came to apply simply to the inception of human initiative.

An identical historical drift across the semantic spectrum can be traced in the English usage of these terms. The verb 'to inaugurate' in a strict sense suggests the *ritual* inception of a major matter. The word is now commonly used apart from its original meaning, simply to indicate an important beginning, usually of public concern. It is worth reflecting that even in our irreligious age the word never entirely loses its ritual connotation; how much more resonant, therefore, will have been that same connotation in the time of the Roman Empire and before.

καταρχω

Three terms from Greek and Latin, with derivatives and connected usages

katarche	auspicium	augurium	(noun)
katarchesthai	auspicari	augurari	(verb)
– a beginning	[– to begin or undertake a business]	[– to begin]	
– to make a beginning (m)*			
– part of (sacrificial) victim first offered	– to seek from omens	– divination	
– to begin the rites of sacrifice (m)		[– conjecture, surmise]	
hence:			
– to consecrate for sacrifice		– to consecrate	
– to sacrifice, slay			
– to celebrate, lead dance in honour of ...			
– primacy, authority, basis	– leading or principal person		
– to rule, govern	– government, authority		

* (m) refers to 'middle voice' in Greek.

'Auspice' is similarly revealing. When we say that some project is under the auspices of some organisation, we are asserting that the venture has *originated* under its *authority*. The word has moved its weight over to these secular meanings; the older divinatory sense of the invocation of sacred authority has passed into the shadows. The question therefore arises of how far this archaic divinatory attitude found expression in early astrology. Before this is possible, it is necessary to describe characteristics of ancient divination, considered at first independently of the question of astrology.

In all ancient cultures, the sacrifice of an animal to praise a god or to gain his blessing was a widespread practice. But who are these gods to whom sacrifice must be made? They may be described as autonomous, or partially autonomous entities, imbued with volition, and constituting a numinous realm beyond man's immediate knowledge or control. Although this realm lies 'beyond', at the same time it interpenetrates the cosmos, nature, and man himself, and lies at the deepest core of his concerns. This interpenetration is both sustained and expressed in the celebration of ritual, worship – and divination.

Divination is here to be understood as the interpretation of the will of the divine beings, as the Latin root of this word 'divinus' suggests.[7] These divine beings include the *daemones* ('demons'), intelligences between mortals and gods. The gods and daemones communicate their will in various ways. They might work directly through inspiration. They might appear in dreams and visions, directly or in disguise, or show themselves in the symbolism of signs and omens, the remarkable occurrences of the natural world. A response could be sought at the famous oracles, such as that of Apollo at Delphi, on one of the holy days assigned for the purpose. At Delphi the supplicant made an animal sacrifice, and the god, entering the priestess, would answer in her utterance.

There is from archaic times a useful distinction between unbidden omens and bidden omens (in Latin, *omina oblativa* and *omina impetrativa* respectively). Unbidden omens are the showing of the god in an unexpected dramatic event, such as a prodigious birth. Bidden omens are those where the god's response is actively sought.

There is early evidence of the ritual impetration or bidding of omens in Mesopotamia. In the third millennium BC there existed the practice of examining the entrails of the sacrificial animal to determine the will of the god invoked. Detailed examples of the art of reading the signs on the liver have been found from around 1900 BC. From this time liver reading becomes increasingly codified, and an extensive aphoristic literature develops, together with the careful recording of actual cases.[8]

Other trusted forms of divination included the watching of omens, bidden or unbidden, from the behaviour of birds. This, together with liver-divination, was transmitted to the Etruscans of central Italy. From this people, the art of livers and the wisdom of the birds passed into the observances of the Roman College of Augurs.

THE NATURE OF AUGURY

The attitude demonstrated in Roman state augury exemplifies a fundamental characteristic of ancient divination:

> The augural art never provided an answer to the question 'what is going to happen?' but only to that much more religious one, 'are the deities willing that we should do this or that?'[9]

This reveals to us one of the most significant of all differences between ancient and modern interpretations of divination, a difference which must extend into our understanding of astrology as divination. Divination is in our times most frequently described – by practitioners and sceptics alike – as a means of *foretelling the future.* Yet on all the evidence across many cultures, this gives an entirely misleading definition of ancient divination, where a possible prediction is in the majority of cases incidental to the main task, which is to *consult with the gods.* To take one illuminating example, studies on the record of historical responses at the Delphic Oracle after 750 BC have shown that around three quarters of all consultations concerned matters of *res divinae*, broadly 'religious law'. The Greek states and their citizens referred to Apollo for the 'foundation of cults, sacrifices and other worship of gods, daemones, and heroes'.[10]

Other responses concerned matters of public and private concern, mainly asking what *should* be done. Very few are couched in the form of a request for straight 'secular' prediction of the future, and there is no indication that this was seen as a significant function of the Oracle.

Divination was understood to reside in the sacred. Although in developed systems the omens might bear at many points on details of the mundane world, the effect of divination was to bring the matters enquired about, the vital concerns of man, within the guidance of the sacred. Seen in this light, a prediction through divination was none other than the revelation of what the gods willed to come to pass.

It should not be inferred that ancient divination can be described only as religious observance. Self-interest seeks gain by manipulating predictions, and the will of the gods is capable of flexible interpretation along lines of prevailing political exigencies. However, the essentially sacral process described above will have been perpetually affirmed by the whole interwoven fabric of belief and priestly authority within which divination was socially acceptable. It required a general decline in belief in the gods to divorce the outward forms of divination, including astrology, from the realm of the sacred.

It takes real imagination to recover the import of the 'dialogue with the gods'. This attitude is opaque to modern thought. In conveying something of its quality, the following example from the Greek historian Herodotus will serve better than many paragraphs of abstract discussion. There is a possibility that Herodotus's report reflects a legendary inflation of the historical reality, but even if this is the case, it still serves to illustrate a widely held conception of the sacred dialogue in augury. The circumstance was the victory of the awkward alliance of Greek states, including the Tegeans and the Spartans, over the Persians and their Greek allies, in 479 BC. This victory decisively guaranteed the future independence of the Greeks. The Persians were led by Mardonius, the independent Greek states were under Pausanias. According to Herodotus, the outcome of this conflict had already been prophesied at Delphi, but the ambiguity of the oracle allowed Mardonius to ignore or misunderstand it. Both sides were employing similar rites of sacrificial divination. Neither had received good omens for an all-out attack, but Mardonius with the stronger forces decided to ignore his diviner's advice. Now comes the critical moment, the decisive juncture of fate, for Pausanias and the independent Greeks, the Tegeans and Spartans:

> Once more as they were about to engage with Mardonius and his men, they performed the ritual of sacrifice. The omens were not favourable, and meanwhile many of their men were killed, and many more wounded, for the Persians had made a barricade of their wicker shields and from the protection of it were shooting arrows in such numbers that the Spartan troops were in serious distress; this, added to the unfavourable results of the sacrifice, at last caused Pausanias to turn his eyes to the temple of Hera and call upon the goddess for her aid, praying her not to allow the Greeks to be robbed of their hope of victory. Then, *while the words were still upon his lips, the Tegeans sprang forward to lead the attack, and a moment later the sacrificial victims promised success.* At this, the Spartans, too, at last moved forward against the enemy...[my italics][11]

Who gives the Greeks their victory? Notice the change of heart attending the appeal to Hera, followed by the immediate reversal of omens. Despite the inexorable, if paradoxical, fulfilment of major prophecies, nevertheless in the particular circumstances in which men find themselves there can be no guaranteed or absolute destiny beyond human influence, or independent of man's participation. It may change from moment to moment, from omen to omen. Men find courage and invoke the gods: destiny is negotiable. The right attitude in ritual and in divination may itself be part of that initiative.

I have so far been stressing Greek and Roman attitudes to divination, but it is important to recognise the identical participatory and reciprocal relationship between gods and humans in ancient Mesopotamia, at the dawn of our astrology. The benevolent gods of Mesopotamia listened to human beings and responded accordingly:

> Deductive divination involved reading *in* events or objects... divine decisions that touched upon the future of the interested party... this future was not a 'real' future, an absolute future which would take place inevitably. It was a future that the gods had decreed *hic et nunc* [here and now], and, just as the ruler was free to revoke his decisions, to give in to requests, and... to put off punishment of someone he had originally condemned, the gods also remained merciful.[12]

The fateful development in astrology of the concept of an unerring heavenly decree has a different original impetus altogether. The whole spirit of augury, the spirit of the katarche, denies such a fate.

THE MOMENT OF AUGURY

It is inferred here that this way of thought coloured the astrological katarche, but before this influence can be exactly assessed, it is necessary to delineate the general form of the 'moment of divination' implicit in ancient practices.

In what time and place is divination? On what grounds does the diviner refer omen to event? He does so within the *templum*, the sacred space created in ritual. The sacred space is that wherein a god may be present. Within the ritual is brought forward man's concern, the worldy matters past, present, or future, in which will be discerned the working of the sacred. The god's response occurs within the sacred space of ritual, spontaneously blessing or touching that which has been ritually presented. The 'time' does not belong to the literal event, but to the sacred moment when an omen is bidden with respect to the event.

Where the omen comes unbidden, the gods speak in a space of their choosing, blessing or touching events present with the omen. Such omens are commonly brought together with events by time, in that they occur contemporaneously.

Contemporaneity is an expression of actual perception and not of some abstracted and theoretical 'objective' nexus of space and time. Significance is not first and foremost an event of physical nature, but is a human quality, whether individual or social, and depends upon the human knower. Whatever is significantly in mind, whatever is clouding the horizon, the dominant uncertainty of present attention: it is this that will spontaneously associate with the appearance of an omen. So when omens have not been bidden yet one makes its showing, then the current main concern is the likely locus of reference. If an eclipse is observed while the king is on an expedition, then *prima facie* the king's expedition is the dominant current uncertainty to which the omen refers. If there is no obvious association for some remarkable event recognised as an omen, then that omen itself becomes the centre of current uncertainty. There will then be an expectation for the immediate future, something unknown but just around the corner, to be speculated upon by the diviners. In this case the future and its sign becomes a matter of present concern, demanding human understanding and ritual response.

In developed traditions of divination, there is fine discrimination of detail of the omen, by analogy, similitude or historical precedent. Thus a particular element in current concern may become the locus of association. Alternatively the diviner can seek a specific locus, and in the process improve, confirm, or disconfirm, his original understanding, by the bidding of a further omen in ritual divination. This process can be discerned throughout divinatory practice. An unspecified solar sign seen at the start of the military expedition of King Mursilis II, around 1330 BC, led to fears for both king and expedition. Further consultation by divination relocated the omen as concerning his queen.[13]

PARTICIPATORY SIGNIFICANCE IN THE OMEN

Since an omen is only an omen if it is recognised as such, it is clear that its significance is dependent on the participation of those for whom it is present. Its validity does not depend in any way on some general or theoretical law governing the production of omens. Its power comes precisely from its unique appearance 'for us, here, now'. For this reason, the significance derived from omens and embodied in ancient divination may be called *participatory significance*. It is significant *for* someone who perceives it as significant. This notion will help us recognise that great divide between archaic and modern modes of thought. It stands in contrast to the modern non-divinatory attitude which assigns an apparently non-participatory *theoretical significance* to events:

> We understand phenomena, not by what makes them peculiar, but by what makes them manifestations of general laws. But a general law cannot do justice to the individual character of each event. And the individual character of the event is precisely what early man experiences most strongly.[14]

The observation of meteorological and celestial omens ran parallel with the development of liver-divination and emerged from the same matrix of participatory understanding. Regions of the sky were identified with areas of the liver.[15] Like the marks in the entrails of the sacrificial animal, celestial omens were seen within the realm of the sacred, and they required ritual response. They were were the substance of divination. Hence they could be referred to other forms of divination, as is evident in the case of the Hittite king already mentioned. In very early times the liver seems to have been the final arbiter in any case of ambiguity.

The passage into Greek thought eventually overlaid participatory significance with theoretical understanding. It thus rendered problematic the original inspiration of astrology as a form of omen-reading. However, vestiges of the older way of understanding remained for long at work in the spiritual and intellectual ferment. Delphi retained traces of its authority after the time of Christ. The priestly practice of liver divination survived the ruin of Babylon, and is recorded at least down to the fifth century AD.[16]

The early period of the Roman Republic saw a competition for belief, on approximately equal terms, between the ancient art of haruspicy, which covers several old forms of omen-watching, including entrails-divination, and astrology:

> There was in Rome contact, rivalry, and reciprocal adulteration between Etruscan divination and astrology, but we cannot tell to what extent they reacted, one upon the other.[17]

The two different modes of thought, archaic and classical, can be traced in the astrology of the Hellenistic period:

> In the temples of Oriental gods astrology assumed, or rather maintained, a very different character from that under which it presented itself in the schools or observatories...[18]

Cumont contrasts the older religious attitude with that of 'a didactic treatise like the *Tetrabiblos* of Ptolemy, where the effects of the planets are traced to physical causes'.

What little is known of the early astrologers bears out the view that augury and astrology were intimate companions. Soudines, a Chaldean who acted as advisor to Attalos of Pergamon around 240 BC, was an authority on divination – including liver-reading – and an astrologer. His lunar tables were still used by Greek astrologers several centuries later. Posidonius, skilled in various divinatory arts, including astrology, pre-eminently represents the fusion of these practices with Stoic philosophy in the first century BC. A contemporary, Nigidius Figulus, was in the first generation of native Roman astrologers. He was immersed in the Etruscan tradition, and amongst his writings were essays on thunder-omens and entrails-divination.

Greek astrology therefore developed out of a complex interaction of various ancient strands, combining Greek science and philosophy, Egyptian cosmology and calendar construction, and Mesopotamian astronomy and astral religion:

> ...the haruspices... evidently had elaborate systems of co-relating signs or natural events with particular predictions; and it is possible to show that they related their doctrine of lightnings with the latest developments of Greek astrology.[19]

The picture is obscure, but certain inferences may be tentatively drawn. It seems likely that for many of these early astrologers, at least part of their astrological experience will have been recognised as having direct association with augury, an association which was the legacy of both Etruscan and Mesopotamian attitudes. Hence the likelihood of 'reciprocal adulteration'. Augury's matrix of understanding could hardly fail to influence the rationale for elements of astrological practice.

By the time of Ptolemy in the second century AD, the development of the doctrine of origin (outlined in Chapter 5) had effectively eclipsed all other possible justifications for horoscopy. Most importantly, the logical foundation for *all* astrology had been entirely reformulated. In the Ptolemaic definition, the archaic participatory significance has been supplanted by Aristotle's theoretical structure. It follows that the later rationalisation of astrology gives us few clues as to formative attitudes of the earlier period. Ptolemy has wiped the subject clean of archaic religious traces.

Some scholars, like Bouché-Leclercq, take the view of early horary astrology as something of a corruption, arising as an unscrupulous or weak-minded response to competition from other forms of divination. The corruption is seen as residing in the apparently arbitrary nature of the moment chosen by the astrologer to provide the pertinent horoscope. But this sort of censure has fallen entirely under the spell of Ptolemy's rationalisation, and is therefore liable to misinterpret the phenomena of early astrology. The whole of our later tradition has led us into a similar forgetfulness, which misses the essential fact that the pre-classical 'moment of astrology' is in significant part grounded in *divinatory practice*, and expressive of a *divinatory logic*. This logic quite clearly determined the character of the astrological katarche, and through this influenced the interpretive foundation of that most complex of omens, the horoscope.

Once we remove the framework of the Ptolemaic rationalisation, it becomes possible to review early horoscopic practices within the light of augury. This reveals the uniting thread of the diverse collection gathered under the name of katarche. Unlike the most usual understanding of natal astrology, where a fate appears to be determined at birth, these katarchic practices share with augury a quality of human *participation*. When Nigidius Figulus judges a katarche for the inception of civil war between Caesar and Pompey, like the other omen-readers he seeks not only a prediction of outcome, but more fundamentally a judgment on the legality or divine accord of Caesar's action: that is, the response of the gods to this freely taken human initiative.[20] Despite the immeasurable authority of the numinous realm called upon by divination, the question of destiny is in effect a fluid and open project – the gods may be propitiated, the sacred may be approached. Unlike the fixed indication which classical astrology has attributed to a natal horoscope – or to an inceptional horoscope treated after the manner of a nativity – the omens of the katarche cannot be guaranteed, they do not constitute an unalterable order of things. Like the legendary auguries of Pausanias, they are open to change as initiative changes.

As with inceptional astrology, the early forms of electional and horary astrology come forward in a new light when considered within the katarchic attitude. An election takes on the quality of the seeking of a blessing, the *authorisation* by the astrological divinities elected. Choosing the day or the hour of the god, choosing the time of his beneficent configuration with respect to one's own wish – such an act of election is consistent with, and expressive of, an archaic religious attitude. That same attitude will equally find expression in more active forms: the dedication of prayer or ritual to the god, or the creation of emblems or talismans to evoke the god's participation. It is the same type of attitude which appears to be the active principle shaping the early katarchic astrology.[21]

Seen in the same light, horary astrology perfectly reflects ancient divinatory practice. It is the seeking of an astrological omen to indicate the will of the gods – and thus the outcome in terms of good or ill fortune – with respect to human initiative brought before those gods. The horary chart is the equivalent of the bidden response in ritual divination: to make a horary is equivalent to beginning the rites of sacrifice.

It was brought forward earlier in connection with the ritual act of divination that *the act itself* creates the sacred space, the *templum* wherein an omen may appear. The omen belongs to this space, and is not an objective property of the event in the world with which it is spontaneously associated. Translating this into the interpretation of horary that has already been demonstrated in the last chapter, the horary moment is significant precisely and only *because* it is the moment that someone has posed a horary question. It is therefore brought into being by both the act of the questioner, and equally by the decision of the astrologer that this will be taken as a horary moment. To apply the language of augury, it is the astrologer who has the authority of the *templum*.

SPONTANEOUS SIGNIFICANCE

As we move from an archaic realm of augury into the early development of our classical astrology, we also move from religious rites to secular human experience. But however interpreted, whether as omens of the gods or simply as meaningful coincidences, the katarchic moment keeps its distinctive quality of spontaneity, arising from the immediate concerns and circumstances of the diviner or the inquirer. Its significance is participatory – that is, it is dependent on the participation of the astrologer, or of the one who will press an inquiry upon the astrologer. The moment is thus associated with what moves someone, what makes an impact in their experience. The katarche, unlike the natal moment as ordinarily understood, does not require a theoretical structure to support it. It has no need of a law of astrological influence or signatures objectively existing independent of the astrologer's participation. Since it is not held within the boundary of the doctrine of origin, where a literal beginning is the definitive theoretical requirement, the katarche finds expression through a range of possible moments for which a horoscope may be judged. This range naturally includes beginnings as a pre-eminent possibility. However, which moment is taken up in each particular case depends entirely on the astrologer, in the light of the circumstances. It is not to be predetermined by any fixed rule, unless the astrologer has chosen to follow a convention or adopt such a 'rule' as part of the ritual of his or her practice of astrology.

What sort of objective moment could therefore become the moment of the katarche? Almost any moment at all could suggest itself, but in practice the moments 'significantly presented' and therefore 'spontaneously associated' commonly fall into one or other of a few self-evident categories. These serve to technically differentiate horaries, which are moments when questions are posed, from inceptionals, moments of starting something.

In the katarche, any initiative or event that is decisively marked out by a critical instant will be associated with the time, and hence with the celestial configuration, of that instant. One moment is not theoretically more important than any other – it is the moment that comes forward in the particular circumstance that counts. When Palchus judges the katarche for the moment of receipt of letters, this is not a secondary moment reflecting some more primal origin, such as the unknown moment of their being written. Had that moment been available, and not the moment of receipt, then doubtless it too would have served for the katarche. The very fact that this earlier moment is not 'presented' removes it entirely from participatory significance.

The question of the status and contribution of the katarche in early horoscopy is much clarified when its essential relationship with ancient divination is revealed. The differences between the Ptolemaic rationalisation and the practices of the katarche go far deeper than questions of technique, or of different areas of application. The katarche embodies a certain stance, one which allows the astrologer the creativity – and the uncertainty – of a significance in which he or she directly participates. The transmission of this ancient attitude into later horary practice is easy to recognise. The modern art of horary can not be adequately described without including the participation of the astrologer in that description. In this way, we come back to the participatory significance of ancient thought, and probably of divination as a whole.

THE MYSTERIOUS DECUMBITURE

It has been two decades since the original work on the katarche opened up discussion on the connection between ancient divination and horary, inceptional and electional astrology. This project was inspired by close observation of current practice. Frustration with the inadequacy of conventional descriptions, and comparisons with other forms of divination, brought into view the essential nature of the question waiting to be asked. This led to a study of the ancient material available, yielding its fruit and confirming the initial inspiration through a combination of historical and etymological approaches.

From the point of view of what this actually means for present-day practice, the development of this understanding has up to now been sluggish. Few horary astrologers – let alone practitioners of other branches of astrology – seem to have the slightest idea about what it might imply. Perhaps it goes too far against the grain of everything we have taught ourselves to believe; and this is a grain that runs deep, and goes back a long way.

There has however been support for the historical side of the argument. The views expressed by Robert Schmidt in his translation of *The Astrological Record of the Early Sages in Greek* underscore the conclusions already drawn concerning the augural origins of katarchic practices. Taking up the sacrificial meaning of katarche, he brings out its pairing with the widely used term *apostelesma* (astrological completion or 'effect'), Schmidt suggests that these Greek words indicate a *ritual* relationship of sign and that which is signified, rather than a causal relationship in the sense of our modern usage of the word 'cause'.[22] Ritual action is as intelligible as the causal action interpreted by modern science, but from the viewpoint of ritual the astrologer looks for intelligent signs in the heavens, and not simple causes. If Schmidt's thesis is correct, we will feel more assured in inferring evidence of an earlier ritualistic and divinatory interpretation wherever the term *apostelesma* was used, therefore including natal astrology.

In the recovery of the ritual attitude implied in the katarche, there has nevertheless been a continuing puzzle concerning the origins of a major practice of ancient medical astrology known as the *decumbiture*. This is the method of prognosis of disease from a horoscope drawn up for the moment a patient becomes ill and takes to bed or 'declines upon a couch', which is the meaning of this Latin word. Although it shares certain features with other methods of the katarche, it does not constitute a class of medical or 6th-house question, which remains a particular application of horary. William Lilly practiced medical horary; he left decumbitures to his physician-colleague Nicholas Culpeper. Decumbitures involve a distinctive set of doctrines, most notably concerning the judgment of crises traced from the condition of the heavens at the times the Moon squares and opposes its original position.[23]

It always seemed to me that although one must avoid over-defined hard-and-fast distinctions, there was nevertheless something here that did not fit the 'initiative' ticket. In raising the topic of katarchic astrology, I was inclined to bracket the decumbiture off as something of a special case. What makes it an awkward fit is that it gives every appearance of being a *natural* origin, given to us by the accidents and circumstances of nature, rather than being a free initiative to invoke auspices and move on them, which I take as fundamental to the katarche. It is easy to fit decumbitures into an organic and at least partly determined world of natural stellar influence, and the invocation of the lunar rhythm predisposes to such a view.

Far from being a special case, however, since the first edition of *Moment of Astrology* I have come to recognise that the decumbiture lies at the heart of the katarche. It may even prove to be the most significant of all the indications of the ritual and divinatory origins of horoscopic astrology. Once the evidence for the connection is pointed out it all seems quite obvious. The link comes through *incubation*, which simply stated is the divinatory practice of lying down either to sleep or to enter a trance state, with the intention of inducing a dream or vision of a god. Peter Kingsley's *In the Dark Places of Wisdom* describes the healing function of this practice:

> Before the beginnings of what's known as 'rational' medicine in the West, healing always had to do with the divine. If people were sick it was normal to go to the shrines of the gods, or else to the shrines of great beings who had once been humans but were now more than humans: the heroes. And they'd lie down.

Furthermore, there was a class of priest who would undertake incubation on behalf of a sick person. Strabo records details of the sacred precinct of the Plutonium – the entrance to the underworld – in a village near the city of Acharaca. There is a temple of Pluto and his consort. Above the precinct is the Charonium, the cave used for incubation:

> People who fall ill and are willing to submit to the methods of healing offered by these two divinities come here and live for a while in the village together with the most experienced among the priests. And these priests lie down and sleep in the cave on behalf of the sick, then they prescribe treatments on the basis of the dreams they receive.[24]

Peter Kingsley shows that Apollo was a 'lord of the lair', and this is understood as the lair in which an animal lies down. One of the Orphic hymns tells the story of Apollo marrying the Queen of the Underworld, Persephone[25], but the motif of Apollo as night Sun was pushed into oblivion by later philosophical and religious overlays. Apollo's human offspring Asclepius (Aesculapius), 'the blameless physician', learned his father's wisdom of snakes and his gift of healing, and temples in his name became sanctuaries for the sick. Now everything is in place for the final piece of the jigsaw. The Greek term which became in Latin 'decumbiture' is κατάκλϊσις (*kataclysis*), which means both 'sitting at table' and 'a lying down'. The word is itself a derivative of κατακλίνω, which holds amongst its meanings, '*to lay* the sick *on couches* in the temples [especially] in that of Aesculapius'.[26]

There are curious and recognised survivals of these pagan practices even into modern times. There are still parts of Greece where dreams and omens are taken seriously by ordinary folk; and there are shrines where, on the eve of the saint's day, sick people lie overnight in the church in expectation of the healing visitation of the saint.[27]

But what of the survival in later astrology? In the absence of historical records, our understanding of exactly how a formal doctrine of the astrological decumbiture evolved from sacral temple practice remains speculative. It is not unreasonable to suppose that the Moon and its phase would be closely observed for the course of the incubation as well as for the progress of the disease, and lunar or other stellar omens might become elements of election in choosing the day of the ritual. It is possible that the astrological approach rapidly departed from its ritualistic origins, so that the technical terms used by astrologers came to represent little more than a borrowing of ritual language, but without ritual content, within one or two generations. But even if this minimalist interpretation is adopted, we cannot ignore the evidence that at a key originative phase of its formation, the doctrine of decumbitures was in a close association with, and framed by, the omen-reading mind-set of the augurs and the priests. At a certain point it becomes impossible to fully separate out ritual from causal-temporal thinking, since these are conceptual divisions that we impose on the material from our quite different world-view, and in long hindsight. A similar problem of historical interpretation arises in tracing the origins of scientific medicine, as shaped by Hippocrates, which nevertheless starts its journey in the same healing sanctuaries of Asclepius.

It is not my intention here to suggest a project for the modern medical astrologer directly founded on these sacral origins. We cannot simply peel back the ages and return to the practices of our ancestors, however much we may hold their world in respect. On the other hand, I believe that what does strongly emerge from these considerations is the participatory, intentional and imaginal component, at the same time essentially religious or mystical in its attitude, disclosed at the origins of our astrology. Perhaps this is what we require to remember, and to discover in our modern practice.

NOTES

1 J.B.Pritchard (ed.), *The Ancient Near Eastern Texts relating to the Old Testament* (Princeton University Press, Princeton, N.J., 1950), p.390.

2 See *The Yavanajataka of Sphujidhava*, Vol 2, translated, edited, and with a commentary by David Pingree, Harvard University Press, Cambridge, Mass., and London, 1978), pp.379-80.

3 From O.Neugebauer & H.B. van Hoesen, *Greek Horoscopes* (American Philosophical Society, Philadelphia, 1959; see nos. L474 – L 487). According to Pingree (op.cit., p.437), 'Palchus is not a compiler of c.500, but is the mask behind which Eleutherius Eleus hid in 1388; the name "Palchus" is a Greek translation of the Arabic al-Balkhi – the resident of Balkh'. Eleutherius has, however, gathered genuinely ancient fragments.

4 Professor Richard Lemay of the City University of New York has kindly confirmed this. It would prove of interest to establish whether the same decay occurred in the transmission of Hellenistic astrology into India.

5 *Odyssey*, III.445.

6 On the Latin for katarche, I have taken the reference given in Pingree (op. cit., see note 2 above), p.xv, to A. Ludwich, 'Maximi et Ammonis carminum de *actionum auspiciis* reliquiae'. The phrase in italics translates 'katarche'. I have seen no evidence to indicate how early authors would decide the translation.

7 Interestingly, the Latin *divinus* for Greek *mantike* is a late usage from Cicero: see *Pagan Priests*, ed. Mary Beard and John North (Duckworth, 1990), p.57.

8 For Mesopotamian divination, see the essay by O.R. Gurney in *Divination and Oracles*, ed. M. Loewe and C. Blacker (Allen and Unwin, 1981): early liver-reading, p.148; solar sign, p.161.

9 W. Warde Fowler, *The Religious Experience of the Roman People* (Macmillan & Co., 1911), Lecture XIII, p.298.

10 Plato, *Republic*, quoted in J.Fontenrose, *The Delphic Oracle* (California University Press, 1978), p.43.

11 Herodotus, *Histories*, IX, 61-2. I have used the lively translation of Aubrey de Selincourt (Penguin Classic), p.576.

12 Jean Bottéro, *Mesopotamia* (University of Chicago Press, 1992), p.33.

13 O.R.Gurney, in *Divination and Oracles*, op.cit., p.161.

14 H.A. Frankfort *et al.*, *Before Philosophy* (Pelican Books, 1949), pp. 24-5. Especially in the first chapter on 'Myth and Reality', this work gives a remarkable and lucid insight into the logic of archaic mythopeic thought, from which astrology ultimately derives.

15 See Jack Lindsay, *Origins of Astrology* (Muller, 1971), p.18. A valuable and extensive compilation from scholarly sources.

16 For fifth-century haruspicy, see W. Warde Fowler, op. cit., Lecture XIII, p.309, note 25.

17 See Bouché-Leclercq, *L'Astrologie Grecque* (Paris, 1899, reprinted under the title *Culture et Civilisation*, Brussels, 1963), ch.16, p.550 (1963 ed.). This work is still a definitive source; over 650 pages by an erudite scholar who loathed his subject. With thanks to Denis Labouré for help with this material.

18 Franz Cumont, *Astrology and Religion among the Greeks and Romans* (1912, reprinted by Dover, New York, 1960), Lecture V, p.87 (1960 ed.).

19 See M. Beard and J. North (eds.), *Pagan Priests*, op.cit., p.65.

20 For Nigidius Figulus on the Civil War, see J. Lindsay, *Origins of Astrology*, op.cit., p220-1, quoting Lucan.

21 This pattern of sacral authorisation of conduct is quite common in antiquity, for example in the Greek rituals as recorded by Homer, prior to the contact with Mesopotamian divination.

22 The Astrological Records of the Early Sages in Greek – tr. Robert Schmidt ed. Robert Hand Project Hindsight, Greek Track X, 1995; Golden Hind Press pp xxvi–xxxii. This is an important discussion on the meaning of key astrological terms, and on the divide in thought between ritualistic and causal-temporal modes. Schmidt suggests the possibility that 'the original translators of the Egyptian wisdom tradition into Greek might have been consciously embedding their own rival view of the nature of things deep in the Greek language itself', thereby making 'a lasting impact on the Greek mind'. It should be noted that Greek mind already retained from its own archaic sources a ritualistic heritage quite apart from any obvious Egyptian or Mesopotamian transmission. Whether or not the choice of Greek terms used in the translations reflects a conscious intent in the way suggested by Schmidt, the imprint of an earlier attitude remains, but it seems that whatever its source its true significance was soon to be overlaid and effectively obliterated. It also appears to have had little lasting impact, until we reach the point that the neo-Platonic inheritors of the Egyptian mysteries – I am thinking especially of Iamblichus – found themselves to be critics of the literalism and causal determinism of the orthodox astrologers of their day. On all the evidence the causal-temporal conception split apart from the ritual mode even before the time of the earliest Greek astrology of which we have records, and certainly by the time of Vettius Valens in the 2nd century AD. Schmidt is probably unwilling to allow such a seemingly negative judgment on early classical astrology, however. The philosophical engine of this change appears to be Stoicism, especially in its cosmological development with Chrysippus (3rd century BC) – see reference to Michael Lapidge below. Stoicism warmly embraced and permanently secured major astrological doctrines yet harbours an anti-katarchic strain in its organic and biological determinism. Within astrology it was eclipsed by the rising authority of Aristotle, carried through by Ptolemy; stoicism nevertheless lives on as a potent presence in the shadowy reaches of the astrological imagination. There is much

more work to be done in understanding the origins and legacy of this vital component in our tradition. I found a useful starting point in several of the essays in the collection 'The Stoics' ed. John M. Rist 1978 University of California; see especially Michael Lapidge on 'Stoic Cosmology'.

Schmidt provisionally translates the term *katarche* as 'inception'. Although this may be strictly accurate, it risks confusion with one part of katarchic astrology that has become known as 'inceptions' (eg the starting-moment of a venture, a business etc). The neutrality of this term also allows the modern astrologer too much leeway to fall back into purely efficient-cause non-participatory thinking. For that reason, I prefer 'initiative', which retains a sense of conscious intention essential to any understanding of astrology-as-ritual.

23 See Graeme Tobyn 'Culpeper's Medicine: A Practice of Western Holistic Medicine' 1997 Element Books esp. pp154-161. I must thank the author for his considerable erudition and help in tracing the origins of the method. See further comments on the decumbiture ch.8 n14, and ch.9, p176.

24 Peter Kingsley *In the Dark Places of Wisdom*, (Golden Sufi Center, Ca., 1999) Quotations are from pages 80,82. Strabo lived from c 54BC–24AD. It was reading this profound and provocative work that directly inspired the understanding concerning decumbitures, under charged 'synchronistic' conditions. All of this only hints at the scope of Peter Kingsley's thesis.

Other scholarly references which open up this topic can be traced through W.R.Halliday *Greek Divination: A Study of its Methods and Principles* Argonaut Chicago (1967 reprint of 1913 first edition) pp128-134. Halliday notes the totemic aspect of the ritual of incubation, involving animal skins in which the querent is wrapped, or on which he is laid.

25 Peter Kingsley op.cit p91.

26 Liddell & Scott's Greek Lexicon.

27 These customs were fully documented at the beginning of last century by J.C.Lawson *Modern Greek Folklore and Ancient Greek Religion* (1910) Cambridge University Press. With thanks for this reference to Anthony Relf 'A study of the development, principally in the Greek world, of oneiromancy as a divinatory practice' (undergraduate dissertation in Cosmology & Divination, University of Kent at Canterbury January 2002).

8

Horary Revived

Discretion, together with Art

William Lilly

THE katarche refers to a domain of experience that is wrapped in the folds of astrology, but in horary this is sometimes revealed in a pure and unadorned form. However, horary's potential to reveal carries a penalty for the unwary.

This might seem a surprising observation. What could be more practical and straightforward than horary? Once past the initial barrier of a distinctive terminology, it is a relatively simple method from a purely technical point of view. Further, it is usually applied to the most common of human concerns, with nothing apparently spiritual or even psychological about them.

Without it being a question of disbelief, many sound practitioners of astrology as well as intelligent lay users feel themselves 'not ready' for horary. For one thing the requirement to come up front with a yes or no answer to a question is too strong a demand, and other forms of astrology are seen as offering better possibilities of consultation or of opening up the symbolic without these all or nothing feats of judgment. But that is not the whole story, either. As we have seen, this supposedly practical method is far from straightforward in either its operations or its implication. Horary's occasionally miraculous directness seems to demand from the astrologer an even greater circumspection and discretion in order to be of any use, and a merely literal-minded treatment soon runs into error. When horary is good, it is good, but when it is bad it is very bad indeed. Most important of all, it begins to reveal an *active* dimension in the working of astrology, no longer reading off heavenly 'information' but implicating client and astrologer in the move that brings to pass the desired effect. The student's reserve is therefore sound. The step into the direct experience of the initiative is also an initiation. These issues reach far beyond the literal statement of the 'rules of astrology' or the meanings of planets and houses.

In order to explore what the katarche might mean for *us*, as opposed to augurs in ancient Rome, we need to illustrate something of the same experience in later astrology, which is a purpose of this chapter. I believe this brings us to the question of a magical attitude at work in astrology. There is nowhere better to start than the horary astrology of William Lilly. I will first return to his captivating 'Fish Stolen', already discussed in Chapter 6 (page 98) and look at the implications of this judgment in the light of our present discussion.

This is one of only two judgments given in *Christian Astrology* that date from Lilly's five year period of isolation in rural Walton, following a melancholic mid-life crisis. It is metaphorically as well as literally about recovery after loss, and it is full of horary's spirit of fun.

As I have already shown, the symbolism of success in the question is immediately clear to us, just as it was obvious to Lilly at the time. There is, however, a further dimension to the working of the astrology. This is typical of a common class of horary where the matter desired cannot be brought to pass unless the querent, taking heed of the symbolism, makes a move. Lilly's fish will never come back to him on the technical perfection shown unless Lilly embodies the *symbolism* in order to bring the promise of the horary to pass. Once he realises he has a horary perfection of significators to work with, Lilly knows his actions are likely to succeed. He is thereby confident in pursuing the tenuous inquiries. This is in no sense the reading of an objective fate to which we are subject. It is a symbolic possibility within which the astrologer may choose to participate. Thus, despite the extraordinary predictive detail, the outcome depends on the *symbolic participation* of the person involved, for the stars are *non cogunt* ('not compelling'). This understanding takes us right back to the ancestral origins of horary in the katarche.

This type of symbolic participation is not simply an isolated occurrence, but the key to understanding several of Lilly's most remarkable judgments. Have a look, for instance, at the first of the two 'Marriage' questions in *Christian Astrology*.[1] Here is a fickle lady, who had continually slighted a suitor to the point where she had given a final and positive refusal to his proposal of marriage. She had then changed her mind, and full of regrets she realised that she indeed wished to marry him. The man had become angry and scornful of her previous treatment of him, and in addition was being led to forget his former hopes by his companions. The case was hopeless, her opportunity lost, and the significators indicated this truth of the matter. On any sound basic reading of horary, the answer had to be 'no'. Yet Lilly was moved by her grief: 'Hereupon, with much compassion, I began to consider what hopes we had in the Figure'. Notice the '*we*'! This is not a slip of the pen – Lilly himself is participating up to the hilt. He then proceeded to weave a thread of possible signification, a remote chance that the two suitors might be brought together again. It is a complex and delicate judgment and Lilly gives it much more space than most of his judgments. I will not try to summarise it for the reader, except to remark that it involves beautiful symbolism, but at the same time it undoubtedly breaks several horary conventions about what can and cannot be perfected. The key to success was a third party, who Lilly described from the figure, who knew both the suitor and the lady. This gentleman was to be a true friend and put the lady's change of heart to the spurned suitor. Based on an exact Jupiter-Saturn sextile some three days later, Lilly gave direction 'that the nineteenth of June neer upon noon, the Gentleman should first move the quesited in the business'. Here is what followed:

> My counsell was followed, and the issue was thus: By the Gentlemans meanes and procurement the matter was brought on againe, the Matche effected, and all within twenty dayes following, to the content of the sorrowful (but as to me unthankful!) Lady, &c.

Let us be clear about what has been done. The astrologer has intervened by astrological election to transmute the pattern of events, in order to bring about good fortune for the client. *Horary is being used not to predict the outcome but to change it.* It is an active role for astrology, not simply passive reporting like a celestial weather forecast. The stars were not even inclining this way, much less 'compelling' the outcome. Lilly's move is possible only where there is a free creative imagination alive in the symbolism. The symbolism can be seen to be entirely appropriate, as if it was meant to be that way all along, but this seeing is after the event. Before the matter was resolved, everything depended on Lilly sensing and creating a unique possibility that can in no sense be put down to a 'rule', and there is no way this judgment could be recommended to a beginner in horary without encouraging appalling craft habits. Although there is a framework of traditional rules, these do not in themselves provide for resolution in cases such as this:

> You must know how to vary your Rules, wherein principally consists the Master-peece of the Art.[2]

I suspect that even the detail of the lady's unthankful treatment of Lilly is revealing, because it is problematic for most people to acknowledge magical assistance, as opposed to a forecast of possibilities. Whether or not this was so for the lady, we should be under no illusions about the dimension of astrology revealed here. The relationship with a magical attitude is apparent.

Any lingering doubts about Lilly's style in astrology having its roots in a magical attitude are dispelled when we read his diaries, edited by his great friend

Elias Ashmole.[3] Lilly was completely familiar with a world of scrying and the summoning of spirits. His first teacher of astrology, the formidable Evans, 'had some Arts above, and beyond Astrology, for he was well versed in the Nature of Spirits'. For a fee of £40 Evans undertook an operation in daemonic magic on behalf of a gentlewoman, to recover title deeds to some land from the home of former gentleman friend who was now holding on to them. A fortnight's pattern of ritual and invocation culminated in the summoning of the Angel Salmon, of the nature of Mars, who was instructed to obtain the deeds:

> In small time Salmon returns with the very Deed desired, lays it down gently upon a Table where a white Cloth was spread, and then, being dismiss'd, vanish'd.[4]

Other aspects of the Angel Salmon's operation were not so gentle, and involved the destruction of part of the house of the gentleman concerned. Lilly reports this straight, and does not suggest trickery, although Evans was an undoubted rogue.

We can hardly ignore Lilly's reports of his own experiments, which are of an explicit magical-astrological nature. In 1634 or 1635 he taught John Hegenius, Doctor of Physic, the use of talismans and dowsing rods:

> ...we did create several Sigils to very good purpose; I gave him the true Key thereof, viz. instructed him of their Forms, Characters, Words, and last of all, how to give them Vivification, and what Number or Numbers were appropriated to every Planet.[5]

In another instance a desperate woman made pregnant and then abandoned by a young lord came to Lilly to find some way through the barrier of lackeys and servants, so that she might confront the young man. On two separate occasions he appointed 'such a Day, such an Hour of that Day' where she had the opportunity to see him. This worked both times. On the second occasion she went to see a play as directed by Lilly and within a quarter of an hour the young Lord chanced to enter the very same box where she was sitting. This could well be skilled astrological election, as in the case of the fickle lady discussed above, but it must also have been aided by a more direct magical intervention from Lilly. We know this from his dark and mysterious statement that follows:

> ...But I grew weary of such Imployments, and since have burned my Books which instructed these Curiosities: For after that I became melancholly, very much afflicted with the Hypocondriack Melancholly, growing lean and spare, and every Day worse.[6]

Lilly's abandoning of certain forms of magic, possibly daemonic, and his subsequent retreat to the country at Walton-on-Thames, suggests the recuperation in his natal horoscope of the Sun in Taurus against the deadly opposition of Saturn in Scorpio in the 8th house (the Black Arts). It is this revival that shines through the early 'Fish Stolen' judgment. At the same time he began to raise his astrology to a higher order altogether, which is several times hinted at as 'prophetical astrology', the basis of his strange hieroglyphic predictions:

> I had not that Learning from Books, or any Manuscript I ever yet met withal, it is reduced from a Cabal lodging in Astrology...[7]

The active participation of the astrologer in assisting the client to create good fortune does not mean that successful astrology depends on explicitly talismanic magic or the invocation of Spirits. However, *in principle* this participation and intervention, well understood as a category of magic, is at work in the most ordinary cases. The following superb katarche from Lilly serves to remind us of this, while demonstrating yet again the remarkable truth that powerful predictive judgments are not necessarily founded in some pre-ordained fate, a common and debilitating error to which horary is especially prone.

THE GENTLEWOMAN AND THE AGED MAN

Lilly's horary on the 'Gentlewoman and the Aged Man', given here in full, was published in his *England's Propheticall Merline* (1644). Perhaps because it had already seen the light of day, it was not included in *Christian Astrology* three years later. It is a classic, in the same league as the finest judgments in his textbook.

A Gentlewoman desired to know if she should have an aged man; yea, or no.

The Querent hath Mercury only for her significatrix. Jupiter is for the aged man and party questioned after. Considering Mercury had lately separated from a Sextile of Jupiter, and the Moon by a Quadrate, I judged there had lately been some treaty about it, (which was confessed:) and that the old man did much importune it, because Jupiter receives Mercury in his exaltation, and casteth a friendly Trine to the degree Ascending; this was so: seeing the Moon carried the light from Jupiter to Mars, and Mercury was going to a Quartile of Mars; I judged the maids affection was alienated from the old man, and that she desired such a man as Mars, viz. a Captaine or Souldier, &c. and that she should be crossed therein, by reason both Mars and the Moon were in unfortunate homes: nor had Mercury or Luna any dignities where Mars was, or in the Signe, and degree where

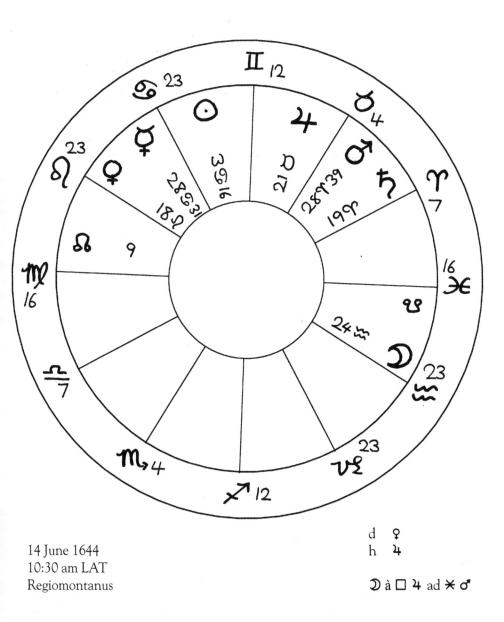

14 June 1644
10:30 am LAT
Regiomontanus

d ♀
h ♃

☽ à □ ♃ ad ⚹ ♂

FIGURE 10 A gentlewoman desired to know if she should have an aged man; yea, or no.

Figure as given by Lilly

himself was: all this was acknowledged with teares: because I found Saturn and Mars in the eighth, and that Mars was the impediting Planet; I bad the maide require a joynture* of the old man, and see what it would do which at next meeting she did, but then it appeared he could not make any, there being an incumbrance upon his Land, as Saturn with Mars, in his second house of substance doth excellently signifie: after this they broke off all termes of marriage, directly as I told her.

The Querent was of a stature tall.... of a good lovely brown complexion and... round visaged, well spoken, modest and judicious. The Quesited I judged to be a man fleshy and full bodied, ovall visaged... brown colour, dark sad hair, his stature tending to talnesse, a man worldly and covetous, for Jupiter being in Taurus the Emblem of Labour, doth influence so much: it was so confessed.[8]

* Jointure: estate settled on a wife, to be enjoyed after her husband's death.

A COMMENTARY ON LILLY'S JUDGMENT

The interpretation is beguiling in its simplicity. Yet these few broad strokes reveal both the secure foundation and the acuity of Lilly's art. By an exquisite turn of symbol he brings the latent possibilities of horary to decisive expression. This expression is far from the simple-minded view of horary as a straightforward predictive method. On careful analysis it becomes apparent that, just like the other cases I have discussed in this chapter, 'resolution' in this horary depends upon an implicit understanding of the astrology of the *initiative* (katarche), and of *symbolic participation*.

The most significant overall feature of Lilly's text may not be obvious on first reading. It is this. Lilly gives a decisive judgment, yet he *does not answer the question, yes or no*. He does not predict whether the woman *will* marry the old man. Neither does he simply advise whether she *should* or *should not* pursue the match. Further, there is no indication that he has privately decided but has not communicated the prediction. A careful reading assures us that, on the contrary, he does not take up the symbolism in such a way as to yield this prediction. He unravels the knot, while leaving the outcome unresolved and subject to the test of further action. From this I infer that for Lilly it is not necessary for the success of the horary that the outcome shall be available to foreknowledge. Despite this, the querent is moved to a definite decision, where all relevant details are appropriately described in the symbolism. I trust the reader now better perceives the weight of my question when I ask, if the astrologer is not concerned to predict the outcome, nor does he advise yes or no, then what is the root of his judgment, and what is its end?

On studying the chart we observe that there can be no simple perfection, since the significators and the Moon are separating their aspects. There is therefore no simple 'yes' to the question as put. The symbolism moves in a different direction. Both Mercury, significator for the Querent, and the Moon, universal cosignificator, apply immediately to Mars. There follows from this the chance that Mars may act as an intermediary between the Moon and Mercury, collecting the light of them both. Moreover the Moon is, as Lilly notes, already carrying light on a separating square from Jupiter, significator for the prospective husband. There might be faint hopes for a compound perfection (translation plus collection) involving the light of both particular significators and the Moon. Faint hopes, therefore, that we might answer 'yes' to the woman's question.

But it is Mars which has the decisive role in the resolution of the matter. This is an example of what is properly termed 'interposition'. Mars is not a significator, but he is directly involved in applications from significators. Mars therefore shows that which intrudes or interposes, a factor which has not been framed within the spoken query. Judgment is conditional upon an understanding of this interposing factor. The separation of significators and the interposition by Mars form the basis for Lilly's pivotal observation: 'I judged the maids affection was alienated from the old man' (separation from the lord of 7th), 'and that she desired such a man as Mars, viz. a Captaine or Souldier, &c.' Mars is here interpreted solely by his universal symbolism, not by particular house rulership or placing. The old man cannot give her '&c'. Crossing her on the square, Mars unspoken shows what the old man *lacks*, and that is why it exerts such a powerful negating force in the question.

The uncompromising severity of Lilly's judgment at this point expresses the square of Mercury to Mars. Some astrologers might think it at least worth a try for the Captain, the Soldier, or the '&c'. After all, Mars is in gorgeous male dignity and the Moon closes on a friendly sextile. Instead, the unequivocal prediction: 'she should be crossed therein'. I believe that Lilly's firm negation stems from his reading of Mars as repressed desire. Mars has no inherent sympathy either essentially or by its zodiacal placing with Mercury, significator of the woman, or with the Moon as cosignificator. The applying aspects to Mars show not sympathy and benefit – how could they since the woman has not dared to speak its name? – but the power to pull awry the matter propounded. Unacknowledged and therefore an enemy, its dignity serves only to strengthen its maleficity with respect to the question as put. Lilly has hit the nail on the head: 'all this was acknowledged with teares.'

Poor Mercury in Cancer only sobs, cannot speak. If both symbolism and tears reveal the woman frustrates herself, then it does not require a gift of second sight to be led to ask whether what she imagines she wants, viz. the security of the old man's estate, is worth setting against her alienated affection. The estate had better be good. Mars is in the 8th and lord of the 8th, the substance of the marriage partner and the house of legacies. So Lilly turns directly from Mars impeding in its universal signification as frustrated desire, to Mars in its particular determination. Mars rules and is placed in the 8th, the man's estate. This 'lamination of the symbol', where one symbol is turned to show two or more apparently unrelated elements in the overall situation of the inquiry, is character-istic of some of Lilly's best judgments, and it is a marvellous possibility in horoscopy.

Lilly's move is not to *predict* the condition of the husband's estate, but to get the querent to *test* it. He directs her to take a course of action that will bring into the open the maleficity of the impeding Mars. There remains the slender possibility that if her repression is admitted, Mars might allow collection of light and a perfection in the matter. In that case, sexual frustration notwithstanding, it might be to her benefit to marry the old man. By acknowledging that she wants him most for his estate or perhaps for the security he may bring, the path is now cleared for her to bring this desire to its test: 'I bad the maide require a joynture... to see what it would do'.

We may infer that Lilly suspects the estate, finding both malefics in the 8th, Saturn corrupt and Mars afflicting the significator for the querent. However, note well that he is *not* concerned with an objective judgment or prediction purely from the chart. The symbolism points to the critical decision, which is to test whether the old man can come up with a jointure. That is all, and that is all that is required for the success of the judgment and the good fortune of the querent. Lilly gives no indication that a secure prediction was possible or desirable. After the event, he is happy to observe that 'there being an incumbrance upon his Land...Saturn with Mars, in his second house of substance doth excellently signifie'. However, from the point of view of directing the woman on a path of good fortune, such a prediction is at best redundant, at worst a hindrance. Following Lilly's direction, she will avoid a foolish error born of emotional confusion however the estate turns out, simply by being mindful in her objective.

In bidding the maid to test the meaning of Mars, Lilly is inviting her to enact the theme of the symbolism, the immediate application of Mercury to Mars. This enactment, freely undertaken in response to the astrology, is what is meant by *symbolic participation.* What is the goal of this participation? It is certainly not to live out some 'objective fate' depicted by the astrology, since knowledge of the outcome (the 'fate') is unnecessary. *Non cogunt* – these things are 'not fated'. The astrology reveals and enhances the querent's free will even while it gives an exact picture of the situation she is in. The goal is to take up the thread of symbol and follow it into the knot of fate – the moment of her own binding initiative. Guided in this way, the choice will be the best fortune that can be hoped for in the circumstances. The course advised by Lilly is hardly distant from what common sense would suggest – and why should astrology seek more, or prove itself by irrelevant miracles of prediction?

This is a masterly judgment, which allows the querent a true resolution of her dilemma.[9] For horary to really mean anything it has to move people and allow them to find their own good fortune, which is what has happened here. Effective judgment in turn depends on radicality and this is a horary with deep radicality.

I do not wish to suggest that all of Lilly's judgments will sustain the sort of close analysis made here, and some are far coarser grained. He was also going for what worked in practice, rather than seeking a consistent theoretical position. Yet identifying the katarchic process in this notable example suffices to indicate that traditional astrology has more subtlety than modern critics have ever imagined. Further, I hope it has demonstrated that the idea of prediction is far from adequate as an expression of the core process of horary.

MY AUNT'S HOUSE

Lilly does not tell us what was going on in his mind. Like the archetypal Sun Taurus he does not indulge in flights of philosophy, and he doesn't theorise about astrological practice. Conclusions about his expectations of astrology made from a study of his judgments must therefore remain to a degree speculative. I will therefore give in detail a horary judgment of my own, since understanding the nuances from the inside I can report them directly in the light of the themes I have raised. The horary concerned led to an important decision, and produced a definite outcome. It is in any case a lively and radical example with some useful points of craft.

The story begins in December 1979. My aunt was a widow of 81. With no children, and now no husband, her lonely life was a cause for concern, especially as her sight was beginning to fail. She was the owner-occupier of a reasonably valuable but deteriorating detached house in a middle-class suburb of London, and this was her only wealth.

A certain Mr. A, a man in his late thirties, turned up seeking cheap furnished accommodation. My aunt, pleased to have another soul in the house, offered him an upstairs bedroom at a rent of £8 per week, which was low even by the standards of those days. The verbal agreement was that he would leave at very short notice should my aunt need to move.

My aunt's health began to slip and I set in motion moves to find her a residential home. Waiting lists were long, so when an offer came through early in 1982 a delay was not feasible, especially given my aunt's condition. As a house owner she would receive no subsidy in the home, and with only small savings as a buffer, it now became essential that the house be sold. The possibility of trying to accommodate my aunt in my own home was beyond the pale of contemplation for various reasons, practical and emotional. Principal amongst these was her difficult and demanding nature.

My aunt therefore went to stay in the old people's home. She left her goods in her house and visited it on occasional afternoons with an elderly gentleman friend from the home. Mr. A became the sole occupier of her house and refused to leave. After a while he began to assert his occupancy over other parts of the house, including a living room and the garden, without any permission. He made unannounced alterations in two upstairs rooms, including the removal of a ceiling rose and an inbuilt Edwardian cupboard. He told me that my aunt had promised him that he could have a second room, in preparation for his daughter moving in with him sometime soon. He also changed the cover of his rent book to show two rooms instead of one. My aunt remembered no such agreement. It became clear that he had a fixed notion of his daughter moving in with him and attending a nearby girl's school.

As the law stood at that time Mr. A had unambiguous security of tenure. The value of the house was much diminished by a sitting tenant and therefore, as the saying goes, he had us over a barrel. My aunt gave me power of attorney over her affairs in order to deal with the situation. After frustrating dealings, Mr. A refused to accept an offer of £5000 to move out. We even contemplated splitting the house into two maisonettes. Mr. A said he would offer £7000 for the ground floor, thus giving him a garden flat of considerable value. I felt that I wasn't in a serious discussion. Our original family solicitor agreed how very difficult it all was, but declared that nothing could be done.

We finally reached the point of advertising the house for sale with a sitting tenant, but Mr. A had his own plans. A builder interested in purchase pulled out without making any offer after he met Mr. A at the house and realised that he was not interested in any deal, including being re-housed on advantageous terms. He indicated that he had rights to the whole upper half of the house, and gave the impression of being a difficult customer. Eventually a second builder took an interest and was prepared to take Mr. A on board. The offer from this builder was of course very low, under half its ordinary value, but given the circumstances, we were lucky enough to get even this offer.

I was exhausted with the situation and inclined to accept the offer. Renegotiation with Mr. A was no option, as I believed there was an unreasoning and destructive element in his position. Further, his claim on the house appeared to be growing by the month.

And then one other possibility emerged. In some frustration with the original legal advice, I had switched to a Shepherd's Bush firm with a more inventive approach. They noted that given her circumstances my aunt would have a good case in court if she were still the *resident* landlady. But how could we achieve this? She had now been in the old folk's home for over a year. The solicitor suggested we should re-establish a nominal residency, with my aunt sleeping in the house. This could then be put forward as 'occupancy' even if most of the time she was being looked after at the old folk's home. It could prove awkward if challenged in court, but there was a good chance of success.

So this is the context of the question. The unusual manoeuvre proposed would firstly mean the co-operation of my aunt in a protracted and unpleasant campaign. The matron at the old folk's home would need to be amenable. Arrangements would have to be made to ferry my aunt backwards and forwards a number of days each week. My aunt was adamant that no way could she stay overnight in the house unless I was there as a bodyguard. These arrangements would have to be continued until the matter had been concluded in court.

The quick sale option therefore had a lot of attraction in the face of this wearisome alternative, especially as ultimate success could not be guaranteed. I was inclined to get the whole thing off my hands and swallow my resentment at Mr. A's destruction of the family resources. It is on this basis that I decided to resolve the matter with the help of horary and I asked the question, 'Should we accept the offer for the house?'

What are the significators? The Moon is right on the ascendant. Given my aunt's nature, her love of amateur music-hall for which she was known throughout the borough, her hats and her dramatic, rather emotional Cancer nature, this Moon in Leo was a perfect description. It is her business and her house, hence the identity with the ascendant, but I am the *motive* force in the question, the agent of initiative, asking for my Aunt. I am therefore signified by the ruler of the ascendant, the Sun. There is a mixed reception between these significators with the Sun in the Moon's exaltation and the Moon in the Sun's rulership, indicative of the intimate relationship between the two parties. As the only close relative I am disposing of my aunt's affairs and determining her circumstances (rulership), but I am also acting in the place that will enhance her affairs (Sun in the sign of the Moon's exaltation). Any doubt about this initial location of significators for the querent is dispelled by the testimony of the Moon as my father's sister (lady of the 12th, being the 3rd – sister – from the 10th, here my father).[10]

My aunt's house itself is shown by the 4th. Its deteriorating condition, with rot in the kitchen from a persistent leak and rising damp downstairs, was well-described by the malefics, Pluto and Saturn, straddling the IC. Venus as ruler of the IC is the significator for the house. Her position in Gemini reflects that it was in dispute and under dual control. Could it even be split into maisonettes to deal with the Mr. A problem?

So if I am the Sun and my aunt is the Moon, where is Mr. A in this chart? The 'other party' to the querent will be the 7th house and its ruler, Saturn. Here Mr. A is revealed in all his wilfulness and maleficity as Saturn in Scorpio intercepted in the 4th, holding firm and residing in my aunt's house. Like Saturn intercepted in the 4th, he was often tucked away silently for hours in his dirty room. Tenants may also be indicated by the 6th house and this also comes under Saturn here. The physical descriptive fit is remarkable. Mr. A is a dark haired and dark-eyed man, sullen and imperturbable, physically strong and on occasion slightly menacing. The Sun closely applies the opposition of Saturn, the aspect of 'perfect enmity'. The lord of the ascendant applies to oppose the lord of the 7th. We are open enemies.

Looking at other significators, the *offer* from the builder is Mercury, lord of the 2nd and dispositor of the house (Venus) – cash for the house. The Moon applies by square to Mercury, describing the situation and the question. This is, therefore, a possible perfection of significators, although it is Hobson's choice. My aunt can accept this offer and have the money, but the deal is a poor one, like the poor perfection of the square.

There are other testimonies to consider. Jupiter, lord of the 9th in Sagittarius, shows the solicitors advising us. As things are, there is nothing they can do with respect to the house. Venus (the house) goes to the opposition of Jupiter (the solicitor), so there is no hope here. But my clever solicitor in Shepherd's Bush had suggested another way of proceeding. Can we see this in the chart?

Mutual receptions commonly show choice in horary, and the symbolic switch of 'mutual reception by degree' shows the likely consequences of that choice. Venus and Mercury, the house and the offer, can be juggled around. If we move these significators by degree, Venus goes to 9 Taurus and Mercury to 20 Gemini. The effect of the move is to greatly improve the cash my aunt will receive for the

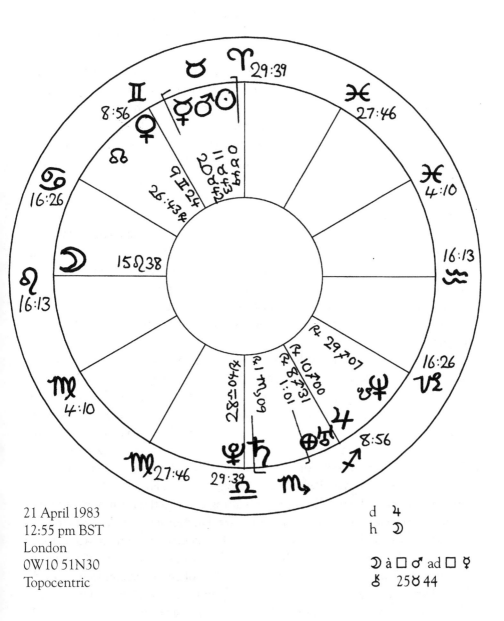

21 April 1983
12:55 pm BST
London
0W10 51N30
Topocentric

d ♃
h ☽

☽ à □ ♂ ad □ ☿
♋ 25♉44

FIGURE 11 'Should we accept the offer for the house?'

house because the Moon goes to a sextile of Mercury in Gemini, rather than to a square. This would be a favourable offer for the house. How is this reception to be achieved? The original unhelpful legal situation, Jupiter opposite Venus, is to be removed. We will get more money for the house if we can take the case to court, and this is indicated by the received Venus going into the 10th where it will join Mars, lord of the 10th. The 10th is the house of the Judge, and higher authority in general. Moreover, Mars shows the power that can evict Mr. A. because Mars disposes of Saturn in Scorpio.

The judgment is therefore as follows: if we take the case to Court we will win, evict Mr. A, and receive the market price for the house, unoccupied. However, the matter can only go to court on the grounds of my aunt as resident owner and I must therefore make the mutual reception and go through with the strategy suggested by the solicitor.

I showed this map to three friends, Derek Appleby, Maggie Hyde and Gordon Watson. We all shared in this interpretation, and we were all agreed about the move I could make and its promise of success.[11] Derek Appleby also said quite decisively that the Moon in Leo on the ascendant meant my aunt would have to appear in court. I particularly noted that remark because the solicitor had assured me that this wouldn't be necessary. I was hoping to avoid such an unpleasant experience for her.

Certain other things the solicitor advised struck me as curiously apt about the Venus – Mercury reception and served to affirm my confidence in our judgment. The solicitor had advised on a comprehensive strategy to gain advantage in the situation, including an immediate change of all locks in the house. This would limit Mr. A's access to those areas that we asserted were part of the original agreement. I thus spent an anxious day, changing the existing lock on the front door and fitting new locks on internal doors, wondering whether our tenant would suddenly return and what his reaction would be. Fortunately I was able to present him with the finished deed and a single key to the front door. Another Mercury trick gave me a potential trump card. Unknown to Mr. A., I had found a second key to the door of his room. I used the opportunity to rummage through the mess in his drawers to find the rent-book, with its indications of tampering, and took it down to the town to photocopy, full of apprehension that he might come back early, before safely returning the rentbook to its place. The value of this information was that our solicitor would now have a good idea of what Mr. A. would and would not be likely to show and tell the court, and we would have damning evidence in the event that entries might be later added or changed. In all of these strategems I was well aware of Mercury's symbolism, and delighted to participate.

I had no intention of making clear to Mr.A what we were planning. Within a day or two I set up my own base camp in one of the disputed rooms and then started bringing my aunt back most evenings, a tedious business involving two buses each way.

Keeping up this mediocre lifestyle meant the sacrifice of a whole summer, one of the finest and sunniest of that decade.[12] With Saturn afflicting I should have been more aware of possible delays. Documents got lost between departments at the solicitor's, costing us many weeks, and the situation dragged on and on. Eventually the case crawled its way into the County Court on 6th October 1983. Fortunately for us Mr. A represented himself, and made a bad job of it. Issues concerning the second room and a dispute about arrears came centre stage, while the ambiguous status of my aunt's residency did not come into the discussion. The Registrar ruled that Mr. A should settle arrears and vacate the premises by 3rd November.

Mr. A was now making extreme and irrational-sounding claims of a conspiracy against him. Although the indications now pointed to us having no further problems, our counsel warned that the Judge might need to re-hear original evidence. We could not therefore take anything for granted. The solicitor seemed to leave it open as to whether I or my aunt should give evidence again in Court. However, I remembered Derek Appleby's advice on the horary, and felt that an appearance by my aunt was now definitely called for in this closing stage of the drama.

Invited to answer questions, my aunt's theatrical ambitions found a minor fulfilment. Acting and being the part at one and the same time, she was an innocent old lady who clearly had been put upon by a scheming rogue. She denied having made any of the promises he suggested, and her appearance in court was completely convincing.

Mr. A had no intention of leaving even after he lost his appeal. In the end, on the 29th November, the bailiff was called in – Mars lord of the 10th in Taurus, the physical manifestation of the authority of the Court. Mr. A wasn't in, luckily, but even so it was surprisingly strong-arm stuff, ripping open locked suitcases for anything of value to impound to cover court fees. Mr. A's goods were dumped outside and I was given a note to show the police in case I later became embroiled in violence.

Looking back, I can more fully see what an important lesson in divination this was for me. At the time, I faced a dilemma of self-interest. The Sun is in Taurus. As the only relative of my aunt the house represented a sizeable possible legacy. Could I be sure that my own self-interest wasn't governing my moves here, against the best interests of my aunt? It is difficult to be clear about one's motives in such a situation. It is precisely in these circumstances that divination is most valuable. That is why I required to be assured by the astrology, one way or the other, in arriving at my final decision. Seeing the signification for eventual success I decided that I did have the stomach for the war of attrition represented by the Sun-Saturn opposition. And I was also convinced from the symbolism that I *should* make the move the solicitor suggested. Neither was there any obvious indication in the symbolism that my own desires were pushing things in a wrong direction.

Early on in the saga, there occurred an incident which was a revelation for me. Several days after the new regime at my aunt's house had begun, I was in the cold, dank kitchen one evening. Mr.A came in with a little saucepan to cook up some tea. I said 'Good evening' and he said 'Good evening'. Then he said, 'So you're here?' and I simply answered, 'Yes, I'm staying'. In that moment, I remembered the Sun in Taurus and I felt exactly that stubborn. Mr. A turned away and did not say another word, but as he did so I noticed his face and had a very strong sense of his presence. As I looked he became black with rage, and it was the threatening blackness of Saturn in Scorpio. In this instant was fully 'realised' and embodied the Sun-Saturn opposition, and I knew it. And just as I knew that, I also knew from the signs that I would beat him, and that my freely elected course of action, moving on those signs, would get for me what I wanted.

So this I take to be a true katarche. The question was asked at a critical moment of decision. I moved on the initiative, and I participated in the symbolism to resolve it along the line of good fortune. In retrospect, it was clearly the good move. Had I not made that move my aunt's money would have run out some years before her death at the age of ninety-one, in September 1989. As it was, her position was secure and comfortable and her money lasted to the end of her life, eventually leaving me with a welcome legacy. My aunt was of that generation that is humiliated by the thought of having to take charity or to be a burden to the state. So honour was fulfilled and the right thing was done.[13]

THE MODERN REVIVAL

There has been a revival of interest in horary in the past twenty years, especially in the English-speaking world. We only have to note the scanty and misleading treatment in the older mainstream textbooks, or Carter's observation of the subject's rarity in the early 1960s, to remind ourselves that times have changed. There always were a few doughty horarists keeping the practice alive, but they never switched the lights on for everyone else. The old lady of astrology has for most of the twentieth century been struggling to rekit herself in modern dress, making every effort to look like a respectable woman. Against such a project horary looks lurid and unappealing, a low-grade medieval throwback.

The upswing in horary's fortunes is part of a wider counter-movement against recent astrology's dismissal of anything earlier than the twentieth century. Traditional astrology is back on the agenda.[14] This is far more than an acknowledgment of origins – it is a means of re-evaluating our modern methods. Robert Hand sees this as a recovering of what has been lost by the humanistic and psychological-astrology programmes. These have been 'restructuring the symbols so that everything in astrology always and at any time can mean anything'.[15] Against the wide but ambiguous possibilities of symbolism as explored in modern natal astrology, practices in the katarche focus on definite results in the here-and-now situation. This usually involves a concrete symbolism attached to the real-world practicalities of a situation, even if abstract or ethical categories are also involved. Inherent in its method therefore, horary symbolism is 'realised' in our immediate ready-to-hand concerns, leading to definite interpretations and results. This is why horary as a practice reminds the astrologer of the value of what Hand calls 'symbolic rigour' and the 'logical interpretation of symbols'. Standing in stern contrast to the woolly New Age subjectivity of much that passes as astrology, horary has made an impact precisely because it is a well-ordered traditional form with a strong craft framework and a well-defined possibility of application and testing.

As to the future of this revival, there is some reason to hope that horary will gradually resume its place as an essential part of the practice of mainstream astrologers. A barrier that has to be crossed, however, is the notion that a worldly and specific craft method like horary is therefore necessarily fatalistic. I believe that by developing an understanding of participation and initiatives – in effect the ancient katarche – a bridge can be built between traditional craft and the psychological and spiritual insight of the best of modern practice.

A significant move in this direction has been the development of 'psychological horary'.[16] This is concerned with the symbolism of what actually moves people and allows them to change, which is the *resolution* in horary, and is not simply content with a perfection-type predictive *judgment*. Its aim is to allow horary to reveal unspoken and possibly unacknowledged motivations of the querent, while showing how those desires work themselves out in our everyday reality. A possibility of this approach is the understanding of the evocative craft-words of the horary method – frustration, denial, evasion, prohibition, etc. – in the light of psychoanalytic concepts. This is also recognised as a dimension of traditional astrology, brought into a modern perspective. Lilly's 'Gentlewoman and the Aged Man' is a marvellous example, and shows horary symbolism allied to penetrating psychological insight.

Horary astrology is an important part of the argument in this book not only because it offers such a powerful method in the analysis of symbolism, but because more than any other standard horoscopic practice it exposes to view features of *all* astrology that are not acknowledged in our existing theories. However, the re-awakening of horary in recent years has been far from an unmixed blessing. The culmination of the upswing was the republication in 1985 of *Christian Astrology* after a gap of three centuries. So much could be hoped for when, once again, a 'LILLY had flowered amongst the thorns'.[17] However, reproducing Lilly has not proved enough to sustain the high hopes of many of us involved in the recent revival. For a supposedly well-ordered traditional form of craft, its demonstration appears surprisingly erratic, even amongst experienced practitioners. Supposedly following in the master's footsteps, horary literature has also been afflicted with a spate of wholly unconvincing 'great questions' – 'Is AIDS a man-made disease?', 'Is the Bible truly the Word of God?' – which I have discussed in detail elsewhere.[18]

Many of the inadequacies of modern horary come down to misunderstandings concerning the limits and possibilities of symbolism. This brings us back to the issues raised for us by Lilly and the magical attitude that informs his work.

THE CRITICAL MAGICIANS

I can best bring out some of these considerations through the censures of the Oxford scholar Elias Ashmole, Lilly's friend and patron. Ashmole was fully an astrologer, equally at home with nativities as with horaries and elections. On various occasions Ashmole referred judgments to the older man, who he clearly regarded as the authority. In 1652 Ashmole published his *Theatrum Chemicum Britannicum*, a compendium and translation of alchemical and Hermetic writings from several English authors, together with his own comments. He makes clear that magic leads to the Philosopher's Stone of alchemy, while astrology is an essential ingredient of 'natural magic':

> Iudiciall Astrologie is the Key of Naturall Magick, and Naturall magick the Doore that leads to this Blessed Stone.[19]

For Ashmole, the category of 'Natural Magic' included the creation of sigils and astrologically elected talismans. The point that I would like to emphasise is that astrology is seen not just within the frame of magic, but as well within the frame of the Great Work of Alchemy. Commenting on a similar reference to astrology in Thomas Norton's *Ordinall of Alchimy* Ashmole observes that

> ...Astrologie (take it with all its Comprehensions) is as Secret or Misterious as Alchimy, and as difficult to be throughly and perfectly understood.

This is the context in which to look at Ashmole's savage critique of the practice of astrology of his day. He was writing in what is often taken to be the Golden Age of English astrology – but it is probably so only because William Lilly made it so. In the light of the imminent demise of astrology, Ashmole's text is a sombre prophecy. (The whole remarkable passage is given in Appendix 5.) Above all, poor horary is a particular problem:

> He that understands no more of Astrologie (nor will make a further use of it) then to quack with a few Tearmes in an Horary Question; is no more worthy to be esteemed an Astrologian then Hee who hath onely learnt Hebrew may be accounted a Caballistical Rabbi...

> ...I know some few Artists have satisfactorily manifested what excellency of Skill there is in Judging an Horary Question... But they are those that are throughly read in all other parts of Astrologie; for such only are able to give a true Resolution to the Querent...

There must have been as much duff horary around in the 1650s as there is now. When Ashmole talks of the need to be 'throughly read' in other branches of astrology, I understand from this the discipline, certainly of traditional astrology, inherently involved by having to study a natal horoscope, or a mundane horoscope, in some sort of extended context. The horoscope has to fit the client's past history, it might need rectifying, and so on. In addition there is usually a pattern of other symbolism involved, that has to be weighed and balanced. So if I try to decide on a job application off a single transit next week, I will also have in mind recent progressions to the MC, and the way my horoscope worked in this area of life in the past. It is not quite the simple yes-or-no perfection/non-perfection issue that we can demand of horary on occasion. With horary, a minimum of technical skill and virtually no consideration of context outside the immediate question gives the astrologer an access to ready-made judgment. It is the immediacy of horary that is so potent, but also such a temptation for thoughtless practice.

The horary astrologers Ashmole condemns do not therefore fail in a purely 'technical' sense – it's not a question of whether they can name the terms of Mars or define 'translation of light'. These things may seem an arcane mystery at first sight to a non-horarist, but they are mostly straightforward to master. If the rules and terminology are all one understands about horary, it really would be 'to quack with a few Tearmes'.

Ashmole is striking at one of astrology's persistent fallacies, 'the illusion of technique'. It is this illusion which lets the astrologer follow a rule, pick a significator, and forget to question whether he or she should be judging at all. To know this is to know something of what is meant by discretion in astrology – and that does not appear in any of the textbooks. Remember what Carter said about the weakness of 'fearing to discard'; it is such a temptation to demand an answer, so that the powers of horary will not be denied; 'straining at the Art', Lilly calls it. Discretion means knowing when common-sense and symbolism together say 'Stop'. 'Many men', declares Norton, 'surmise that they understand what they read, when they have not understood'. Following the rules of horary with a technical and literal understanding is no understanding at all.

Ashmole's criticism brings us full circle back to the attacks by Ficino and Pico on the judicial astrology of their day. A moment's reflection will show that although the conclusions of these men are quite various, they share a common background in the world of magic. Magical consciousness seems to be very impatient of the literal style of much astrology. The modern traditional astrologers who are ready to quote Lilly also have to take on board that he too was fully versed in magic. In fact, we can hardly avoid the suggestion that it is the imaginative dimension of magic that adds spirit to the letter of astrology's rules, and depth to its practice.

NOTES

1 William Lilly, *Christian Astrology* (1647; second edition 1659, reprinted Regulus, London, 1985), p385.
2 ibid., p.192.
3 For the diary of William Lilly, see *The Last of the Astrologers*, ed. Katharine M. Briggs (Folklore Society, London, 1974).
4 ibid., p.22.
5 ibid., p.93.
6 ibid., p.33.
7 ibid., p.63.
8 '...' in note shows text which is illegible in my copy. From *England's Propheticall Merline* (London, 1644).
9 The illuminating distinction of these terms (which appears to be only implicit in Lilly and other traditional authors) was first emphasised by Maggie Hyde. It is a particularly important distinction for 'psychological horary' (see note 16 below).
10 Note that 10th sometimes shows the father, sometimes the mother (vice versa for the 4th). I incline to the 10th as the mother, as a first choice in practice.

11 Interestingly, we four were the co-founders of the Company of Astrologers, which started on its course later that year as a Teaching Body of the Astrological Lodge. Sometimes good judgments need colleagues in astrology to come together, and then the symbolism becomes enhanced, and more firmly resolved through the agreement.

12 It was only a long time after that I realised how pertinent was the mixed reception of Sun and Moon, especially by bringing my significator into the 12th. This is an imprisonment and a sacrifice undertaken prior to coming to court. In court however, the significators revert to their radical positions (Alan Jones pointed this out to me).

13 Additional observations and data: the two court hearings, on 13th October and 3rd November, were both set for 10:30am (south-west London). The execution of the warrant for possession was 2:30pm 29th November. The house was sold on 4th May 1984.

    Concerning the 'realisation in the kitchen', this probably occurred around the 3rd or 4th May 1983, but I did not at the time consider it as an instant distinct from the actual horary which was so strongly in my mind.

    There are many resonances in a map of this order of radicality. For instance, I am natally a strong Saturn type, so the opposition of the horary Saturn to my significator the Sun is striking. Mr. A (Saturn) opposes me (Sun). Just as Saturn hates and darkens the Sun I can hardly avoid the possibility that Mr. A manifested as a 'shadow' for me, in the sense so powerfully described by Jung. Further, this case seemed a suitable one to illustrate certain themes of this book. After deciding to include it, it dawned on me that there is a connection with the *Moment of Astrology* original articles – I started Part I in my miserable evenings stuck in my aunt's house in the spring and summer of 1983. Time and the seed moment – Saturn and the Sun! Also, when I originally planned this current chapter, I never realised the obvious connecting theme with Lilly's crisis of magic – Saturn and the Sun. There is always more to our choices of symbolism than we realise at the time.

14 The modern revival of traditional astrology: It should be recorded that the horary revival in the UK was in very significant measure directly inspired by Derek Appleby, who originally taught himself astrology, and along with it Horary. Derek Appleby turned on a small group of us at the Astrological Lodge in the early 1970's. We knew of horary through several of the modern authorities, yet the subject seemed to slumber. I now know that I couldn't properly 'see' horary. Like others, I was amazed when Derek Appleby demonstrated the capacity to bring horoscopes alive and make the symbols dance with radicality. From this impetus came the desire amongst various traditionalists at the Lodge to recover Lilly from his obscurity. Maggie Hyde then researched various almanacs and publications of Lilly in the Guildhall Library, and in addition we copied sections of Mavis Miller's copy of *Christian Astrology* (a legacy from Charles Carter). Later in the 1970's Olivia Barclay's photocopy edition promoted Lilly and horary further, and the first stage of the recovery can be said to have been completed with the facsimile reprint of *Christian Astrology* in 1985. Since this time there have been a number of important disagreements on approach between the various earlier activists. It is regrettable that the influence of Derek Appleby's work has not been more widely acknowledged: see his *Horary Astrology* (Aquarian, London, 1985, the year of Lilly's reprint).

    The rebirth of the Decumbiture from virtually total oblivion before the 1980's parallels the revival of horary. The decumbiture is the horoscope cast for a crisis or start of an illness and it indicates both the prognosis and the correct course of healing. Maggie Hyde researched and revived the decumbiture methods of Culpeper and Lilly, presenting her conclusions at a ground-breaking seminar in London on 3rd November 1984. From this point this ancient practice has begun once again to flourish in both UK and US medical astrology, and it could prove an important element in the modern reconnection of astrology and herbalism.

The most significant of all recent developments in the restoration of traditional astrology is the extraordinary Hindsight Project, a programme of translation of original Greek and Latin texts under the inspiration of Robert Hand. Every serious astrologer should support this (Golden Hind Press/Phaser Foundation Inc. 532 Washington Street, Cumberland, MD 21502).

15 Robert Hand, in his Foreword to Olivia Barclay's *Horary Astrology Rediscovered* (Schiffer, Penn. 1990).

16 See Maggie Hyde, 'Psychological Horary' in the *Astrological Journal*, (published by the Astrological Association) vol 35, no.6, November/December 1993.

17 See my 'Afterword' essay in the 1985 edition of *Christian Astrology*, op.cit.

18 Letter analysing the failure of some modern 'Great Questions': 'Horrible Horaries' in the *Astrological Journal*, vol. 31, no.3, May/June 1989.

19 Elias Ashmole, *Theatrum Chemicum Britannicum* (London, 1652). See especially pp453-4.

9

Some Genius or Spirit

ONE of the defining moments for twentieth-century astrology was the Mansion House Court case of 16 July 1917. This led to the successful prosecution of Alan Leo on the charge of 'pretending and professing to tell fortunes'. He was fined £5, with £25 costs, and was granted leave to appeal. The judge, apparently sympathetic to the dilemma of astrology and in no doubt as to the sincerity of Alan Leo, made it clear that he would like a higher court to ensure the whole issue was properly reviewed.

This was a test case, and it followed an earlier unsuccessful prosecution in 1914, which failed on technical grounds. It was aimed at Leo because of his public standing, and also because he stood at the respectable end of his profession. A successful prosecution here would make similar prosecutions a mere formality.

Much to the consternation of other professional astrologers, Leo decided not to appeal. He knew that given the state of the law and of public opinion at the time, the central problem of a predictive capacity to astrology could not be adequately defended, however it might be dressed up as 'trends and tendencies' He decided instead on the arduous task of rewriting his volumes of books and reference sheets for postal horoscopes. He wanted to purge them of fatalistic inferences and concentrate on the motif of 'character is destiny'. This was in any case consistent with his long term criticism of traditional astrology's materialistic tendencies. As Patrick Curry remarks, 'Leo's conviction for fortune-telling really only pushed him further down the same road'.[1]

Although the UK law has since changed[2], the fundamental issues have not. Is astrology fortune-telling, and what does this imply? This is an old dilemma. For two thousand years astrology has been identified as a celestial science of objective fate, with prediction as its ultimate goal. Like Alan Leo, I see this as a vicious narrowing of perspective that has been the bane of traditional astrology. I also recognise the immense difficulty of broadening this perspective.

Leo is a significant figure for us because he stands at the centre of the modern European revival of astrology. He also represents its highest spiritual aspirations, which he sought through a union of astrology and Theosophy, and his efforts have shaped the course of organised astrology in the U.K. down to the present day.[3]

One of the main themes I have brought forward in this book has been the long-standing divide between astrology and the magical-religious imagination. The effect of this has been to push into obscurity a whole domain of the astrological experience. This consideration gives us the context for Alan Leo's dilemma, for as well as being a craft astrologer he was an *occultist*, inspired by the late nineteenth-century rise of wisdom-teachings associated with Theosophy. The crisis facing Alan Leo is really the ancient divide, but now in modern guise.

Alan Leo did not succeed in resolving the crisis, and his attempted solution in terms of esoteric astrology has not proved enduring.[4] Quite apart from this project, however, there are many indications in his writings of an attitude fundamentally at variance with more orthodox astrology. Towards the end of his life he was beginning to express an angelic vision, a move towards Christianised *daemones* as the guides of our astrology:

> I believe every human being belongs to a Father Star in heaven or Star Angel as did Jesus Christ according to our Scripture.[5]

There is an indication of Leo's attitude in a story told by his colleague Alfred Barley. In 1901 Barley had been consulted by a woman anxious for her two daughters after having had a dream of death, and she wanted the astrologer to be completely honest about the dangers for the girls. In particular, she wanted to know which of them the dream referred to. In the horoscope of one of the daughters Barley saw a similar configuration to one which he had seen in the chart of his own sister, who had died when he was a child. He asked Alan Leo for a second opinion, but Leo told him to abandon giving such judgments to people until he ranked himself amongst the prophets. Leo commented on Barley's judgment, and affirmed its likelihood, but then said this:

> I should have to work out the directions to be sure, and this I am not inclined to do. I have already enough Karma upon my shoulders without incurring any more.[6]

Such a judgment is possible, but it *should not* be made. The reason is something more than a conventional ethical position – although it certainly includes that as well. Introducing the notion of the astrologer's karma means that the astrologer is *implicated*, and cannot stand apart from the prediction as if it is something wholly objective and apart from his own destiny. It is a telling detail that Barley's attempt to decide the question objectively is symbolically rooted in his own dead sister. However we may interpret this, observe here the total contrast in spirit between Leo's occult attitude to prediction and the position taken by the astrologers who laud the death of Pico.

Alan Leo never completed the task of revising his astrological judgments, for within six weeks of the Mansion House case he died of a sudden stroke, at the age of fifty-seven. Perhaps the burden of astrology's karma had become too great to carry.

One of his colleagues recorded a dream that Alan Leo had in the early days of July 1917, with the Mansion House case pending. This seems to tell the whole story:

> He found himself walking by the sea-shore, carrying something in his hand, and looking at it he became conscious that it was lifeless, and so said to himself 'It's no use carrying a *dead* thing,' and threw it far into the sea. He watched it splash into the water and disappear, but from the place of its disappearance there came up a water bird, whose head shone with vivid peacock-blue colouring; and it swam to the land and walked about, shaking itself free of water and growing larger and more brilliant as he watched it.[7]

So what is this 'dead thing'? I believe this is the Saturnian bondage of time and objectivity which has for two millennia afflicted astrology and suppressed its genius, symbolised by the brilliant, peacock-blue bird. When it is not seen through, this bondage makes of astrology a deterministic system, a heavenly machine grinding out the fate of mankind. To take on the dilemma with which Alan Leo struggled, we must return to the sources of our tradition and the origins of this fateful conception.

ORIGINS OF THE MACHINE OF DESTINY

From long before the Hellenistic period, the ability to predict awesome eclipses and the appearances and disappearances of the great gods must have produced an exaltation amongst the Mesopotamian priests who attained this knowledge:

> It is impossible to exaggerate the religious importance which an eminently superstitious people attached to these discoveries...by establishing the unchangeable character of the celestial revolutions [they] imagined that they understood the mechanism of the Universe, and had discovered the actual laws of life.[8]

Yet the Mesopotamians had not abstracted their gods, and the physical planets were therefore not separable from those gods. The predictive certainty of the astronomical cycles carried over, by a potent imaginative association, into a calculable certainty of fate itself. This possibility gave astral divination an ascendancy over all other forms, including liver-reading, well before the spread of astrology in the Hellenistic period.

The Mesopotamian astrologers did not achieve a reliable chronology, the foundation of a scientific astronomy, until the eighth century BC. The record of ancient eclipses utilised by Ptolemy starts in this period with the eclipse of March 721 BC. Accurate monthly ephemerides, computed in advance, date from the sixth century BC. The technical development in the next few centuries appears to have been continuously sustained up to the end of the second century BC, by which time perpetual ephemerides had been constructed.

The extraordinary technical capacity to construct an ephemeris in advance becomes integrally linked with a pervasive philosophical stance underlying much astrological practice. Since the stellar omens show destiny, then destiny itself is determined by the heavens in orderly, periodic and – in principle – calculable cycles. It is a short step from here to astrological determinism, and this is a step which on all the evidence was taken – or taken for granted – by our predecessors in astrology.

As with most beliefs when carried over into ordinary human life, this was not a total or consistent position. In Greek and Roman astrology it seems to have been possible for katarchic methods and a more fatalistic approach to be practised side by side. Whether this mix is a legacy from Babylon remains an open question. However, there is no reason to suppose that the two forms were generally seen as mutually exclusive. Life is commonly perceived as a paradoxical mix of fated and free elements, and these conflicting attitudes will find different expressions of the same religion to support them. Early critics of astral divination were quick to point out the 'illogical' behaviour of both astrologers and the common people, who would seek out propitiation and magical or spiritual alleviatives at the same time as they accepted the notion of fate.[9] This mix of methods is only absurd when measured against the philosophical conception of an absolute predetermination of fate.

As our classical astrology begins to take on definition in the Hellenistic period, we can trace three principal themes moulding its character and serving as its philosophical justification. These themes may be broadly described as *originative power*, *order*, and *abstraction*. Unity and harmony are at the very heart of the Greek *cosmos*, which arises with Greek logic and science – a new and orderly concept of the cosmos revealed by intellectual inquiry and philosophical analysis. The orderly movements of the heavenly bodies above all represent and govern this order. The heavens are the source of change and the abode of the greatest gods. Hand in hand with these conceptions is the withdrawal of the gods, the divine world intertwined with man, intimately responsive to his propitiation. Beginning with the early Greek schools, there is a move to locate the action of the divine in a realm of abstract principles, and away from the anthropomorphic Homeric pantheon. The Zeus of the philosopher becomes a different creature from the Zeus of popular belief.

Plato, at the turning-point of philosophy, reveals at the same time the turning-point for astrology. His great cosmological work, *Timaeus*, founds the whole later Platonic conception of astrology within a soul-sown harmony of the spheres; at the same time it demonstrates the change in perception and conception which must eventually sever the umbilical cord between astral omen-reading and Greek astrology. It would, says Plato, be labour in vain 'without an inspection of models' (ie an armillary and a planisphere),

> to tell which of the gods come into line with another at their conjunctions, and which in opposition...and at what periods of time they are severally hidden from our view and again reappearing send panic fears and omens of the future to men who are unable to calculate.[10]

'Men who are unable to calculate'... the term *mathematicii* was to become synonomous with 'astrologers'. The direct experience of celestial omens in 'panic fears' becomes transformed into the ordered vision of the heavens in mathematical and geometrical models. From this era on, philosophy can claim for itself a model of the cosmos, open to inspection, measure and inquiry, where the most fundamental motion, the diurnal motion of the Primum Mobile – is itself the source of intelligence.

The stately order of the heavens, open to computation from remote antiquity to the distant future, allows of no deflection. It is mathematical law which determines the movements of the gods themselves, and it is beyond even their power to command. Once the symbolism of astrology is bound to this great order, the loss of the old participatory consciousness of omen-reading creates a fateful conception of the cosmos, a Machine of Destiny. In its extreme form, in the interpretation of later Stoic cosmology which so influenced the astrologers, this is the understanding that mankind's fate, either collectively or individually, is predetermined with a similar order and precision as that manifested in the observed cycles of the planets.

The abstraction of the gods lifts their field of action far beyond the old concerns of tribal deities. One great sky covers all races, nations and times. Seen in this perspective, astrology goes beyond the local gods, its omens cannot be just 'for us, here, now'. By its greatness and unerring inevitability, the machine grinds to dust any hope of intervention in its decree.

This conception exercises a powerful attraction for the monotheistic imagination, because monotheism is the first step in the abstraction of a more or less accessible divine realm into one great impersonal determining power. The idea of divine beings intimately close to us, responsive to and interpenetrating our human intelligence, will and action, is especially uncomfortable for Christianity, which tends to see in this the survival of the pagan gods. Divination and magic, which embody and acknowledge our relationship with the divine realm, are necessarily suppressed. Their function is wholly taken up within the authority of the Church and its authorised priests, who have the sole public responsibility for intercession with God, in the name of Jesus Christ. Outside this sanction, all other relations with the divine become in the original meaning of the term 'superstition' – practices and beliefs not permitted by authorised religious law.

The monotheistic and transcendent definition of the divine throws other conceptions into its shadow. This has led to a damning and 'demonisation' of divination and magic in Christian culture. It also gives us a distorting mirror when we try to understand the magical practices and beliefs of primitive cultures, and we lose the ability to comprehend the various fate-beliefs that survive from our pagan pre-Christian heritage. As the studies of Alby Stone have demonstrated, in the paganism of northern Europe there were many fates, or taboo-patterns where certain consequences were likely to follow from the breaking of the taboos. Yet the living of life entails the breaking of taboos, and the hero is frequently shown having to choose between two conflicting possibilities, each with its 'fated' penalty. Although there is a cosmogonic framework of these fates, this is far from immutable pre-ordination. In this conception, magic is a participation in destiny, a means by which can one can *create* by ritually binding together the fate-threads. Divination is the other side of the same magical freedom, because it is the means of revealing the situation and foreseeing the consequences of choice:

> To foretell is to assume the mantle of the Fates, and thus to create the future. In
> this way, the constant process of creation is maintained, and although the future
> has indeed already been written, *its shape is constantly being redrawn*. Magic is, in
> effect, the means by which this is done. [11] [*my italics.*]

Here is the theme we find repeated again and again, against the tendency of our culture to impute to fate the absolute power that we see in the great forces of the cosmos. This is the spirit that we can discern from the earliest records of Mesopotamian culture to the practices of the haruspices and augurs.[12] It is the same spirit of the katarche that shows us our implication and encourages our participation in the symbols of astrology.

DECAY OF THE KATARCHE

The Machine of Destiny conception destroys the inner coherence of the astrological katarche. Vettius Valens (second century AD) records the matter succinctly:

> It is impossible to defeat by sacrifice that which has been established from the beginning of time.[13]

What an extraordinary contrast there is between this lofty and overwhelming statement of classical astrology, and the spirit of the Mesopotamian haruspice praying to the stars for successful divination! Vettius Valens was obviously attacking some other view of the divine, perhaps a challenge that augury could still, in his day, pose to his vision of astrology. If astrology speaks of a divine order established for *all* time, then how could a mere mortal imagine that his propitiations might alter this, and bend the fate already determined at the moment of birth. Daemones and gods will not listen. Even if they did, they cannot assist, for they too are bound in the ageless law. Destiny is no longer negotiable.

A century and a half earlier Manilius laid down the same fundamental law in his beautiful poem:

> Fate rules the world, all things stand fixed by its immutable law, and the long ages are assigned a predestined course of events. At birth our death is sealed, and our end is consequent upon our beginning...no man by prayer may by prayer seize fortune if it demur, or escape if it draw nigh: each one must bear his appointed lot.[14]

The astrology of Manilius reflects the philosophy of Stoicism, which had great influence in Rome in his day. Amongst the Greek schools the Stoics were, with a few exceptions, defenders of old practices of divination. Astrology in particular seems to have caught their attention. The fragments of Stoic philosophy which have survived suggest that their vision of fate was completely modelled along the lines of the Machine of Destiny. Divination worked – not because of a relationship between man and gods – but because of the absolute harmony which existed throughout the cosmos, where even an omen was itself predestined to indicate that which it presaged. Although this attitude permitted practices of divination to continue, it is at root incompatible with the active spirit of negotiation with the divine that characterises the katarche. From the Stoic point of view, we must bear our appointed portion of fate with philosophical serenity, hence the meaning of the word 'stoic' that has come down into modern usage.

Stoicism of the style of Manilius took hold in the fatalistic interpretation of the natal horoscope. From a theoretical point of view this completely deterministic conception rapidly yielded to the more flexible conception derived from Aristotle, and carried into astrology by Ptolemy, but in practice the Stoic attitude resonates throughout later astrology. Perceptive later critics such as Ficino and Pico are in effect rejecting the false logic which dresses Stoic attitudes in Aristotelian guise. For the Aristotelian interpetation, the Machine of Destiny is grinding out universal themes, not particular fates. Contingent circumstances, and therefore human intervention, can hinder or further the general direction produced by the primary causation. It is in the Aristotelian formulation that we can say, 'The stars incline, they do not compel'. It should not be forgotten, however, that the participatory imagination of the katarche loses out in both of these approaches, which between them define the limits of virtually all debate in the tradition of astrology.

Compared with the spontaneous and chaotic quality of astral omen-watching, the conception induced by the Machine of Destiny encourages an objective attitude to the signs and showings of astrology. Above all, astrology is associated with a model, the physical model of the heavens, conceivable in the mind's eye and capable of visual demonstration. It thereby serves as the basis of theory. The participation of the astrologer transmutes into his or her ability to visualise a universal ordering of all destinies, 'in theory' laid out before our gaze as the endless cycles of the heavens are unrolled in the pages of the ephemeris.

THE POTTER'S WHEEL

Nigidius Figulus (first century BC) illuminates the style of astrological thinking founded in this new conception. Nigidius, who has already been briefly mentioned in Chapter 7, is an important representative of early horoscopy since he stands at a point of contact and transition between archaic and classical practices. He was a Pythagorean philosopher, recognised in his day as one of the most learned men in Rome. He used both natal and katarchic astrology, together with haruspicy and, probably, magical practices. If a man with this range of attitudes and practices was under the spell of the Machine of Destiny at this early period, then there seems little likelihood that any other conception of astrology had a chance of developing.

There survives a story which indicates his attitude to the natal moment. The argument about the differences in the destinies of twins troubled him greatly and his answer to the problem earned him the nickname 'Figulus, the Potter'. He spun a potter's wheel at speed, and then made two marks with ink in rapid succession, apparently at the same spot. When the wheel stopped these marks were found to be far apart. Nigidius explained that the same principle was at work for twins. The sky whirls around so rapidly that even when two people are born close in time, that represents a large difference in the sky, and therefore in the horoscope indications of the different destinies. Augustine is unimpressed:

> This parable is even more fragile than the pottery made on that wheel. For if a change in the constellations which cannot be observed makes such a difference in the sky... [then] how can those astrologers have the boldness to examine the constellations in the case of those who are *not* twins, and then foretell matters which depend on this unobservable mystery, and connect them with the moment of birth?[15]

This has always been considered to be one of the most damaging of all objections to astrology. The sometimes tiny change between the horoscopes of twins with different characters and lives renders every other horoscope interpretation absurd, because few natal charts are timed to the precision of one of those marks on the potter's wheel. Nigidius is in no way considering the natal horoscope as if it were an occasional and spontaneously observed omen associated with birth. He sees it as an instance drawn from a theoretically continuous pattern of celestial correspondences operative universally, and he takes as a model for this the continuous turning of the wheel, the analogue of the Machine of Destiny.

Astrologers remain defensive on the subject of twins, and Augustine's observation continues to be unanswered and unanswerable. Nigidius's position makes no sense, and most astrologers have not succeeded in making any more sense of the twins problem down the ages. One sees over and over in modern astrology the same Potter's Wheel fallacy. Astrologers will turn out a brilliant display of technical discrimination which they never demonstrate in any other natal map, using midpoints and ultra-fine aspects to differentiate a degree on the ascendant in an otherwise identical map for dissimilar twins.[16]

I have no wish to make fun of Nigidius, or of later astrologers caught out in the same position. Given the fundamental conception of classical astrology, they hardly have a choice. The Potter's Wheel is a remarkable parable because it dramatically reveals the impossibility of a certain type of rational justification for the horoscope, a rational justification that our whole tradition has been impelled to adopt. The Machine of Destiny has a powerful hold on astrological consciousness, to the point of forcing intelligent astrologers into an irrational defence of their symbolic reality.

Reflecting the impressive discovery of the periodicity of all planetary motions, the Machine of Destiny moved to the heart of astrological belief. Katarchic practices could not offer any independent conception, and were, therefore, in an ambiguous position. With the general decline in belief in ritual divination and the old anthropomorphic gods, the spirit of augury died. The astral-omen imagination could only survive in hiding, latching itself on to the rational justification offered by the Machine of Destiny.

PTOLEMY'S ACHIEVEMENT REVIEWED

This gives us a further insight into the context for Ptolemy's extraordinary achievement. In the melting pot of the origins of classical astrology, various philosophies were competing for attention and might claim the allegiance of astrologers. The general tendency was in the direction of a rational framework for astrological phenomena, even if that explanation might take as its first premise a Pythagorean or Platonic mystical tenet. Ptolemy's major achievement was to give a convincing rational explanation for natal astrology, the single most important divinatory astrological practice. The effect of this was to permanently embed divinatory-horoscopic astrology in a natural-scientific model.

Ptolemy is on the whole consistent in his project, sometimes down to details which might pass unnoticed on first reading. For example, Bouché-Leclercq draws attention to Ptolemy's development of the method of reading predisposition to illness from the natal horoscope, and especially from its 6th house.[17] Why should that be significant in the light of our present discussion? It seems certain that he was freeing astrology of dependence on a venerable and well established katarchic variant – the system of medical astrology attributed to the Egyptians, and about which Ptolemy is quite respectful. This has survived in later astrology as part of the doctrine of Decumbitures, which we have discussed in Chapter 7; this involves prognosis from a horoscope for the moment of falling ill. Figures cast upon receipt of a sample of urine also stem from this tradition. Either practice is certain to be anathema to astrologers of any period imbued with the 'Ptolemaic attitude'. For them, everything must be subsumed to the causal-temporal origin, and therefore sickness is to be found in the 6th house of the *natal* chart.

Ptolemy's rationalisation of the causal-temporal origin represents a modification and a softening of the earlier Stoic conception, and it is on that account far more defensible. From the *Tetrabiblos* on, the identification of the moment of astrology as a moment of *origin* was fully established, with the natal moment as its pre-eminent representative. As Bouché-Leclercq observes, this development produces an inevitable cleavage between katarchic and natal astrology, a result of

... the metaphysical coup d'etat by natal astrologers, who pretended to integrate
in a unique moment the totality of causes predetermining the destiny.[18]

The natal moment subsumes every other moment in life, and therefore the natal
horoscope subsumes every other astrological signification of life. It is as if
everything else in life is pre-determined by the overwhelming potency of the
heavens, stamping out their signature at the moment of birth.

Yet despite Ptolemy, the various katarchic practices appear to have had strong
traditions of practice behind them, and they no doubt continued to work in the
opinion of their practiioners. However, independent of the Ptolemaic model, they
lose any power of theory and this is why the katarche becomes merely a generic
term for a motley of non-natal moments. As a legacy from Ptolemy, *philosophical
debate about horoscopy is almost entirely dedicated to the doctrine of origin*, and the
doctrine of origin is itself most commonly expressed in the imagery of birth. It is
this combination of circumstances that places the natal horoscope at the centre
of astrological practice and makes of its symbolism a passive record of a seemingly
objective fate.

THE DAEMON

However objective we astrologers try to be about our material, however much we
may experience it as a clockwork machine, there is always something else going
on just beneath the surface. When our astrology is really successful, it can be as if
some unexpected blessing or providence has led us to our conclusions. In the
seventeenth century, the mathematician and astrologer William Oughtred

... confessed that he was not satisfied how it came about that one might foretell
by the Starres, but so it was that it fell out true as he did often by his experience
find; he did believe that some genius or spirit did help.[19]

In this experience we often feel ourselves strangely taken up in the symbolism, or
equally implicated in it. In discussing the descent of astrology from augury in
Chapter 7, a distinction was made between participatory and theoretical significance. The showing of signs and omens does not come from some abstracted
universal working of things, some natural law, but from a participatory
consciousness. An omen is understood to be *for* someone who perceives it as
significant. This means that the omen *addresses* us, just as God spoke to His
people through the Prophets.

The Ptolemaic model of astrology has obscured the foundation in participatory significance by treating symbolism as an expression of causes, or as an

expression of some objective cosmic order. This puts the world it illuminates in the third person, as an IT. Mars influences or signifies anger and angry men as a universal fact of things, and as an astrologer I can see this correlation in the world. However, this is an objective arm's-length sort of knowing. Even if I look at the astrology for my own character and life history, I am looking down on myself from a distance, as if I can objectively view my life story from the point of view of the cosmos.

However, once we see astrology as a formation of omens, then the world it illuminates is the world of participation: *my* world or *your* world. Participatory significance is known in the first person and speaks in the second person. The showing of astrology speaks to me or to you, and it addresses us individually. Mars in a particular chart still signifies an angry man – but the astrology is showing *me* that – not as a universal truth of nature but as a relative but effective truth for my understanding in what concerns me, here, now.

So what is this intelligence that prompts or addresses us? This entity has been named since antiquity as the *daemon*. To avoid the entirely negative connotation (demon) found in Christian culture, the Greek spelling -ai or – ae is often used. It approximates to what is indicated in modern spiritualism by the guide or the guardian angel. For the modern mind it is appropriate to consider the daemon in the form of the 'genius', as a higher function or modality of the soul, but it nevertheless tends to manifest as other to our ordinary consciousness.

Despite the open-ended definition of the daemon, certain well-established characteristics can be described. For the reader of Jung, the Latin approximation *numen* will be evocative.[20] The daemon is numinous in its presence, and those who experience it feel themselves touched by the supernatural. The daemones reveal themselves as part of the domain of the sacred, intermediate between mortals and the great gods. In ancient times worship and rites were offered to the daemones as well as to the gods, and they were generally considered to be beneficent, helping us to know and understand things beyond our ordinary conscious range.[21]

As 'guardian angel', one of the tasks of the daemon is to assist the individual to find fortune and destiny. Discussing the natal horoscope, Ficino believes that we are formed by the heavens for some honourable work and way of life, and the heavens favour us to the extent that we follow this calling:

> That assuredly is the thing for which the heavens and the lord of your horoscope
> gave birth to you. Therefore they will promote your undertakings and favour
> your life to the extent that you follow the auspices [*auspicia*] of your geniture,
> especially if that Platonic doctrine is true (with which all antiquity agrees) that

every person has at birth one certain daemon, the guardian of his life, assigned by his own personal star, which helps him to that very task to which the celestials summoned him when he was born.[22]

We are in the same league as Alan Leo's 'Star Angels' here. Once again it is obvious that this attitude to astrology is a world away from either determinism or the rational model of Ptolemy. Ficino develops his theme to show that an individual may have two daemones, 'one proper to his nativity, the other to his profession'. The key to good fortune is identity or harmony between the two. He goes on to discuss the horoscopic signification of the daemon, especially in relation to the Part of Fortune.[23]

At first sight Christianity appears to have driven the 'demons' down into the realm of Satan, but that is only half the story. The old beneficent daemones have survived as angels, and the archaic belief that the souls of dead heroes become daemones is paralleled in the saints of Christianity. When divine intercession is needed, the good pagan prays to the daemones and the good Christian appeals to the saints and angels. The story of Lilly's teacher Evans, mentioned in the previous chapter, illustrates the survival of daemonic magic in Christianised form – Evans summons the *angel* Salmon to do his bidding.[24]

An Arabic story I once heard tells the story of the djinn ('genie'), who are exactly the same daemones. The mention of the genie is an immediate reminder of Aladdin and his lamp; the djinn have the power to make things come true and grant our wishes. How does this wish-granting work? The Almighty One has Word and Power. His Word is made Truth. Men have words but no power, while the djinn have power but no words. That is why the djinn wait close to men, so that when men speak, the djinn can attach themselves to the words and empower them for their own purposes. For this reason we should always beware of what we speak, especially if we speak of bad things.

Significantly, a Greek term for a sign or omen is *daemonion* ('the divine thing' or, literally, 'the daemonic thing'). Divination is a mode of communication with a god but equally with a daemon. It is also important to take account of the suggestion, which we already know from the story of Socrates, that the daemones communicate through signs and symbols.[25] The language of symbol is the primary medium of this realm that crosses between human and divine, and it carries unknown and unknowable potencies. Everyone who practises in the symbolic languages should know that the words spoken in connection with symbols are far from small-talk.

The ancient conception of the daemone is well understood by St. Augustine, and it is indeed significant that he uses the idea as part of his attack on astrology.

His analysis of astrology connects up what we now call 'synchronicity' with the power of the daemones. In his *Confessions* he discusses a conversation with his friend Vindicianus. We know from his own account that in his youth Augustine was fascinated by astrology, and this conversation must have occurred while he was still grappling with the subject. Augustine asked how it was that many true things could be foretold by astrology. Vindicianus replied that

> ... the force of chance, diffused throughout the whole order of things, brought this about. For if when a man by hap-hazard opens the pages of some poet, who sang and thought of something wholly different, a verse oftentimes fell out, wondrously agreeable to the present business: it were not to be wondered at if, out of the soul of man, unconscious what takes place in it, by some higher instinct an answer should be given, by hap, not by art, corresponding to the business and actions of the demander.[26]

The argument is a beautiful exposition of divination. Although the study of astrological correspondences cannot constitute a true discipline or art, nevertheless Vindicianus allows that merely chance occurrences may also be wonderful and meaningful. Here is an equivalent to Jung's synchronicity. These coincidences are genuinely meaningful because a certain higher faculty of the soul, of which we are unconscious, seizes on the occasion to inform us of something we should know. Extending Vindicianus's observations, we may say that the unconscious prompts consciousness through signs.

The 'wondrously agreeable' correspondence, applied to symbolism, is the vital power in divination. It is but a short step from this 'higher instinct' of the soul to the more sinister suggestion that behind the realisation of astrological symbolism is the agency of an evil spirit (daemon), an external malevolent intelligence penetrating into the soul. According to Augustine, this is the true inspiration behind astrology:

> ...one has some justification for supposing that when astrologers give replies that are often surprisingly true, they are inspired, in some mysterious way, by spirits, but spirits of evil, whose concern is to instil and confirm in men's minds those false and baneful notions about 'astral destiny'. These true predictions do not come from any skill in the notation and inspection of horoscopes; that is a spurious art.[27]

The suggestion that evil spirits wish to imprison our souls by bending them to the false notion of stellar fatality is the same 'work of the Devil' argument that has been employed over the ages against astrology.

Astrology lost Augustine, who converted to Christianity. In this is reflected the vast historical dilemma of astrology and religion. It is obvious both from various comments of Augustine's and from our knowledge of the astrological tradition, that the majority of astrologers of his day offered fate-prescriptions supposedly determined by the stars, and attainable through their scientific judgments. The stance of orthodox astrology must have been no different from that of the time of Pico a thousand years later, and just as intolerable. There is therefore a curious irony in Augustine's analysis. He is wrong to assume that the daemones instil bad ideas in the soul. They give the astrologers signs and omens of true things, but it is the *astrologers who misinterpret the daemones* by locating their divinatory signs in a 'false and baneful' determinism of the machine of destiny. It is not the daemones who have corrupted astrologers, but astrologers who have corrupted the daemones.

NOTES

1 Patrick Curry, *A Confusion of Prophets: Victorian and Edwardian Astrology* (Collins and Brown, 1992), p.157.

2 For the 1989 Repeal of a section of the Vagrancy Act, see P.Curry, op.cit., p.171. The legal position is, I understand, still uncertain in parts of the U.S.A.

3 Alan Leo (William Allan), born 7 August 1860, rectified time 5:51:28am GMT, Westminster, London; died 30 August 1917, 10am, Bude, Cornwall. Quite apart from his influence through his writings, Alan Leo's genius has shaped the whole course of organised astrology in the UK through the most successful of the various organisations he founded, the Astrological Lodge of the Theosophical Society (13 July 1915, 7:15pm North London, 51N36 0W11). From the 1920s, under the presidency of Charles Carter, this grew to be the leading body in UK astrology, taking on many non-Theosophical members. Out of the Lodge was formed the prestigious Faculty of Astrological Studies (7 June 1948, 7:58pm BST, Queen Square, London WC1); this became independent of the Lodge in 1954. The ambiguity of the Astrology-Theosophy connection and dual membership finally brought the split that led to John Addey's founding of what rapidly became the largest and most influential body in the UK, the Astrological Association (21 June 1958 8:22pm Queensberry Place, London SW7). Between 1982 and 1986 the Lodge itself finally split under the unresolved paradox of its origins. Following in the footsteps of John Addey's earlier attempts in the Lodge, under my presidency and in the face of obduracy from the Theosophical Society, a compromise dual constitution was created and the previous commonly used but unofficial name, Astrological Lodge of London, was formally adopted (15 November 1982, 9:24pm GMT, Queen Square). This was a fateful inception and the compromise was, it turned out, doomed to fail. It did however produce fruit in the founding of the Company of Astrologers (originally as a Teaching Body of the Lodge: 14 November 1983, 9:29pm GMT, Queen Square). The major part of the body continued as The Astrological Lodge of London, retained the publication of the long-running *Astrology* journal, and split with the tiny Theosophical core. This latter renamed itself as the 'Astrological Lodge of Great Britain' at the elected instant of the 75th Solar Return of the 1915 Lodge inception on 12 July 1990 (11:13:26pm BST, Queen Square

WC1). It surrendered its Theosophical Society Charter on 14 November 1992 (9:10pm GMT, Battersea, London), and finally wound up its affairs on 21 January 1994 at 9:58pm, Queen Square (not elected). Its last act timed for this instant was to renew in perpetuity the auspice granted to the Company of Astrologers, and pass into the keeping of the Company its ritual. Leo's attempt to marry Theosophy and Astrology was at this point dissolved, at least in its organisational expression. Underlying the many contingent circumstances of these splits and developments may be traced an *ideological* question about the nature of astrology, unresolved in Alan Leo's own mind. He talked of the 'curse and blessing' of astrology, indicating that its practice is negative unless it serves an occult revelation. Leo believed that Theosophy, with its teachings on karma and reincarnation, showed where we may seek for the blessing. For a discussion of Leo's legacy in organised astrology, see my article, 'The Astrological Lodge from Alan Leo to the Present Day', *Astrology Quarterly*, vol.60, no.1, Spring 1986.

4 Charles Carter called Leo's book on esoteric astrology 'a big volume containing virtually nothing worth reading'; see his article, 'The Astrological Lodge of the London Theosophical Society' in *The Best in Astrology from IN SEARCH*, ed. Charles Jayne, vol.1 (Association for Research in Cosmecology, New York, 1974).

5 Bessie Leo et al., *The Life and Work of Alan Leo* (Modern Astrology Office, London, 1919) p12. Carter was characteristically scathing about Leo's 'woolliness' about Star Angels – see his 'Reminiscences of Alan Leo' in *Astrology Quarterly*, vol.39, no.4, Winter 1965-6. Carter's comments suggest the gap between a rationalised notion of 'spiritual principles' (*logoi*) underlying the planets, contrasted with the explicitly daemonic conception that we pick up from Alan Leo.

6 B.Leo et.al., op.cit., p125-6.

7 ibid., pp.141-2. The peacock symbolism in alchemy indicates that the transformation process of the coniunctio is near. See, for example, Jung, *Collected Works*, vol.9 part I, paras. 685-6 (Princeton University Press, Princeton, N.J., 1980).

8 Cumont, reference n9 below, p13.

9 See, for example, comment by the Peripatetic Alexander of Aphrodisias quoted by Cumont in *Astrology and Religion among the Greeks and Romans* (1912; also Dover, New York, 1960), Lecture V, note 30, p.87 (1960 edition).

10 Plato 'Timaeus' 40 C & D Warrington transl. Everyman's Library 493 (1965) London.

11 Alby Stone, *Wyrd: Fate and Destiny in North European Paganism* (Borough of Newark, 1989, reprinted Newark Chamber of Commerce, 1981), p.35. On the question of 'taboo' (*geis*), see pp.15f. See also the author's main conclusion on p39: 'There is very little to suggest that the northern Europeans had much of a belief in an inexorable and predetermined Fate. Inexorable perhaps, but certainly not fixed and beyond appeal.' This important study deserves to be better known.

12 Jean Bottero, *Mesopotamia* (University of Chicago Press, 1992), and other references in chapter 7 above.

13 Vettius Valens, quoted by Cumont, op.cit., Lecture V, note 30, p86.

14 Manilius, *Astronomica*, 4:14 ff., trans. Goold (Loeb Classical Library, 1977), pp223-5.

15 Augustine, *City of God*, V.3, trans. Bettenson (Pelican 1972), p.183.

16 I believe that only a divinatory interpretation gives a practical solution for the astrologer faced with the twins problem. This was proposed a few years back and it seems to have caught on. Briefly, this abandons the notion that we 'own' a birthchart, and reposes the issue in the 'context' form, ie. of the astrologer presented with a horoscope-of-twins. The task is then to see two different signatures (for instance in two major aspect groups) in the

horoscope that reveal the two different people. A small change in cusps can then highlight this differentiation. For discussion and example see Maggie Hyde, 'Twins, or Can You Have Half a Chart?' (Company of Astrologers, Bulletin no.1, Summer 1987). Except for a brief extra note this is a reprint from *Astrology Quarterly* (Astrological Lodge of London), vol59 no.2, Summer 1985.

17 For Ptolemy on disease, see *Tetrabiblos*, III.12; also note Ptolemy's respectful discussion of Egyptian medical astrology at I.3.

18 Bouché-Leclercq, *L'Astrologie Grecque* (Paris, 1899, reprinted under the title *Culture et Civilisation*, Brussels, 1963), ch.13, p.462 (1963 edition).

19 John Aubrey, *Brief Lives...set down by John Aubrey between the Years 1669 and 1696*, ed. Andrew Clark (Clarendon Press, Oxford, 1898), vol.2, p.105. Oughtred was an expert in algebra, a member of the Royal Society, and plainly an astrologer.

20 An excellent starting point in exploring Jung's views is the essay by James Hillman, *The Pandaemonium of Images* published in his *Healing Fiction* (Station Hill, Barrytown, New York, 1983).

21 See, for instance, Plato, *Cratylus*,398 tracing the etymology of daemon (= knowing). The discussion follows Hesiod in associating daemones with the golden race of the first men. Plato (through Socrates in his dialogue) suggests that when a good man dies he joins the daemones, and his wisdom in life is 'more than human'. The etymologies in this dialogue are considered to be generally fanciful and unreliable. For our purposes this is less important than the fact that Plato chooses to understand 'daemon' in this way, giving us a profound insight into the nature of interpretation.

22 Marsilio Ficino, *Three Books on Life*, trans.C.Kaske & J.Clarke (State University of New York, Binghampton, New York, 1989), pp.371ff.

23 Ficino gives a lengthy discussion on this topic, mentioning several ancient opinions. He appears to favour the rule of Firmicus Maternus, which first locates the Part of Fortune (but reversed for a night birth: Asc+Sun-Moon) and then takes the Lord of the Term in which that falls, as the daemon. I have, however, found the various opinions between Firmicus Maternus and Ficino contradictory and in need of further clarification.

24 For the assimilation of daemones and magic into Christianity, see the comprehensive survey by Valerie Flint, *The Rise of Magic in Early Medieval Europe* (Clarendon Press, Oxford, 1991).

25 See, for example, the discussion in Plutarch, 'On the Sign of Socrates', in *Moralia* (Loeb Classical Library), VII, 579f-582c and 588b-589f.

26 Augustine, *Confessions*, trans. Pusey (Brittanica Great Books, University of Chicago Press, 1952), III.5.

27 Augustine, *City of God*, trans. Knowles (Pelican, 1972), V.7, p.188. Augustine marshals a formidable battery of arguments against astrology.

10

The Unique Case of Interpretation

I N the formation of our traditional model of astrology, something essential has been overlooked. The very possibility of talking about astrology as divination has become obscure. There is a curious syndrome about the description of astrology in that intelligent sceptics who stand outside our subject have little difficulty in recognising astrological practice as divination. Pico della Mirandola's great critique is against '*divinatory* astrology'. By contrast, most astrologers shy away from the comparison, or are genuinely puzzled when it is made. However, it is not adequate to say that astrologers have misunderstood their own subject. The real problem lies with the definition of divination itself. Divination is a homeless wanderer with no easily definable location within the categories of knowledge. To understand this problem, it is necessary to plumb a perennial philosophic issue, the old divide between subject and object, internal and external realms of reality.

DIVINATION AND THE SUBJECT-OBJECT SPLIT

It is a habit of unreflective thought to take for granted that the world can be described without particular reference to the act and context of perception, where the nature of things and the laws underlying phenomena are treated as having a neutral ground of existence independent of any consciousness positing that ground. We even come to see ourselves objectively as human-things, jostling with all the other things in that neutral existence. In speaking of life and experience, we then imaginatively adopt a position somewhere outside, looking down upon 'our' life, 'our' experience, instead of *being* that life, that experience.

The way of scientific imagination, with all of its marvellous gifts, depends on the exercise of this objectifying faculty; through this mankind appears to have mastered the material substance of reality. On the other hand, it is doubtful whether anything of *human* significance can be known in this way: 'science manipulates things and gives up living in them'.[1]

The ingrained and largely unquestioned cultural habit of valuing the 'objective' has tended to the degradation of understandings deemed to be 'merely subjective'. This affliction undermines not only art and divination: even philosophy, once a supreme goal of thought, has been relegated to secondary status compared with the real work of the natural sciences. Western culture has carried through an earlier Greek and Christian attitude which has divided the realms of spirit and matter, but it has reversed the original philosophical and religious inspiration by learning to seek the foundation of truth in the world of literal and material facts. The conventional description of reality has become sundered into sharply divided objective and subjective realms. European culture and science has emerged within languages whose very syntax embodies a precise subject-object demarcation. Further, within science, a clear method appears to have been attained by which to strip away subjective elements from the exact definition of the universally and objectively true. Since our habitual leaning is to equate the real with the world of objects and material substances, the world of facts, the arbitration of the real is given over to the objective domain. The content of the subjective world 'inside our heads', the totality of ideas and intuitions, theories and imaginations, whether collective or individual, has reality value only to the extent that it allows us to correctly perceive the objective world. The 'really real' is outside our heads, the really real things are outside our thoughts about those things. At its extreme, this tendency reduces consciousness and life itself to epiphenomenal status, a secondary concomitant of processes that may be completely established at the material level.

An interesting contrast can be made between an older conception of science as *description* and the modern paradigm of science as *instruction*.[2] 'Instructional science' establishes a reality that can be manipulated and turned into algorithms, and stands as exemplar of the objective means for sifting and sorting 'real facts' about the world. A set of explicit instructions, capable of theoretically infinite repetition, and removed as far as possible from the vagaries of subjective interpretation, can be given for obtaining reliable results. Add x to y and the result will invariably be z. The world is understood and theorised insofar as it can be reduced and manipulated in this way. Naturally it is recognised that there are relatively few areas of useful knowledge where facts can be obtained according to this strict computational and science-laboratory model, but the key to the powerful hold of this approach lies in the belief that 'in theory' or 'in principle', the really real facts about things ought to be capable of such demonstration. Even some of the humanities, such as psychology and sociology, fall prey to this belief and place excessive trust in quantitative and statistical methods which are supposed to carry the rigour and reality value of hard science.

Much is heard these days about the new physics which is supposed to change all this. From the time of the discoveries of relativity, great inroads have been made into the scientific bastion of objectivity. Observer participation in the results of the experiment has come on to the agenda, and the irreducible role of subjective interpretation has been acknowledged. Sophisticated science has arrived at the understanding that a final presuppositionless description of reality is in principle unattainable. I am not convinced that these developments offer any immediate hope of solving our problems of the adequate description of astrology, because we are still talking about entirely different orders of perception, rooted in two different modes of thinking. In any case, such subtleties hardly begin to touch the dead weight of *scientism* – a science-like objectivity turned into a crude philosophy of life.

The habitual attitude which is so entrenched in a divide between subject and object, thought and fact, is only effectively questioned by philosophical insight or spiritual discipline. Doing astrology stirs the mud but does not of itself offer a guarantee of illumination. What frequently happens is that as soon as astrological practice demonstrates to the practitioner that it is *real*, the phenomena are cast across the divide, and are seen as *objective*, as opposed to being 'merely' subjective. As Maggie Hyde observes:

> [astrologers] use the physical world in a ritualised framework to discourse on the human condition, and then assume that the physical world embodies an objective truth pre-existent to man, which they have uncovered *about* man.[3]

Where the subject-object divide is accepted without question, and reality value is finally located in the objective half, then divination loses its ground. At best it becomes the possibility of a 'paranormal means for obtaining facts or predicting events'. Its paranormal nature is seen in that no explanation of its working is likely to be found within conventional reality. What is shown in divination arises by chance, and not by some traceable and objective natural process or law which could connect divinatory method with the 'facts' that it seeks to discern. Its subjectivity is taken to lie in its arbitrary and non-replicable quality, since its successful performance appears to depend on chance circumstances mediated by the imaginative skills of the diviner. In sharp contrast to the procedure of conventional science, whatever instructions might be given for the performance of divination, these instructions do not in themselves offer the guarantee of results. They are not even approximations to the instructions of science, since they are of the nature of ritual expressions. For instance, the methods of interpretation given in divinatory systems such as the *I Ching* can hardly be compared with the universal laws sought in science, since the significance of each divination lies precisely in the unique circumstance in which the case arises. The unique circumstance is constituted by the participants in the situation, including the diviner. From the standpoint of a world divided into subjects and objects, divination refers to a dimension of subjectivity to the extent that its significance depends upon what it means for the participants. Generalisations from the situation are therefore pointless, since other circum-stances and other participants will require wholly other divinations. This important topic, which above all marks off divination from science, will be taken up again later in this chapter.

Within scientific discipline, imaginative and interpretive strategies are suspect unless they have a demonstrable relationship with the objective facts and processes described by that discipline. Any understanding nurtured in partici-patory significance must be theoretically reworked to purge it of the taint of subjectivity. Whatever startling results symbolism may from time to time yield, the symbolic attitude is necessarily devalued or, if utilised at all, is subverted by instructional science. Metaphor may assist, but will not suffice. Modern mathematics funnels through a wild dream of Descartes, a vision of the unity of all sciences which he saw on 10 November 1619. Chemistry took a leap forward when Kekule broke the secret of the benzine ring after he dreamt of the serpent that eats its tail. Yet the scientist believes that reality adheres to the benzine, not to the serpent. However helpful to the scientific imagination such exercises may be, however conducive as they are to lateral thinking, nevertheless dreams and serpents, Heaven, Earth, wind and mountain, the Fool and the Hanged Man have *in themselves* no place in chemistry or management studies. Nor should diviners be unduly perturbed that this is so.

From the conventional subject-object stance of modern culture, therefore, divination has at best only a tangential relationship with the realm of the fully real (=objective). Given this dubious status, it is understandable that the defence of divination appears an uninviting basis for the justification of astrology. When the difficult question of divination is side-stepped, we are tempted to lose sight of the distinction between the two orders of significance, and we then try to make astrology consist of a set of 'objective facts'.

As has already been suggested in Chapter 4, it is only in the field of natural (scientific) astrology that such straightforward facts can be presupposed or attained – and this is just as much an empirical observation as it is a logical and philosophical one. Let us start from where we actually are and recover interpretive astrology's own ground, which is that of divination. If this ground is to be recovered, however, the conventional subject-object cut across reality must be transmuted. A description of divination is required that does not take for granted such a divide, with its disabling location of reality value on the object side. Our difficulty is that the paths laid out in ancient or modern thought have not been oriented to the particular problem of describing divination, which simply does not seem to exist as a category of philosophical concern. We have to undertake the main part of the task for ourselves. In this project I believe that astrology, by virtue of its vast symbolic scope, its cultural significance, its intricate yet coherent technical range, and its formidable tradition, has the possibility of leading the way for all forms of divination in general. First, however, astrology needs to develop an adequate language of description of its own phenomena. A good place to start is the question of 'astrological significance'. From this I hope to arrive at what I believe to be the key precept of the 'unique case of interpretation'.

ASTROLOGICAL SIGNIFICANCE

The question of what we mean by significance when we say this or that piece of astrology is 'significant' seems hardly to be a problem at all, until with a little reflection we encounter the archetypal subject-object dilemma once again.

One part of our concept of significance is yielded to the rule of science. This is so important that I trust the reader will allow me to repeat observations already made in this chapter. The scientific significance of things is universal, usually subject to quantification, and available to algorithmic or instructional treatment. It is the objective knowledge we have of the world around us. As knowledge grows of whole populations of things, from dogs to gas molecules, the various subject-sciences are built up.

There is another meaning to 'significance'. It is the unique significance of each life, its meaning for each and every one of us, and it cannot be separated from the human-being in which its creation is founded. This gives us the category earlier discussed in Chapter 7, of *participatory significance*, which depends upon the individual who finds it significant. It is the world we each *live* in, as opposed to merely *exist* in as animated bodies, that is the primary world of astrological significance. Everything I have ever experienced and understood about astrology leads me to this conclusion. The point I am making here, when put in the way I have put it, seems obvious and even banal. I could even be accused of labouring it, were it not for the fact that this supposedly obvious distinction between the orders of significance of science and of individually experienced human life is continually forgotten in astrology.

Dane Rudhyar made one of his most notable contributions on the question of the distinction of the orders of significance. It is a position from which he never wavered, and it forms a cornerstone of Humanistic astrology:

> Science deals always essentially with collective factors. But what I consider as 'astrology per se' – astrology as a sui generis thought-discipline – has as its true field *individual existential situations*....this distinction is of absolutely capital importance for the astrologer.[4]

Further, the 'individual-existential' character of astrology means that its truth is significant only for a person who finds it to be so:

> It is for the individual to let...symbols organise themselves into significance.[5]

Modern science and astrology represent two different disciplines of thinking, each the appropriate road to their own domains of knowledge. On this basis of a distinction of theoretical-scientific and individual-existential orders of truth and significance, Rudhyar regards scientific research as irrelevant and misleading when applied to the questions of astrology.

The stance of Rudhyar's humanistic astrology is no threat to science, nor to a strictly scientific level of inquiry into what I have termed 'natural astrology', and which Rudhyar refers to as the 'raw materials which the astrological discipline uses'.[6] This stance is, however, a defence of astrology against *scientism*, since it renders null and void the claim sometimes made that the method of scientific astrology is the only valid mode of arbitrating significance in all of astrology, full stop.

It comes as no surprise therefore that Geoffrey Dean should single Rudhyar out for bombardment right at the beginning of *Recent Advances in Natal Astrology*.[7] Geoffrey Dean commits the basic philosophical error of scientism, which is to assert or imply that there can be logically only one class of truth, and that any truth of individual experience is only verified by referring to collective experience. Scientism necessarily denies the principle of orders of significance, and turns individual and participatory significance into a secondary 'merely subjective therefore not-fully-real' by-product of existence.

As is (or should be) well understood in statistics, the behaviour of large populations of individuals has strictly *nothing* to say about any one individual in that population. But our humanly experienced significance is *wholly* founded in the individual. Even though the individual necessarily experiences life as one with others, this collectivity is always a group of individuals, you and me and another.

Statistical understanding, like scientific theory as a whole, represents a highly specialised and rationalised abstraction of human significance. So far have we come down this seductive road of abstraction, that the derivation of 'science' as a particular and narrow focus of human concern is obliterated, and the truth of science is turned into the truth of humanity. Popular imagination and bad science assume that there is only one road of truth, and that individual significance must somehow reduce to a law of large numbers. Astrology is just one of the modes of human knowing to be crippled by this modern disease of the imagination.

What Rudhyar calls an issue of 'capital importance for the astrologer' requires, I believe, a description of the principle of the *unique case*. This is at the heart of divinatory astrology. It refers to that experience of reality that is essentially and of its nature irreducible to quantification. There cannot meaningfully be a 'population' of these cases. The primary ground of this irreducibility is You and I. Rather than try to define it further in the abstract, it will be far better established by reference to our everyday experience of astrology, where it shows itself over and over again. I will therefore try to demonstrate this, and bring out the impossibility of a rational-scientific interpretation of the same phenomenon, through some examples.

THE UNIQUE CASE: A SATURNINE ILLUSTRATION

As an example, I will make a brief astrological comparison of two women of power who dominated the British psyche in the latter part of the twentieth century. In an important sense these two were rivals for influence – I am referring to Queen Elizabeth II, and to Margaret Thatcher.

In principle there are many ways we could compare and contrast these horoscopes, just as there are many ways in which we could compare the two people. However, a relatively few salient features stand out, on which the great majority of astrologers will concur. Most astrologers will, for instance, note that both women have the Moon in Leo – female figures prominent in public life. At the planets in signs level this may be taken as significant, although admittedly Elizabeth does not strike us as having a flamboyant streak.

More significant, they both happen to have Saturn in Scorpio, being born within a little over six months of each other. In itself, that hardly means much for comparison, other than showing us that they fall in the same part of a particular generation. However, the horoscopic placings of Saturn are immediately striking. For Thatcher, Saturn is *rising*, right on the ascendant. For Elizabeth Saturn is *culminating*, right on the Midheaven.

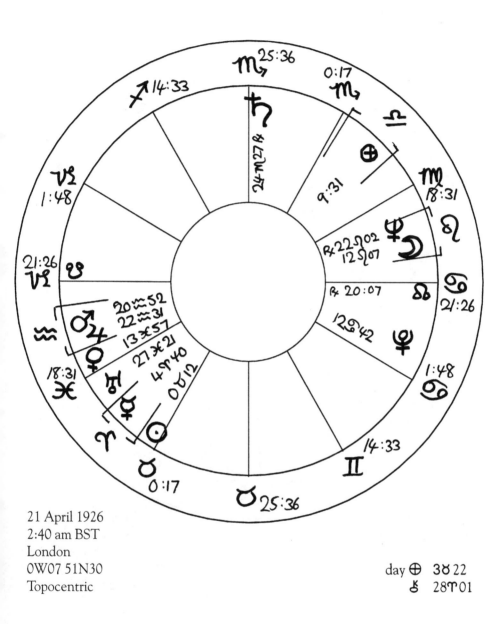

21 April 1926
2:40 am BST
London
0W07 51N30
Topocentric

day ⊕ 3♉22
⚷ 28♈01

FIGURE 12 Elizabeth II

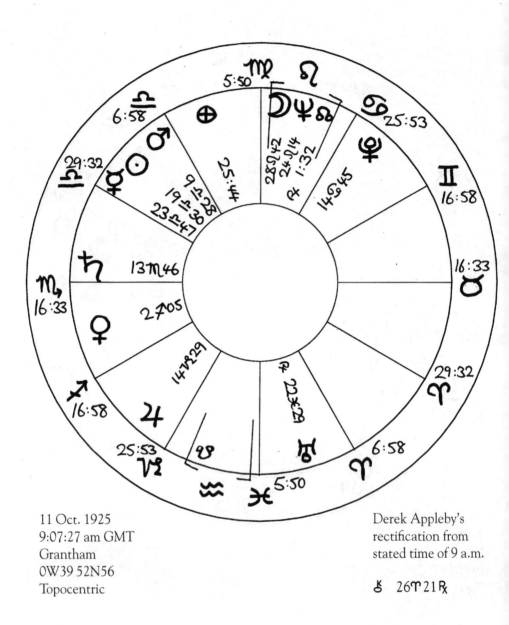

11 Oct. 1925
9:07:27 am GMT
Grantham
0W39 52N56
Topocentric

Derek Appleby's
rectification from
stated time of 9 a.m.

⚷ 26♈21℞

FIGURE 13 Margaret Thatcher

Saturn in both cases is the closest planet to angles. It seems to be announced to us that these two women are Scorpio Saturn women. Cold, stubborn, tough-minded – critics might even say emotionally constipated – but it is difficult not to admire the determination and durability, the dour holding power signified by this placing. Even at their best Saturn qualities are not loved, though they may be respected. The Queen, with Sun Taurus, is shown to have the advantage in holding her own, but Thatcher persisted in her wilful way a remarkably long time. She was in power far longer than most prime ministers, and Elizabeth's reign has been a lengthy one. In worldly affairs time is cruel. There is a baneful quality about power achieved through Saturn, as if there is always somewhere in the story a loss of favour or a fall from grace. Margaret Thatcher wrought large changes but it cannot be said that her legacy is warmly regarded, beyond a hard-core conservative minority. She has been somewhat cast into the shadows as something of an embarrassment even by her own party, the Tories. The hard law of Saturn has been equally unforgiving towards Elizabeth. Despite her great personal standing as a model of duty, her long reign passes with the sad decline of the House of Windsor. The question is not so much about her, but the monarchy itself – the source of authority, Saturn on the MC.

Yet for a few years these two powerful maidens bestrode the stage of British political history. Simply out of the circumstances of their time, they were brought together 'by fate'. It is as if their two Saturns have to pay heed to each other. Perhaps Margaret Thatcher wanted her Saturn to culminate, which was often suggested of her, especially when she began using the royal 'We' – 'we are a grandmother', she declared. She also upstaged the monarch on several occasions by manifesting prominently at the scene of major disasters – Saturn in the sign of death.

I am sure that any reader versed in traditional astrology will accept at least the broad outline of these simple interpretations, even if they might disagree on this or that detail or feel I have not gone far enough. Let me break down the likely agreement between us into several component parts. Firstly, beyond what Saturn means independently in each separate horoscope, the Saturn-pairing does represent an astrologically significant comparison. Secondly, my interpretation is consistent with conventional astrological method and symbolism. Thirdly, I think it will be acknowledged that taken as a whole, the Saturnine comparison is true in the world – we have something of an accurate reflection not only of the separate characters of the two women, but also of the *perceived comparison* between them. In this last agreement – that this really is so in the world – we have the mystery of the working of astrology. But let me leave that for now.

There is here, is there not, astrological significance? We say, on recognising this significance, 'Yes, that's so'. It's like the nose on someone's face, obvious and part of a person once you know them. But where does this astrological truth exist? I have purposely chosen a comparison of charts for this first example because it brings out more forcefully the completely unique nature of all interpretation. In this case, the symbolism that becomes so relevant is more than the sum of two separate Saturn-on-angles interpretations. The interpretation only 'exists' *when I bring the two maps together*, and set it against a conventional reading of Saturn. Of course, the two women have their real characters and destinies whether or not I bring their horoscopes together. These are not any two women either. The fact that it is the Queen and her Prime Minister provides the significant and one-and-only context for a comparison. Furthermore, the piece of art which we astrologers can make here depends entirely on the act of interpretation. On the other hand, it is not merely a 'subjective impression'. It crosses the subject-object divide by showing a truth of symbolism that will be self-evident to most astrologers.

The significance of the interpretation takes on a shared existence, beyond my subjective impressions. It is therefore 'objective'. But it does not give us some theoretically universal significance for all times and all places, simply because this unique case can only exist for Elizabeth II and Margaret Thatcher as brought together in the light of one selected detail of our astrology.

The only 'universal' factors here are the theoretically constant meaning of the planets and signs, but *these meanings which we share in our tradition have no meaning at all until they are brought into symbolic relation with actual situations and people*, against whom they are interpreted. There is no such thing as a population of other cases like this, only countless equally individual cases which we come to know about only when we actually set out to interpret them.

The comparison of Saturn in these two charts is useful in our discussion for another reason altogether. The factor that emerges as significant, Saturn on angles, suggests an immediate contrast with the work of Michel and Françoise Gauquelin, concerning the diurnal distributions of the planets. The placings are definitely in Gauquelin sectors or plus zones suggestive of the Saturnine temperament.[8] So is that where the real truth of these placings will be found to lie? This is not the answer, because this statistical work does not give us a significance that is exactly located *on* the angles. The Elizabeth-Thatcher Saturn comparison would not strike us as very interesting at all apart from the close angular conjunctions. The interpretation I made above is *wholly rooted in the coincidental placing of Saturn closely on angles*, and cannot be derived from the relatively small statistical fluctuations of Gauquelin data, or from the sectors that Gauquelin has discovered. It is therefore not capable of being derived from the behaviour of some other supposed population, as if there could be hundreds of Margaret Thatchers. Significance comes from, and returns to, the unique case and the qualitative interpretation. The significance I am talking about is *of a different order*. Whatever significance is involved, it is not amenable to scientific verification, and it is completely unreplicable. The significance of the unique case exists once and once only in the context in which it is interpreted.

The unique case quite characteristically and as a natural part of its development includes two, three and perhaps four cases. To explain this seeming contradiction, I would refer back firstly to the Elizabeth and Thatcher example, which although I am taking primarily as a comparison, does also involve two independently quite significant Saturn conjunct angle placings. The comparison interpretation is, therefore, a unique case which also consists of two unique cases. Significance frequently arises for an astrologer when there is the fortuitous juxtaposition or coincidence of the same or similar factors in similar situations. For example, we may encounter two clients in turn with the same configuration, and know that we are being invited to draw the inference in the second case that we have already had demonstrated to us in the first case. It seems to be almost a rule that once we have a particular symbolism in mind, it will be almost immediately spontaneously manifested a second or even a third time. It is off clumps of two or three cases of this sort that most astrologers learn their own 'hints and wrinkles' of astrology. These instances are still part of the unique circumstance of astrology meaningfully arising, and the replication of symbolism involved is a replication in a few significant instances, not an abstracted population of cases.

KOESTLER AND SUICIDE

I will now give a further example of the astrology of the unique case which I hope will be decisive for the reader. By way of context, this requires us to bear in mind the total null result of the New York Suicide Project discussed in Chapter 3. Thousands of horoscopic patterns were applied in the birth-charts of a large and carefully controlled sample of New York suicides, and *nothing* was found that even remotely suggested the tendency to suicide.

In my practice of astrology, I have not had occasion to deal directly with the possible signification for suicide in more than a tiny handful of students or clients. Yet on a couple of striking occasions, I have seen the strong signification of suicide or potential suicide. I approach my practical astrology on the understanding that in this, as in every other category of behaviour or event that can be imagined and talked about, there is an appropriate symbolism for it. So I am not surprised if on rare occasion, the possibility of an astrological judgment of suicide does become valid.

Clearly, if I take the results of the New York Suicide study as bearing on the horoscopes I see, I must be deluding myself in entertaining such a possibility. This dilemma is well brought out by the life and horoscope of Arthur Koestler, together with Dennis Elwell's perceptive interpretation in his book *Cosmic Loom*.[9]

Koestler was well known as a scientist, writer and researcher, with a deep interest in all things paranormal. One of his passions was his support for voluntary euthanasia. This was truly Koestler's last great cause, for after a progressive physical decline he ended his life in a carefully organised suicide pact with his wife, taking an overdose of barbiturates on 1 March 1983.

Is there a possible symbolism for suicide in Arthur Koestler's natal horoscope? Dennis Elwell locates the theme in Neptune on the 7th cusp, and there can be no doubt that this is a true attribution. This well denotes both the manner of death through drugs, and points to the sacrifice by his wife who 'had no life of her own; she lived through Arthur [Koestler]'[10]. Neptune is in sextile with the 8th house Sun, thus fulfilling Charles Carter's observation that in suicide Neptune is usually in some relation to the 8th.[11] Neptune is perfectly portrayed by Koestler's single philosophical or spiritual reference in a detailed and practical suicide letter (Sun Virgo 8th) which he had prepared eight months earlier. I give this moving passage in full, because I believe it to be a significant statement of the symbol:

> I wish my friends to know that I am leaving their company in a peaceful frame of mind, with some timid hopes for a de-personalised after-life beyond due confines of space, time and matter and beyond the limits of our comprehension. This 'oceanic feeling' has often sustained me at difficult moments, and does so now, while I am writing this.[12]

A conclusive piece of evidence for the large role of Neptune around the time of the suicide will be found in the secondary progressions with progressed Neptune's *exact* return, by retrograde motion, to its natal place (10 Cancer 0). Such zero-orb contacts involving trans-Saturnians are of a rare order in secondaries: here it suggests life returning to its origin. Koestler's oceanic feeling at death brings him back to his birth.

There is a second major theme of symbolism relating to Koestler's death, as well as to his life, announced in the close dissociate opposition of Mercury and Saturn.

Look at that opposition: it is the central axis of Koestler's horoscope, part of a dissociate grand cross based in the mutable signs. The two planets are joint final

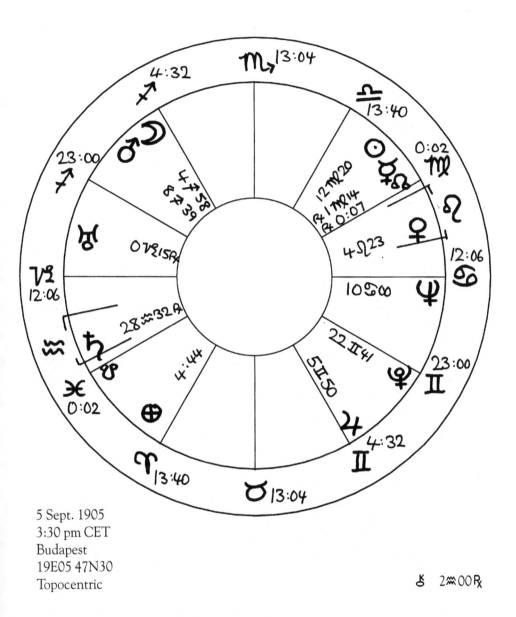

5 Sept. 1905
3:30 pm CET
Budapest
19E05 47N30
Topocentric

FIGURE 14 Arthur Koestler

dispositors, together with the mediating Uranus. Saturn is lord of the ascendant, retrograde and on the South Node; Mercury is lord of the 8th on the 8th cusp. The line of the Nodes underscores the opposition along the 2nd-8th axis. The house of death is further emphasised by the Sun, under the dominion of Mercury. The right to choose one's own death as a great public cause: we must have here the signature of 'death by one's own hand' (lord of ascendant opposite 8th ruler Mercury in the 8th). Koestler's friend George Mikes describes the suicide as 'a brave and dignified act; and – most fittingly – a weighty argument in an important debate'.[13]

Timing confirms the role of Saturn; for the year of death the Sun progresses to the square of natal Saturn, with progressed ascendant square progressed Saturn.[14]

Koestler had attempted suicide once before, and the symbolism seems to evoke Neptune, but also brings in the Saturn-Mercury opposition. It was sometime in 1934, which puts it in the period leading into the Saturn return.[15] In misery and depression Koestler set out to gas himself (Neptune). As he lay down a book 'fell from the shelf above and hit him full in the face', knocking him to his senses. Mercury on this occasion opposed an untimely departure, with the help of gravity (Saturn).

But let us come back to the problem with which we started. By whatever route, we have arrived at a symbolism suggestive of Koestler's suicide. Dennis Elwell bases his interpretation on the Neptune symbolism and declares that this is linked not just with the attendant details but with the act *per se*. His astrology shows him that here is a case where 'suicide is the last resort of Neptune'.[16] As I have shown, I can fully bear out the correctness of this interpretation in the case of Koestler. When we do this sort of work in astrology, it is important to note that poetic and protean though the symbolism is, our astrology is not to be reduced wholly to a matter of hunches and intuitions. Part of its work is a rational inference from conventional significations given by the tradition of astrology, and capable of quite exact craft discrimination. It is in this that astrology is more amazing than we sometimes realise, because it takes on the form of language, whereby one astrologer can communicate, agree or disagree with another.

On the basis of rational inference from symbolism, I would assert that any competent astrologer will agree that Dennis Elwell has made his case. Neptune appropriately placed in the horoscope appears as a signifier for at least one of the main motivations to suicide. This is also quite consistent with observations made by other authors, such as Charles Carter.

Now we are in a much stronger position to take head on the paradox suggested by the results of the New York Suicide Study. Suicide 'shows' in the

Koestler example. Suicide does not 'show' in the New York Suicide Study. Since it cannot be reasonably claimed that the New York Study hasn't covered the relatively ordinary horoscopic factors discussed here, then the following conclusion suggests itself: the Koestler example is not a member of the population of cases ('all suicides') being sampled in the New York Study.

The reason for this is that the Koestler example, like all individual examples taken up by astrologers, is a unique case, and the unique case in astrology is not a member of a population. It should by now be obvious that statistical studies of astrology have no demonstrable bearing on, or logical relationship with, the successful interpretation of a symbol in any single instance of divinatory astrology. This is what is meant by the argument for the unique case in astrology. It is a fundamental principle of divinatory astrology. Koestler's remarkable death is just one such case, and it remains – unique.

However, as I have already remarked in relation to the Saturn on angles symbolism for Margaret Thatcher and Elizabeth II, there is no reason why we should not find a family of unique cases, just as we meet families of individuals. Another suicide that attracted astrological attention at the time allows me to emphasise this important point. Pierre Beregovoy, a former socialist Prime Minister of France, took his own life on 1 May 1993, and his horoscope is given a convincing interpretation for this sad event by Lynn Bell and Charles Harvey in *The Astrological Journal* (July/August 1993). The authors, not surprisingly, feel constrained to defend their interpretation against the dead weight of the New York Suicide Study. They give its negative conclusion, then continue:

> ...Yet one knows from experience that the astrology of each tragic death would most probably have made clear symbolic sense if studied within the specific context of that person's life and situation.

This statement needs to strengthen only one element to make it a true expression of the unique case of interpretation. That element is the participation of the interpreting astrologer. Astrologers never will study 'each tragic death'; but in the very few individual cases that circumstance or special interest makes it meaningful for an astrologer to study, then he or she can hope and expect to find symbolic sense in the specific context of the suicide's life. This expectation arises simply and naturally out of our experience of astrology.

The conclusion we have reached in this chapter has an obvious corollary: our interpretations cannot be secured, in theory or in practice, by an appeal to a large-number demonstration. The only appeal is to the fittingness of the interpretation in the unique case itself, and whether in that case it opens the possibility to further inferences or accurate predictions.

When we interpret a horoscope, it is always a new one-off situation, completely unique and individual. We never study averaged populations, just as we never meet average people. The remarkable thing about our astrology, therefore, is that we also expect the next one-off and completely individual horoscope that we study to answer to the canons of interpretation of astrology – which mysteriously they generally turn out to do. Yet those canons have been shown over and over again to have no relevance whatsoever for large-number populations of cases.

UNIQUE AFTER THE EVENT

It is frequently brought against astrologers as a criticism that they don't see anything before the event, but afterwards they can give all sorts of clever reasons in symbolism as to why something should have happened. Instead of shying away from this or trying to deny it, it is much better to recognise that this reflects an essential characteristic of the unique case interpretation, in that interpretation only arises *after* that which we wish to interpret. This will often be experienced by astrologers who set out to interpret character and destiny for the horoscope of a baby. This can be one of the most boring exercises in all astrology, simply because there is nothing there to interpret. There is a flat and necessarily speculative quality to an interpretation whenever there is no real substance and colour from events, incidents and accidents. The interpretation takes off, however, the moment we pick up a spark of synastry, or see the symbolic fittingness of the fourth house for the parents as we perceive them. It is only in a Machine of Destiny interpretation that we come to routinely imagine that life and character are laid down in advance for the hapless infant. Even if this was so, we may doubt whether the astrologer is going to be given the key to meaningfully interpret it. This observation is not intended to deny a certain role for this category of interpretation, but rather to remind us again that symbolism seizes upon the *given* content of our perception. The best inferences and predictions, the liveliest insights of interpretation, are founded in the symbolism of what we *already* know, and not what we necessarily cannot know.

The proof of the unique case rests in experience, not in logic. The reader who has patiently followed my discussion over the last few pages will appreciate that it is difficult to lay out a completely logical argument in support of the unique case. I have done my best, but my assertions have their fair share of potential ambiguity and tautology. However, and perhaps fortunately, the unique case does not depend on logical demonstration, because it would seem to be a category of perception, or a way in which astrologers tend to look at their material. Once described, most astrologers will recognise the idea immediately, and see that it is an effective description of the phenomena they encounter in practice.

Although everything we do as astrologers is founded in it, the concept of the unique case easily slips out of our grasp. One reason for this is its ambiguous status in a reality which is conventionally divided between subject and object. The unique case is not easy to justify as a part of 'objective reality' – and if it *is* part of objective reality, astrology's critics will say, then it must show in large populations and really be a collective multiple case of significance.

The concept of the unique case is a starting point for exploring astrology as divination, but we cannot stop there. If astrology is not founded in objective-empirical factors observed in large populations, then *what* is it founded in? And what sort of truth is it that we discover in each unique case of interpretation? It is to these questions that I will now turn.

NOTES

1 Maurice Merleau-Ponty, *The Primacy of Perception & Other Essays*, ed. J.Edie (Northwestern University Press, Ill., 1964), p.159.

2 'Instructional science': this useful definition comes from the work of E.F.Schumacher, *A Guide for the Perplexed* (Cape, 1977). It is contrasted with descriptive science. Dr Michael Shallis has pointed out the importance of this distinction for astrological research: see his discussion in 'Science & Astrology' I, *Astrology Quarterly*, vol. 58, no.3 p.120. Also, a fuller discussion in his book *On Time* (Burnett Books, 1982), ch.7 pp.137-8.

3 Maggie Hyde, *Jung and Astrology* (Aquarian, London, 1992), p.165.

4 Dane Rudhyar, *In Search* (Astrological Center, New York, Fall 1961), p.135.

5 Dane Rudhyar, *The Astrology of Personality* (1936, reprinted Doubleday, New York, 1970), p.439 (1970 edition).

6 D.Rudhyar, *In Search*, op.cit, p.135.

7 Geoffrey Dean, *Recent Advances in Natal Astrology* (Analogic, 1977; distributed by Para Research Inc., Rockport, Mass.), Introduction, p.2.

8 Gauquelin 'plus zones' are four areas of the diurnal circle broadly around the four angles, but centred distinctly in the cadent houses 12,9,6,3. Thus the rising 'plus zone' corresponds to the 12th house and the third of the 1st house closest to the ascendant. The peak of significance for Gauquelin is not right *on* the angles, but well back behind them.

9 Dennis Elwell, *Cosmic Loom* (Unwin/Hyman, 1987; revised edition Urania Trust, 1999) ch.4.

10 George Mikes, *Arthur Koestler: The Story of a Friendship* (André Deutsch, 1983), p79.

11 Charles Carter, *Encyclopaedia of Psychological Astrology* (Theosophical Publishing House, 1970), p.172.

12 G.Mikes, op.cit., p79.

13 ibid., p.77.

14 Converse secondaries are fully consistent: the MC opposes natal Saturn, which is at the same time trined by converse Sun. This emphasis on a dignified Saturn as lord of the ascendant

suggests Koestler reaching his terminus in his own good time. He took responsibility for the opposition with the lord of death, when he realised that 'his number was up'. It is also worth mention that converse Mercury closed on to natal Pluto – the perfect conjunction measuring to within three weeks of the exact date, 1 March 1983. Hermes fulfils his ancient role as guide to the dead.

15 Iain Hamilton, *Koestler – A Biography* (Secker & Warburg, 1982), p29-30.

16 D.Elwell op.cit., p.79 (revised edn p.110). The undeniable nature of the symbolism at work in Koestler's horoscope is well brought out by Elwell, but he is at the same time put into an inconsistent position because of statements he elsewhere makes concerning the New York Suicide Study. In the first edition of *Cosmic Loom*, in discussing the 'cosmic vocabulary' (p.13), he states: 'a number of important biographical indices fall outside the scope of our contract with the heavens altogether, and many people will rejoice that suicide is one of them'. This uncomfortable statement has been dropped from the revised edition (p.12), and the discussion on the weaknesses of statistical analysis has been amplified, but in my view the argument is not successfully sustained. He suggests quite reasonably on the basis of psychological and sociological research that suicide is not a homogenous category, but follows with the *non sequitur* that 'given the generality of the act, any astrological tendency would show up only in a much larger sample'. This stretches our credulity in the face of the meticulous 300-case New York study, given the enormous range of astrological indicators tested. Even if each subject is a potential suicide under extreme conditions, it would nevertheless be perverse to deny that certain personality-types or character-traits have more of a disposition to self-destruction, and therefore feature somewhat more than chance expectation in any large sample of suicides. Elwell undermines his own astrology if he argues that there is *no* astrological indicator for those types and traits. The Koestler case is a perfect instance of the only answer a horoscopic astrologer can give – the case that belongs to the individual alone, the 'unique case of interpretation'. The problematic exposed in the suicide issue, recurring throughout Elwell's work, is the split between abstracted speculative theory and practical symbolic interpretation and prediction. He is one of the finest astrologers of our generation when it comes to concrete symbolism, yet his cosmological and philosophical theory is incapable of justifying his actual results. This is not however a special reflection on Dennis Elwell – it emerges more explicitly in his work because he has made a genuine attempt at an overall theory. As I have sought to show, the dilemma on which Elwell's approach founders goes to the heart of our astrological tradition, and must be faced by each of us in our practice. For further discussion of this theme, see my review of *Cosmic Loom*: 'Coming Apart at the Seams' Company of Astrologers Bulletin no.2 June 1988.

11

Appearances: The Symbol in Context

MOST disciplines develop a set of descriptive categories above the how-to-do-it level of practical instruction, but in this respect astrology does not compare at all well. Despite its vast quantities of interpretive text, its *theory* is little discussed and usually taken for granted. What a symbol means is one thing (interpretation); how it comes to mean what it means is quite another (theory). One of my concerns has been to question the taken-for-granted bits of astrology's theory by showing their inadequacy to describe the phenomena we experience. This recognition pushes us into the struggle for more adequate theory, to better comprehend the extraordinary thing that we astrologers do.

With this end in view, it is appropriate to introduce the concept of 'takes', which has proved especially fruitful in the treatment of astrology as divination. This concept also permits a more exact description of the unique case nature of astrological interpretation, and thus follows directly on from the concerns of the previous chapter.

We lead into this material through the 'signature'. Occult philosophy has always understood this term to refer to the manifest sign or declaration of an occult reality: 'meaning is the revelation of secrets through the sign' (Raymond Lull).[1] It is also understood as the way anything – a flower, a herb, a human being – may express its essential nature by an outwardly manifest sign or appearance. In a similar way we 'sign' ourselves – and a written signature on cheques and letters is a definitive token or identifier for the person.

At first glance using the term 'signature' in astrology amounts to little more than the conventional position that a horoscope declares its subject matter. The most characteristic case of astrology is of course that of the birth horoscope, which is understood to be a signature for the life and destiny of the native. Yet naming it as signature nudges us one step beyond the conventional position because the connection between the horoscope and its supposed subject has to be made *explicit*, and cannot be just taken for granted.

We need to be explicit about the connection when a horoscope is taken beyond the conventional expectation of our astrological tradition. So I have used the word signature to describe the chart used in the 1975 *Humanist* attack on astrology, and in Chapter 2 I have declared this to be an 'anti-astrology *signature*'. There I attempt to demonstrate through ordinary horoscopic methods that this apparently randomly derived moment from 1907 *signifies* the 1975 attack. But this is only one level of the signature. I have further suggested that this horoscope has the power of signifying the wider historical issues of the astrology/anti-astrology debate, and it is this that allows the title I have given it. The connection between this horoscope and the natal chart of Pico is a testimony to such a signification.

The idea of the signature leads us back to the question of the origin of significance. *Every signature must have been assigned its significance.* It is not enough to declare that God has assigned all these signatures, since it is the first step in magic to know that this god is also part of our conscious and unconscious motivation. Our mode of perceiving grants significance to the signature, which takes on a reality that is both objective and subjective at the same time. Science requires the object; symbol requires subject and object together.

Exploring the concept of the signature in astrology has led me to suggest the idea of 'assigned time', pointing to the way in which we *assign* a certain time as having significance. The notion of signature therefore allows us to step outside the Ptolemaic concept of significance as that which is given wholly objectively at the moment of origin, as if by Nature.

It is a rule of natal astrology that, without reserve, significance is assigned to the horoscope of birth. Because there are no ifs and buts to this assignation it becomes routine, and its routine taken-for-granted nature lulls us into continual forgetfulness about the boldness and uncertainty of the astrological project. However, when an astrological signature is derived away from its conventional location, as with the anti-astrology signature, then the non-routine nature of this act allows the essential creativity of *all* astrological interpretation to stand out.

Although the idea of the signature can move us towards assignation, and bring in the creative role of the astrologer, nevertheless as soon as it is well-established a signature tends to take on an objective, pre-ordained or pre-given appearance. The more successful the interpretation, the more indisputably the signature is established beyond any particular astrologer's subjective perception, then the more completely will the horoscope carry this objective status.

In order to hold onto the creative dimension of the signature, and from this to tease out the creativity of all interpretation, the further concept of 'takes' is helpful. What is the idea of takes? This is a term used in the film industry – one takes a shot of something, and one can take it again a second time, in a different way. By naming a fundamental procedure of all astrological interpretation as a take, our attention is brought fully to bear on the question of the participation of the astrologer in the creation of astrological meaning. The take also suggests the mis-take, where a creative attempt simply does not hold. When this happens, neither life nor symbolism can sustain the interpretation.

So to interpret the horoscope given in the *Humanist* attack as also signifying that attack is one take, while interpreting it for the whole question of astrology/anti-astrology is a further and more ambitious take. Both of these use camera angles which are never employed when Ptolemy directs the movie. Necessarily to talk of one take suggests that there may be or could be one or more re-takes on the same horoscope, but for convenience we might as well call them all, simply, 'takes', except where we need to especially emphasise the multiplicity of interpretations.

Some further examples of takes will help our discussion. A well known example that set something of a pattern was provided by Maggie Hyde, working with the natal horoscope of the actor Jack Nicholson. This was convincingly demonstrated as being a signature for the *story and main characters* of a major film in which Nicholson starred, *One Flew Over the Cuckoo's Nest*. Actors are a rich source of takes, and their horoscopes will often be found to yield distinct symbolism for characters that they play. This particular type of take has been frequently demonstrated, as for example Vernon Wells's treatment of the horoscope of the actor Christopher Reeves, re-taken as signifying the character and life-story of his most famous part, Superman.[2]

I will give another example that comes closer to conventional views of astrological interpretation. The horoscope of Karl Marx can be plausibly re-taken to show the whole political and philosophical movement to which he has lent his name. Anyone who observed the transit of Pluto opposite the solar eclipse in Taurus in the 2nd house of his chart (*Das Kapital*), coincident with the collapse of East European Communism, could hardly fail to be impressed by this possibility.[3] Now this particular take doesn't seem so far from a more orthodox move in astrology which sees a system of thought as derived from the natal horoscope of the originator. This way of deriving a symbol can be squeezed into the conventions of the causal seed-moment, with Marx's own birth as the 'birth of Marxism'. However, there is a crucial difference in the two ways of approach to this issue. The conventional view allows us to interpret the symbolism of Marxism as a secondary derivation from the primary meaning of the horoscope, which is taken to be the life and destiny of Karl Marx. However, the re-take approach insists on seeing another subject – Marxism – as having a *primary* signification in the same horoscope. It is Marxism, not Marx, that is indicated in the Pluto transits of 1989.

The actual method involved in a creative re-take will not strike more imaginative astrologers as far removed from their own explorations of symbols. Yet I would suggest that until recently the idea of the take has not been recognised for what it is, and its implications and possibilities have been limited, simply by virtue of its uncomfortable fit with our established theory. This renders re-takes as little more than curiosities, marginal to the main practice of astrology. I am suggesting here that far from being marginal, the concept of takes reveals the essential characteristic of *all* horoscope interpretation.

The first definitive exposition of the nature of takes from a theoretical point of view was made by Gordon Watson in an illuminating article published in *Astrology Quarterly* in 1983. In this he sets out the development of the idea from the original impetus of the anti-astrology signature, and gives four categories which define the parameters of the take. These are:

(i)   *The nature of astrological symbols.* They must support the interpretation and there must be a genuine fittingness of symbolism to subject.

(ii) *The subject matter.* This limits the scope of an astrologer's personal or fanciful associations to the material. In natal astrology we have the native's actual biography, and this has to be followed. In re-takes, not just any combination of subject-matter and symbol will do:

Christopher Reeves plays Superman, not the Lone Ranger or Skywalker.

(iii) *The meaningful context* in which the chart arises. This *frames* the interpretation:

When an astrologer puts forward an interpretation of a chart, that understanding is not neutral or objective because the astrologer's participation is a significant element of the context in which the chart is interpreted.

(iv) *The astrologer's creative imagination.* A take is based on the first three considerations, yet

a creative interpretation forever goes beyond the astrological tradition, subject matter and context relevant to the chart. There is always 'something else' that seems to be created, that cannot be reduced to the elements that have gone to make up the interpretation.

Like most items in any theory of astrology, takes have to jump across the ubiquitous subject-object divide. The first two of the above four categories – the shared conventions of symbolism, and the actual subject matter – strike us as relatively objective, while the latter two – context and creative imagination – are more subjective. Once a take becomes convincing and established – in effect, once it becomes perceived as a signature – then our attention is drawn towards the *objective* appearance of a subject matter matched by appropriate symbols. It is easy then to forget the *subjective* component, representing the participation of the astrologer. Creativity becomes an add-on, as if the 'facts' of astrology somehow exist without that creativity. The concept of the take acknowledges the objective matching of symbolism to subject but at the same time it unambiguously draws our attention back to the making of meaning by the astrologer.

Gordon Watson's analysis establishes interpretation as *creative production*, as opposed to a mechanical discovery of some pre-supposed objective significance. The answers we receive from astrology are determined by the questions we put, and the questions we put are in turned framed in the meaningful context in which the questioning through astrology has been undertaken.

We have arrived at the crucial idea of *context* in astrological interpretation. With this in place, we can describe with greater confidence the exact character of the 'unique case' introduced in the previous chapter. The unique case is not a subset of some other generalised presupposed meaning occurring all the time. It is a quite unique combination of circumstances, integrating symbol and subject matter together with the context which gives the interpretation its meaning. This union occurs in the mysterious fourth term, the alembic of the imagination of the astrologer. Once the truth-speaking take has been made, it is capable of moving the understanding of everyone involved, and proves or makes tangible the tradition in which the various symbols have been assigned their meaning as 'this' rather than 'that'.

We encounter here the issue of levels of experience and understanding in astrology. Context and participation are not difficult ideas to understand in a generalised theoretical way – but *they are always forgotten* the moment we do actually 'see' symbolism and establish successful interpretations. This forgetting is not a matter of stupidity or ignorance. It is part of the essential character of objectifying consciousness as it moves to grasp its object. This poses a singular problem in the teaching of astrology, because until one has 'seen' the working of astrology in a full and indisputably objective sense, all talk of the subjective component introduces confusion and threatens to undermine the act of faith that is required to see in the first place. The re-take, which so explicitly points towards creativity and the context of interpretation, cannot be introduced before the student has successfully made the first take, and secured astrological truth as a fact of what we determine to be objective reality.

SELF-REFERENCING

The concept of the take allows us a way of approach to what is one of the most unsettling and challenging experiences in astrology, that of 'self-referencing'. The recognition of this phenomenon is a significant landmark in any astrologer's quest. Perhaps more than any other single factor it signposts the path to the understanding of astrology as divination. However, it can only be genuinely appreciated when an astrologer has matured in his or her craft, otherwise it is simply not effectively realised except as a speculative and theoretical possibility. Broadly speaking it describes the potential for astrological symbolism to refer not only to the subject-matter to which it is assigned, according to the ordinary conventions of practice, but also explicitly to the circumstances in which the astrologer has taken up the interpetation. This may be extended to the possibility of reference to some other concern that the astrologer has in mind. As with the various examples of the take already described, the astrological symbols cross over the conventional boundaries that we set for them, but in this case the symbol loops back and the re-take points directly to ourselves or to the immediate subjective context of the interpretation. In effect we become the subject of a horoscope that we set out to interpret for something other than ourselves.

In a muted and generalised form this phenomenon is well known to modern astrology under the title of 'affinity effect', where for example consultant astrologers find that they attract several clients in a row with similar problems or configurations, and in turn this is found to resonate with some problem of the astrologer and to be reflected in the symbolism of the astrologer's own natal horoscope.[4]

It should be noted that the horary and decumbiture traditions have always been alert to the astrologer's implication by signifying the astrologer's action directly in the horoscope. This is the symbolic origin of the important stricture of Saturn in the 7th in a horary. In such a figure the greatest discretion is required if the astrologer, despite all good intentions, is not to hinder the good fortune of the client. The greatest discretion of all is simply to fulfil the signification completely and beneficially by denying the client an interpretation. It is characteristic of the deep divide in attitudes between the main branches of practice that modern natal astrology has nothing in its methods to match this process of self-referential consideration we find in horary and the katarche.

APPEARANCES

I will now describe a delightful occurrence which lends itself well to demonstrating the dependence of the take on context and subjective participation. It is in that fascinating category of astrological event, 'of things suddenly happening', where there is no other horoscope to refer to other than that of the event itself.[5] This involves us in horoscopes of omens, funny coincidences, and other spontaneous phenomena about which superstitious people – or people with the symbolic attitude – ask: 'What does this mean?' Frequently these horoscopes are simply not radical and do not add anything to the incidents for which they have been cast. However, when they do choose to play, they can give remarkable signatures and insights. Even more obviously than with horary, this class of horoscope stands free of roots in some prior causal-temporal origin, simply because it shows a situation that has come out of the blue and generally has meaning only in the immediate circumstances of its occurrence.

Here is the story. The event occurred when I was a tutor on a weekend retreat organised by Central Wandsworth Adult Education Institute in the 1970's. These weekends gathered mature students of Buddhism, mythology, dreams, parapsychology, astrology, the I Ching, and several other uncommon subjects. Many profound insights, illuminating synchronicities and stimulating occurrences happened on these weekends, and some remarkable pieces of astrology emerged over the years. The current example is quite typical. The theme on this particular weekend was 'Appearances' – questioning the nature of reality and illusion. As always, the inceptional horoscope of the weekend was cast, but only *after* the theme had been chosen. There was only one obviously significant symbolism in play. The Moon was translating light by sextile between a close Sun-Mercury conjunction. No special interpretation of this was made before the event, and it was assumed that – as often happened – the symbolism would reveal itself in due course.

A feature of these weekends was that the whole of Saturday afternoon after lunch was left free for walks by the sea or in the old cinque port of Rye. The group split into two main parties and went on different walks. Now it so happened that both groups independently saw something that struck them as significant. Given the theme of our weekend, various members of both groups recognised their respective events as an appearance for us all. One group, the party I was with, saw a *dead sheep* on the rocks by the seashore. It had been washed clean by the sea, and one of its eyes was open, gazing at us as if it was ready to come to life. The cause of death was not apparent, but by the way the

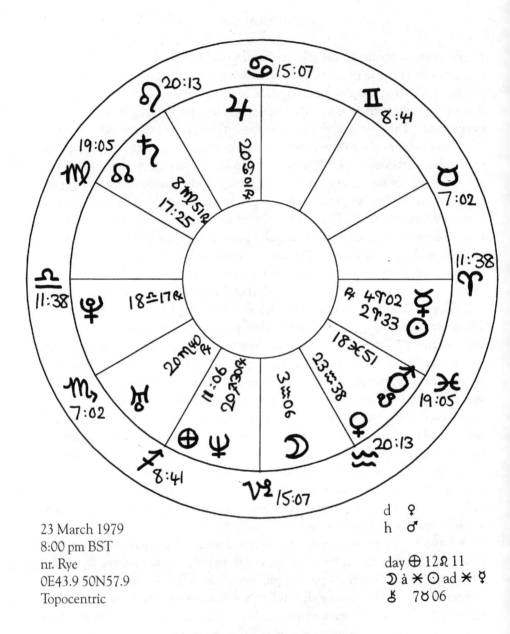

23 March 1979
8:00 pm BST
nr. Rye
0E43.9 50N57.9
Topocentric

d   ♀
h   ♂

day ⊕ 12♌11
☽ à ✶ ☉ ad ✶ ☿
⚷   7♉06

Figure 15 Commencement of a weekend course

sheep was jammed in the rocks, there was a possibility that it had got itself caught and then drowned. However it may have died, this is how it 'appeared' to us, in the manner of a sea-death.

We timed this as about 3:10 pm. When we got back to the house at teatime the other group reported that they too had seen something remarkable. Driving along the sea road, they had seen a *flamingo* perched motionless in a marshy field. It was an unexpected sight for them in an English country setting. The bird was large and deep pink, and very beautiful, with a striking mythical quality and a sense of stillness. Everyone in the party felt it was a significant sighting, that it was meaningful for them. The group timed their appearance at 3:17 pm.

For everyone involved, the coincidence of these two separate appearances had a marked and completely undeniable quality of synchronicity – a 'meaningful a-causal coincidence in time'. It led to an excited stir of conversation as various people compared their stories. Both groups had experienced events which their respective members felt to be significant, and the two incidents had occurred within minutes.

The astrological correspondence is just as intriguing as the actual fact of these events, and brings them into an extraordinary focus. Both appearances had occurred within twelve minutes of the precise conjunction of Mercury and the Sun at 3:06 pm. Several of the astrologers were aware of the time of that conjunction, but taken by itself it is not an especially notable configuration, and I do not remember any great interest being declared in it before the event. Certainly I had not given it much attention, since my main focus was the original symbolism of the weekend inception chart. Neither I nor anyone else in my party realised the close coincidence of our sightings with the astrological occurrence until it was later pointed out to us. In other words, there was no sense of arming ourselves with time-pieces and hunting down events simply to match, and we had not consciously set up the moment to be 'significant'.

At this point I decided to compute a horoscope for the exact Mercury-Sun conjunction, and discovered that this fell on the 9th house cusp. The nominal time of the conjunction was given as 3:06 pm, but by taking this as a starting point and working down to the minute of arc level of accuracy, which is a few seconds span of time, it was possible to produce a figure with the Mercury Sun conjunction on the 9th cusp, partile (exact)!

So what does all this *mean*? We already had our appearances in reality and now we had the horoscope for those appearances as well. The astrologers were quite excited by the horoscope. It is highly radical. The 9th house, apart from signifying astrology itself, indicates higher meaning, prophecy and prophetic dreams, angelic visions and UFOs. If the appearances we had seen were true omens, they might well be indicated by the 9th. The Sun, lord of the ascendant, should also represent that which is being announced. Look at its power, exalted in Aries and at the heart of the appearance, on the 9th cusp. However, it is Mercury who does the announcing and guides us to that truth. The appearance was presaged at the inception of the weekend, in the Moon's movement by aspect between the Sun and Mercury; now the appearance has become reality.

The way the sign is shown in objective reality is revealed in the symbolism. The dead sheep was immediately striking. The Sun-Mercury conjunction is made in Aries on the 9th. How does the appearance appear? Mars, emphasised by the line of the Nodes, is lord of the 9th and holds the conjunction in his sign, Aries. Aries the Ram, ruled by Mars in Water (Pisces) in the 8th house of death: *the dead sheep*. Mars also applies square to watery Neptune, lord of the 8th and god of the sea.[6]

The flamingo was slightly less obvious. It was pink, so this could also be the Mars, although I was not convinced by this possibility. After much discussion the consensus was that the flamingo was like the setting Venus because of its beauty and tranquillity, and because Venus is in an air sign. The flamingo in turn suggests the phoenix, an image of *rebirth*. Although we were three weeks short of Easter Day, this time of year, with the Sun just past the spring equinox, carries something of the Easter symbolism. This suggests that the dead sheep is also the sacrificial lamb (Mars in Pisces square Neptune).

I have since shown this horoscope blind on several occasions, including once to a large conference. With a minimum of prompting to concentrate attention on the 9th house, it is usually easy to get astrologers to guess correctly what might appear at such a moment. Someone will quickly seize upon the dead ram image. When one then asks, 'What sort of death?', death by water is the obvious answer. There is no doubt at all about the public and objective nature of the radicality of the symbolism for this first of the two appearances. The second appearance can hardly be guessed blind, but in context its fittingness with the general symbolism of the horoscope becomes apparent.

There remains a question mark about what all this means. Exhilirating though it was, there was a big 'so what' about the whole dead sheep and flamingo incident, as our Buddhist friends were quick to point out. It is not uncommon for unbidden omens and synchronicities to start off fizzing like sparklers and end up going nowhere. We should not mistake the initial recognition of symbolic signifi-cance for truth-speaking, by which I mean astrology's goal in effective and moving interpretation. Like the retrograde of Mercury, none of us at the time pulled through an understanding of why a symbolism of sacrifice and rebirth might be some sort of resolution to our collective question concerning the nature of 'Appearances'. The incident and its symbolism remained like a puzzling gift.[7]

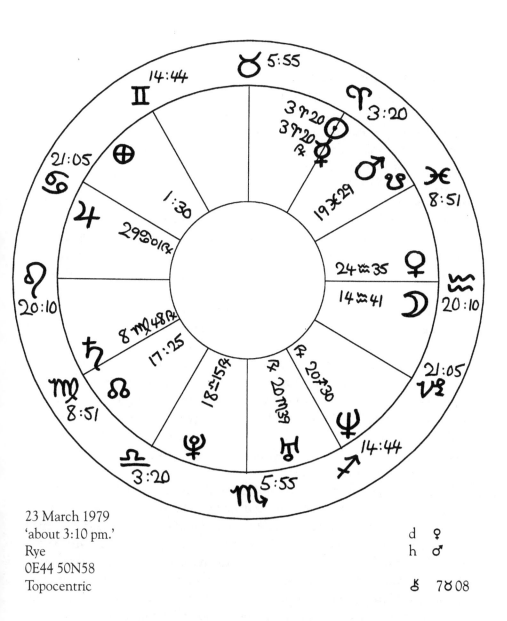

23 March 1979
'about 3:10 pm.'
Rye
0E44 50N58
Topocentric

d ♀
h ♂

⚷ 7♉08

Figure 16 Dead sheep and flamingo

This chart is for ☿ ☉ on the IXth cusp: 3:05:39 pm GMT.

CONTEXT AND APPEARANCES

Despite its tantalising lack of resolution, this story illuminates the questions of context and the participation of the astrologer. I will stay with the more obvious symbolism of the dead sheep for this purpose. We only have to take one step back from the situation to see what an extraordinary thing it is to say that in a horoscope for this part of southern England at a little after three on a Saturday afternoon, Mars signifies a dead sheep. A myriad unaccounted and unaccountable things are happening in the surrounding region at this time. Birds are flying, babies are being made and born, people are watching TV, somewhere in Rye rubbish is being put out, someone else is setting light to a chip pan. But of all those innumerable things whose signification hasn't been taken up, there is just one that has been taken up: we have discovered that Mars signifies *this* thing, a particular dead sheep on a beach. Or rather, Mars signifies a dead sheep *insofar as a group of people seeing the sheep have taken it as significant*. The sheep was there for hours before and no doubt hours after, if not days, but of all possible moments it is only the moment of *our* discovery that becomes significant. The same is true for the flamingo; out of its life story it has taken this moment to give it an astrological signification.

Further, both sheep and flamingo have been taken as significant in the unusual context of an intense residential weekend dedicated to the theme of 'Appearances'. If it had been a weekend course on 'Starting a Small Business' then *nobody* would have been moved apart from the minor curiosity of flamingoes in Sussex, or the problems farmers must have with wandering livestock. How could anybody but a group of diviners and Buddhists actually think these sightings might 'mean something'?

In this example, astrological symbolism is discovered 'objectively' in literal things in the world – the sheep and the flamingo. The astrology really does work. Looked at from a purely external point of view the whole event might be termed a paranormal occurrence, a possible manifestation of psi; but the point should not be lost that this is *context-psi*. Significance in the situation finally *depends* on the context which frames the discovery – and that is the conscious concern and intentions of the group of people who make the discovery, including the astrologers who will want to make a horoscope for it. This brings us back to what we have already established as the divinatory logic of *participatory significance* discussed in Chapter 7. It is this participation that is the foundation of takes.

THE LIGHT OF ASTROLOGY

In his book *Culpeper's Medicine*, Graeme Tobyn describes an astrological coincidence which demonstrates the potential of symbolism once we unbind its self-referential genius. It is in a more apparently extreme category of interpretation compared with the examples already discussed in this chapter, for any notion of a causal or temporal connection of the astrological signification with that which it signifies is here forced to breaking-point, unless we strain what we understand by such connections beyond the limit of coherent expression.

Tobyn happened to be working on a horoscope published at the end of Nicholas Culpeper's *English Physitian*, in preparation for presentation at a conference on astrology and medicine. The figure was sent to Culpeper by a young man, a student 'both in physick and astrology', concerning a lady taken sick, and wondering whether she was naturally ill or 'under an ill tongue' – ie bewitched. The approach adopted by both the student and by Culpeper strictly speaking places this case in the category of medical horary rather than that of decumbiture; the student has cast the figure on receipt of the question from the lady, since concerning the onset of disease 'the certain day and hour she is not able to nominate'. However, Culpeper employs the same approach to differential diagnosis as he would in a decumbiture. He locates the source of illness as hot and dry distemper of the womb. He also observes the strong possibility of pregnancy, 'there being a most forcible reception betweeen the Moon and Venus from fruitful signs...the Moon being in the fifth house' (Moon in Pisces applying trine Venus, ruler of the ascendant, in Cancer). He does not give a decisive conclusion on the issue of pregnancy; however, Tobyn's analysis of the treatment recommended shows that Culpeper is guarding against miscarriage. Although we do not know the outcome for the lady concerned, the figure does indeed indicate pregnancy.

At a family lunch in the month before the conference at which this case was due to be presented, Graeme Tobyn's wife peeled an orange and revealed a perfect smaller orange inside; his sister promptly declared this to be a symbol of fertility. It so happened that the wife's period was by then delayed, and she felt off-colour. In the following week her concern led to a pregnancy test, but this proved negative. However, the sickness continued, and Tobyn considered casting a decumbiture. Then the realisation arose:

> It suddenly dawned on me that the divination was already in front of my eyes in the 1651 horoscope I was working on. I decided to compare the decumbiture from Culpeper with

my wife's natal chart: Mars in Scorpio was *exactly to the minute* conjunct her 5th house and fertile Jupiter; Venus in Cancer was conjunct her ascendant (orb 30') and the nodes were conjunct but reversed (orb 30'). Such startling synastry between major significators persuaded me that both women were pregnant![8]

And so it turned out for his wife. There were hitches on the way which seem to have been presaged in the Culpeper figure. A notable feature was the needless anxiety and humiliating pressure of her local doctor and the obstetricians who tried to frighten the mother into a hospital birth with tales of haemorrhaging and possible death – 'under an ill tongue' – but Culpeper had already forecast that there were no life-threatening dangers to concern us here. Like the perfect little orange all came out well with a 'smooth birth at home without drugs or stitches... when the Sun was transiting the ascendant of the 1651 decumbiture'. To underscore the genuine radicality of this manifestation across 337 years, baby Lydia's natal ascendant falls on the Part of Fortune of the original horoscope. The solar symbolism of the orange, the little sun born on the 1651 ascendant, is spell-binding. As Graeme Tobyn observes, this case 'reveals... something of the nature of astrology itself'. It is an instance of symbolic depth and grace, and from it shines the light of astrology.

Earlier, in discussing the katarche, I observed that the choice of the moment for which the horoscope is cast depends on the context and on the decision – the take – of the astrologer, and there is no fixed rule pre-established outside the actual situation that can guide us. Going back to Culpeper's original material, we observe that the student takes for his figure the time the question is put to him, since the woman is unable to remember the day and hour of falling sick, which would allow a decumbiture. There seems little doubt that had the nominal decumbiture moment been available this would have been given precedence, yet that does not make the moment chosen a poor second best, for this becomes of necessity the moment that will – or will not – show. Culpeper has no need of a further moment, such as his own receipt of the student's letter, since he has sufficient authority from the horoscope presented to him by the student. From a phenomenological perspective the astrologers respond to the symbol *as presented*, and not primarily through a consideration of what ought to show according to some abstracted explanatory theory of astrological influences. Here is the hallmark of divination, and not of science. The test is our momentary realisation and fitting response in the face of the presentation of the symbol to consciousness. Graeme Tobyn's judgment on his wife's pregnancy captures the unpredictable nature of the unbidden omen which comes as gift and is caught on the wing; it brings out the significance of context, implicating the astrologer and

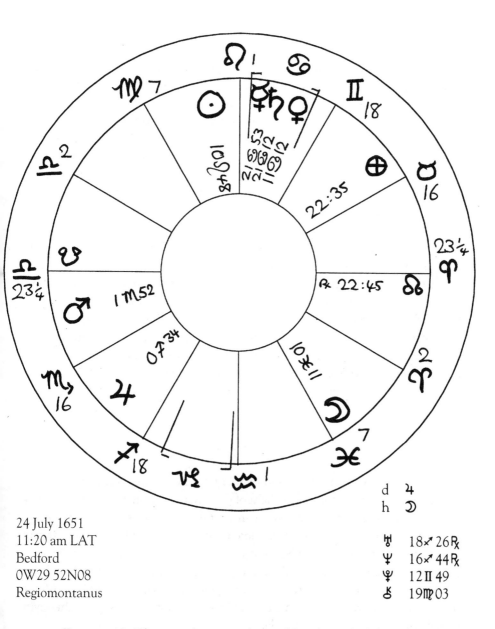

24 July 1651
11:20 am LAT
Bedford
0W29 52N08
Regiomontanus

FIGURE 17 'Physic without astrology is like a lamp without oil'

Figure from Nicholas Culpeper (based on recomputation by Graeme Tobyn
Culpeper's Medicine fig. 17)

framing the interpretation; and it reveals the moment of creation, for it is in the take that the gift may be given.

So what is the relationship between the move of divination and the conventional canons of horoscopy? A characteristic feature of the re-take is the demand for heightened radicality, demonstrated here in the unusually close and pertinent synastry contacts between the 1651 horoscope and the modern natal figure. Had the contacts not been close and relevant, they simply would not have struck home as significant. A much closer fit is needed to justify a re-take that steps across conventional expectations; and it is not enough to simply have strikingly close contacts – the symbolism involved must, as in this case, 'make sense' and be sustained in the re-take. And by 'making sense', we mean it requires to be *interpreted*, authentically and convincingly, for without the interpretation, the take, there is strictly nothing there.

It is likely that by this point some readers will be entirely bemused, because accepting Graeme Tobyn's re-take as a true showing of astrology appears to make a nonsense of any framework of guidelines or rules. It could look close to advocating 'anything goes'. But a little reflection shows that this and the other cases I have discussed are far from allowing any and every horoscope to be read for anything-we-fancy. We catch glimpses of an ordering, a *logos*, in divination, and astrology-as-divination seems to have unique status as a manifestation of that ordering; but to secure the first steps into this obscure terrain requires a conceptual move that at key points runs counter to our usual way of describing astrology. We are at such a critical juncture here.

LAND ZODIACS

Both the dead sheep and flamingo incident, and Graeme Tobyn's rereading of Culpeper's 1651 horoscope in the light of the omen of the little orange, bring into view the context-specific nature of interpretation, and show the subjective dimension of our takes even where there is an undeniably objective and worldly manifestation of symbolism. There is no doubt that the move through the issue of context to the question of subjective participation in the symbol is deeply uncomfortable. For many astrologers, giving up the olympian authority of pure objectivity conferred by the classical model of astrology leaves us, as the saying goes, between a rock and a hard place.

I would like to illustrate something of the dilemma we are in through a brief digression into the issues raised by the land zodiacs.[9] The Glastonbury Zodiac, and the more recently discovered Kingston Zodiac, reveal in microcosm questions about the symbolic attitude and the participatory dimension which lie just beneath the surface of all astrology.

The Glastonbury Zodiac, discovered by Katherine Maltwood in 1925 and researched and refined over many years by Mary Caine, consists of zodiacal 'giants' or figures in a 10-mile-diameter circle around the West Country town of Glastonbury. These figures are traceable in the features of hills, streams, roads and paths, and there are some striking coincidences of human artefacts, place names and local legends which match the pattern. Katherine Maltwood believed that this was the original Round Table of Arthur, and the whole constitutes a gigantic 'Temple of the Stars', a spiritual site of great significance for the British Isles.

The general opinion amongst proponents of the Land Zodiacs is that these are geographical formations produced by nature in accord with spiritual forces, creating a geomantic mirror of the constellations, especially those of the zodiac. The mystery was recognised by early inhabitants and worked into their religion and mythology, and it was carried and transmuted into Celtic Christianity and the Arthurian legend. It is believed that the figures have a capacity to recreate themselves even in modern times, drawing modern people to fulfil the design.

Understandably the authenticity of the figures is far from easy for the modern rational imagination to accept. Doubtless to the amusement of the total sceptic, even some astrologers find the land zodiacs just too much to take. My concern here, however, is not directly the question of their validity. I am interested in the *way* in which they become validated by those who see them, and what this might imply for astrology in general. The figures are on the subject-object threshold of reality, and it is obvious on looking at the maps and photographs that to 'see' them we have to enter the material in a certain way. In a foreword to Mary Caine's text, Geoffrey Ashe remarks:

> If you discuss the figures in a purely objective way, as if they could be proved and accounted for like a prehistoric burial or a Roman villa, you are discussing them wrongly. Those who do not see them do not see them, and should not be argued with, or treated as obstinate or wilfully blind. What matters is the experience of those who do see them – the wide-ranging meditations which they can set in motion, the complex imagery which they can conjure up.[10]

It is the second sight of symbolism that is required to know such things, for they exist in an alternative symbolic world – or a second vision of this world. As to signposts in this world, omens and personal synchronicities will soon steer the understanding and allow discrimination, confirmation and disconfirmation, just as happens in our ordinary astrology.

Ashe's recommendation to get past the 'purely objective' consideration of symbolism highlights what it is that makes the land zodiacs so awkward for most astrologers. This can best be illustrated by the story of John Addey's discovery of yet another terrestrial patterning from the stars: the Cheam Road Zodiac.[11] Addey began to observe a definite order of symbolism at work in the block of houses around his home. Starting with his own home as Cancer, he observed that the next house clockwise was the home of identical twins, and there were two other sets of twins in nearby houses: obviously the Gemini area. Further on there were solid houses with well-kept gardens, including the home of an ear, nose and throat specialist: Taurus. Successive groups of houses yielded an ex-army character for Aries, and an eye-catching fish-pond for Pisces. So it went on, in a complete zodiacal circle of twelve zones with appropriate residents and houses, until he returned to his starting point.

Before announcing this exciting discovery, he decided on a control experiment. What would happen if his own house was treated as being in the *Aries* zone? Now he realised that he had earlier overlooked the fact that next door they were keen wine-makers, and in any case they had a fish-tank: clearly Pisces. The previous Taureans showed up as Aquarian eccentrics given to good causes, and the throat specialist became a leading scientist. The military type turned out to love mountain climbing, so he must really be in the Capricorn zone, not Aries as earlier supposed. And so on, until the original symbolic picture had melted away.

The conclusion we are being invited to make is that neither of these supposed zodiacs is 'really' there. As Charles Harvey comments, in considering land zodiacs

> we cease to be concerned with whether there is or is not an actual zodiac, rather we are using and allowing the rich symbolism of the concept of a zodiac to order our experience.[12]

Charles Harvey is differentiating the process involved in interpreting the celestial zodiac which is really there (= objective), from the interpretation of the terrestrial zodiac which is not really there, but which we imagine (= subjective). We are back to the logic of exclusion (either-or-ness), characteristic of science. This has little to do with the logic of inclusion (and-ness), characteristic of symbolism. This logic of exclusion also treats the subjective realm of imagination in a purely passive and individual role, and does not take on board the possibility that the symbolism of the land zodiacs, like symbolism in general, actively induces and creates experience which can be shared as language between many people.

It is appropriate at this point to make a comparison with other modes of mapping the heavens upon the earth which are more favoured in astrology. The leading form of this mapping is astro-cartography.[13] It is easy to see why this appears to have a quite different symbolic status for the astrologer. Because it is universal and applicable to all times and places, it can be employed for any birth or event. It is therefore a valuable extension to the astrologer's practical technique. But quite apart from this I believe its validity will be *taken for granted* by most astrologers in a way that could never happen with the Glastonbury Zodiac, because it is a natural projection of the movements of the heaven and earth. It can be created as a computer algorithm, at which point any suggestion of a subjective and contextual component in interpretation becomes entirely obliterated.

By contrast, the Glastonbury and Kingston Zodiacs cannot be turned into an algorithm, and the relative and contextual status of their imagery is exposed. They are an uncomfortable reminder, against the objectifying either-or tendency, that the whole of our practical astrology requires a similar act of creativity. Of course there is a vast difference in magnitude between the awesome universal order symbolised by the heavens and the local manifestations of the Glastonbury and Kingston Zodiacs. However, I see no essential difference between the *way* we form meaning in the land zodiacs and the way we form meaning in the rest of our astrology. Pegging our horoscopes to real-time movements of literal planetary bodies, we astrologers easily forget that for astrology to have meaning, our *celestial* zodiac and planets depend on the second-sight of the symbolic, just as much as do the figures of a *terrestrial* zodiac. Perhaps John Addey's inspired Cheam Zodiac has more truth to it than we might care to admit.

NATAL ASTROLOGY AND THE INTERPRETATION OF CONTEXT

The creative and participatory dimension of interpretation is normally implicit, and therefore forgotten. It only becomes an explicit issue in considering the katarche or in some uncommon applications of astrology, such as the examples given earlier, or when the raw nerve of symbolism is exposed as with the land zodiacs. It may also become explicit in cases where the interpretation is taken against the grain of conventional expectation, as when a natal horoscope is re-taken. However, it is in the ordinary practice of natal astrology, for ourselves or with clients, that insights arising from the divinatory approach may turn out to bring the most substantial benefit.

I will first reiterate some remarks that I hope have become clear about context and the natal horoscope. In the previous chapter the horoscopes of Margaret Thatcher and Elizabeth II were brought together in an objective context of comparison of the angular Saturn placings. It was this comparison that dictated the direction of the brief interpretation that I offered. I therefore chose one speculative, but I hope true, line of interpretation out of an indefinite number of possible (and possibly true) interpretations. My choice was dictated by the fact that in terms of conventional craft, these Saturn placings are amongst the most significant in each of the horoscopes taken separately, but there are many other true things that can be said about these horoscopes, and indeed many other lines of comparison.

The same applies to each client and each client's horoscope. We should not imagine when we take up a line of interpretation that it is the bottom line, or the final and best interpretation. Rather, it is the interpretation that we have taken up in the light of a particular question that we are concerned with, in a particular context and at that moment in the client's life. The best and truest interpretation is what the client needs to hear now. The significations of the astrology will then answer to the context, in the truly mysterious way that astrology works. To put it another way, if astrology is psi, and if the psi is context-psi, then we need to comprehend the relevant context of our discussions with the client in order to usefully interpret the symbolism that presents itself to consciousness.

This understanding of context is a liberation of practice from the shadowy bondage of having to know everything, which is the fateful lure of the Machine of Destiny. Even the velvet-coated model of modern psychological astrology has not succeeded in disentangling itself from that lure, such is the enduring momentum of our Ptolemaic tradition.[14] Far from astrology having access to everything, we realise that the astrologer can know almost nothing. If the mystery of divination occurs, what we see in the natal horoscope is the symbolism of a few vital things that concern us. Properly understood, that is more than enough.

Once we put together the interpretation of a context which includes the astrologer making the interpretation with the possibility of a re-take, then we arrive at one of the most important of all revelations from the natal horoscope, but one which is virtually inaccessible to the classical tradition. A significant development in recent astrology has been to follow through the implications of context and self-referencing into natal practice. This opens up the question of what Jung has termed the *secret mutual connivance*, drawing the astrologer into the client's material.[15]

These phenomena are well known in psychoanalysis under the general heading of transference, and we can learn a great deal from the experience of the analysts here. There is, however, a crucial difference in the psychoanalytic and divinatory interpretations of the transference. The analyst is not expected to read an *omen* produced by or around a client, unless it is limited to a psychosomatic or hysterical condition manifesting *in the body, speech or action of the person.* The divinatory interpretation reads transference as *metaphor*. The very word 'transference' is from the Latin, via the Greek word 'metaphor'. For the astrologer, transference crosses the psycho-physical boundary of the client and is read in the metaphor of the heavens.[16]

The following case illustrates something of these themes of transference and self-referencing, applied to the natal consultation.

A BAG OF BONES

I worked for several years with an elderly man, whom I shall call Mr. B. He had already learnt astrology to a basic level of competence. He was fascinated by the subject and an important part of the work for him was the detailed study of his own natal horoscope, including its progressions. I suspect he was using the astrology to put the long vista of his life in perspective, and to get a line on it. As so often happens, at the same time he had become drawn into doing charts for others. We agreed to a programme of regular supervision which, where necessary, would have an element of instruction.

Mr. B had come to the discipline of astrology late in life and he was a slow learner, but I felt he allowed himself to become hindered by technical complications. This seemed expressive of his natal Virgo ascendant, his only Earth, afflicted by the South Node and the square from Saturn. I often became frustrated that he did not seem able to take the step that cuts through all techniques, the step of no return, after which the whole of symbolism comes to life. I was probably asking for fire, which he did not have.

Astrology may also have been playing the role of the feminine for him, like the Moon in the 7th. He had long since left behind the company of women, and had divorced his wife many years before. Now I certainly do not think I was playing out the muse for him, because it soon became clear where I was in the chart – the Saturn. This is conjunct the MC and is the authority in his life. In the particular situation we were in, that meant me, the teacher. This was where everything important came to the crunch between Mr. B and me.[17]

Early in our work it became obvious what a major part this angular Saturn had played in his life. He had always felt under the shadow of his father, a strong-minded man who found his son slow-witted and weak. This is a classic possibility for Saturn on the MC, leading to a sense of failure and non-fulfilment throughout life if not courageously addressed. Saturn dominates the whole chart, especially with a stellium in Aquarius.

The Mars retrograde in Cancer does not help the 10th house. Mr. B had never settled to a fulfilling career and had not managed to reach several academic goals he had set himself. The same pattern of circumstances designed to defeat him was in danger of repeating in his study of astrology. There is, however, much to be done through the trines to Saturn, especially from the Sun, and from the mutual reception with the ascendant ruler Mercury. This latter is weakened by its combustion, which seems to mimic the weakening of the ascendant by the Node. However, if the inherent weakness can be overcome, the configuration of Mercury, ruler of the ascendant and the MC, with Saturn, the planet on the MC, could offer a brilliant possibility of finding the right path in life.

There was a story of Mr. B and his parents that plays out this configuration of Mercury trine and mutual reception Saturn in Gemini, going between the 5th and 10th houses. It was one of the strongest memories of his childhood. The family was quite poor in the early days, so there were few luxuries for the children. When Mr. B was a boy of six or seven, his most heartfelt longing was for a clockwork train. One Christmas morning, he found a small bag at the foot of his bed. Could this be his longed-for little train? He opened the bag – but all it contained were some old bones. His father thought this a fine trick, and his mother also saw the funny side. Mr. B never got his clockwork train, and for the rest of his life, he never forgot being given a bag of bones.

When the astrologer takes up the natal horoscope, then he or she steps into that life-context and takes up a position. It is no surprise, therefore, that as a Saturnine individual in the authoritative role of supervisor, I am a suitable hook for projection and will soon assimilate myself to the role of Saturn, the father, whatever my conscious intentions.

This is all very obvious in retrospect. At the time I preferred to only half-acknowledge it, getting on with this or that discussion of practical interpretation, or Mr. B's latest blockage on some technicality. The true issue became fully apparent to me, however, with the following incident.

Mr. B had set about making a full written horoscope interpretation for a small girl, the daughter of an acquaintance. He had in mind that it would be valuable now for the parents but his text was addressed to the child, for the time when she would be old enough to understand it. The little girl had Saturn in Scorpio prominently placed, and this, as Mr. B had correctly judged, was a focal point of interpretation. This was only one amongst many factors dealt with in an extensive and on the whole quite convincing interpretation. I agreed to study his notes before our next meeting and to go over them with him before he completed

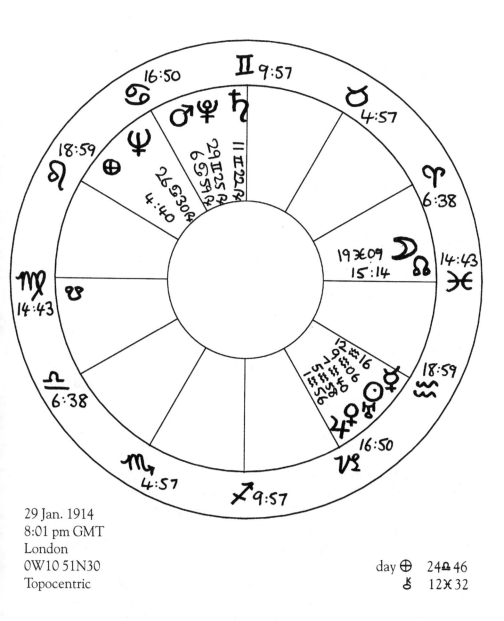

29 Jan. 1914
8:01 pm GMT
London
0W10 51N30
Topocentric

day ⊕ 24♎46
⚷ 12♓32

FIGURE 18 Mr B

it for the client. The papers he gave me were straightforward except for one sheet which was awkwardly folded. I had to unfold this sheet in order to read a short section on a close Moon-Saturn square, including this passage:

> Look upon Saturn as a young middle-aged, circa 45, <u>crusty</u> <u>disciplinarian</u> type of man – but fair and just, kind-hearted too. Saturn is the teacher of the planets and <u>you</u> <u>can't</u> <u>pull</u> <u>the</u> <u>wool</u> over his eyes. <u>Anything</u> <u>badly</u> <u>or</u> <u>slip-shodly</u> <u>done</u> comes back to you with a curt – <u>try</u> <u>again</u>
>
> *[underlining in the original].*

I was at this time in my mid-forties. Mr. B was puzzled when I made a joke about it later. There is no likelihood that he knowingly intended me to take this passage for myself. It is a spontaneous eruption of symbolism.

Let me unfold this a little, just as I unfolded the paper (Saturn in Gemini) in order to read what he had written to me (Mercury trine Saturn). As I take the place of Saturn, Mr. B is like Mercury (ruler of the ascendant) speaking to me. He is evoking the Sun-Saturn trine: 'fair and just, kind-hearted too'. This is how Sun Aquarians generally see themselves, but it is also what he wants me (his father) to be. He is trying to please me, just as he has spent his life trying to please his father – but you can't pull the wool (why wool?) over the eyes of crusty Saturn. Mr. B has to pass the test which allows him to leave behind his father, his old ways, and take his own authority, his own MC. Then he can leave me behind and get on with his astrology (his life) for himself. If at first you don't succeed... but he hasn't succeeded; 'try again' is the curt reply.

In the end, I wonder whether I too had given Mr. B a bag of bones. All my elegant interpretation is no substitute for moving in the world. We are back again to the rarity of effective *resolution* in astrology. I do not think I was able to help Mr. B turn things round, or be of that much help in his studies. One of the reasons for this is that the pact into which we had entered, the conscious intention of our sessions, had been framed to the task of objective astrological technique, rather than to the possibility of self-revealing. As symbolism and the unconscious broke through this frame, the realisation in the situation was confined to me.

Of their nature, the moments of revelation in symbolism come unexpectedly. When they steal upon us, the symbols loom out of the shadows of the context, in details that are particular to the unique situation of the client, as this has been brought to life for the astrologer. For Mr. B, out of all the possible things in the world his Mercury-Saturn configuration *could* be, it showed itself first and most powerfully as the story of the longed-for train and the bag of bones. This story is something more than an illustration; it is a personal symbol encapsulating a dimension of his childhood experience. It is these personal symbols, in all their concrete detail, that are often found to have the most illuminating astrological signification to guide the astrologer. Further, it is in such exact symbolism that we can validate and make real the conventional theoretical take, as when I assume on first contact with the horoscope that this Saturn probably has something to do with the client's father.

The issue of context is even more strikingly revealed where the symbolism directly implicates the astrologer, as in cases of transference or the secret mutual connivance. Out of all the countless ways Mr. B's Mercury-Saturn configuration could have shown itself *between us*, it requires this completely unpredictable turn of the folded note to give me the message about me and Mr. B's father. This incident is something more than an illustration; it is a mutual symbol encapsulating the relationship between Mr. B and me. The whole possibility and meaning of this depends on the context in which both of us might be able to 'take' this up as meaningful. The symbol shows its context, and indeed, it has no meaning outside of its context.

NOTES

1 J.E.Cirlot, *Dictionary of Symbols*: see under 'sign' (Routledge & Kegan Paul 1972).

2 Vernon Wells, 'Takes – Superman' *Astrology Quarterly*, vol.57, no.2, Summer 1983. The same example is quoted by Dennis Elwell in his *Cosmic Loom*, p.110 (1999 edition p139). I have not so far come across instances of this approach to the horoscopes of actors etc prior to the introduction and demonstration of the idea of takes in the late 1970's and early 1980's. Its adoption as a practical possibility of horoscope method marks a subtle erosion of the Ptolemaic and causal-temporal legacy in favour of a more divinatory approach.

3 Karl Marx was born within hours of an eclipse in Taurus (5 May 1818, 2 am LMT, Trier, Germany: Moon 11 Taurus 17, Sun 13 Taurus 56: data from Rodden, *American Book of Charts*). Pluto passed opposite his Moon-Sun conjunction from December 1987 and completed its final pass opposite the Sun just a month before the symbolic disintegration of the Communist bloc with the pulling down of the Berlin Wall (9 November 1989). This two-year period marked the annihilation of Communist authority. The 2nd house Taurus eclipse has often been interpreted as Marx's attitude to capitalism. Significantly, the USSR Sun at 14 Scorpio 00 is closely opposite Marx's eclipse, thus suffering the same destructive transit (data from *Mundane Astrology* by M.Baigent, N.Campion and C.Harvey (Aquarian, London, 1984), p443.

4 Affinity effect: there is a useful discussion in Geoffrey Dean *Recent Advances in Natal Astrology* (Analogic, 1977) pp20-21. However, a measure of Dean's departure from a divinatory understanding is shown by his concluding comment: 'If affinity effects are real then they will require special precautions in research to ensure that they do not influence the results'. Dean doesn't realise that affinity effects are part of the 'results'.

5 See the section in William Lilly, *Christian Astrology* (1659, reprinted Regulus, London, 1985), p.148, which in effect establishes a distinctive subset of the katarche for the interpretation 'Of a thing suddenly happening, Whether it signifieth Good or Evill'.

6 In view of the other showings of Neptune in this text, I have to acknowledge this may be the daemon showing again.

7 This story is also recounted by Michael Shallis, in his *On Time* (Burnett, 1982) see ch.10; he comments on this case as an illustration of the 'powerful meaning inherent in astrological symbolism... like other languages it is both vital and communicable'. The context of my own reworking of the material for this book has itself developed my perception of its meaning, and long after the decision to include it, the symbolism of the Mars-Neptune-Uranus configuration became more suggestive. Although I have no doubt this will now be obvious, I only recently properly realised the closeness of the connection of the ideas of Appearance, Signature and Symbol; this was brought home to me by the fittingness of the Sun-Mercury cazimi on the 9th for what the Christian tradition says about biblical allegory: man signifies meanings by words, but God may signify meanings by things themselves. It is not appropriate here to go further on a re-take of this horoscope, but I trust this illustrates the point that active symbolism remains live and open, and always capable of further meaning in some new context.

8 Graeme Tobyn *Culpeper's Medicine: a practice of western holistic medicine* (1997 Element Books) appendix 2. The case was first published as 'An Omen in the Light of Astrology', Company of Astrologers Bulletin no.4 Summer 1991. See also Maggie Hyde's comments in *Jung and Astrology* (Aquarian, London, 1992), pp 194-5. Tobyn draws attention to a psi-Neptune signification at work in the mother's horoscope. Lydia's birth occurred on 14th October 1988. Introducing the horoscope, Culpeper says: 'To such as study astrology [who are the only men I know that are fit to study physick, physick without astrology being like a lamp without oil], you are the men I exceedingly respect...'

9 Katherine Maltwood, *A Guide to Glastonbury's Temple of the Stars* (James Clarke, London, 1964); Mary Caine *The Glastonbury Zodiac: Key to the Mysteries of Britain* (Grael Communications, Torquay, 1978); also *The Kingston Zodiac* 2nd edition (1978), available from the author (25 Kingston Hill, Kingston-upon-Thames, Surrey).

10 M. Caine, op.cit., p.16. Ashe's criticism of 'pseudo-archaeology' with respect to the Giants is a parallel to my criticism of 'pseudo-science' with respect to astrology as a whole.

11 Unpublished Astrological Association Conference lecture, September 1981. The case is reported and comparisons with land zodiacs discussed by Charles Harvey in *Mundane Astrology*, op.cit., pp307-8. Addey's remarks here appear to contrast with his earlier more enthusiastic (although still qualified) comments: see his Editorial in *Astrological Journal*, Vol IX, no.1, Winter 1966-7.

12 Baigent, Campion and Harvey, op.cit., p308.

13 Astro-cartography, as developed by Jim Lewis, maps for any given moment geographical lines linking all places on the earth's surface where a given planet is either *exactly* on the horizon (rising and setting) or on the meridian. A location on a birth-moment planet line (eg Jupiter rising) is understood to be significant for the individual as an expression of that planet and angle. Locations where two lines cross are especially significant.

14 See, for example, Maggie Hyde, *Jung and Astrology*, op.cit., especially chs. 5 and 6.

15 ibid., especially ch.10.

16 I believe that psychoanalysis can be viewed as a form of secular divination, at which point the taboo realm shared in common by astrology and psychoanalysis comes into light. For further discussion on these themes see my article 'Psychoanalysis, Divination, Astrology' in Company of Astrologers Bulletin no.4 (1991).

17 I should observe that my natal Saturn is within the degree conjunct Mr. B's Mars, which suggests an erotic connection with the father figure. It certainly emphasises the 'hook for projection' theme. The symbolism which emerged between us at that time did not to my mind speak directly of this Mars. Given the events that actually unfolded, I was being prompted to my place in fulfilling the role of his own Saturn on the MC, thereby allowing is his own Mercury-Saturn to speak. My natal Uranus is within two degrees of Mr. B's Saturn, but at the time I took this as a general synastry contact rather than as an exact signature of the situation between us. In practice I find little is gained (and often much clarity is lost) by going further than one degree orb conjunctions and oppositions for this type of high-signature work. In retrospect, however, the Uranus contact has a definite appropriateness to the situation.

12

Images of Birth

Perhaps it was a perverse streak in me right from the beginning, but I have always found the subject of wrong charts intriguing in so far as they throw light on what we do in our interpretations. This is not a popular topic with most astrologers. 'Wrong charts working' was my subject matter the first time I was invited to talk at the Astrological Association many years ago, in the days of its large meetings at the National Liberal Club in Whitehall. It was significant that sharing the evening with me was Chester Kemp. He was demonstrating his rectification of the natal chart of the fictional character Horatio Hornblower, from the novels of C.S.Forester. Chester Kemp's exploration of technical precision in the craft of astrology, together with his demonstrations of the essential playfulness of symbolism, were a primary impetus for the divinatory and hermeneutic astrology discussed in this book. Between us that day we were chipping at the foundations of Ptolemaic orthodoxy.

In my talk I used fairly high technique to demonstrate that in a natal horoscope which was being studied for the native's road accidents, an error of one hour on the daylight saving produced a chart which nevertheless worked exactly and with genuinely relevant symbolism. By 'working' I do not mean a loose psychological fit that is in the end incapable of discrimination. I mean 'working' in terms of precise directions of appropriate and descriptive significators involving the angles and house cusps in secondary progression. On discovering my error with the original calculation, I found that the corrected chart showed the accidents with different but appropriate significators, although not quite so aptly as the 'wrong' chart. Which astrologer is there who has *not* had this experience, or one very similar?

With all the opportunities there are for error, compounded by the hazy memories of mothers, wrong records, time-zone teasers, calculation catastrophes and general sloppiness by the astrologer, getting an accurate horoscope based on reliable data sometimes appears to be a noteworthy achievement. The unwelcome opportunity for experiments with wrong charts therefore arises over and over again. From all the anecdotal evidence of many years of being with astrologers, I conclude that the curious phenomenon I have reported – of the wrong chart apparently working – is a fairly common occurrence. Because it does not fit our preconceptions – it is in fact destructive for them – this puzzling commonplace tends to get pushed under the carpet. Usually it is only the critics of astrology who try to rub our noses in this embarrassing mess.[1]

RADICALITY OF THE HOROSCOPE OF BIRTH

The problem of wrong charts puts into question the presupposition about what consitutes a right chart. What is meant by 'right'? Our classical approach to nativities, founded in the Doctrine of Origin, gives a simple answer: the causal-temporal origin of the person or thing concerned is the Radix. This word means 'root', so we are asserting the causal-temporal origin as the root of astrological symbolism. At birth the human being emerges and it is the meaning of independent human life that is represented in the natal horoscope.

Linked to this idea of the radix is the concept of *radicality*. Radicality is the assumption that the horoscope is a true symbolic representation of its subject. Here we find that natal astrology differs significantly from all katarchic forms of astrology in one crucial point of method: in the birth chart, radicality is given, already assigned. If we have a true time of birth, that horoscope is by definition radical for the person born then, and we therefore without question assign that horoscope as a radix. If it should happen that the chart does not seem to work for character and events then we have to admit we are baffled, or think we have to shuffle our techniques. Provided we are really sure of the accuracy of the birth time then its status as a radix is unlikely to be seriously questioned, and it would breach a fundamental axiom to say, 'Mr.X's birth-moment does not yield a radical horoscope for him'.

This pregiven assignation of radicality for the natal horoscope derives its authority from several sources. Unlike moments *in* life, birth itself is of an entirely different order, being without a shadow of ambiguity the moment of significant origin *of* life. It is the ultimate origin, the ancestor of all the other little origins in life. There is no decision involved about whether it is significant, or whether it is less significant than some other originating moment. The moving experience of birth cannot fail to deeply affect everyone involved. Where birth is uncomplicated, the coming of the new human being can be timed down to seconds, and if this time is accurately recorded, then there is little space for doubt in anyone's mind that we have 'this moment and no other'. If astrology means anything at all, the horoscope so derived must be taken as the symbolic marker of the human being.

The difficulties we may face in pinning this moment to an event in the physical process of birth, for example first breath, or cutting the umbilical cord, does not affect the theoretical positing of a single definitive astrological moment of birth. This is taken for granted as the foundation of natal astrology, the signature of the soul, granted at birth.

For reasons that will become clear, I will refer to this ideal picture of the moment of birth, perfectly timed, as the *astrological image of birth*. In emotional association with this image are all the powerful feelings and beliefs, conscious and unconscious, called up by our experience that others are born, and by the recognition that we ourselves have been born.

This has well enough answered the question of what is conventionally meant by the 'right' moment for the natal horoscope, but I would like to return to the dilemma with which we started. Since wrong charts may work *where does the apparent rightness of the wrong horoscope come from?*

THE TANTALISING ASTROLOGY OF DIANA, PRINCESS OF WALES

I will illustrate this subtle question of the nature of astrological significance through a well-studied and intriguingly problematic horoscope, that of Diana, Princess of Wales. The topic was treated in the first edition of this book in 1994; Diana's demise in 1997 brings the story to its tragic close, and if anything compounds the insecurities we face in determining what exactly horoscopes may be said to reveal. The starting point for our difficulties is that the relevant birth data has from the time of its first announcement in 1981 led astrologers a merry dance. The story's twists and turns have a great deal to show us about astrological significance in the 'unique case of interpretation'.

When news broke of the engagement of Prince Charles and the young Lady Diana Spencer, there was a tremendous media hubbub and wide general interest. Who was this Lady Diana? Of course we astrologers were equally interested – what sort of horoscope had she got, especially in relation to the horoscope of the Prince of Wales? In no time the data came onto the astrological hotline, and I remember the situation well because I was teaching an astrology class that week, and given Diana's topical interest, timing the proposed Royal Wedding would be a useful exercise for the class. Roger Elliott was the first to obtain the birth data from an official source: 2pm 1st July 1961, Sandringham. I shall term this 'Diana I', making this clearer where necessary by referring to the Libra ascendant.

I did some work on this horoscope to check out synastry and timing, and the symbolism looked interesting and lively. The astrology fitted the media image

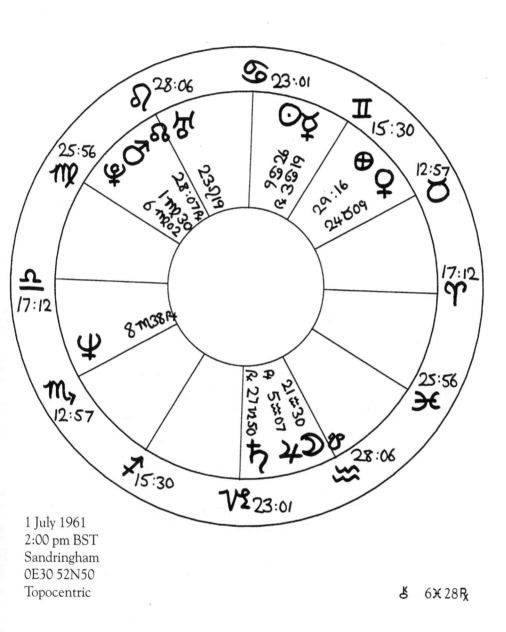

1 July 1961
2:00 pm BST
Sandringham
0E30 52N50
Topocentric

☊   6♓28℞

FIGURE 19 Diana – version I (Libra)

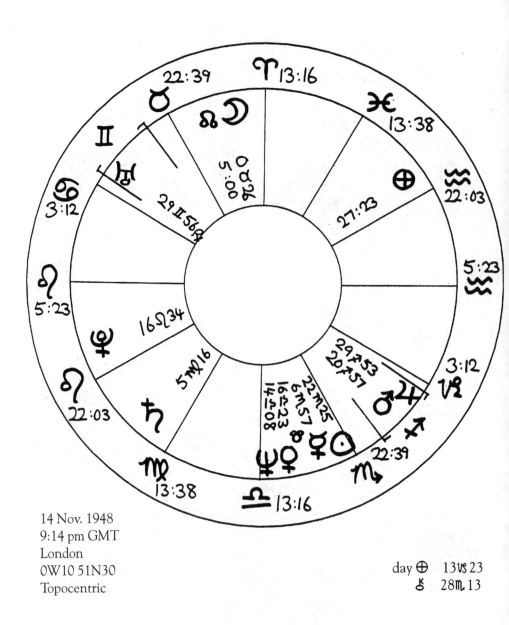

14 Nov. 1948
9:14 pm GMT
London
0W10 51N30
Topocentric

day ⊕   13♑23
        ⅋   28♏13

FIGURE 20 Charles

that we were all being given, and it was easy to see the beautiful Diana in Libra rising, Venus in Taurus. Yet it is the synastry with Charles which is really fascinating because 17 Libra, the rising degree, is on a key configuration for Prince Charles. He has Venus at 16 Libra 24 with a Venus-Neptune conjunction on the IC in Libra. Ascendant plus Venus-Neptune in Libra – what more beautiful image could you have for this media romance, the fairy tale wedding? That was the image we were receiving in public and that is the image of the astrology. Just as the general public was captivated by the romance of Charles and Di, the various astrologers who saw this configuration were equally captivated.

This chart is more than just a surface hit on one piece of symbolism. It measured on secondaries very powerfully to the Royal Wedding. The direction involved is progressed ascendant sextile natal Mars, lord of the 7th of marriage, just 9′ arc applying. The progressed *descendant* is therefore trine Mars, its ruler: the natal promise and the actual perfection of marriage. The progressed descendant of 1 Taurus is also conjunct Charles's natal Moon at 0 Taurus 26. All in all, this is a definitive textbook example of progressions, underscored by appropriate synastry. Such astrology points to the possibility of sound judgment, accurate inference and plausible prediction. Yet no sooner had this chart, 'Diana I', displayed its brilliant image than it was gone.

Shortly afterwards, news came through that this was the wrong chart. Buckingham Palace now gave the time as 7.45pm BST, not 2.00pm. This new time gives an ascendant of 18 Sagittarius, and I will term it 'Diana II'. This chart rapidly established itself amongst astrologers, and a good case can be made for its symbolic appropriateness. Note in particular how the Jupiter synastry with Charles makes a lot more sense than it did in the previous chart. This is now the ruler of her ascendant and it falls on Charles's 7th cusp – a typical marriage contact. Further, her ascendant is fairly close to his Mars, lord of his 10th and 5th and in the 5th. That is a sexually active connection, and good for the blood line of the House of Windsor.

In either chart, Diana has a dramatic T-square configuration of the Moon opposite Uranus square Venus, and in the Diana II chart, Venus is in the 5th house. Venus as ruler of the MC in the 5th shows her primary vocation – to produce the royal offspring. Yet it is a tremendously disruptive T-square and many astrologers on seeing that were wary and inferred upsets to come for Lady Diana, for her marriage, and for her future status.[2]

The negative potential of the T-square manifested itself in 1992 when the royal marriage unravelled publicly and painfully over the course of the summer, starting with the media-grabbing publication of Andrew Morton's book, *Diana:*

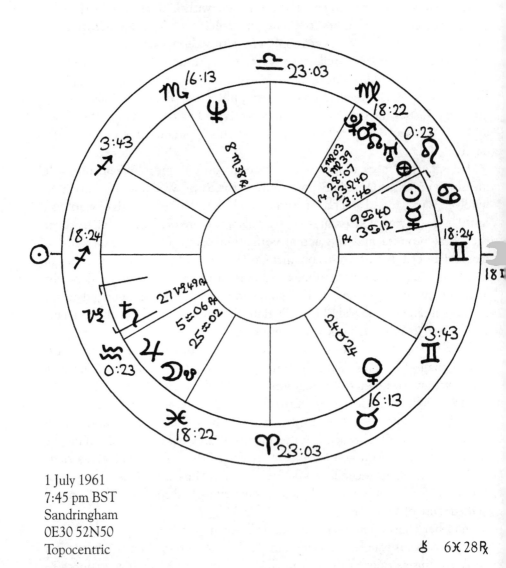

1 July 1961
7:45 pm BST
Sandringham
0E30 52N50
Topocentric

☒   6♓28℞

FIGURE 21 Diana – version II (Sagittarius)
showing the eclipse of 9th December 1992

Her True Story. Revelations in this book, authenticated by sources close to Diana, shook to the roots the royal family and the British psyche.

Throughout 1992, the Princess was subject to the transit of the south Node across her 7th House Sun. This meant that her Sun, like her husband, suffered a pattern of eclipses. This culminated in the total solar eclipse on 30th June, one day before her birthday, at 8 Cancer 57. This eclipse blighted her Sun, threatened her marriage and seriously damaged the royal family.

Damaging extracts from Morton's book were first published in the *Sunday Times* on 7 June 1992, so I used this nominal date to investigate secondary progressions for the beginnings of public scandal. There is a most remarkable, once in a lifetime direction in this period, *formed by progressed Uranus at 25 Leo 03, just one minute of arc applying opposite the natal Moon at 25 Aquarius 02.* One minute of arc for progressed Uranus takes us back to exactitude in the previous winter of 1991-92, probably when the most damaging allegations were being set up with Morton. Here is a rare class of trans-Saturnian progression manifesting the disruption promised in the natal T-square. Attention-seeking attempts at suicide are very like Uranus in the 8th house, and the affliction to the Moon is suggestive of bulimia. The Moon is part ruler of the 7th, dispositor of the royal Sun in the 7th and of Mercury, the afflicted lord of the 7th – it is the marriage which is threatened.

This remarkable direction of Uranus opposite the Moon is an explosive revelation. The Princess was allowing the world to know, in a most dramatic way, that her marriage was not the fairy-tale affair we had all been led to believe.

In terms of traditional astrology, this is the major symbolism for the troubles of the Princess in her separation from the Prince. There is, however, a minor exact transit formation which is appropriate to the actual publication of Morton's revelations. Neptune was at 18 Capricorn 24 retrograde as the *Sunday Times* was rolling off the presses – in an exact semi-sextile to the nominal natal ascendant of 18 Sagittarius 24. Saturn at 18 Aquarius 25 was also sextile the ascendant and semi-sextile this transiting Neptune. At the level of transits, therefore, we find a pattern within 1' of arc involving slow-moving planets. Minor though the aspects are, the whole configuration is symbolically apt. The involvement of Neptune at this time is especially obvious. We may even have the 'suicide' reference here, as this was one of the most insidious and damaging of all the revelations concerning the marriage. I believe that in this chart, Diana II, Neptune in the 10th, lord of the 3rd, represents rumour and scandal and the possibility of public disgrace. At the wedding, the progressed Moon was conjunct this Neptune, and therefore trine the seventh house Sun. What a beautiful illusion that was, the 'stuff of which fairy tales are made'.[3] But the other side of Neptune is the dissolving of the illusion created for and by the media at the wedding.

I made the point above that I am working with the nominal natal ascendant of 18 Sagittarius 24. The Saturn-Neptune transits with their minute-of-arc relationship to this ascendant can only indicate the *exact* date of publication of Morton's extracts, 7 June, if I am assuming that Diana's birthtime is accurate to within a few seconds of the stated time of 7:45:00 pm. How can I make such a claim? If I am not making this claim of stop-watch accuracy about the birthtime, then is the exact transit formation I have shown, despite its symbolic fittingness, *merely chance*? As far as I am concerned, this is a valid demonstration of astrological symbolism, and it is based on the efficacy of what may be termed the 'stated time phenomenon'. However, Princess Diana will have to take us a little further into the revelation of astrology before I can justify this statement.

Diana had shocked everybody, just like Uranus opposite her Moon. But there was also a shock with the birth data itself. This came in the autumn of 1992 via Penny Thornton who had been informed directly by the Princess that the chart we had been studying for a decade – Diana II – was wrong. In fact Diana I (Libra), based on the very first information obtained hot on the heels of the engagement, was believed to have been right all the time! So now this earlier chart came springing back to life.

We now had to do our progressions all over again, on a new horoscope. How do the two charts compare? Progressing Chart I (Libra) up to Diana's 1992 troubles, it *loses the Uranus opposite Moon* direction which was found in chart II. From this point of view it really cannot compare in terms of symbolic liveliness with chart II, but that is not the end of its story. Uranus still wants to show itself in chart I. The ascendant for the nominal stated time in this chart is 17 Libra 12. On the morning of the *Sunday Times* revelations, Sunday 7 June, Uranus was 17 Capricorn 12 – *Uranus zero orb square the ascendant*. When astrology is working well we often see a transit exactly confirm a progression. This has happened here – but *across two charts*. The transit of Uranus in Diana I confirms the progression of Uranus in Diana II, and now it is timing the publication of the revelations to within a few hours.

Each of these two stated-time charts is therefore showing a continuing power of signification, and is recognisably giving minor testimony to the showings of the other chart. It is the same symbolic factor in play in both, and we are talking, remember, about zero-orb or near zero-orb astrology.

How has it happened that *both* charts can tell a story and even back each other up? It shows that what we ordinarily think of as 'wrong' and 'right' in terms of objective time and horoscopes is at best oversimple and at worst completely misleading. The classical Ptolemaic theory with its prescription for the objective time moment does not offer a reliable description of what actually happens in our astrology.

Let me indicate another type of explanation altogether, this time consistent with the idea that astrology is about our subjective experience of significant *images* of reality. It is as if in a context of perceived significance, an image such as that of the 17 Libra horoscope for Diana is drawn forward. It comes into psychic play, as if to yield a picture of its own significance. The image that came forward, that of the fairy tale princess and the fairy-tale romance, is the image that cracked in the publication of the book extracts. Those precise contacts may well be more about the cracking of the image, Moon opposite Uranus, than they are about the actuality of the marriage. The marriage had after all reached the dire state that was now being reported years earlier, well before the time Morton began his nosing around.

Do these things come forward to us in the exact way they do because they are on our mind, in the public eye? Is this what the astrology speaks to? Everything we know, especially from Jung, concerning the nature of these curious coincidences suggests that this is the process at work.

Let me make clear why I have shown this particular example to you. It is not a special case, as if it is somehow different to the usual working of astrology. This applies to *all* of our astrology. What I have done is to demonstrate, as clearly as possible, the *way* in which horoscopes 'come up' for us. I think we all know this in our astrology. The problem is that our traditional edifice of theory has hindered talking about it.

DIANA ECLIPSED

After the revelations of the summer of 1992, events moved rapidly towards the formal separation of the Prince and Princess of Wales. This produced an omen of the highest potency. On the afternoon of 9th December, the business of the Commons was interrupted for the Prime Minister to formally announce the separation and to outline the constitutional position, which was that the right of the Princess of Wales to succession as Queen was not affected. This claim was to be later questioned, but that very night everyone with even a grain of symbolism had a more immediate and dramatic celestial indication of the true state of affairs. Around midnight, there was a total lunar eclipse, with the shadowy ball of the Full Moon high in the sky, crossing the meridian of London.[4] The Full Moon is the Sun and Moon in opposition, the King and the Queen, but with the shadow of the world between them. The noble Diana, like her namesake the Moon, enthroned at the midheaven yet darkened. How could she now be Queen?

Here is an autonomous, fully real and visually impressive phenomenon of the heavens, a striking parallel to human events. The astronomy of this is completely objective but the *astrology* of it is entirely dependent on our shared symbolic images, reflecting the unique context of the public breakdown in the Royal Family. The omen here is an astrological image working in the realm of public consciousness, compared with the more usual private realm of symbolism emerging for astrologer and client. Whatever our views of the royals, they are public icons and carriers of collective imagination, hence the appearance of omens around them.

For any astrologer who saw this eclipse, the implication was immediate and undeniable, and it completed the earlier pattern of eclipses on Diana's natal Sun. Yet apart from the significance of this omen as a public astrological appearance, it has a more specific horoscopic reference, as might be expected. The *eclipsed Moon at 18 Gemini 10 falls right on the 7th house cusp, the marriage cusp, of the Sagittarius ascendant horoscope.* Here is the image of the destruction of a marriage. The contact is close, within 14' of arc, and therefore a strong testimony to the radicality of the Diana II variant.

MORE TWISTS AND TURNS

The eclipse symbolism looked set to decide the question of the Diana's horoscope in favour of the 18 Sagittarius ascendant, allowing us to treat the the Libra horoscope as a red herring. Several months after this eclipse, an astrologer colleague with well-placed connections sought out Diana's opinion on the conflict of birth times. According to this source, the Princess affirmed that her time of birth was indeed 7:45pm (Diana II, Sagittarius ascendant). But then, a few weeks later, another astrologer colleague with separate but equally well-placed connections independently informed me that it is known in the household that there was confusion concerning the recollection of the birth times of Diana and a brother who died at birth, one of them being born at 2pm and the other at 7:45pm.

Nicholas Campion then came up with another variant of the puzzle, reawakening old doubts. In the summer of 1993 he sought out Diana's view of her birthtime through an intermediary and she responded with the time of 2:15pm, thus giving us a slight but significant variant of the original Libra version. On sending a message back asking for clarification Diana replied that the correct time of birth was 7:45pm. So even after she had no doubt become aware of the significance of the astrologers' queries, Diana on different occasions asserted two entirely different versions of her birthtime. The issue has ever since remained open to question.[5]

It is worth a moment's reflection to consider how, in cases such as that of the Princess and her ambiguous data, our attitude as astrologers twists and turns in response. The balance of probabilities and the strength of the symbolism does now favour one version (Diana II, Sagittarius) over the other, but it is quite conceivable that this opinion could still be overturned. Whichever choice we make, the main point arising from the problematic case of the Princess should not be forgotten. Since two mutually incompatible ascendants and their horoscopes (17 Libra and 18 Sagittarius) show appropriate symbolism, including synastry and exact timing, there emerges the possibility of an effective natal signification which, though assigned to the life and character of the native, is nevertheless not a function of the clock time of birth. Rather than looking to the 'clock of the heavens' as the source of astrological symbolism, we would do better to look at the nature of the act of imaginative assignation by which we make time itself significant.

ELUSIVE SYMBOLISM AT THE DEATH OF DIANA

We might hope that from the death of Diana in 1997 we would attain a decisive piece of symbolism to unlock the secrets of her birthchart. The high-speed crash in a Paris underpass was such a shocking occurrence, and the tragedy moved so many people world-wide, that we could not imagine it passing without a manifest symbolism of astrology pushing itself forward. So was there appropriate symbolism of a convincing order? As with so much in our astrology, the answer has to be both 'yes' and 'no'. In one sense yes, potent symbolism appears to have been in play; but from the perspective of regular natal practice it would have to be admitted that the astrology was oddly mute, and not really on.

Let us deal with the disappointing part of this rhetorical answer first. It is not my intention to offer a full analysis of that sad September night in Paris, either in terms of its own intrinsic symbolism or in its relation to the nativity of Diana. I will simply observe that thousands of astrologer-hours must have been spent gazing at computer monitors and poring over ephemerides in order to hunt down every trace of signification, just as I too have spent many more hours than I had intended playing the same game. When it comes to the question of how far the natal horoscope of Diana directly prefigured the event, then I have to say that out of all this effort nothing especially convincing has emerged into print or into astrological discussion.

A similar conclusion has been arrived at in a trenchant critique by Maggie Hyde, as a result of her study of various published interpretations concerning the symbolism of Diana's death. Many astrologers were struck by the proximity of the death to a solar eclipse two days later, falling three and a half degrees from her natal Pluto. This is arguably the most significant transit phenomenon, and it does describe something of the prevailing mood of the following days. Eclipses were significant markers at several key points in Diana's life, but on tighter orbs and more obvious symbolism than this partial eclipse. There are outer planet transiting oppositions a fortnight away (Uranus to natal Jupiter, Neptune to natal Saturn) but their symbolism is not obviously relevant, and there is nothing to mark out this weekend as fateful for Diana:

> If we are honest about our astrology, her death is not especially obvious by our conventional timing measures. In this case her natal chart does not appear to be an adequate frame of reference to signify the vast collective emotions released by Diana's untimely death. A different order of the symbolic seems to be called for...[6]

Maggie Hyde demonstrates a striking symbolism involving comet Hale-Bopp which had manifested over England in the spring and summer of 1997. This takes us to the 'different order' of mundane astrology, and we will discuss this topic, including its relevance for Diana, in the next chapter. Returning to our present consideration of the natal horoscope, however, it is essential that we do not try to cover over the inadequacy of the symbolism and our corresponding sense of dissatisfaction. Otherwise, as Maggie Hyde observes, 'we simply scrape the barrel with a mechanical application of methods and fragile interpretations'.

We are particularly tested out when it comes to great public events and figures, observed after rather than before the event. Most astrologers are sensible enough to recognise that projecting into the future is at best hazardous. Of its nature, astrological prediction is beset with uncertainty, especially in the wide open realms of signification which characterise natal and mundane astrology, since there are so many levels and modes in which any particular symbolism might work itself out. However, while they acknowledge the *pre facto* problem, many astrologers have more difficulty accepting that the symbolism might not be there at all, and that there may be nothing much to see *post facto*, either. That certainly appears to be the case with Diana's natal horoscope with respect to her death. Yet it is rare to find such an admission in the discourse of astrology, where the taken-for-granted assumption is that for all major events in all natal horoscopes there must be a true signification that is 'really there', if we only had the technique, ability or intuition to grasp it. This assumption is our great legacy from the Ptolemaic tradition, the belief that astrology has as its subject matter a universal and objective phenomenon, universally lawful and consistently operative. To suggest that this may not be the best way of approaching astrology is seen as shaking its very foundations.

In response to my observations here, proponents of the classical tradition can be expected to come out fighting. And of course, I can offer no simple answer to the objection that when our interpretation fails then some other technique or method, other than the one we happen to have employed, will reveal the truth. Similarly, there is no answer to the declaration that the birthtime must be wrong and the horoscope needs to be rectified before it will reveal the cosmic pattern. These tenets of practice are not in their own narrow compass untrue, but their limited efficacy is secondary to the overwhelming ignorance wrought by the attitude that so wishes astrology to be all-powerful and all-significant that it is rendered incapable of discriminating weak from potent signification, general half-truth from specific insight, and mere speculation from the light of symbolism. Such an attitude cannot bear to let go and allow that in the mysterious way of symbolism, sometimes we are shown things, sometimes we are not, and most times we are not sure one way or the other.

Although using our common methods Diana's natal horoscope does not give sufficient symbolism for the timing of her death, there is, as was suggested earlier, an order of potential signification in the events themselves, and several astrologers have accordingly moved free from the limitations of the nativity and spun a web of meanings from the death chart, and from various coincidences surrounding the event.[7] Dennis Elwell's treatment in the revised edition of his *Cosmic Loom* is revealing in that he does not tie his interpretation of her death to the natal horoscope, although we can be sure that had there been a convincing natal indication an astrologer of Elwell's calibre would certainly have found it. Instead he discovers a patchwork of coincidences linking Diana with Mother Theresa, Marilyn Monroe, the Duchess of Windsor, and the assassinations both of Kennedy and of the archduke Ferdinand in Sarajevo, which precipitated the first World War. In this mass of material there are indeed some curious parallels, and several of these will intrigue anyone with a symbolic attitude. They do not, however, bear the weight of interpretation that Elwell strains to give them, of revealing an objective and impersonal 'cosmic matrix' sustaining the 'invisible mechanism that underpins events'. In my view such connections are better seen as *symbolic traces*, tantalising beginnings of possible threads of interpretation, and they should not be mistaken for developed expressions of symbol. When these traces are heaped up without being gathered into the ordering power of symbol, then they become chaotic and appear slightly dotty.[8]

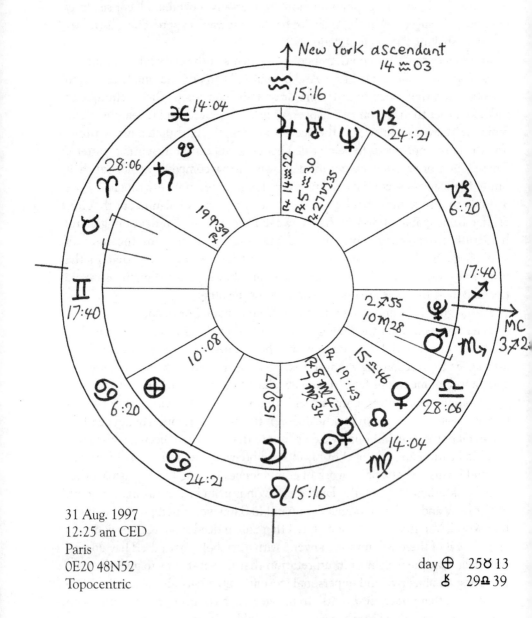

31 Aug. 1997
12:25 am CED
Paris
0E20 48N52
Topocentric

day ⊕ 25♉13
☍ 29♎39

FIGURE 22 Death of a Princess

I am however bound to acknowledge a beautiful symbolic theme observed by Dennis Elwell that does indeed demonstrate ordering power, and carries potency precisely because it has been discriminated through astrological craft. The moment of the fatal crash in the Alma tunnel was recorded as 12:25am in Paris, three and a half hours before the formal announcement of Diana's death, after a hopeless fight to save her. The figure for this moment is remarkable for the exact meridian passage of the close Moon-Jupiter opposition, with the Moon in Leo on the IC separating from the opposition of Jupiter, culminating in Aquarius. This does not in any way look like a car-crash or death; it is however a brilliant signature of a royal (Jupiter on MC, Moon Leo) princess (Moon, Diana). To ensure that we take this horoscope seriously, it yields an ascendant in the 18th degree of Gemini, within a degree reversing the horizon of Diana II. As the horizon reverses the soul of Diana begins to depart.

This horoscopic foundation enables a striking interpretation of an emblematic feature of the scene of the tragedy. In the plaza above the Alma tunnel, and destined to become a popular shrine to Diana, is a replica of the torch of the Statue of Liberty. As a symbol of freedom in the form of a female figure, the Statue of Liberty finds a perfect expression in this same Moon-Jupiter/Aquarius configuration. Now Elwell proves his take: if we relocate the moment of the accident to the New York home of the statue, the Moon-Jupiter lies exactly across the horizon, with Jupiter to the degree rising. At the same instant Pluto culminates, an image of destruction. As Diana met her fateful end under the torch of liberty, liberty was rising (Jupiter in Aquarius) and a princess entered the underworld (Moon in Leo, setting).

THE QUESTION OF RECTIFICATION

Our preceding discussion on the problematic significations in Diana's horoscope throws open the whole question of rectification, which is the correcting of a horoscope and its clock-time from the evidence of events, and from other purely symbolic methods. I never came across anyone's rectification of Diana I because it was around for such a brief time, but prior to her death a plausible rectification of the Diana II chart was undertaken by Adrian Duncan, and this adds its own significant testimony to the theme of astrology-as-divination.

Duncan's approach pushes the birth time back 16 minutes and gives an ascendant of 15 Sagittarius 14.[9] There are several appropriate directions timing to the royal wedding, but the foundation of Duncan's symbolism – the definitive take on which he bases his rectification – would seem to be the movement of

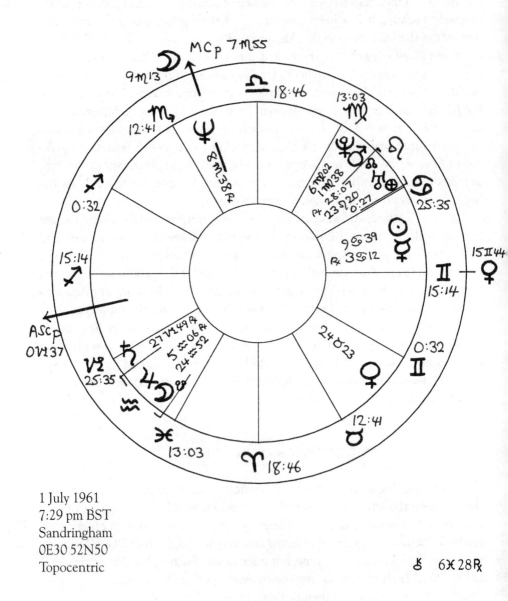

1 July 1961
7:29 pm BST
Sandringham
0E30 52N50
Topocentric

FIGURE 23 Diana – Adrian Duncan's rectification
with progressions to the Royal Wedding 29th July 1981

Venus onto the 7th cusp. This is a textbook direction, not only for the universal symbolism of Venus as planet of love, coming to the angle appropriate to marriage, but by virtue of the Venus rulership of Princess Diana's MC.

As with most rectifications it would not be difficult to argue a point against for every point brought forward in support of Adrian Duncan's choice. The turn of fate does however give a testimony in his favour in the secondary progression of the 15 Sagittarius horoscope to Diana's death. The angles configure strongly with Mars, Uranus, and the 8th house – a clear signature for violent death. The progressed asc. of 16°33' Capricorn is sesquiquadrate within 5' arc natal Mars, which afflicts from the 8th; at the same time progressed MC at 23°18' Scorpio is sextile progressed Mars and square natal Uranus to just 2' arc, a characteristic example of Uranian high-timing. Any astrologer who has worked secondaries to any degree of precision will acknowledge the validity of this symbolism, which is all the more impressive given the seeming weakness of the other major contending figures: within the particular framework of the methods adopted here, neither Diana I (17°12' Libra) nor II (18°24' Sagittarius) yield adequate directions.

Please note the qualification I have just employed: 'within the particular framework of the methods adopted here'. The problematic of form and technique is exposed in this far from innocent phrase. Every detail of our method, each technical choice we knowingly or unknowingly make, frames and structures our assignation of significance, and the results we obtain are a function of that assignation. When it comes to timing measures other than transits, the method I employ in this book as in my practical astrology is secondary progression, applying solar arc in longitude to the MC. Had I employed mean solar arc in RA (the 'sidereal time' method, or Naibod arc), or the much less common but revealing true solar arc in RA, then we would expect substantially different angular timings, giving a variance of several years. If we apply solar arc directions to chart factors, as commonly practised in American astrology, then the picture changes again. And we have not even begun to consider converse measures, primaries in all their numbing variety, tertiaries, symbolic measures, planetary periods, profections, returns, etc etc. This welter of possibilities is further magnified if we step outside the broad interpretive form of conventional modern natal interpretation, and engage the specialisms of midpoint trees and harmonics, let alone parts, asteroids, hypotheticals and degree symbols. And wider still, we are in the territory assigned by western tropical astrology and not sidereal or Vedic.

Like the 17 Libra 'Diana I' version, Duncan's rectification changes the natal Moon position and therefore loses the remarkable progressed opposition from

Uranus to the Moon for 1992, the year in which Diana's marriage publicly unravelled. The transits for the traumatic *Sunday Times* denouement beginning on 7 June 1992 are also less pertinent, except for one little detail. It is a small detail but nevertheless suggestive. Venus was transiting the rectified natal descendant on the morning of 7 June. What does this tell us? I suggest it reflects Adrian Duncan's original major secondary *direction* for the wedding, Venus progressed to the natal descendant. So this exactly rectified time has its story to tell, even if on other grounds we declare it to be 'wrong'.

There are other connections between the various events and the several charts, as if these charts link together. Yet of course they link together, in the images we have of the Princess, her marriage, and her tragic life. The images that move us, and to which we respond, have a place in the public imagination. When we symbolically negotiate those images using the discipline of astrology, *the horoscopes we seek to validate take their meaning in the imagination of we astrologers.*

Every astrologer knows that charts come forward when they are ready, symbolism appears under curiously significant circumstances. A wrong chart, or a particular rectification, comes forward to be the image that is required, the unique image that allows a reading of the situation. We *assign* certain moments as significant, so our art is not one of reading off an objective influence in material reality. It is an act of assignation. We both create and respond to significance, and our interpretation reaps the fruits of our assignation. We find that reality is revealed when we take this step – and this reality includes facets of life and character which we could not otherwise have known about. This, I am sure you will see, is divination, and this is the foundation of our practice: divinatory astrology.

DIVINATION AND RECTIFICATION

While it is obvious that the major part of practical horoscope interpretation does not require fine-tuned birth timing, the issue of rectification is far more than a detail of technique. Even a basic transits approach adopted by many beginners has to take this into account, since any attempt to date outer-planet transits to angles may be completely thrown by a modest difference in the birthtime. A Pluto transit of the ascendant can easily be nine or ten months adrift on a matter of a few minutes in the original birth.

Adopting the divinatory approach to the assigned time of birth has a number of implications for practical astrology, including work with clients, and I will briefly indicate some of these here. Take firstly the capacity for 'stated time' charts to work with exactitude for that stated time. If the time of birth is asserted to be 7:45pm, this is nevertheless tacitly understood to be simply a round time. As has already been suggested in relation to Princess Diana, it is noteworthy how certain exact transits and directions play a game with the astrologer and insist on showing *as if* the exact time of birth is, as in the 'Diana II' data, 7:45:00pm, timed by a stop watch. This does not preclude the equally accurate working of a rectified chart close to the stated time (e.g. 7:42:37pm), nor indeed the equally accurate working of a rectified chart some distance from the stated time, as in Adrian Duncan's version of 'Diana II', 7:29:00pm.

Once it is understood that we are working with astrological *images* of birth, and only indirectly with some supposed objective *time* of birth, then the stated-time phenomenon takes its place as one more possibility for the showing of symbolism. As a matter of ordinary practice, the stated time chart is usually adequate and is capable of surprising precision. A useful motto here is: 'If the cap fits wear it'. We need to bother with rectification only where the stated time gives us blatantly non-radical symbolism, or when the astrologer wishes to enhance the precision and symbolic relevance of the horoscope with regard to some outstanding feature of life.

This latter possibility leads naturally on to the phenomenon of the 'definitive direction'. The definitive direction is usually discovered in rectification where the astrologer has to choose between different directions testifying to several different possible birthtimes. The same procedure can obviously be applied to transits, but I will here treat these under the general heading of directions. It will often be found, though not always, that the solution is *not* to average out a moderate fit for several of the major directions. The more effective solution is to *choose one direction which is highly revealing for a significant event* and produce an exact rectification from this alone, even if this means sacrificing altogether several other possibly relevant directions which now fall out of acceptable orb for their supposed events. The frequent result is that this decisive and singular rectification is later found to yield equally decisive measures to certain other events, past or future, where the 'averaged out' rectification, true to its origin, continues to give soggy results.[10]

Before leaving the realm of rectification, a comparison with the ancient technique of the pre-natal epoch will prove instructive. This method finds a moment nine months before birth which yields a mutual swap-over between the horizon and Moon of the conception and the birth-moment. Some of the old astrologers, and modern proponents of the method such as E.H.Bailey, talk as if this really is the actual moment of physiological conception. In many cases it quite demonstrably does not give the clock-time of conception. What it will give is the clock-time for a horoscope that in our tradition serves as an astrological *image* of conception. In this respect, it is quite analogous to the image of the natal horoscope with respect to birth.

I will now summarise these practical observations as they bear on the birthtime:

(a) Where a birthtime is recorded the astrologer is strongly inclined to define this as the 'right' moment for a natal horoscope. This is the birthtime with the authority of the hospital clock behind it. It is unlikely, although not impossible, that this will be found to give a 'wrong' horoscope – i.e. one that does not 'work'.

(b) The stated time given to the astrologer may or may not be the same as the recorded time, because of lost records or errors of memory. However, it frequently gives a chart that works well, sometimes to uncanny precision when taken to the nominal second of the stated time. If it does not work well, the astrologer enters a creative process of rectification.

(c) Rectification is likely to yield variants of the horoscope, each of which work, and are therefore 'right'. Sometimes rectification may lead back to a previously unknown recorded time which is later proved to be true.

(d) The entirely 'wrong' horoscope produced by misinformation or gross error not infrequently (but not always) works just as if it is a 'right' horoscope.

This brings us back to the observation that the working of natal horoscopes is not essentially a function of the clock-time of birth. This tallies with the broad conclusion already already arrived at with respect to divinatory astrology in general, namely that 'the coming-to-pass of astrological effects or showings is not founded in a coincidence in objective time of heavens above and event below'.[11]

OBJECTIONS TO THE DIVINATORY INTERPRETATION

Against the divinatory interpretation I have been discussing, it is sometimes supposed that we should set another argument to neutralise it. The astrologer, finding a poor fit between the chart and the character or events, infers on astrological evidence alone that the birthtime has been wrongly given, and when rectified the chart is later independently confirmed by historical evidence. Correcting the clock by the internal evidence of symbolism alone is not common, but it undoubtedly does happen.[12] However, a little reflection will show that this in no way counters the possibility that the wrong chart may also work. All we may safely conclude is the rather obvious suggestion that *not all* wrong charts work, but that a right one may be expected to work. The main import of my argument here is that astrology works for us whether or not it can be sustained by an objectively correct time, because the working of astrology is not logically or physically dependent on that objective time. There are even cases where astrology works with *no moment of time* at all, as has been effectively demonstrated by Maggie Hyde.[13]

Some astrologers will be tempted to resolve the dilemmas posed here by suggesting that the 'real' natal moment throws off reflections into other moments, and these produce all the other wrong charts that nonetheless give some true indications. It is difficult to see how such a last-ditch defence of the Ptolemaic position could be disproved. All I could say is that this assertion of the 'really real' physical moment as the foundation of astrology is *unnecessary* and inhibiting, since it does not help our description of what we actually encounter in practice. It also lumbers us with a burden of astral determinism, however we might dress this up.

Once we recognise the divinatory move we are always employing in our astrology, even the embarrassing phenomenon of the wrong time working takes its place as a valid possibility of symbolism, capable of allowing fruitful interpretation. As with all symbolism, but in complete contrast to the theoretical significance of things established in modern science, astrological interpretation depends on what comes into consciousness as meaningful. The 'right time' has this status only if we happen to establish it, and this precept remains true above and beyond the objective authority of the hospital clock. If nobody remembers what the hospital clock actually showed, then from the point of view of meaningful experience it has not shown us anything.

In dealing with symbolism we need to subvert the exclusive either-or logic of right and wrong in favour of the more open and uncertain possibility that things are more or less meaningful, depending on the context. Now this could look as if I am advocating some astrological anarchy where anything goes, and any chart can be read for anything we like. This doesn't follow in practice, however, because we limit the assignation of astrological significance to a few categories or our perception where an imaginative association ensures that our emotions are to some degree engaged, as with the story of a person's life which we associate with the physiological origin of that life, at birth. As soon as the imaginative association is broken, then emotion and meaning withdraw. When we discover a chart to be wrong, it immediately loses its hold. We are bound to withdraw our assignation and will even end up convincing ourselves that of course it was wrong all along.

I am under no illusion as to how readily the divinatory interpretation of natal astrology can in practice be accepted. The supreme status of the natal horoscope, coupled with the powerful objectifying tendency inherent in all astrology, make it especially difficult to shake off a lingering desire to found the 'really real' natal origin in an objective physical event rather than in a symbolic assignation. In the end, attitudes to this question come down to imagination and experience. If the terms mean anything at all, the distinction between an 'esoteric' and an 'exoteric' astrology is found exactly at this point.[14]

LEVELS IN ASTROLOGY

It must be understood that by advocating a divinatory re-interpretation of most of our practice of astrology, this should not mean that we abandon the natural-science physical and material showing of astrology, such as that established for us by the Gauquelins. This brings us back to the idea of levels.

It is a disease of modern rational thought to imagine that a thing is either this or that, and if it is this, it cannot be that. A characteristic of primitive thought, and of the symbolic imagination we enter in our astrology, is that it is possible for things to be this *and* that, at the same time. Modern rationalism tends to exclusivity – either-or-ness – while symbolic and mythopoeic thought tends to be inclusive, and-ness. The concept of levels allows us to deal with and-ness. On this account it would be self-defeating for a divinatory understanding of astrology to deny the validity of an objective and scientific natural astrology. The divinatory approach, remember, is sustained in multiple interpretations but this does not work in reverse. Modern scientific and rationalistic paradigms of astrology cannot handle levels and they disallow any suggestion of astrology being founded in a divinatory or even a genuinely symbolic approach.

SYMBOLIC IMAGES OF BIRTH

In our natal astrology let us get away from the illusion that we are really dealing with an 'objective' birth moment. From the potent totemic truths of the Sun-signs all the way to the sober sophistication of the horoscope, we are trading in psychic and symbolic images of birth. This means that when we see a client, the historical fact of physiological birth is simply not the issue for his or her here-and-now reality. Unless the astrologer was actually there at the birth, or engaging with the emotions of a client who was actually there at someone's birth, the historical and physiological moment is not likely to be a component in the existential reality of the unique case of interpretation. From the symbolist's point of view even the recorded time on the birth certificate is but one more potent image assigned to the client. The natal horoscope reads for ontology, not physiology.

I believe that any technically proficient astrologer who examines his or her experience will find that the suggestions I have made in this chapter match what is regularly encountered in practice. Acknowledging this does not, however, save us from a massive conceptual disruption, because these ideas run directly counter to the habits of thought instilled by two millenia of our tradition. The disruption is most deeply felt in natal astrology as we cut the bindings of its old determinism and its implied claim to read some ultimate pattern of destiny in the objective moment of birth. Modern horoscopic astrology no longer needs the theoretical chimera of a final truth indelibly coded at physiological birth. Interpretation is an open-ended moment of astrology, changing over time and circumstance, and varying with the context in which the horoscope symbols have been taken up. We assign our natal astrology to the hospital clock to see what the divination gives us – but the horoscopes we work with are not astronomical records of an event in the physical world. They are symbols in a world of human significance.

NOTES

1 In *Recent Advances in Natal Astrology* (Analogic, 1977; distributed by Para Research Inc., Rockport, Mass.), especially pp. 19-20, 30-32, Geoffrey Dean has collected some interesting reports of the 'wrong map working'. One example will suffice here, from Carl Payne Tobey: 'A very prominent woman astrologer told this story about herself. A woman client entered her office. The astrologer took a chart from the files, correctly told the client why she had come, what was occurring in her life, and the ultimate outcome. The client was astonished at how much the astrologer knew about what had been going on. After the well-impressed client left, the astrologer discovered she had withdrawn the wrong chart from the files. It was the chart of a different client' (p.19). For Dean, cases such as this raise the ESP/intuition issue: the possibility that when it works, it is not astrology but ESP. He is also interested in showing how astrologers arrive at different (and 'wrong') convincing rectifications, thus – as far as Dean is concerned – demonstrating the arbitrariness of all astrological judgment.

2 See Penny Thornton's accurate judgment in her *Synastry* (Aquarian, Wellingborough, Northants., 1982), p140.

3 The Archbishop of Canterbury, quoted by Andrew Morton in *Diana: Her True Story* (2nd edition, Michael O'Mara Books, 1993), p66.

4 The eclipse of 9 December 1992, 11:41pm GMT. At this instant of the Full Moon in longitude (18 Gemini 10), the Moon was under three degrees from the London meridian (15 Gemini 18), which it then transited fully eclipsed. This is such a significant symbolism that several astrologers speculated that the timing of the separation announcement might have been astrologically elected by those working against the Princess of Wales.

5 Nicholas Campion mentions his story in his editorial, *Astrology Quarterly* vol. 64, no.1,

Winter 1993 p4 (published by the Astrological Lodge of London). He suggests that '2:15 represents Diana the private person and 7:45 Diana the princess'. This is a plausible and natural interpretation. It also illustrates the theme of my chapter, because Campion has made the divinatory move off the symbol as presented to consciousness (i.e. two different presentations of Diana) instead of the theoretical notion of a single correct birth-time and a single horoscope. His interpretation would be almost impossible to justify from the perspective of the Ptolemaic causal-temporal origin.

I am sure there may be further twists with the data. Andrew Morton in *Diana: Her True Story* reports Diana's birth as 'late on the afternoon.' In between Libra (2pm) and Sagittarius (7:45pm), we might well end up with Neptune rising in Scorpio, which would be quite appropriate.

6 Maggie Hyde 'Diana, 1066 & the Legacy of Hale-Bopp' COA Bulletin 29 (30 Dec 2001).

7 Interpretations of the death of Diana: see Nicholas Campion 'Diana, Princess of Wales' Astrological Journal 39:6 Nov/Dec 1997; Dennis Elwell 'Cosmic Loom' 2nd edition pp254-261; the two phrases quoted are on p255. Both of these studies of Diana are criticised by Maggie Hyde, op.cit. *Data for the death of Diana*: the formal announcement of her death was made at 4:00am Paris (Asc 3 Leo); the accident occurred at 12:25am – see Campion op.cit quoting the *Times* 1 Sept 1997. In an interview in the *Daily Express* 2 Sept 2000, Frances Shand Kydd, Diana's mother, says that she had been informed that her daughter had died an hour before the public announcement: 'protocol required that heads of state had to be informed before it was made public'.

8 Dennis Elwell's peg for his raft of associations is the partial and unseen eclipse two days after Diana's death, falling at 9°34' Virgo. Given the relatively tangential status of this eclipse in relation to Diana's horoscope, this is not the most secure of moorings. He launches off to configurations at the death of Marilyn Monroe (5 Aug 1962), with Pluto at 8°55' Virgo, opposite a Chiron-Jupiter conjunction at 9 and 11 Pisces. But this is not in itself a very convincing or interesting connection, especially as we are not dealing with near-zero or even ordinarily close orbs: Marilyn Monroe died a year after Diana was born, and slow Pluto, the only substantial point of contact with the eclipse and Diana, has hardly shifted. Further, at the time of Marilyn Monroe's death Pluto was not making any significant contact to her natal planets or angles (1 June 1926 9:30am PST Los Angeles, ascendant 13 Leo: source Rodden). The loose nature of the connections would still be acceptable if a genuinely astrological interpretation had been sustained; but Elwell leaves it entirely vague as to how the symbolism of the eclipse, or of Pluto in Virgo, or of Jupiter in Pisces, connects the two women or fits the theme of Marilyn's song, *Candle Blowing in the Wind*, rededicated to Diana by Elton John in the funeral service. From this point on, Elwell uses degree area contact connections at 9 degrees of the mutables without adequately interpreting either the astrological factors or the events to which they refer. I do not suggest that these associations are meaningless; my objection is that they have not been worked, by which I mean convincing symbolic interpretation and horoscopic testing. Most of the evidences assembled remain at the incoherent level of symbolic traces and have not been 'gathered into the ordering power of symbol'.

9 Adrian Duncan *Doing Time on Planet Earth* (Element, 1990), pp.62ff.

10 I was first introduced to what I term 'the definitive direction' in the work of Chester Kemp, who has in this and a number of other ways directly influenced the development of the concept of astrological divination outlined here.

11 See ch. 2, pp.37-8; ch. 5, pp.82-3.

12 A remarkable case in my practice involved correcting my own faulty watch to the second against the horoscope of the wedding of Princess Anne in 1973, with an independent confir-

mation of the timing. This case is reported in detail by Michael Shallis in *On Time* (Burnett Books 1982, Penguin, 1983), pp.186-7.

13 Maggie Hyde, *Jung and Astrology* (Aquarian, London, 1992), pp.155-8. The 'operation baby' case discussed here is highly relevant to the themes I am raising in this chapter.

14 'Esoteric astrology': this designation is usually completely misleading, with authors imagining that they have to provide a secret technical code. Every single thing in our conventional astrology is 'esoteric' if the nature of symbol is properly understood.

13

Images of the World

THERE is a particular attitude to astrology that sees itself as practical, middle-of-the-road, and no-nonsense, the epitome of common-sense. It held sway in the period before the revival of interest in traditional and classical astrology in recent decades, and it remains near to the heart of many sound astrologers. The common-sense approach doesn't warm to fancy symbolism, Arabic parts, or iffy items such as dark moon Lilith and clairvoyantly-derived degree symbols. It loves character description but is not at home with depth psychology. It will be loathe to dip its toes into horary, which gaily abandons all pretensions of common sense. This approach prefers real-time techniques, especially cycles and transits, and is uneasy with purely symbolic explanations for methods such as secondary progressions, seeking instead a description in terms of energies.

From the discussion developed in previous chapters, it should be obvious that this attitude is to the highest degree resistant to the description of astrology as divination; indeed, it finds it incomprehensible. One reason for this incomprehensibility is the very success of our whole Ptolemaic tradition in fusing the symbolic with the literal at the moment of birth. I ended the previous chapter on the theme that our natal horoscopes are symbolic and not astronomical records, but in our ordinary practice the two realms are not separate, nor do they need to be separated. It requires problematic exceptions, with wrong maps and conflicts of symbolism as in the case of Princess Diana, to clearly reveal the theoretical distinction.

What is being teased out here is a fundamental question of attitude that goes to the heart of what we imagine astrology to be. This can be categorised as a cleavage of view between two poles of interpretation, the *literalist* and *symbolist*. They are often difficult to disentangle, and the approach of many astrologers seems to fall in some ill-defined in-between position, without this ambiguity weakening the usefulness of their ordinary practice. Both approaches employ symbols and both approaches may interpret literal events and situations in the world, but the key to distinguishing the attitudes is that the literalist employs symbols literally, whereas the symbolist interprets literal things symbolically. The literalist will tend in the direction of *causes*, albeit cosmic-harmonic, spiritual-energetic or sympathetic; the symbolist thinks in terms of *signs*.

I now turn to mundane astrology, which to the common-sense imagination might seem such a reliable and objective testing-ground of practical astrology, yet where the divide between literalist and symbolist interpretations becomes even more explicit. Mundane astrology, the astrology of the world, covers global, national and political events; it is about the collective, rather than the individual. We find in the mainstream tradition two distinct orders of method; this division broadly follows the logical structure of universal and particular realms of the astrological effect, as given to us by Ptolemy. The universal working of the heavens is shown in 'the more complete eclipses and the significant passages of the planets' (cf p. 85), which acts upon 'whole races, countries, and cities'. This is also the level of meteorological influence, in 'storms, heat, and winds'. The Arabic astrologers developed the study of this first order through the cycles of Jupiter and Saturn over the whole of recorded history, chronocrators for the rise and fall of religions and civilisations. Modern astrology has extended its range with the cycles of the trans-Saturnian planets, but the perspective is otherwise identical. This astrology is non-horoscopic but it is nevertheless judicial; that is, specific judgments and predictions of a collective nature may be offered on the basis of the interpretation of symbols. However, especially in the field of economic and financial astrology, this approach merges with a proto-science of cycles, where the symbolic component in interpretation becomes more and more attenuated, and we are searching only for correspondences of rhythm.

Once we reach the level of cycles, astrology takes on an appearance of natural law-like objectivity, with the astrologer in the role of an empirical scientist, seeking to determine regularities and patterns in phenomena. This is an enduring impetus in the astrological imagination, but it needs to be recognised that at this point we are at an ambiguous borderland that lies between judicial and natural astrology. I in no way discount the possibility of a certain insight as we step fully into the natural-science way of examination. That remains a possibility within the greater project of astrology. However, in the terms of the thesis presented here, it is important to observe that in taking this step we leave behind the unique case of interpretation, and with it the illumination that a judgment within the symbolist and divinatory mode brings to the individual case.

Ptolemy's second order gives us the outworking of the universal heavenly pattern onto particular events. By the same logic that gives us the natal horoscope, we study inceptions of collective and public ventures, including the horoscopes for nations, and for towns, cities and corporations, timed for their grant of charter or their legal incorporation, or for some notable moment in their formation. This second order accounts for the main part of the field, for when we say 'mundane astrology' most modern astrologers will think first and foremost of horoscopes, and will be at a loss if there is no single moment in time and space that can be assigned in this way.

A distinctive feature of the astrological imagination may be noted here, which is that since horoscopic astrologers make their 'takes' by the method of assigning the unique moment of a horoscope to an entity such as a nation, they are inclined to interpret the history of that entity along the lines of its dependence stemming from that moment, as some sort of seed-moment of its destiny. There is a circular process at work here, whereby the astrologer is led to the mode of historical interpretation that emphasises *turning-points in history*, decisive and heroic events decided at critical junctures of fate by world-historical individuals, the Napoleons and Caesars. This may indeed be a definitive and revelatory mode in symbolic-historical interpretation; however, the astrologer would be wise to bear in mind the extent to which this mode is set in advance by the imaginative process by which the assignation of significance has been made in the first place, that is by the desire to pin down a horoscope. If the astrologer is unaware of this circle of interpretation, a species of determinism slips quietly in under the cover of symbol. Only by a divinatory understanding can we effectively retain the assignatory potency of the horoscope without having to labour under the burden of historical or seed-moment determinism.

UNPREDICTABLE OMENS

Mundane astrology has since antiquity sustained a tradition of observation of unpredictable celestial phenomena that fall outside the regular cyclic movements of Sun, Moon and planets. An unusual meteorological phenomenon used to marvellous effect by William Lilly was the appearance of parhelia or 'mock suns' seen in London on the birthday of Charles I, 19th November 1644. In this apparition two phantom suns flank the real sun, signifying a mutation in the fortunes of the king. By a combination of astute judgment, boldness, and good fortune, Lilly published his *Starry Messenger* pamphlet, utilising a vivid woodcut illustration of the mock suns, on the very day of the overwhelming parliamentary victory at the battle of Naseby, 14th June 1645. This marked the virtual annihilation of the royalist cause. Lilly's sure-footed prediction of the decisive outcome of the battle propelled him – and his astrology – to a pinnacle of reputation. He was also skilfully weaving the strands which would come together in his remarkable prophecy of the ultimate fate of the king.[1]

The most significant of all non-predictable portents, and matched only by rare supernovae, are the great comets. A famous instance that has become embedded into England's historical imagination was the appearance of Halley's comet in 1066. King Harold faced a double peril, on the one side from incursion by his banished brother Tostig, but more threateningly from William of Normandy, who by the spring of that year was laying down preparations for the intended invasion. Now, to strike fear into the Saxons in these cruel times, came a marvellous 'hairy-star' or comet. It was at its greatest brilliance in the evening skies of 24th April to 1st May, probably disappearing early in June. For the Normans, at least in retrospect, it becomes an omen of good fortune, celebrated in the Bayeux Tapestry. Astrologers of a later era can hardly avoid the symbolic recognition that the 1066 comet announced the end of Saxon England.

There is a parallel to this theme that becomes more remarkable the more it is pondered, in the brightest manifestation of Halley's comet in the modern epoch, that of 1910. First sighted on 18th January, this became a stunning sight in the night skies of May that year, with its closest approach to the Earth on the 10th May – three days after the death of Edward VII. Contemporary reports of preparations for the state funeral on the 20th run side by side with discussions of the comet. It is however only with long retrospect that we have a measure both of large-scale historical events and of the celestial symbolism that figures them, and what seems obvious and ominous to us will have been obscure even to symbolically-aware participants. From our vantage point we see this comet as marking the last bloom of European monarchy. The Great War that was soon to come destroyed the political power of the network of royal families which joined in blood and marriage the Tsar of Russia, the German Kaiser and the British King-Emperor, together with various lesser thrones. In the funeral cortege were no less than nine reigning monarchs and a host of lesser royals, and in the evenings in that brief period, gathered by the death of Edward, they together observed the comet that portended the end of old Europe.

For mundane astrologers comets are perhaps the greatest of manifestations, yet they are amongst the least capable of being rendered into concrete meaning: we know for sure that a comet must 'mean something', but *what*? They readily lead to complete credulity and wild imaginings, and at first sight appear to break all boundaries of any settled divinatory method. Yet even here we observe the process of craft, which is the fundamental desire to articulate phenomena into language and communicable meaning. From antiquity comets have been categorised by their appearance and their duration, and finally captured in the all-embracing symbolism of the zodiac, as their movement is tracked along the ecliptic and they become subject to planetary rulership. Lilly, as ever, sets the standard of craft practice, as when he weaves an impressive celestial visitor which appeared in 1618 into the Jupiter-Saturn cycles, and into his pattern of predictions concerning the monarchy.[2] Although we moderns understand the periodic and orbital nature of comets, and can therefore predict the return of some of the greatest of them, such as Halley's, new comets are always appearing. As a category, therefore, they remain as they always were for astrology, an essentially out-of-frame manifestation cutting across our orderly planetary rhythms.

So what is the status of this order of showing, when compared with the ephemeris-bound indications of our regular astrology? Commenting on Lilly's use of the 1618 comet, the Japanese astrologer Ryuji Kagami suggests that such portents formally reintroduce into our practice 'the omen factor' and remind us of the essentially spontaneous nature of the astrological phenomenon:

> Today, with such powerful computer software, we can calculate exact motions of the planets, and under such circumstances, it is easy to forget that our astrology started as a form of omens or divination. More and more it has come to sound like science, but comets may bring breaks into the horoscope, sudden eruptions which break the continuous pattern of things and upset the smooth order inherent in the ephemeris. By implication, this serves to break up astrological determinism and its fated understanding of human destiny.[3]

A striking instance in recent history of the 'sudden eruption' of a comet into mundane symbolism occurred with comet Hale-Bopp, a prominent visitor to our night skies in the spring and summer of 1997. Astrologers at the time did not, I suspect, give it the consideration that it deserved, but as the study by Maggie Hyde has shown, Hale-Bopp had a particular significance for Britain, bringing an intense focus to the most important of the nation's inceptions, the Coronation of William I on Christmas Day 1066.[4] The first telescopic sighting of the comet took place on 23rd July 1995 when it was at 9 Capricorn on the 1066 Sun, while the ascendant for its stated moment of discovery is 25 Aries, which is identically the 1066 ascendant. Its maximum visibility, at perigee, occurred 22nd-23rd March 1997, when it had come to that very degree, 25-26 Aries.[5]

Several of us watching from the north Kent area that spring observed the tail of the comet flaring over Essex to the north of the Thames Estuary, and a local joke was that this must be the end of 'Essex man'. Pollsters had identified this right-wing archetype – plebeian, materialistic, and self-satisfied – as a key to Tory support in the Thatcher and post-Thatcher era. The prognostication proved correct when New Labour swept to power on a landslide victory on 29th May, obliterating Conservative prospects for years to come. More fundamental and appropriate to the level of such a portent, Tony Blair's reforming government made irreversible constitutional changes through devolution, which gave Scotland its own parliament, the first for two centuries; and through the stripping of aristocratic hereditary powers in the House of Lords, which had been the subject of inconclusive debate for the greater part of a century.

In retrospect, we see that Hale-Bopp was hinting at a darker possibility, consistent with the well-attested ancient theme that has always linked comets and the deaths of princes.[6] In this case the death was that of Princess Diana, whose Sun at 9 Cancer, on the 1066 IC, was opposed by the comet at first sighting. This thread of symbolism is confirmed by the comet's transit at 5 Leo 56 at Diana's death, opposite her Jupiter, ruler of her ascendant for the Sagittarius map.[7] This degree is Prince Charles's ascendant, his principal synastry with Diana, leaving him scorched in the comet's blaze. Given this connection, we may wonder whether Hale-Bopp will eventually be seen to cast a long shadow over the future of the House of Windsor.

WHAT MAY BE PREDICTED?

The symbolic connection between a comet and the tragic death of a Princess reminds us yet again, if we needed reminding, of one of the most imponderable of all questions, which is, what may be predicted? Even for those astrologers who rightly see the main task of their art as illuminating actions and events rather than predicting them, the raising of a predictive possibility exposes our creaking theories and tottering metaphysics. The topic requires more development than can be undertaken here, but we can hardly avoid addressing the issue, even if only in a provisional manner.

The first observation is subtle and metaphysical. It concerns the illusion of fate that arises every time we 'see' symbolism at work in our present circumstances or in some historical situation or nativity that we happen to be studying. We forget that seeing symbolically is interpreting, and our interpreting is the picture we are being shown *now*. Here is a cardinal mystery of divination, and a key to the moment of astrology. By forgetting our interpreting we give over the reality of the symbolism to the literally-understood *then*. This is the fallacy of literalism. Because astrology is a divination of time, in forgetting our interpreting we equate planetary movement with fate and imagine ourselves bound to the cycles of time, past, present and future.

The second observation is empirical. It is clear both from the tradition and from practical experience that successful and useful specific prediction is the exception rather than the rule, and there is no obvious need for it on many occasions where astrology is being meaningfully employed. We have already seen in relation to katarchic astrology how futile it is to substitute mere predictive judgment for a successful resolution or illumination of an issue for a client, and the same consideration is even more relevant in natal interpretation, which humanistic and psychological astrologers well understand. The very concept of 'prediction' is something of a misnomer, implying as it does an objective stance whereby the astrologer supposedly stands outside and before ('pre') the material and utters facts about its future *ex cathedra*.

The third observation concerns the craft of divination, and is the recognition that like all effective judgment, a telling prediction arises within a specific and limited context of participation. When a true prediction is framed, it is as if the astrologer stands within a circle of symbolic threads, and realises by a gift of inspiration which thread calls to be followed from the past and present into the future. This is quite different to the machine of destiny conception that the planets grind out universal fates at all places and all times, and that somehow the techniques of astrology will crack the heavenly code.

These somewhat abstract observations come into their own when we seek to comprehend various manifestations of mundane symbolism. With this in mind I will take up an example of historical significance for our epoch, the 9/11 attacks on New York and on the Pentagon in 2001. This event marked a turning-point in the world affairs of recent times, threatening violence, instability, and the terror of mass destruction to come. The attacks were the catalyst for an aggressive and preemptive stance in US foreign policy. The fall of the twin towers was so tragic and awesome that it would be almost impossible for anyone with a symbolic attitude to avoid being drawn into a search for a deeper meaning. And of course, the heavens matched the event with the brutal signification of a close Saturn-Pluto opposition. Pluto in Sagittarius shows deadly terror by religious fanatics, Saturn in Gemini is the twin concrete towers, the opposition shows perfect enmity. So undeniable was this symbolism that like most other astrologers I felt a chill of fearful recognition and a grim foreboding of far worse things to come, induced by the symbols themselves.

There is however a further feature marking this out as a potent manifestation of mundane symbolism. Amongst several commonly used horoscopes for America is one for the Declaration of Independence, 4th July 1776, for around 5:10pm (Sibly 12 Sagittarius ascendant), together with its rectified variant (Rudhyar 13 Sagittarius ascendant). Either of these charts has the Saturn-Pluto opposition closely across the horizon, Saturn at 14 Gemini 45, Pluto at 12 Sagittarius 38. This is a transit of devastating potential. With this specificity of location the sense of awe is multiplied, because the configuration is seen to be figured *there* as well as *then*, seemingly a fate determined in both space and time.

The configuration is itself a symbol of the unseen and retributive power of vast unconscious forces, bound to the inevitability of time; its contemplation induces a mood of terrible fatalism. But the operative word here is 'seemingly'. Although we were right in the middle of a series of three Saturn-Pluto oppositions (the first one had been on 5th August and the next one was due 2nd November), there was nothing special in terms of astrological symbolism to mark out the day of the attack, or that week. There have been many published discussions of the symbolism, and I have no doubt only seen a minority of them, but so far I have come across no persuasive indication of the exact timing for the attack. Some astrologers had before the event picked up the possibility of a summer or autumn attack from Islamists on America, from the Pluto symbolism, but to my knowledge nobody had specified either a useful dating or the symbolism of the twin towers, even though this latter appears in retrospect grimly obvious. We therefore have to admit that these important events were *figured* yet not usefully *prefigured*, either in principle or in practice. The distinction between figuring and prefiguring is of vital importance if we are to understand how astrology actually works in practice, as opposed to some idealised and universalised notion of how it ought to work.

THE SIBLY SAGA

In the previous chapter I used the problematic working of the horoscope of Diana, Princess of Wales, to illuminate the essentially divinatory process by which significance is derived in natal astrology. Now I will apply the same procedure to the debate that surrounds a fascinating mundane horoscope, that for the American Declaration of Independence, which event is often treated as the 'birth' of the United States. The Saturn-Pluto opposition of 2001 brought the Sibly horoscope for America, or at least one version of it, bouncing into prominence. But even apart from its transitory showing for the tragic events of that year, this must be considered a horoscope of primary significance, since it is the first known exact astrological record of the American Declaration of Independence.

If we follow the evidence provided by the English astrologer Ebenezer Sibly, then the timing of the declaration is placed somewhere around 5pm on the 4th July. We must first acknowledge that there are conflicting historical accounts of proceedings of Congress and the timing of events on the day, and these have led astrologers to widely different variants. However, the view that the signing occurred on the late afternoon of the 4th July has convincing support from good historical sources.[8]

Sibly's famous horoscope features in an engraving titled 'Revolution of America' in his *New and Complete Illustration of the Occult Sciences* published in 1784. The plate shows an infant with a parchment on which appear the words 'Federal Union'. The infant is being watched by a chubby native Indian and a British officer, sword lowered and gesturing in acknowledgment of the new-born babe. Behind stands a blindfold figure of Justice with her sword and scales. A trumpeting angel bears aloft the horoscope scroll, titled 'America Independance'(sic), showing cusps, planets and chart data, 4th July 10h10m pm 1776.

The horoscope in the angel's hand shows Placidus cusps cast for the latitude of London, which at first sight seems an odd choice. The stated time, 10h10m pm, also appears to refer to local time for London. Adopting this assumption, the horoscope may be relocated to the place of the signing, Philadelphia, almost exactly five hours behind London. Taking this approach produces an initial determination of the time for the Declaration of Independence of 5:10pm Local Time 4th July 1776, with an ascendant of 12 Sagittarius 21. This latter figure is commonly, although wrongly, taken to be the Sibly horoscope for America.

Where did Sibly get his data? His voluminous work *Occult Sciences* is dedicated to the 'Ancient and Honourable Fraternity of Free and Accepted Masons', to whom he commits 'this venerable pile of ancient Astrology'. The Masonic connection appears to be of real significance, since the majority of the young nation's founders were Masons, including George Washington and Benjamin Franklin. Michael Baigent has researched Sibly's background and established that he was a member of Masonic Lodges in Portsmouth and then in Bristol, both cities with trading connections with the former colonies. Baigent argues that he was particularly well placed to hear from fellow Masons an account of the momentous events leading to independence. Indeed, one gets the sense from reading Sibly's discussion of the horoscope that the data itself is taken for granted as a matter of fact. There is nothing in his text to suggest that the timing derives either from speculation, or from astrological rectification. On the other hand we have no sound basis for discounting these options, and it is apparent from *Occult Sciences* that Sibly employs precise rectification in his practice.

Given its support from historical evidence, we might imagine that the case for Sibly's timing is cast-iron. Sadly, however, his effort has been obscured for succeeding generations of astrologers; instead of recognition he has attracted

Revolution of America

FIGURE 24 Sibly Engraving

bewilderment and condescension. He is undone by a huge and seemingly intractable obstacle, which is that data and horoscope details in the published engraving show gross errors and are a complete mismatch, and however they are juggled they cannot be made to make sense. It is a matter of some irritation to any astrologer following in his footsteps that juggling and guesswork has to be used to arrive at a speculation concerning the final chart, with several different versions emerging from the mess. Later attempts to work out what Sibly intended have led to two main solutions to the problem, producing variants of Sagittarius 8 and 12 degrees rising in the horoscope relocated to Philadelphia.

The tangled data has continued to defeat those few researchers who have bothered to look. The confusion makes Sibly's original look like an amateurish and ignorant concoction, undermining the credibility of the author and his timing ever since. Even his historical and symbolic sense looks off-beam when he locates the significance of the Declaration of Independence in London and not in America. Given these obscurities, it is not surprising that Sibly's labours, including his perceptive astrological interpretation of the Revolution, have sunk into oblivion. However, the botch-job theory leaves us with a puzzle. Even a casual examination of his ambitious text *Occult Sciences* will soon indicate that quite apart from a man of wide learning and an inquisitive mind, we have encountered an experienced and technically sophisticated astrologer. We will do Sibly and our quest for the US horoscope a favour by seeking some other explanation.

The solution comes when we realise that the errors are not computational in origin; they are typographical, and derive from ignorance or sloppiness at the hands of the printer or the engraver. The obscurity has been further compounded by lack of awareness amongst later researchers of the method of computation employed in 18th century astrology. These conclusions are demonstrated in detail in Appendix 6, which I trust will clear up once and for all the question of the 'correct' Sibly horoscope, that is, the computation that he intended and the timing he used as his basis.

THE REAL SIBLY

We can be sure that Sibly understands the Declaration of Independence to occur on 4th July 1776, at or about 9:53pm GMT. When we adjust this for Philadelphia the best estimate of the data is 4:52:41pm, for a longitude correction equivalent to 5h00m36s West of Greenwich. This is the correct determination for the 'Sibly 8 Sagittarius', with an ascendant in Philadelphia of 8 Sagittarius 47. As to what relation this has, either historically or symbolically, with the event it is supposed to represent is quite another question. What should not be in doubt is what Sibly wants us to understand concerning the birth of the new republic. Since it is certain that he was a technically competent astrologer, there is no good reason to doubt his actual computation. The timing given here therefore has to be the starting point for any historical and astrological consideration of the Sibly horoscope.

So what was done on that day and at that hour? It is not in itself one of the initiating moments of the revolution, and neither is it the most important event from a constitutional point of view. Nevertheless at that hour an epochal decision was announced to which all the former colonies eventually assented, acknowledging de facto independence and recording its formal justification before God and men. It is this document with its exalted language that has come to seize the American public and political imagination as the proclaiming of the nation's independence, and it is this spirit that is distilled in Sibly's engraving and his horoscope.

If we have arrived at the real Sibly, then other versions which have been suggested to solve the problem, whatever their symbolic merits, must be 'wrong' in the strict sense that they are not astronomically derived from Sibly. This includes the version proposed for 4:50 pm LMT, with 8 Sagittarius 14 ascendant – the logic here is to suppose that the time in the engraving is a mistake for 10 minutes before 10 to the hour, GMT, which converts on a straight five hour difference to 10 minutes before 5pm in Philadelphia.

The variant commonly found, for 12 Sagittarius rising, is arrived at by ignoring Sibly's London angles and cusps altogether and assuming that the time in the engraving is a statement of GMT, giving a time in Philadelphia of 5:10pm. But, as is demonstrated in Appendix 6, this is simply an error and does not square with Sibly's method, nor with the actual horoscope calculations.

CLOSING THE SYMBOLIC CIRCLE: RUDHYAR'S RECTIFICATION

By one of those extraordinary movements in which symbolism reworks science to produce the desired astrological effect, Dane Rudhyar has arrived at a potent development from Sibly's original. In *The Astrology of America's Destiny*, published in 1974, Rudhyar reproduces the engraving, which he titles 'George Washington receiving the horoscope of America from the Angel Gabriel'.[9] He proposes a version for an ascendant of 13 Sagittarius 10, for a time of 5:13:55 pm LMT Philadelphia. This is derived from his rectification of the Sibly 12, mentioned above, and demonstrated in an ambitious study of American history.

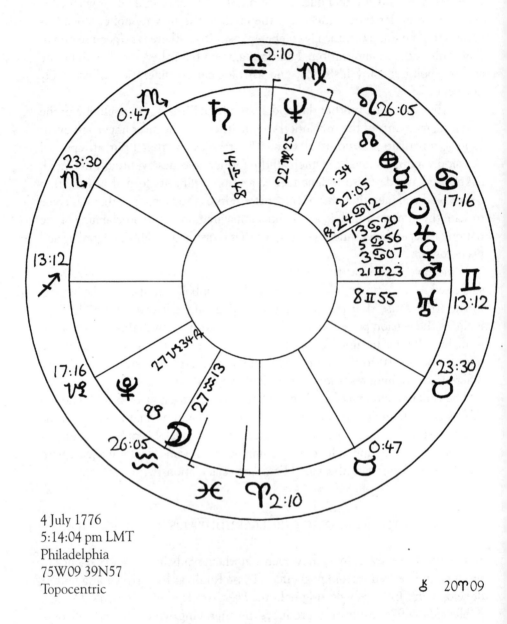

4 July 1776
5:14:04 pm LMT
Philadelphia
75W09 39N57
Topocentric

FIGURE 25   United States Declaration of Independence
from Dane Rudhyar's rectification of the Sibly horoscope

Now the Sibly 12 Sagittarius is essentially a fiction, but the symbolic reconstruction undertaken by Rudhyar is not – whatever we may think of his craft methods, this exemplifies the imaginative work at the heart of astrology. He leaves Sibly behind, yet in doing so he has created a marvellous re-connection with the original London horoscope: the Rudhyar ascendant of 13 Sagittarius 10 is just 2′ short of the Sibly London MC of 13 Sagittarius 12, with one as the reflection of the other. It is also obvious from Rudhyar's text that his rectification is, at the conscious level, quite independent of any wish to reflect Sibly's original. He has almost certainly not registered the connection as significant; if he had it is difficult to imagine him not bridging the 2′ gap.

Knowingly or unknowingly Rudhyar has closed the symbolic circle of the Sibly horoscope for the USA. If we were to represent this closure we would make a very slight change to the rectified horoscope, to place 13 Sagittarius 12 on the ascendant for Philadelphia 5:14:04pm LMT. This brings us back to Sibly's intention in showing the figure for London. His discussion in *Occult Sciences* is concerned to demonstrate the political effects on Britain of the Aries and Cancer Ingresses for 1776, and he follows through the symbolism of the Aries Ingress to the decisive moment of the break with the colonies. His entire emphasis is on the movement of fate and the heavens with respect to the seat of power, which up to the instant of the breach is the government in London, ultimately rooted in the semi-divine authority of the monarch. Following Rudhyar's intuition and his rectification, the circle is complete in the image of the Mother, Britain (13 Sagittarius on the MC) and the new-born Child, America (13 Sagittarius on the ascendant).

Perhaps we as astrologers get too caught up in the idea of one precise moment, and can easily miss the drama of the world event unfolding that afternoon in Philadelphia. Following Sibly's unknown source and his astrology as our starting point, and Rudhyar's poetic interpretation as our terminus, we are invited to assign the worldly event to a space of twenty-two minutes and a five degree ascending arc of the sign Sagittarius. In that turn of the heavens the destiny of America devolves from England (London and the 8 Sagittarius) to the genesis of a common declaration binding the various independent States (Rudhyar's 13 Sagittarius). That is the spirit that has been captured in Rudhyar's imaginative symbolism, and I believe it constitutes a true and revealing way of working with the Sibly representation of the Declaration of Independence.

It is worth interpreting certain features of this remarkable horoscope in order to reveal its radicality. Jupiter, exalted in Cancer, is lord of the horoscope and ultimately determines its destiny. Jupiter's authority is announced through the Moon, ruler of Cancer, and we therefore observe that this figure is a signature of the event it represents, namely a *declaration*, since the Moon is on the 3rd cusp. Staying at this first level of interpretation, we may trace the logic of the Declaration of Independence through main significators, taking the Moon as our starting point. As the text states in its introduction, its purpose is to put the case, to justify the breach, and to announce its reasons both to the world and for the assurance of the former colonists themselves. The act of rebellion is shown by Uranus, co-dispositor of the Moon, passing under the western horizon now that the deed is done. Mercury in the 8th, retrograding to an aspect of Neptune, shows the move to 'dissolve the Political Bonds which have connected them with another'; Mercury rules the 7th of the other and is in semisquare with Uranus, the planet that has finished the deed. With Mercury mute we should bear in mind how unspeakable this concept might seem for ordinary folk in the context of an earlier and pre-Uranian epoch. Government could change, lands change hands, dynasties might come and go, but it was a radical idea to advocate the *separation* of an independent people ruled neither by a home-grown king nor by an imposed one, but wholly by their own elected government. Above any king are 'the Laws of Nature and of Nature's God', which authority I believe is here signified in the Sun-Jupiter conjunction. This is the philosophy of the New Order and not of the Old, and it is why the declaration does something more that offer a juridical analysis of the tyranny of the British monarchy; like its Moon in Aquarius, it moves to a plain-speaking yet eloquent philosophical justification for the principle of democratic independence.

> We hold these Truths to be self-evident, that all Men are created equal, that they are endowed by their Creator with certain inalienable Rights, that among these are Life, Liberty and the Pursuit of Happiness...

Thus opens the argument (3rd house), the self-evident showing of humane Aquarius in its care for the people, the Moon. Behind the essential simplicity of this statement lies the political philosophy of Thomas Paine, a true Aquarian; it was his revolutionary pamphlet 'Common Sense', printed and reprinted in 100,000 copies and talked about in countless homes and gatherings, that finally inspired the resolve of the colonists and brought them together in common cause. In testimony to this origin Paine's natal Jupiter in the 28th degree of Aquarius is on the Declaration Moon.[10]

The rights specified are 'Life, Liberty and the Pursuit of Happiness', and we surely have here the three graces of the renaissance philosophers, Sun, Jupiter and Venus. The greatest of these is Liberty, in the cause of which the human spirit will sacrifice everything, even life itself. This is why it is Jupiter that rules the horoscope, and why in the document the pursuance of liberty depends on the capacity of a governed people to pass their own laws for their own security (Cancer) and public good. From this flows an attitude to government which characterises both Thomas Paine's liberal philosophy and the later fibre of American politics, which is that government is not a *source* of these blessings of humanity, and not a good in itself, but a *necessary means* by which the rights of the people are maintained and defended. The power of government is therefore always to be held in check. Rudhyar notes the placing of Saturn in the 10th and observes that in contrast to most other democratic systems 'American sociopolitical processes are dominated by time measures', with terms of office exactly predetermined, and little flexibility in the system.[11] Here we see Saturn as significator of the constitution and the government, exalted and elevated in the place of authority yet square to the Sun and subservient to Law – Venus its dispositor is with Jupiter – in an eternal balance of powers.

THE AMERICAN HOROSCOPE: LITERAL OR SYMBOLIC?

Rudhyar's rectification takes us towards the far pole of symbolic interpretation. As has been established, there is no basis to the 12 Sagittarius figure as a derivative of Sibly's computation, and therefore Rudhyar's starting point is, from a literal point of view, 'wrong'. His next step rubs salt into the wound as far as our common-sense literalists are concerned. He rectifies the ascendant by a degree, not on the direct evidence of transits or progressions, but on the basis of Sabian degree symbolism.[12] When we unpack the layers of his text it is obvious that it is the Sabian symbol of one single degree that is decisive, which is the ascendant in the 14th degree of Sagittarius (13°00' to 13°59' of the sign). Its image is: 'the Great Pyramid and the Sphinx'.

The Great Seal of the United States, authorised by Congress on 20th June 1782, shows the eagle, embodying an easily understood evocation of power and national pride. The design on the reverse of the seal is much less immediate in its appeal: it is an unfinished pyramid of thirteen stones capped by a triangle, in which is an eye. There is a Latin inscription *novus ordo seclorum*, 'a new order of the centuries', together with the date 1776. Various esoteric interpretations are suggested, but it suffices here to say that the design has usually been taken to reflect Masonic and Rosicrucian symbolism. Rudhyar holds that this reflects an unacknowledged stream of the American destiny with sources in ancient cosmology. The triangular apex of the pyramid demands spiritual and not simply material completion, and the figure as a whole suggests a purpose still awaiting fulfilment.[13]

Rudhyar supports his reworking of the chart from degree symbols on the other angles, especially the MC. In terms of the Sabian symbols, his choice is an effective one and the immediately surrounding degree areas for an earlier or later timing do not appear to give appropriate degrees on the angles.[14] I have found no indication as to why he chose the exact minute of arc on the MC or ascendant, and his use of transits and progressions to prove his chosen angles is quite loose. A careful examination of the angles in timing reveals that this figure does on the whole yield reasonable signification for a number of important events in American history, and works as well as most mundane horoscopes can be expected to work.[15] By giving first place to degree symbols over and above more enduring craft methods, Rudhyar sacrifices much of the authority that his interpretation might otherwise have, but that does not affect my conclusion that this is an effective rectification yielding genuine symbolism, and carrying a hidden inspiration in its re-connection to Sibly's original figure. Further, whatever the craft astrologer's justifiable caveats against Rudhyar's techniques and his theorising, I believe he has given voice to a spiritual dimension of the destiny of America.

This is a good point to come back to the base-line relocation derived from Sibly, namely the 8 Sagittarius horoscope, for this has its own story to tell. Its most striking feature is Uranus exactly on the descendant, with just 8′ orb. Uranus is not mentioned in *Occult Sciences*, which was published in 1784, but it is likely that even if Sibly had been interested in the new planet at the time of writing his text, accurate knowledge of its position back in 1776 would not have been available. For us seeing it in hindsight, it emerges as an archetypal and spontaneous manifestation, proclaiming its celestial role in overthrowing kingship and bringing an entirely modern mode of political and social revolution – in truth a New World and 'a new order of the centuries'. Its placing closely on the western angle is the instant of breach, the cutting of the bond tying it to the English – and European – other.

The striking role of Uranus brings us to a curious symbolic reversal of horizon that occurs around the Independence horoscope. The Sibly 8 Sagittarius chart is a mirror image to the most commonly found of all the versions of the American horoscope, cast, with small variations, for around 2:15am on 4th July. This shows 7 or 8 Gemini on the ascendant, with Uranus now exactly rising. In the course of his researches on the origins of the various US horoscopes, Nicholas Campion suggests from his experience that 'at least half of American astrologers who express an opinion, perhaps more, regard this unequivocally as the horoscope of the United States', and this despite the fact that there is no documentary evidence to support the timing, and the evidence we do have runs completely counter to it. Campion traces a possible origin of this tradition back to the

American astrologer Luke Broughton, writing in 1861, who asserted that Gemini 'rules' the United States, and that the passage of Uranus at 9 Gemini brought the Declaration of Independence. The symbolism appears to have become conflated to suggest an *ascendant* of 9 Gemini, with Uranus rising, although it is not obvious that this was Broughton's intention:

> It would seem, therefore, that the Gemini rising chart originated either as a rectification not based on historical timing, or as a symbolic chart which was not intended to represent a precise historical moment.[16]

Campion observes that 'an entire mythology' has grown up in order to justify the Gemini chart, including the claim that it must have been astrologically elected by the founding fathers. I do not wish to deny this chart's validity for those who have tested it and found it to be significant, but the idea that it was elected is improbable, not least because of the condition of the ruler of the ascendant, Mercury, impeded by being both retrograde and under beams. Add to this the fact that Cancer is traditionally mute and we would have to admit that this horoscope would be unlikely to be chosen by an eighteenth-century astrologer to declare anything, let alone a nation's independence.

* * * * *

My concern is not to finally resolve the question of the true horoscope of the United States – even if such a question is capable of being decided, that decision remains the responsibility of my American colleagues. My task here is to bring into view the *process* by which all such decisions are made in horoscopy, namely by the imaginative assignation of significance. The literalist attitude seeks to sidestep this necessity, as if the determining of a literal and historical fact could be in itself the guarantee of significance. We astrologers impose the metaphor of birth on a timed and dated national or constitutional incident and treat it horoscopically as if it is a turning-point in history. So far so good, and astrology can and does proceed on this basis. The error of theory comes when we imagine that it is the literal and historical fact of the incident that grants significance to the astrology, instead of recognising that it is our image of the event and our take on history which locates the literal incident as significant. In mundane astrology imagination is often submerged in the rational language of factual and historical analysis, but in most instances we only need to scratch the surface for the symbolic and non-literal nature of the assignation to shine through. Nowhere is this more apparent than in the horoscope for the Declaration of Independence, treated as the birthmap for the USA.

The attachment astrologers have for the 4th July 1776 horoscopes in relation to the destiny of America makes the case for me. It is an effective counter to literalism since whichever horoscope we choose, Gemini rising, Sibly 8, 12 or 13, or some other on the day, we come up against the most obvious of purely historical questions: why 4th July? As proponents of other dates for the American horoscope have often pointed out, what happened on the 4th was less important from a strictly historical point of view than what happened on several other dates.[17] In particular the crucial 'resolution of independence' was accepted without dissent by the Continental Congress on 2nd July. John Adams, seconder of the motion, declared 'I am apt to believe that it [2 July] will be celebrated by Succeeding Generations as the great anniversary Festival'. Yet within two years the celebrations were recorded as occurring not on the 2nd but on the 4th, and there they have stayed ever since.[18] If we follow in that train and find the symbolism of the 4th July revealing for the story of the United States, then our astrology gives expression not to some supposed literal fact of history but to the living historical imagination of the American people. These are the people *for whom* the Declaration of Independence is significant, and there is nowhere else for significance to be found. It is in the living historical imagination that the narrative of the United States unfolds, and if the symbols of astrology are to have any place at all, it is in that narrative. The answer to the question, 'why the 4th of July' is that this is what American culture and the American people have given us. That is all and that is enough.

The conclusion drawn over the course of this chapter is that our mundane astrology works not with some literalised world supposedly available to objective criteria, but with *images* of the world established within the collective imagination of a culture, and it is this that constitutes divination. We read great celestial signs as spontaneous omens, and we pattern a narrative of the past in planetary cycles. We assign our mundane astrology to dramatised moments of history to see what the divination gives us – but the signs, omens and horoscopes we work with are not astronomical records of historical events in the physical world. They are symbols in a world of human significance.

NOTES

1 Lilly's use of the mock suns, and the development of his prophecies concerning the fate of Charles I, are described in the extensive study by Ann Geneva, 'Astrology and the Seventeenth Century Mind: William Lilly and the Language of the Stars' (1995 Manchester University Press) especially pp99-114. Lilly's predictions concerning Naseby are also discussed in Derek Parker, 'Familiar to All: William Lilly and Astrology in the Seventeenth Century' (1975 Jonathan Cape) pp134-140.

2 Ann Geneva, op.cit. pp214-8.

3 Ryuji Kagami (Akihiro) 'Comets and the Unpredictable' COA Bulletin 30 13th January 2002.

4 Maggie Hyde's study *Diana, 1066 & the Legacy of Hale-Bopp* is in COA Bulletin no.29 (30 Dec 2001); this same issue includes her discussion *Wharton on the Interpretation of Comets* reprinted from *Astrology* Quarterly vol.59:4,1985. This is an abstract of the methods given by George Wharton in his *Gesta Britannorum* (1657). The 1066 horoscope should be computed for true local noon at Westminster Abbey, 25th December (UT 12:05:49 Sun/MC 9Cap55'24" Asc 25Aries13). The coordinates of the high altar at Westminster are: 51N29'54" 0W07'30". There is no historical record of the hour of the event, so the noon horoscope is a symbolic choice for kingship, but it has been found to work consistently with these exact angles. The chart is sometimes given for noon GMT, but this is a lazy compromise for an era long before the concept of standard time meridians.

5 Hale-Bopp discovery: 23rd July 1995 12:10am MDT Cloudcroft New Mexico, asc.25Aries39. Comet approx. position 9 Capricorn (data: Mark Lerner).

6 Predictive and retrospective approaches: I do not know of any astrologer who was guided to consider great danger for Diana on the particular weekend she died, and as we have already discussed (ch.12) there is hardly a convincing interpretation of the tragedy from the symbolism of the natal horoscope even after the event. However, as so often happens it was later obvious that there were symbolic clues that could have guided us had we located them in the right context, while Maggie Hyde and others raised the question of the threat to the monarchy and a direct connection of Hale-Bopp with Diana in a Company of Astrologers meeting of May 1997.

7 A further sad testimony concerning Diana comes through the report of Nicholas Kollerstrom, who saw the lunar eclipse following her death: 'The next Full Moon two weeks later became totally eclipsed after it rose. A crowd of us (on Hampstead Heath) watched it reappear, with grief in our hearts, with a sense of mystery amongst the mists, as if Diana's image were becoming merged with that of the Roman moon-goddess, her namesake.' (Nick Kollerstrom 'Lady Di – The Eclipse Princess' AA Journal vol 42:6 Nov/Dec 2000. Quoted by Maggie Hyde op.cit.) The curious signification of Hale-Bopp is woven into the symbolism through the place of the eclipsed Moon, 24 Pisces – the degree of Saturn, lord of the comet (ruler of its sign) at its discovery. The sombre visual appearance of a lunar eclipse and the trace of a great comet combine to remind us of the dependence of our astrology on 'the omen factor'.

8 For a comprehensive and well-researched review of the various issues concerning the timing and significance of the Declaration of Independence, see Nicholas Campion *The Book of World Horoscopes* (Cinnabar Books 1996) p401ff.

9 The text of Rudhyar's *The Astrology of America's Destiny* is available on-line in the Rudhyar archives at www.khaldea.com

10 Thomas Paine: 29 January 1737 OS (= 9 Feb NS), Thetford, Norfolk, England. The chart has sometimes appeared incorrectly calculated as if the data is New Style, but Great Britain and its dominions did not change calendar until 3/14 Sept 1752. To the best of my knowledge only the date is known through the published biographies. Marc Penfield (2001: The Penfield Collection, Vulcan Books, Seattle 1979) suggests a speculative time of 11am, for an asc. of 7 Gemini 14, probably chosen to place the US Uranus on Paine's ascendant and rising Moon; this does yield a perfect symbolic election which repays close study. Neptune is closely trine Paine's Jupiter, from Gemini to Aquarius, and this Neptune is in mutual reception with Mercury at 8 Pisces 54, ruler of the ascendant. The Moon applies directly square Mercury, making this planet a key significator for Paine's writings. Mutual reception by degree brings

Mercury to 8 Gemini 54, 1' arc conjunct the US Uranus, an undeniable signature of identity. The whole is suggestive of a mystical and quasi-transcendent philosophy of popular democracy as the inspiration for the American revolution.

11 Rudhyar op.cit chapter 6.

12 The Sabian Symbols were derived from the clairvoyant images of a psychic, Elsie Wheeler, working under the direction of Marc Edmund Jones. Each degree of the zodiac has an image, and to this is appended an interpretation, developed by M.E.Jones. Rudhyar made his own variant of these interpretations. The Sabian Symbols became a principal component of his later astrology. See Dane Rudhyar *An Astrological Mandala* Vintage Books 1974; also M.E.Jones *The Sabian Symbols in Astrology* Shambhala 1969.

13 Rudhyar op.cit chapter 4 part 3.

14 There is a degree symbolism which Rudhyar does not point out, but which seems to me quite compelling in relation to the obverse of the Great Seal, where the eagle bears a sheaf of thirteen arrows, for the thirteen original states. The Sabian symbol for the 9th degree of Gemini, the degree of Uranus, reads 'A quiver filled with arrows'.

15 This is not the place to attempt a proof of the 13 Sagittarius horoscope through timing, but a few specific indicators of radicality are worth mention. All the afternoon horoscopes show appropriately for 1861 and the crisis of the Civil War through the progressed full moon in the 5th degree of Aries (exact for the Sagittarius horoscopes in May 1861); the prior progressed New Moon in the 21st degree of Virgo marked the War with Mexico (started 15 May 1846), and here the angles of the 13 Sagittarius figure show ICp to Uranus (solar arc in longitude). This horoscope responds to the Kennedy assassination (22 Nov 1963) with asc.p semisquare Uranus radix 3' wide, and other significant contacts including asc.p to Mercury rad and Mercury p. conjunct desc.p. The events of 9/11 appear to be subsumed under some greater symbolism reflected in progressed Sun to the conjunction of radix Moon. Given what has transpired since, this perhaps indicates the dilemma of international relations facing modern America in its dealings with the rest of the world, and is a test of its faith with respect to its original humanitarian principles. How does America declare itself now? The progressed asc. in the 13 Sagittarius figure has at the same time been moving through the dangerous Mars-Neptune square, with asc. radix semisextile Neptune. This reinforces the indication of the progressed Sun-Neptune quincunx, and close Sun-node quincunx. I do not wish to suggest that the 13 Sagittarius figure is significantly more sensitive to timing measures than are other 4th July variants; they each have their strong notes and their dumb notes, and any astrologer who has worked closely with rectification will know what I mean. But as I hope I have sufficiently indicated Rudhyar's rectified Sibly is well able to hold its ground.

16 Campion op.cit p406-9.

17 See for example the historical analysis by Joseph Milburn in *Astrological Americana* (1949, American Federation of Astrologers: Research Bulletin no.3) p107ff. Another contender for the title of birthchart of the US should be mentioned here; this is the 'Scorpionic America' horoscope researched by David Solté, for 15 November 1777, which marked the first attempt at a cooperative government. Solté's rectification is for 12:46pm LMT, York, PA, with an asc. of 22 Aquarius (see for eg Mountain Astrologer April/May 1997 p109; also Campion op.cit. pp419-20). From this perspective the events of 4 July 1776 involved a group of thirteen independent states, and not one single national entity.

18 Nicholas Campion op.cit quoting Adams p405. The reference to the dating of the celebrations is given p414, recorded by the historian Channing; according to this source the celebrations of 1778 began at 5pm, and appear to have similarly celebrated at this time in other years, supporting the Sibly timing.

14

The Fourfold Symbol I:
Divination and Allegory

REORIENTING astrology as divination leads to a realm of uncertainty with few signposts to guide us. Despite the fact that divination is an enduring belief in the general population, the question of its possibility and scope leaves unruffled the complacent surface of academic thought. Divination is not taken seriously from the point of view of philosophy, and cannot even be observed by science. Since divination has always been a repressed topic in Christianity, it is a non-entity for official culture. How ironic, therefore, that astrology – Western civilisation's most beautiful and sophisticated divinatory language – far from taking a lead, has not even been registered as 'divination' by the majority of its adherents.[1] This blanket ignorance of divination is further compounded by the understandable tendency for practitioners to get on and do it rather than to talk about it.

In the light of this combination of factors it is not so surprising that an adequate way of describing and analysing divination seems never to have developed. There are numerous elementary texts purporting to tell us *how* to make divination, but there is far less discussion of what it means that we experience divination at all, and virtually nothing by way of reflective criticism of the practice.

As a contribution to the discussion of astrology as divination, I would like to introduce the 'Fourfold Interpretation of the Symbol'. This is directly based on a hermeneutic – a model of meaning and interpretation – which was developed to a high degree of sophistication in early and medieval Christianity. This model also inspired Dante in the creation of his *Divine Comedy*. It has remained relatively little known outside historical theology, and in any case never found sympathy in the Protestant reform.

The fourfold method is a marvellous legacy of the Western mystical tradition. When the method is carried over to the description of the divinatory symbol, its capacity to reconnect our astrology to that mystical tradition will, I hope, become evident to any astrologer who takes the trouble to enter into its spirit. The connection with the concerns of Christians lies in the fact that astrologers likewise face the task of interpreting the 'divine sign', which is the original literal meaning of divination. Interpretation is the key here. Divinatory astrology, it must be remembered, depends upon an *interpretive act*; it is not a thing or a fact that is afterwards interpreted. In the light of these considerations, we would expect patterns of analysing interpretation derived from religious inspiration to be illuminating for us. Further, this hermeneutic establishes its modern credentials by its capacity to incorporate insights derived from psychoanalysis and Jung's analytical psychology. In the next chapter, I will make a rough-and-ready attempt in this direction.

The first task, however, is to describe the Fourfold Hermeneutic as originally conceived, in sufficient detail to bring out its scope.

THE FOURFOLD HERMENEUTIC OF MEDIEVAL CHRISTIANITY

He changes the water of carnal sense into the wine of spiritual intelligence

Albertus Magnus[2]

Early and medieval Christianity developed the allegorical method, which is the hermeneutic of levels or senses in scripture, in order to interpret the inner meaning represented by the literal text of the Bible. Actions and events literally recorded in the Bible are understood to carry further allegorical meanings, and these are the Word of God no less than the literal text. This approach is the descendant of a much wider tradition of symbolic thinking. Examples occur in early Greek thought, for instance where the stories of the gods are reinterpreted as symbolising philosophical ideas. The first Christians also had behind them the tradition of the Judaic non-literal interpretation of Scripture known as *midrash*.[3]

Origen (*fl.* third century) is credited as the first author of the method within Christianity. He developed a three-level interpretation of literal, moral and mystical senses of Scripture. The level he described as 'mystical' was later divided into allegory and anagoge to give the fully developed four levels approach.

As far as Origen was concerned, the accounts in the Scriptures do not require to be literally true, as for instance in the account in Genesis. Did God literally make Eve from Adam's rib? The Word of God uses real history where this reveals a mystical truth, but weaves into this account non-literal events where the mystical function requires it. Other Church Fathers, notably Jerome and Tertullian, disputed this, believing that the allegory was permissible only when it

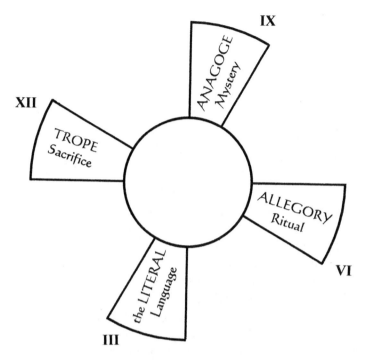

FIGURE 26 The hermeneutic cross in the cadent houses

was founded in a literal truth. Origen's approach won over an influential convert when it succeeded in answering the philosophical doubts of Augustine: 'the letter kills, but the spirit gives life,' said Augustine.[4]

By the time of Thomas Aquinas in the thirteenth century, the four levels hermeneutic had become widely accepted as the means by which Scripture was to be interpreted, its method summed up in a well-known verse:

> The letter teaches you the facts
> Allegory what you should believe
> Morality how you should act
> and Anagogy what to hope for.[5]

I will illustrate the method with the example of the story of the Exodus, as given in Psalm 114:

When Israel went out of Egypt, the house of Jacob from a people of strange language; Judah was his sanctuary, and Israel his dominion.

Let us see how this short text is understood to carry the teachings of Christianity in its layered meanings:

- The *literal* text tells of the historical Exodus of the Jews from Egypt. It is an event of sacred history that is also real human history.
- The *allegorical* is the 'shadow of Truth'. This reading transforms the literal into an allegory of the mission of Christ in world history. The Old Law (Old Testament) becomes a prophecy of the New Law brought by Christ. The Exodus is a prophecy of the Redemption, whereby Christ leads out souls (Israel) from sin (Egypt). Through this interpretation the Old Testament and the New Testament are brought into unity and the creed of the Church is established. The individual accepts these teachings as a matter of *faith*.
- The *tropological or moral* is the 'image of Truth'. It is the turning point for the individual soul, where it is directly addressed by the Word of God. The term 'trope' comes from the Greek *tropos*, to turn, as in the tropic of the Sun's turning at the solstices. The soul turns towards truth. Moved by the literal and allegorical truth shown through Scripture the soul comprehends and enacts its own conversion from its state of estrangement (the strange language) to the state of grace (its own chosen land). This level is *charity*; it transforms knowledge of the Christian teaching into compassionate and charitable action by the individual, which is a primary concern in the lay mission of the Church.
- The *anagogic or mystical* reading is 'Truth itself'. It is a prophecy of the passing of the sanctified soul to everlasting glory at the end of time. This level is *hope*. In lay terms we hope for the Kingdom of God to come. It represents the goal of mystical illumination; the soul, addressed by the Scripture, is illuminated in direct relation to God.

A main part of the task of the four levels approach was seen as bringing the Old and New Laws (Testaments) into unity, through a double structure of prophecy. Since the events in the Old Testament prefigure the mission of Christ, the Old Law is a prophecy of the New (allegory). The New Law in turn is a prophecy of the Kingdom of Heaven upon Earth at the Second Coming (anagoge). Understanding the allegories of the Bible was also the gateway to reading the moral meanings of the various stories, as a guide to Christian conduct (trope). For the ordinary priest who might find the four levels hermeneutic difficult to comprehend, texts of standard interpretations of Bible stories were devised to aid in the composition of sermons.

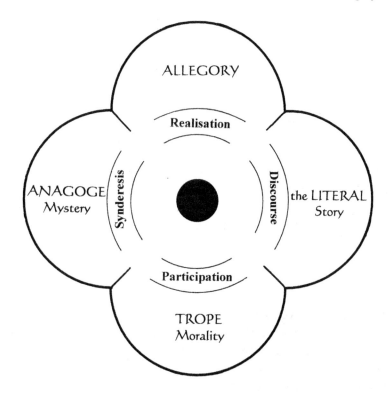

FIGURE 27 Functions of the symbol in divination: Discourse, Realisation, Participation and Synderesis

DANTE AND THE FOUR LEVELS

Up to Dante's time at the turn of the fourteenth century, it had been understood that only Holy Scripture could reveal these four levels of interpretation. Secular poetry or literature might carry a single allegorical sense over and above the literal meaning of the text, but no more. Often this was little more than simple personification, where for example one character in a story stands for Love and another for Hope. Dante gave poetry the potential for a sequence or hierarchy of revelation that had hitherto been reserved exclusively for Scripture. He explained the method he employed in the writing of the *Divine Comedy* in the following words:

The meaning of this work is not of one kind only; rather the work may be described as 'polysemous', that is, having several meanings...

He makes his claim on revelation through poetry by referring to the passage on the Exodus, quoted above, outlining the traditional four levels interpretation. Concerning the three levels above the literal, he observes:

> Although these mystical meanings are all called by various names, they may one and all in a general sense be termed allegorical, inasmuch as they are different (*diversi*) from the literal or historical; for the word 'allegory' is so called from the Greek *allcon*, which in Latin is *alienum* (strange) or *diversum* (different).[6]

The approach I have adopted has some analogy with Dante's translation of the four levels to poetry. By a similar translation, I hope to show that this hermeneutic may help us unfold some of the mysteries of the symbolic order within astrology.

THE FOURFOLD IN ASTROLOGY: AN OVERVIEW

The following brief overview of astrology in terms of the four levels is quite different to any previous description of astrology that the reader is likely to have come across, and the definitions will no doubt seem cryptic and strange at first. As some of the more important implications of this translation will be expanded later, I hope the possibilities of the whole will become much more obvious.

After this overview, the remainder of the chapter takes up a definition of astrology as allegory. Chapter 15 will develop the allegoric description of major features of the craft of astrological interpretation, and describe astrology's tropological and anagogic senses, bringing in comparisons from depth psychology.

I The Literal

> *Literal*: taking words in their usual or primary sense and applying the ordinary rules of grammar, without mysticism or allegory or metaphor.
>
> Concise Oxford Dictionary

The Literal is a representation in words, or in straightforward language-type signs (for example, road signs). The literal level is that of the facts of the matter, which can be *historically reported*, and in principle decided as true or false. The key to the definition of this level is that it appears as an objective truth of the world, which can be posited (or denied) non-metaphorically in ordinary or technical language.

Modern science confines itself to the literal. It is an error to think of this level as material or concrete; time, love, God and infinity can be treated literally. All ideas, abstract concepts, thoughts and emotional states can exist and be spoken of or written about at this level. Even symbols also exist literally. Like the Sun, Moon and planets, all the ephemerides, text-books, clock-times of birth, horoscope judgements, thoughts, emotions, conferences and opinions of astrology exist in such a way that they can be talked of literally, whatever further symbolic meaning may be assigned to any of them. Hence, in terms of astrology, the literal level would be that 'you have the Moon in Leo in the 10th', a literal statement of astronomical fact.

II Allegory – matching astrological symbols to things

Allegory is assigned as a meaning over and above the literal meaning, derived in an explicitly non-literal manner. It takes the astronomical fact – 'you have the Moon in Leo in the 10th' – and interprets it to mean 'you should go for a career in the public eye'. Such an interpretation is *derived non-literally* from the symbolism and conventions of astrology. As against the 'facts of things' posited at the literal level, astrology as a whole stands as a *total* allegory for all things through which those things may be revealed, discriminated or inferred through the act of divination.

III Tropology – knowledge and action

To know and not to act is not yet to know.[7]

Both the literal and the allegorical levels have a quality of objective understanding in which the observing consciousness presumes itself to be apart from the things observed or allegorised. In contrast, the trope reveals the context of interpretation, beyond the things initially taken up in the interpretation, and this includes the participation of the one interpreting.

Natal astrology, especially applied with psychological insight, is strongly tropological because it offers a powerful means for the individual to turn his or her life meaning around. From the time of Alan Leo, the mainstream of Western natal astrology has been striving for this sense of the symbol.

IV Anagoge – the symbolic path

The anagogic is the mystical nature of symbol, and on this account resists positive interpretations. It is the unspoken goal of the project and the direction towards which the turn of the trope turns. It is the future – and eternal present – in prophecy, and it finds its reflection in the astrologer's desire to predict. As the goal of astrology it orients the other senses of symbol, which would have no sense without it.

Despite the impossibility of description of the anagoge, it is close to all who have been touched by the genius of astrology, whatever their shade of theory and practice. This is demonstrated by the common recognition of mystery at the heart of the possibility that astrology works at all. The anagoge graces every occurrence of allegory.[8] Perhaps this is why many astrologers seem to have an instinct that it is important enough just to make astrology in the first place, independent of any supposed benefits. This casts astrology in the light of religious observance, with its practice is its goal.

THE HERMENEUTIC CROSS

As astrologers we better appreciate ideas by locating them within our own symbols. The four levels can be represented as attributes of the horoscope houses that are primarily concerned with interpretation and meaning. There is in the horoscope a hermeneutic cross formed by the cusps of the cadent houses taken in the order of the 3rd, 6th, 12th and 9th, and they represent in turn the literal (the story), allegory, trope, and anagoge. This suggests an affinity with the traditional sign rulerships of Mercury and Jupiter. Thus Mercury rules the literal story (3rd) and the allegorical method that is applied to it (6th). Jupiter rules morality and the sacrifice that arises through participation in the trope (12th). Jupiter also rules prophecy and mystery through the anagoge (9th). By viewing the houses in triads, analogous to the elements in the signs of the zodiac, the angles and the succedent houses are symbolically related to, or metaphorically interpreted by, the cadent houses. The following account briefly introduces this metaphor, especially through the 3rd house of the literal and the 6th house of allegory, and it will be readily capable of development by the reader who has an intuitive sympathy with the ideas presented here.[9]

'Language is the house of Being' (Martin Heidegger). Human beings exist in language, and things that we know are spoken. This is meaning in the literal, and this is the story we tell about our lives. Language also expresses the primary relationship between human beings, and in this way the 3rd house (language) interprets, gives meaning to, or tells the story of, the Other (the 7th). Even when we tell the story of our own life, we objectify our actions and our life, as it would be seen by some Other. Out of this exchange comes the community of thought, the body of ideas, and the collective cultural reality (the 11th). When a client comes to an astrologer, he or she has a story to tell, and this is literally given in words. The story is what is now or has been, and is therefore a 'history'.

Within language there is the imaginative power of metaphor. A meaning is transferred from its literal reference to enable some other meaning to be expressed. In mythic, religious and symbolic language the literal is allegorised in a perpetually extended metaphor to create an alternative vision of reality not attainable within the simply literal. In a divinatory allegoric such as astrology, the allegory is governed by a method and a set of conventions which have to be learned and then formally applied. These rules of astrology are best understood as ritual, although from a literal point of view they appear to us as a technical means to some practical end. These are also two sides of the 6th house, ritual and technique. If we consider an example of the 6th house hermetic *craft* of astrology, then the natal astrologer applies classical astrology's doctrine of origin together with the conventions of symbolism. This enables the birth horoscope to yield an allegorical 'as if' translation of the literal story of the client into a series of astrological symbols.

The earthy 6th-10th-2nd triad reflects the fact that at a certain point this 'as if' quality takes a grip on the material and the allegory becomes manifested or made real. Things are signified no longer by words (eg the literal word 'lion') but directly by things (eg the constellation or the tropical sign of Leo). Much practical astrology does not go further than this. The mysterious capacity to create an objective allegory between planets and events allows us to generate inferences that can be translated back into judgments concerning literal and worldly possibilities.

The conscious attempt to create the objective allegory involves a counter-movement that is usually hidden from view. This is indicated in the other cadent houses, starting with the 12th. In the ordinary application of astrology, this counter-movement brings about actual emotional and psychic change resulting from the use or interpretation of astrology. It is the *resolution* of problems and issues beyond the 10th house *judgment* on them, and it brings into play potent manifestations of the working of astrology. The sacrifice implicit in the 12th involves a little death of the ego, or an undermining of its objectifying conscious hold. Where this level of symbol breaks through autonomously and captures the field of consciousness then the bottom drops out of our symbolic reality as we encounter shadows and signs of our own participation in the symbol. This realm is not 'our' creation however, and here we discover, perhaps for the first time, the agency of the daemones.

The 9th house has from early astrology been associated with prophecy, and its associated triad symbolises the defining relation of the human and the divine. Where the allegory allows symbols to represent beings, the anagoge is the interpretation of Being, which in terms of the horoscope houses is signified by the ascendant.

ALLEGORY AND SYMBOL

I will now turn my attention to what actually happens in astrological interpretation, using the four levels model as a guide.

From the point of view of astrology, Jung is the most significant of the minority of modern thinkers who make a sharp distinction between the symbol and the literal (semiotic) sign.[10] The symbol points to an unknown content which of its nature cannot be otherwise or better represented than through the symbol. It is not simply a likeness or simile, nor is it a symptom, or something left behind by psychic processes, as in Freud. For Jung the symbol presents as a true match for an unknown content, and it invites consciousness to test itself against that unknown content.

Any particular interpretation drawn out of the symbol is still less than the symbol, and does not exhaust its meaning. However, a true symbol may at one and the same time fulfil the function of a literal sign. The Cross is a profound symbol, but at the same time it stands as a literal indication of the presence of a community of Christian worship, just as it shows a church on an Ordnance Survey map.

In considering astrological symbolism, it is useful to make a further distinction between what may be termed 'natural' and 'artificial' symbols. Astrology constructs its major significations from natural things treated symbolically – the literally observed objects, Sun, Moon and planets. We can easily distinguish the astrological Sun taken as symbol from the literal Sun of non-symbolic experience, including astronomy.

Jung's work on symbol properly belongs in the context of his development of analytical psychology, and there has been a tendency amongst astrologers to oversimplify the problems involved in bringing Jung's descriptions over into our practices. At the level of reference usually employed by Jung, celestial symbols such as 'Moon' or 'Mercury' are given a vast range of potential meaning. The individual placements that we use in practical horoscope interpretation hardly seem to qualify in the same way. There is a marked difference in level between asserting the whole horoscope, or the great cross of the four angles, as a symbol, and astrology's familiar locating of a specific *significator*, say for a brother or a second-hand car. If we choose to call astrological significators symbols, then they are at a different end of the symbolic spectrum to the mandala or the Cross. On these lines Maggie Hyde has questioned the assumption commonly held in psychological astrology that we can take the universal symbolism of Jung's archetypes and equate them with horoscope symbols without further qualification:

> Jung's concept of the archetype is akin to an astrological symbol only where this latter is considered as a 'universal'. As soon as that symbol has a place within an individual horoscope, it takes on a particular meaning and becomes part of a method of interpretation.[11]

Ordinary horoscope interpretation draws on only a fraction of a planet's potential symbolic range of meaning, and in any given take the universal symbol is reduced to a narrow and specific meaning. Even where a planet's universal meaning is in play and we are using the language of abstract concepts, the astrologer is generally not seeking beyond a simple and conventional category of meaning, as for instance Jupiter = expansion, Venus = love.

So how should we describe what we are doing? In our conventional interpretations we are undoubtedly closer to what is understood as *allegory*. We need to put aside relatively modern objections to allegory, which is now equated with contrived artificiality and has a poor reputation in modern literature. Allegory is usually defined as 'extended metaphor', and this well describes the work of the astrologer in bringing together individual metaphors in a closely woven logic of meanings. In this way a multiple reference, or a complete story, can be laid out. Here is an example from Margaret Hone's influential text-book, interpreting *ascendant in Libra with Venus trine Uranus*:

> Marriage should be successful so long as the over-independent streak is kept in control. Your wife should be stimulating, active and interesting.[12]

This adds up to a complex image synthesised from elementary factors. Each of these possibilities of life and character is denoted by an astrological factor or configuration which stands as simple allegory for it:

– marriage = Venus
– concern with relationship = ascendant Libra

– over-independent streak = Uranus with ascendant ruler
– interesting wife = Uranus with Venus
– success = trine aspect.

The interpretation is sound, consistent with the established canon of horoscope symbolism, and may reasonably be expected to be of use to the client. Add to it a timing by progressions and transits and we could have a potent judgment with some predictive capacity, carrying all the mystery of astrology when it comes true. It involves a certain element of skilful combination or synthesis, yet there is nothing in this allegorising procedure of the craft of horoscopy which defies the grasp of rational mind, or presents us with the incomprehensible realm of the numinous, even though great celestial symbols have been employed to make the interpretation.

It is important in the analysis of our practice that we should accurately describe this allegorical procedure. Allegory is *part* of symbolism, but not the whole, and by acknowledging this we avoid limiting the broader concept of symbol. This also makes comparisons with Jung's treatment of symbol more meaningful.

ASTROLOGY AS ALLEGORY

Astrology as a total system is known by its practitioners to be omniscopic, capable of symbolising all things that can be conceived in the imagination. Since the astrological allegory stands wholly other to the things it represents, the astrologer does not confuse the symbolic showing of Mars with the actual angry man it may represent, even though a complete identity of meaning is established.

Like other divinatory systems, such as the Tarot or the I *Ching*, astrology's total allegory is constructed from a finite number of distinct elements, principally planets, signs, houses and aspects. Since the literal reality that it potentially holds in its scope is infinite, the symbolic elements of astrology must serve over and over again in countless different circumstances. Each element of symbolism is essentially polyscopic, having a multiple set of potential references. It will depend entirely on the circumstances of the 'unique case of interpretation' as to how a particular literal thing in the world is to be symbolised.

The definition of each factor in the allegory is achieved by the contrast with other factors. In its essential symbolism, Saturn is not a significator for a young man, for example. On the other hand, if that same young man is in charge of a group of children, then he may easily be cast in a Saturnian light. Conversely, when we take up a horoscope symbol, for the purposes of allegory we select one or two significations out of the whole polyscopic range, to match our picture of the situation and the exact question under discussion. It all depends upon the context, and our take. A moment's reflection on horoscope interpretation will soon show this highly selective process at work. In my 'Aunt's House' horary (chapter 8) I was shown by the Sun in Taurus. I am distinctly un-Taurean from a natal and character perspective, but in this context I was truly Taurean. Mr. A., my opponent, was a youngish man, but he was here shown by Saturn, and given the context, this became an allegory for his malevolence, not his age.

Together with all the various interpretations and individual bits of symbolism that go to make up the meanings of astrological factors, this allegorical level also refers to the rules of the game of astrology. That is, part of astrology's allegory consists of the *conventions by which the various factors are assigned* to literal reality. This is the body of theory in astrology. Consider classical astrology's absolute convention, the Doctrine of Origin, which we discussed in chapter 5. By this doctrine we apply allegory to the literal realm at the causal-temporal origin of whatever it is we wish to study. Time is *assigned* by the convention of the allegory, in contrast to the objective or clock-time of literal reality.

In working with allegory, when one is saying that Mars shall stand for this, the 10th house stands for that, these are the rules of the language that we use, these are the rules of the allegory. The rules of astrology are in some ways like the rules of chess; they are cultural creations that cannot be found anywhere in nature and they exist in the domain of human significance. By playing the game a certain result is achieved, just as by applying the precepts of astrology a certain interpretation is attained. Within the agreed conventions of what a bishop can do and what checkmate means there are countless possibilities of gambit and strategy, masterly moves and pedestrian moves. All of these can also be followed and communicated in the community of chess-players, just as the fine points of craft can be debated in the community of astrologers.

The use of allegory reminds us continually that we are engaged in an 'as if' exercise. By keeping to the conventions we are not necessarily asserting that in any particular situation in which the allegory is being applied that this 'really is so'. We are saying, let us treat this 'as if' this is so, and see where our speculations will lead.

With the description of astrology as a divinatory allegory in place, we are in a position to explore phenomena of astrology that are otherwise awkward to differentiate under the catch-all name of 'symbolism'. The next chapter takes up some features suggested by the fourfold model that could bring illumination to aspects of practical interpretation.

NOTES

1 Before the mid 1970's, when the arguments represented here were first advanced by the group of 'hermeneutic astrologers' centred at the Astrological Lodge of London, there was virtually no discussion within modern English-speaking astrology on the question of divination. I should however draw the reader's attention to the last piece of work undertaken by John Addey, in March 1982: 'Astrology as Divination' (*Astrology Quarterly*, vol. 56 no.2, Summer 1982, published by the Astrological Lodge of London). Although it appeared before the original 'Moment of Astrology' articles were published, it remains to the best of my knowledge the only substantial rebuttal that the current divinatory reinterpretation has so far drawn forth. Addey argues that astrology is related to divination only 'on one side of its nature'. Further, divination should be divided into three different main types. The first type, which properly gives us the word 'divination', concerns the invocation of divine agencies to guide human conduct. Addey notes the relationship with prayer and states that this type of divination 'does not concern astrology'. The knowledge we seek in a horary, for example, employs symbolism but not 'knowledge of divine things', nor does it seek angelic or divine aid. The second type of divination is not spiritual but involves a 'psychic sensitivity', as in dowsing, and is therefore a form of subtle perception. 'Higher human faculties of reason and intuition are not involved'. The third type 'is based on symbology', the interpretation of symbols to reveal unrecognised truths about things.

   Astrology properly belongs to this realm, where 'we open the field to the higher human faculties of reason and intuition and to science and philosophy in their true and integral sense'. Symbolism reveals to us the expression of every kind of existence, according to the ten categories of substance, quality, quantity, relation, place, time, condition, situation, activity and passivity. Addey closes with a strong defence of scientific empiricism as a necessary element in our astrology, especially as it relates to the 'brute facts' supplied by the Gauquelin research. John Addey has in effect to differentiate omen-reading from rational symbology. This position does not allow for an intermediate 'spiritual' agency in interpretation (e.g. daemones). He is also taking his stand on an Aristotelian interpretation of an objective time-signature independent of the observing consciousness.

2 *Ipse etiam mutat aquam carnalis sensus in vinum spiritualis intellectus:* Albertus Magnus (thirteenth century) is referring to the first miracle performed by Jesus, where he turned water into wine at the marriage feast of Cana. 'This beginning of miracles did Jesus in Cana of Galilee, and manifested forth his glory; and his disciples believed on him' (John 2). The method of scriptural exegesis using allegory is in turn allegorised by Albertus – a perfect demonstration of allegory. See H.F.Dunbar, *Symbolism in Medieval Thought and its Consummation in the* Divine Comedy (Yale University Press, London, Humphrey Milford, Oxford 1929), p.262.

3 For discussion of these early origins of Christian allegory,see H.A.Wolfson, *The Philosophy of the Church Fathers* (Harvard University Press, 1970) especially Vol.1, ch.2. Many different mystical strands weave together in the development of the Four Levels hermeneutic, and there is a significant parallel with certain much later doctrines found in Qabalah. This could point the way for a Qabalistic interpretation of astrology.

4 Augustine, *Confessions*, trans.Pusey (Britannica Great Books, University of Chicago Press, 1952), VI. 4, ch.9, n.25. Augustine heard this approach expounded by Origen's pupil, Ambrose.

5 *Littera gesta ducet /quid credas allegoria/ Moralis quid agas/ quid speres anagogia.* See Dunbar, op.cit. for further discussion.

6 Dante quotations are from William Anderson, *Dante the Maker* (Hutchinson, London, 1983), pp.333-4. This gives an illuminating account of the Four Levels in the *Divine Comedy.*

7 Wang Yang-Ming, *Instructions for Practical Living*, trans. Wing-tsit Chan (Columbia University Press, New York, 1962). I could not resist the temptation to introduce this key neo-Confucian teaching, known as 'the Unity of Knowledge and Action', from Wang Yang-Ming (1472-1529). He was the most influential philosopher of the Ming dynasty, and his approach has had great influence on Japanese Bushido. It is relevant to note his comment on divination (specifically in reference to I Ching, the *Book of Changes*): 'Divination involves principle and principle is [a form of] divination. Among the principles in the world, is there any greater than that of divination?' (p210).

8 There is a reflection of this in the historical development of the Christian hermeneutic, which was occasionally represented in three levels, with allegory and anagoge together as the 'mystical' sense.

9 Triads of houses: I have adapted for present purposes the mode of symbolising the houses of the horoscope, well-known to modern astrology, which owes its original inspiration to Morin de Villefranche. See 'The Cabal of the Twelve Houses Astrological from Morinus' (Wharton's translation of 1659), *Astrology Quarterly*, vol. 58, no.3, Autumn 1984 (published by the Astrological Lodge of London).

10 For Jung on the symbol, see especially *Psychological Types* (Princeton University Press, Princeton, N.J., 1976), section X. 814-833 (Definitions). *Definition of the symbol*: in Greek *sumbolon*, tally. The tally broken in two halves allowed each holder of the tally to be completely identified. This suggests that the manifest symbol of the unseen thing matches exactly the unseen thing, as its other half.

11 Maggie Hyde, *Jung and Astrology* (Aquarian, London, 1992), p.91.

12 Margaret Hone, *The Modern Text-Book of Astrology* (Fowler, 1973), p.219.

15

The FourFold Symbol II:
Water into Wine

ACCORDING to Jung, the attitude of *intentionality* brought to bear is decisive in determining the existence of the symbol:

> Whether a thing is a symbol or not depends chiefly upon the attitude of the consciousness considering it.[1]

We understand the literal world as public, objective, and open to all, within the five senses. There is a sharp distinction to be drawn between this public world, the world open to everyone in general, and the world as seen in the light of symbol. Others with us, here, now may require to be told about a symbol before they too 'see' it, and even then they may still not quite see it. Symbolic reality cannot therefore be reduced to the notion of a theoretical reality standing apart from the act of perception.

Symbolic seeing is real and communicable for those who share it, yet it is not a literal seeing. To express this, we may use the metaphor of sight and talk of 'second sight'; or the metaphor of the five senses may be used to give a 'sixth sense'. These descriptions are usually thought of in relation to clairvoyance, ESP and similar phenomena. They are equally applicable to the exercise of the symbolic attitude employed in the seeing of divination.

SPECULATIVE AND REALISED INTERPRETATION

The description of the second sight of the symbolic attitude leads to a distinction in modes of astrological interpretation, between the 'speculative' and 'realised' modes. On the basis of our tradition, we *speculate* that the ruler of the 10th shall signify the career of the person. If that happens to be Venus, without further information from the client, we may speculate on various Venusian careers. If we have detailed information and the career fits the symbolism, then we 'real-ise' it as a true signification. When this occurs, the symbol takes hold in our imagination as an image of the thing symbolised. Real-isation is the mysterious function by which the allegory is *seen as* reality and thereby we *make real* the allegory.

It is possible to go some way into astrology without ever 'real-ising' it, but once an individual has realised symbolism to any extent then the attitude to astrology is profoundly altered. It is like a bodily sense, indescribable to one who does not experience it. However, its subtlety and non-literalness means that symbolism tends to require affirmation by others to develop, which accounts for the frustration sometimes found amongst self-taught or isolated astrologers cut off from like-minded friends.

Even though they usually go hand-in-glove, the idea of *symbolic realisation should be clearly distiguished from a rational inference involving symbols*. A rational inference runs like this: so and so has Saturn conjunct the Moon, therefore I infer he will be a melancholic character. Or, so-and-so is a melancholic character, I wonder whether that ties in with his Saturn conjunct Moon? Every astrologer makes this type of inference in every interpretation, and it sets the scene for the much more definite and positive recognition that comes when we sense the Saturn-Moon 'as' the man's melancholy. Such recognition is a spontaneous phenomenon and it has an absolute and undeniable quality to it. Applied to horoscopy, this is the foundation of radicality, and interpretation flowing directly from this recognition is *realised interpretation*, in contrast to the more commonly enacted *speculative interpretation*.

A comparison with Jung's description of synchronicity is illuminating, because the recognition I have discussed above is most often encountered in the 'undeniable' quality of synchronistic experiences. As with synchronicity there appears to be some emotional affect attending realisation of the symbol; within Jung's terms, this affect is a consequence of the activation of unconscious archetypal contents, as they erupt momentarily into consciousness.

A related aspect of this affectivity is that real-isation passes between people, and it is in this way that astrologers can turn each other on. A transmission of symbolism may occur between teacher and pupil, or may occasionally manifest in a group of astrologers in what appears to be a developing program of interactive symbolism and significations. A similar induction of symbolism can also occur between astrologer and client.

NEGOTIATION OF THE SYMBOL

With the distinction in place between the realised and the speculative allegory, we can see that much work in interpretation, much of what happens when we think about a horoscope or discuss a horoscope with a client, involves a complex process of negotiation.[2] We negotiate between the two poles of realised and speculative interpretation, trying this and then that take until we hit upon the 'real' symbolism and we 'see' what this or that factor 'means'. When an astrologer makes a truthful observation from radical symbolism, then that which is told or foretold is quite literally and materially realised in the world. That is astrology proved and made real. On the other hand, good astrological practice depends on a clear sense of the difference between speculative and realised interpretation. However well synthesised, laying out blocks of interpretation against all the main factors in a horoscope – as in the method employed by Margaret Hone – is no more than assembling lists of speculations that this is what these symbols might mean. It is the starting-point for speculation, not the end result of interpretation. *Very few* of these interpretations are in the end likely to be convincingly realised as meaning these things. Understanding this simple but important point is the first step of discrimination in interpretation, and also a corrective against the illusion that somehow we can lay out the whole meaning of a horoscope.[3]

INTELLIGENCE THROUGH SYMBOL

The symbolic act, and the immediate task of interpretation in astrology, is to turn water into wine. That is, a purely literal understanding in any situation is worked symbolically and then a certain 'intelligence' is achieved, and with it a knowledge which benefits the individual concerned. From the point of view of traditional astrology horoscope interpretations are turned back towards literal benefit and good fortune for the client. It is in the ordinary world of our senses and activities that our desire comes to life, is represented to consciousness and is finally made real. By the successful use of divinatory allegory, therefore, we can in some measure tell this fortune.

There is however something else at work that makes this possible, and something further that needs to be told. This relates particularly to the third part of the fourfold symbol, the tropological or moral.

A small instance will illustrate what the tropological level is about, and show that it is a common part of our experience. It also illustrates the turning-point quality of this aspect of the symbol. This incident impressed me about the value of astrology early in my teaching of the subject. The class I was taking was mainly female – which is usually the case in astrology. On one occasion at the end of the first term one of the women became upset and emotional about a personal relationship issue that had come into the spotlight when she looked at her newly calculated horoscope. There was sympathy for her from most of the students – except one. This was a strong-minded woman, a successful professional who was the boss over a number of staff. I saw her natal horoscope some time after the incident concerned, and if I say that she was a strong Aquarius-Leo type, lacking Water, I imagine the astrological message will be clear. Here was a tough cookie who did not find 'feminine' emotionality appealing. This brought about something of an argument in the class. In a memorable outburst she declared 'what I can't stand about some women is the way they turn on the water-works just to get sympathy from men'. I had an uneasy feeling that, as the male teacher, there was some further sub-plot involving *my* sympathies here, but that did not become explicit. The class eventually settled back into good manners and the incident was forgotten. However, as the year wore on the Aquarius-Leo lady seemed to soften. Near the end of the course, I happened to have the opportunity for a private conversation with her and I asked her what she was making of astrology. She said it was all very interesting, but the main thing she had learned was that she may have had the wrong end of the stick in her opinion about weepy women. She referred back to the incident in the class. She now knew it was as much *her own* problem as it was theirs, and it was her lack-of-water nature, clearly revealed to her in her natal horoscope, which could not see the world from the water point of view. I knew from the way she spoke that this had been a revelation, which had moved her and changed her attitude towards others.

Somewhere between the catalyst of the exchange in the class and our end-of-year conversation, the moment of astrology had occurred. By this I mean a movement of attitude and conduct revealed, and real-ised through astrological symbolism. This is the sort of knowing that is properly known, because the subject is now participating in that knowing. It is basic psychology and no more than a first step of self-knowledge, but precious. The world would be a better place if this sort of insight gained a hold.

Several features of this story are worth considering in the light of the analyses of interpretation I have been suggesting in previous chapters. Firstly, it is *nothing special* in terms of technique and sophistication. It is first year astrology – naturally, because it has arisen in a student's first year. It is at such an elementary level of horoscope interpretation that it would be easy to discount its significance. Many of us will know this sort of elementary meaningful symbolism from around the first time we looked properly at our own natal charts, and it is a taken-for-granted base line of astrological realisation. It hardly follows, however, that increasing technical sophistication of a second- or third-year study of astrology guarantees any comparable gain in results. Astrology's descriptive possibilities (allegory) will be enriched and made increasingly articulate as the student learns the techniques and language, but an effective turning to good (trope) may be no nearer than it was in the first moments of taking up astrology. Simple but profound and moving insights of symbolism can be and are regularly attained at the simplest level of all, the Sun-Sign, which any astrologer who has not been blinded by sophistication will admit. There are good grounds to suppose that the ever-present 'illusion of technique' may actually hinder the symbolic turning point by setting us into vain technical pursuits for a significance that is already present right before our eyes.

In chapter 4, we noted the curious results of blind trial tests, suggesting that inexperienced astrologers produced results as good as experienced astrologers, and that different technical approaches made no difference either. The fourfold hermeneutic gives us an intriguing insight into this curiosity, in that it suggests that these results are a species of 'blind' Trope.

A second general observation about this no-water incident is that the moving interpretation was *context-specific*, and depended on a creative *take*. The context is the situation in the class, and in particular the catalysing incident which brings the issue into conscious focus. Out of all the many simple horoscope factors it could have been, it was actually this one to do with element-balance that worked and was realised. We can also say that this is the particular astrological image of herself that the woman brings into play in this situation, allowing her to articulate in common language – and therefore bring to light – a feature of her own attitude (allegorised as no-water), and then to compare it with the attitudes of other people (allegorised as with-water). The knowledge here was no longer speculative but realised and carried into effect, and 'water' as an objective description of a temperament trait has been transformed into the wine of intelligence.

A third observation is that this case neatly illustrates what many astrologers implicitly accept, that the practice of astrology leads to the development of compassion and sympathy for others – water again.

PSYCHOANALYSIS AND THE FOUR LEVELS

The introduction of creative interpretation and imagination into the very definition of divinatory astrology leads to the possibility that the psyche as revealed through modern psychology may be the hidden worker in the astrological phenomenon. Approaches inspired by psychoanalysis and its derivatives have indeed proved of great value in investigating divination in general and astrological interpretation in particular. Where we astrologers have got stuck in an intellectual time-warp that has lasted for two millennia, psychoanalysis has dug back towards the roots in the mysterious field of the soul wherein astrology grows. Astrology can gain great riches from these modern researches into the psyche without in any way fearing reduction or annexation, provided we never forget the magical-religious roots of our Art.[4]

Of particular interest for astrologers is the work of Herbert Silberer, which demonstrates two orders of meaning at work in dreams and visions. A psychoanalyst of the Vienna school and a contemporary of Freud and Jung, his study on *Hidden Symbolism of Alchemy and the Occult Arts* pre-dates Jung's comparable interpretation of alchemy by a generation.[5]

Silberer takes a long alchemical parable from the 18th century and shows a psychoanalytic interpretation of its symbolism. He then contrasts this with a spiritual-alchemical interpretation of the same parable, showing in effect how the same story can be read two ways. On this basis he is demonstrating two orders of meaning at work in products of the unconscious such as dreams and visions. One is the primitive and regressive level revealed by Freud, and leading most frequently to the Oedipal interpretation. The other is a forward-moving teleological level, which has always been the subject of religious and mystical symbolism. Silberer refers to this level as 'anagogic' or mystical.

One of the most fruitful ideas for the purposes of the analysis of astrology is Silberer's treatment of the idea of 'functional' symbolism, which will be found to equate with the trope and the anagoge in the fourfold hermeneutic.[6]

A simple instance to demonstrate what Silberer means by this level of symbolism is his own hypnagogic vision, stimulated by Goethe's mysterious 'Mothers' imagery in *Faust*, Part II. The Mothers exist in an unreachable and infinitely lonely domain beyond space or time, amongst the forms of all things past present and future. Faust is given the key to this domain, which is also the key to his spiritual restoration. Pondering these themes just as he was drifting off to sleep, Silberer had a powerful, spontaneously generated image of himself 'on a lonely stone pier extending far into a dark sea. The waters of the sea blended at the horizon with an equally dark-toned mysterious, heavy air.' The image represents a 'multiple determination' or 'condensation' of various elements, woven into associations traceable to Goethe's imagery. From the Freudian point of view the Oedipal desire to penetrate the mother is manifest and forms a significant element of the symbolism.

But there is another dimension, and which Silberer terms as 'functional': the state of consciousness passing from waking to sleeping *is itself being symbolised* by the reach into the sea. The hypnagogic image is then determined not only by the symbolic reflection of his conscious concern (Faust and the Mothers) but equally by the experience of the psychic process occurring for him there and then (passing from shore to sea, from wakefulness to sleep).

Now this is a simple instance; dreams telling us we are falling off to sleep do not tell us much. However, the implications are considerable if this leads us to see dreams and other spontaneously generated images as reflecting the psychic process in general. Silberer believes that this functional category of symbolism is found in the process of introversion undertaken by the aspirant in alchemy and other mystical practices. Symbolism that arises is then a statement of the *relative state of the soul in its progress along the path*. Under these circumstances, the symbolism is at one and the same time presenting to the aspirant's conscious attitude a symbol of that path. Part of this functional symbolism in mystical systems is therefore prefiguring the direction that the psyche is to take, and it is in this sense prophetic and teleological. This symbolism lays out what Silberer terms a programme of potential achievement, which the aspirant gradually actualises in fulfilment of the symbol. Described in this way, the comparison with the anagogic level in the Christian hermeneutic becomes apparent. Real-ising the symbol of the Path is none other than the Christian hope for the Kingdom of God.

We have already observed in the laminations and turns of astrological symbolism a process akin to the psychoanalytic multiple determination and condensation in dream symbols. Silberer's analysis suggests that in addition we should look for participation, process and Path symbolism (trope and anagoge), at the same time as we are engaging with astrology's object-oriented allegory. This is difficult and obscure terrain, but the way forward has been shown through the application in astrology of certain of Jung's ideas, to which I will now turn.

DEVELOPMENTS FROM JUNG

Although the connection between psychology and astrology has been one of the most striking features of twentieth-century astrology, in the main this has been a one way ticket, restricted to matching astrological factors with components of the psyche (allegory). This has led to the concept of the natal horoscope as a 'map of the psyche', where the astrologer sees psychological categories in the planetary placements. The continuing hold of the objectifying and causalistic Ptolemaic model has, however, ensured that even in the most sophisticated recent developments of psychological astrology there has been no taking up of the *psychology of symbol formation*. Maggie Hyde has bought the return ticket, and in her study of *Jung and Astrology*, she signposts the way in which the psychology of the unconscious must apply to the *astrologer* as well as to the client in the astrologer-client relationship.[7] This radical possibility in psychological astrology fleshes out some of the practical implications of a 'levels' approach for our work with clients. Through various examples, she illustrates what is involved in taking on board Jung's description of synchronicity and the secret mutual connivance of the astrologer. This brings us back to the question of the trope.

The case given in *Jung and Astrology* of the 'Goldsmith Dream' is especially illuminating in unfolding the fourfold symbol. In this case the client had a striking dream following her first session with the astrologer, and the symbolism of the dream fitted the natal horoscope, most notably in its formidable square between a Leo stellium and Saturn in Scorpio. The dream suggested itself for a Jungian-style interpretation, along the lines of possible symbolism for individu-ation, the Self and the Shadow. At this stage of the interpretation, the astrologer is still treating the symbolism of both dream and horoscope as giving an objective indication of the client's psyche (allegory).

However the astrologer then makes the move that liberates the interpre-tation. She *re-takes* the dream for the transference developing between herself and the client. The journey undertaken in the dream becomes a journey of the client experiencing the astrological reading. The symbolism now shows a psychic process, which makes it a functional interpretation in Silberers sense (trope). Functional symbolism characteristically draws into its folds the *context* of the appearance of that symbolism, which must also include the astrologer. Maggie Hyde shows how the whole course of the consultation, the very context in which the symbols appear, including the astrologer's moves to interpret objectively, is described in this same Saturn-Sun square. In the re-take the astrologer and the astrology become symbolised as Saturn.

This is the point at which the astrologer comes off the fence of detached observation (objective allegory). As the symbolism unfolds to reveal the context, psychoanalytic transference may occur as the astrologer becomes implicated in the client's context. As Jung suggests, this is the point at which the synchronicity trickster begins to play his games. This is no longer an 'objective coincidence of things' however, because it is directly involving the one seeing the coincidence, the astrologer. Reinterpreting Jung's definitions along the lines suggested in *Jung and Astrology* we could say that Synchronicity II (participatory a-causal coincidence) is an expression of trope symbolism, and is likely to involve the astrologer in its unfolding.

In the case discussed by Maggie Hyde, a particularly shocking synchronistic crossover occurred. Just before the second session with the client, and with the Saturn-Sun affliction in mind, she received news that her boss at work had suffered a heart attack. Tenth house Sun in Leo, square Saturn in Scorpio, the threat of death to the source of life, involving an authority figure. It is characteristic of symbolism working on the tropological level that it unpredictably breaks down the objective boundaries we set with our conscious intention interpreting 'this' horoscope for 'that' set of literal facts. The most challenging possibility that we can face is that the symbolism will turn to fully implicate the astrologer, and not only move the client's soul (the turning of the soul towards its truth), but also move the astrologer in his or her path of astrology. On the occasion that this is realised we have the conscious expression of the 'turn' (trope) *for the astrologer*:

> Like the alchemical uroborus devouring its own tail, astrological symbolism must be turned not only to what is going on between the astrologer and the client, but also to the astrologer in the act of practising the art itself.[8]

It is the exception rather than the rule to be able to bring this into expression, however attentively we seek for it. Such occasions are remarkable gifts, although often – largely depending on how favourably or unfavourably we are shown – we are tempted to bury them for good. Finding the little light of our conscious intention exposed in a cross beam from an unknown source is not usually a pleasant experience. On very rare occasions we are able to move the material and catch the symbolism on its turn, fully and consciously participating towards a resolution of the symbolism.

BINDING AND UNBINDING

The turn is also the place where we 'ritually bind the fate-threads',[9] and determine, whether we know it or not, the destined course of our life. However, at this point we hit a difficult ethical question for astrology. As John Heaton says:

> One talks of being bound by fate, shackled by fate, whereas somehow one isn't shackled by destiny. So astrology is.... helping to unshackle people from being bound by fate. But of course it's just a further shackle...[10]

John Heaton makes the shackling comparison with psychotherapy, which may replace one obsessive binding with another. In the case I have quoted of the no-water student, has her small gain in human understanding been at the cost of binding herself into a narrow astrological self-image, with which she imagines she has been fated at birth? Put like that, it is a high price to pay.

The deterministic astrologer does not see an ethical problem here, since the no-water state is taken as a simple fact of nature, like having brown eyes. It is the divinatory astrologer who has to take on the question of 'mind-forg'd manacles'; and I believe we have an adequate answer only if we presume our practice of astrology to have as its origin or destination a genuinely spiritual dimension, and not simply a pragmatic usefulness. My answer is along the following lines. Firstly, we are all conditioned one way or another by images and ingrained family and cultural patterns, and there is not some ideal bind-free human existence. Now, to the extent that the astrology has any impact in 'turning' the person, *explicitly symbolic* binds are being substituted for other, more conventional binds. These symbolic binds are available to language – the language of astrology – in a way that most of our mind-sets are not, and allow a direct and creative participation. But here we come to the crucial step, which must remain in the highest sense an article of faith, and trust in the nature of reality. Astrologers have an innate trust that what is shown and understood, is good to be shown and understood. In other words, the soul finds its own ways to achieve its ends, and the symbols of divination are a particularly effective means to achieve this goal. And further, I believe we will find at the core of the belief of most astrologers, the assumption that there is about these showings something that is spiritually authenticated. This is the anagogic nature of symbol, that permits it to point through the shadows of reality, to the reality itself. Astrology is then the use of images to unbind images.[11]

To return to practice, these complex ideas suggest that we astrologers are in a weak position if we do not properly acknowledge the symbolic and divinatory nature of what we do. Our lack of clarity about the project of astrology permits the old deterministic bonds to stay in place, especially for natal astrology. This question of the ethic of astrology returns us to a central argument of this whole book.

NOTES

1 C.G.Jung, *Psychological Types, Collected Works* 6, (Princeton University Press, Princeton, N.J., 1976), section 51.

2 I believe this process can be clearly observed, but its significance is likely to be missed in semiotic inquiries that do not make the speculative/realised distinction in the phenomenology of divination. I have in mind *The Semiotics of Fortune-Telling* by Aphek & Tobin (John Benjamins, Amsterdam/Philadelphia 1989), where a semiological analysis is undertaken of the dialogues between various fortune-tellers and their clients. From my point of view, Aphek and Tobin do not distinguish the *orders* of allegorical assignation being employed

(they suggest that each element employed by the diviner is 'omniscopic', where the transcripts they give indicate that although this is true in some cases, in other cases the factors are clearly being employed by the diviner 'polyscopically'). They also see the course of the dialogue as rationalising the diviner's authority and the universal correctness of his or her statements, but in my view they miss the equally possible interpretation that the diviners are seeking to adduce a symbolic fittingness – and therefore are negotiating their symbols. Standing outside the symbolic material they assume only a species of speculative interpretation and do not see that part of the 'script' for the diviner is symbolic recognition.

3 This is a foundation of the approach to horoscope interpretation known as 'locating significance' and developed in the Company of Astrologers.

4 I have elsewhere argued that at root psychoanalysis shares a common unrecognised divinatory method with astrology: 'Psychoanalysis, Divination, Astrology', abridged from a talk given at the Philadelphia Assocation, London (Company of Astrologers Bulletin no.4, Summer 1991).

5 Herbert Silberer, *Hidden Symbolism of Alchemy and the Occult Arts*, trans. S.E.Jelliffe (reprinted Dover, 1971).

6 Silberer's 'functional' symbolism also strictly covers what is here treated as anagoge. In his terminology, he contrasts 'functional' with 'material' symbolism. As an example of material symbolism he quotes the dream of a man with a homosexual desire, which converted in the dream to picking raspberries in a valley. Following Freud, the psychoanalytic interpretation of dream imagery is almost wholly concerned with this mode of translation of desire into material symbolism.

7 Maggie Hyde, *Jung and Astrology* (Aquarian, London, 1992).

8 ibid., p.191.

9 see reference to Alby Stone's discussion of 'dooms' or taboo-patterns in chapter 9, pp.172

10 John Heaton, *Metis – Divination, Psychotherapy and Cunning Intelligence* (Company of Astrologers, 1990), p16.

11 I would add that a Buddhist image is revealing for us here: that of the Bodhisattva, who, in any sphere of reality in which he or she appears, has the power while in that reality to point back through the reality. Divination properly understood is a function of this. (From 'Divination and Buddhism', an unpublished lecture given by the Buddhist scholar Michael Hookham at the Astrological Lodge of London on 26 February 1979).

16

Astrology as a Gift of the Soul

It was well said, A te & a scientia.
William Lilly

'BY YOU and by the science', *a te & a scientia*. On these few words turns the practice of astrology; how they are interpreted determines the definition of astrology; what lies hidden in them is the treasure of astrology.

With this aphorism as a guide I hope to indicate in this final chapter how the various themes we have been considering may come together. An illuminating clue given to us by Lilly places this understanding firmly in the craft tradition. This further allows me to affirm that the moment of astrology thesis does not spring fully formed from nowhere, but is a modern formulation of an insight that can in various guises be traced from antiquity. But before we take these concluding steps, it is worth restating the original goal with which this work set out, namely 'a radical reinterpretation of the main part of astrological practice, by considering horoscopy in the light of divination'. And if it is conceded that we have gone a good way along this winding path, this only serves to bring into view the problematic question of the nature of divination itself, the full working-out of which must be the subject of further inquiry, beyond the scope of this current work.

This is the place to correct a possible misconception about the moment of astrology project, which is to see it as a comprehensive and definitive theory of astrology. Theoretical constructions have been used in the preceding chapters, but these are better seen as stepping-stones rather than as resting places. The creases have not been ironed out, and the attentive reader will perhaps be able to trace mismatches between various of the constructions if these are pushed to a logical conclusion. In this sense each separate theme – causes versus signs, natural versus divinatory, context and the unique case, participation and initiative, the imaginal, daemones, the fourfold symbol – is provisional and exploratory. Although there is a guiding thought at work, each theme is a starting-point towards a phenomenology of divination, rather than being a settled conclusion.

The intention has been to establish a broad terrain of astrology-as-divination, and to break down the barriers that up to now have obscured this from view. Although astrological practice on occasion carries us deep into this realm, it remains unsecured and at best obliquely described, not least because of limitations of the theory under which astrology has for so long laboured. In naming the terrain I am rather fond of the phrase from Al-Biruni, 'a field of omens and divinations'.[1] If a symbolism is desired to express this abundant and mysterious state, and to show what it is we are seeking, then the reader is referred back to the anti-astrology signature in Chapter 2, and to the turn and return of Mercury in that horoscope.

From the standpoint of theory, the primary obstacle to opening up the territory of astrology-as-divination remains Ptolemy's interpretation, binding the lineages of the tradition to the objective moment of time and to the authority of Aristotle. This is a bond that is all the more powerful by not being recognised for what it is, and this blissful non-recognition, widely shared by classical, traditional, humanistic, psychological and scientific astrologers, has in my view been the single most debilitating weakness in the modern revival. It is for this reason that the current project has required a deconstruction of the Ptolemaic model as an essential step in its critique of the conceptual foundations of Western astrology.

In prising astrology away from Ptolemy's grip, the failure of scientific research will come to be seen as having played a significant and even positive role. The whole excruciating exercise had to be undertaken if only to purge us of simple-mindedness about the 'facts' of astrology and their relationship to science. The charge of scientism and pseudo-science that can rightly be levelled at various sceptical commentators does not let us off the hook. Collectively, and with rare valiant exceptions, astrologers have shown themselves as feeble-minded in the face of science on two related counts. Firstly, we have all too often naively colluded in the scientism of the original research, as if we somehow hoped that science could validate symbol. Then, on the manifest failure of this project, we retreat into a limbo of non-discussion, not paying heed to what our own ordinary practice and the results of research suggest, and with only the woolliest of responses given to sceptics and potential allies alike. And still some call out, 'let there be more research!' This dismal analysis points inescapably to an epistemo-logical void, a collective failure to identify our knowledge-base and to describe what a symbol is, and what manner of knowing is evoked in reading a horoscope. A shake-up of the way we think about our astrology is therefore long overdue.

Immediately registered in the *a te...* formulation is the suggestion of a change in the centre of gravity of our concerns. This pulls us back from over-fixation on the supposed objective reality of a science of astrology and restores the essentially human question of the nature and purpose of mind within which symbolic reality is known. There is, after all, no music without a musician, no language without a speaker, no astrology without an astrologer. The contrast with what we now call science could not be more obvious, for although it is logically correct to say that there is 'no science without a scientist', nevertheless the modern project of scientific rationalism is predicated on a strict bracketing-off and exclusion of any consideration of this necessity. In this exclusion lies its enormous power of focus and its mastery of the material and the literal, with the attendant curse that such forgetful mastery brings.

It follows that *the way* in which we make our symbolic practice, what we turn it towards, and how we act in relation to the symbol, is just as much part of the meaning and therefore the definition of astrology as is an objective statement of its principles and rules. This in turn opens our inquiry towards the most important of all questions, the nature of the ethic of astrology, which is another way of saying, the nature of its good.

THE ETHICAL SYMBOL

Ethics rules the daemon. At the beginning and at the end of all we do as astrologers, we choose to act or not to act, to speak or stay silent.

> The Greek words *daemon* and *daemonion* express a determining power which comes upon man from outside, like providence or fate, though the ethical decision is left to man. He must know, however, what he is deciding about and what he is doing. Then, if he obeys he is following not just his own opinion, and if he rejects he is destroying not just his own invention.
>
> C.G.Jung[2]

In Greek the word daemonion is used for a showing or omen, and it means literally the 'sign of the daemon'. Each symbol is a showing through which this daemonic power speaks, and when we realise it, it seizes the mind as a *compelling and inspired interpretation*, for this too, as Plato suggests, is what the word originally indicates.[3] Yet the relationship with conscious intention is crucial, because we do also *choose*. Bringing into the light of consciousness a power that compels us changes our relation to it and creates a possibility that could not otherwise exist. It is this relation, establishing the stance of human to divine, or consciousness to unconsciousness, that is the final source of ethics.

The world is full of necessities and natural laws, as well as the psychological or occult consequences of actions. It is therefore full of fates, but we are in some degree able to choose between those fates, and above all decide our attitude to them. A fatalistic attitude gives away the ability to create and choose, but even this giving away is also a choice. Here, then, is the first sense in which we locate the '*a te...*' of our guiding aphorism, in the responsibility of the astrologer for his or her interpretation, and responsibility for the action taken as a consequence. Divination, rightly understood, locates us at the heart of our creative freedom to choose, at the place where our fate binds and unbinds. The symbols of astrology reveal the movements of things and show the secret ways of the soul, yet there is always a decision that cannot be given away, ahead of or beyond the symbols we are presently shown.

I opened this book with a stark issue of astrological ethics. Were the astrologers who, it is said, foretold the death of Pico della Mirandola going beyond what is good and true for astrology? It is not whether they *could* predict his death, but whether they *ought* to have done so. From my view of the nature of astrology, they quite possibly had it in their power to do so and they were wrong – unethical – to do so. It is not a question of the social mores of the time. It is a question of the source and nature of the astrological phenomenon.[4] Clearly I have framed a significantly different conception of astrology to that embodied in the practice of the Florentine opponents of Pico; and the rest of this book has laid out an interpretation at odds with a tradition which could applaud a curse as a demonstration of its truth.

I consider that astrology's ethical status takes its ultimate form in relation to prophecy. Such a view is not amenable to proof in any ordinary sense of this word, yet it may be grasped by a certain intuition. I hope to at least indicate it as a theme, once again with the help of William Lilly. Astrology's prophetic power, as archetypally revealed in the story of the magi and the Star of Bethlehem, established for our Christian tradition a potential defining relation between astrology and the divine. On this interpretation, the spiritual purpose of astrology is that it should reveal Christ. This connection is esoterically suggested by Lilly in his *Christian Astrology*.[5]

Most of us encounter the question of astrological ethics at a more humdrum level, where it becomes the issue of what is and is not proper practice for the professional astrologer. We should not imagine that this ethical question has been somehow resolved in a general consensus. We only have to look back to Alan Leo's problem over prediction, brought into painful focus in the Mansion House case, to realise that what was unresolved in 1917 is equally unresolved now.[6] The current lack of legal constraints on our practice does not mean our own ethical uncertainties have disappeared. It is of common concern for the professional astrologer, but at the same time it touches our ultimate definition of astrology.

However hazy our beliefs, they nevertheless underlie everything we do in practice. Any practical 'code of ethics' or way of deciding good and bad conduct in astrology is directly related to this basic stance. An ethic in astrology is not therefore something that stands outside the subject, and we should be wary of portmanteau professional ethics that are supposed to carry over to every major vocation. The ethics of medicine and healing, or of law, are not necessarily the same as the ethics of astrology because we are dealing with distinct categories of human and spiritual relationship. The source of astrology's ethic, and the arbiter for each astrologer's conscience, cannot be wholly separated from something in the fibre of symbolism, at the centre of its phenomenon. It is engaged in every interpretive decision we make.

Conscience is the ethic internalised; it is the individual experience of an ethical relation. This leads to an important but little explored consideration about astrological experience: that astrologers characteristically take the symbolism of their astrology as an *expression of conscience*. Here is the crossing point from the idea of an ethic being laid upon astrology from the outside, to the understanding of the astrological symbol as itself ethical.

Now this may seem all very high-flown and abstract, but it is actually a matter of everyday astrological practice. It follows immediately from the recognition that the horoscope does not show what 'will' happen, out of some blind fate, but what 'should' happen if we participate in our destiny. This is an inspiration for the revival initiated by Alan Leo, although it may be traced back through astrology's neo-Platonic thread, as expressed by Ficino. It has become a predominant theme in humanistic astrology, from Rudhyar to the significant modern formulation of Dennis Elwell.[7] This goes one step beyond the notion that things grow in accordance with their seed – the Ptolemaic foundation – to seeing the symbols of the horoscope as purposive and teleological, calling us towards a future that we should consciously choose to fulfil.

I should add at this point that the whole question of ethics becomes much more relevant if we can shake off false piety, which becomes life-denying at the point that it produces a separation between fortune and conscience. What we 'should' do is to seek warm-blooded human good fortune, for ourselves and for our clients. This good fortune flows with creativity and delight. It is a negative consequence of an interpretation that frequently comes to dominate in transcendental religion, that we think what is good for us must be starchy and unpleasant.

In traditional astrology we see the ethical symbol in the construction of the katarchic 'Should I do this?' type of horary question, as opposed to the fate-prescription 'Will it/he/she/they do this?' In asking '*should* I do this' I am necessarily placed in a position of free choice, but seeking from the astrology an indication of that which it is fortunate – which is at the same time that which I ought to do. When in addition to this we are knowingly participating in the symbolism, the projection of conscience into that symbolism means that we are symbolically participating in a decision of our own conscience. This act of conscious participation towards the beneficent fulfilment of objective symbolism is a further and profound sense in which we may understand *a te & a scientia*, 'by you and by the science'. This act is at one and the same time the move from astrology as *objective allegory* to astrology as *tropology*, understood in the light of the fourfold hermeneutic discussed in Chapters 14 and 15.

RESOLUTION VS. JUDGMENT

The idea of being ethically guided, so that symbolism is a medium of conscience, is characteristic of developed forms of divination, and it has achieved its exemplary expression in the Chinese oracle Book of Changes, *I Ching*. The divinatory understanding also leads to the conclusion that since divination puts us in a creative relationship with our fate, the practice of divination is *in itself* conducive to the good fortune that is being inquired about.

What attitude, therefore, should we take to possible negative interpretations or predictions of unfortunate things? An ethical attitude does not necessarily mean avoiding unfortunate events, or a realistic assessment (judgment) of misfortune when this is required. Rather, it means showing the most effective attitude or move (resolution) in the circumstances. In addition, there is within the scope of astrology another possibility, as on those rare occasions when, like clairvoyants and psychics, astrologers have clear presages of some disaster, as if there is a purpose to warn or avert.[8]

This ethic of astrology does not preclude talking about death, because death at the right time and well accepted is not a misfortune but the last act in the fortune of life. Consider for a moment Lilly's horary 'Whether the Sick would live or dye, and what his Disease was?'[9] Most modern astrologers, even those of traditional inclination, would refer this to medical opinion, and wisely so, but put that to one side and ask what might be the *purpose* of Lilly's judgment here? For a start, if the man 'by election of his will' has freely chosen to ask, then it should be taken that his soul seeks these showings. We should always remember with traditional medical astrology that its katarchic foundation ensures that the astrologer/doctor shall always seek a cure while there is any hope at all. Here, however, the man is departing this life and already dying, and the sign of that truth appears in the symbolism. On the significators Lilly gives him no more than ten to twelve days: 'I persuaded the man to make his peace with God, and to settle his house in order'. That is clearly the purpose of this horary, which brings to light the last positive act of his life.

In these cases where negative conditions are being symbolised, there is always a simple test to apply, which is to ask 'what is the good fortune that comes from this?'; or even more precisely, 'how can the interpretation allow this matter to be resolved to good fortune?' This test is certainly required wherever a strongly objective and predictive astrology is being attempted, natal, horary or mundane. It especially helps to clarify why 'horaries of fearing' are dangerous unless the astrologer knows how to turn them. Horary perfection symbolises the soul in its desire drawing the thing asked about towards itself. Direct questions which simply present the fear of an unlucky outcome, such as 'do I have cancer?' and 'will father die?', threaten to imprison imagination in fear. The danger here is obvious; that the creativity of symbol is being turned into a negative fulfilment of that which is feared.

It is reasonable to suggest that bad fortune will result from the use of astrology where the symbolism has become a vehicle for disintegrative elements in or around the client – in other words, the bad daemon anciently symbolised by the 12th house, and probably for us moderns a negative manifestation of Neptune. The astrologer's own discretion is required as final arbiter here, beyond any craft rule. It is insufficiently appreciated by horary astrologers how far the use of the 'strictures against judgment' serves as a ritualised protection against seizure by the bad daemon. It is not a question of whether the astrologer can or cannot predict through a stricture, but whether he or she *ought not* to do so. Which particular strictures the astrologer observes – Moon void of course or via combust, Saturn in the 7th, first or last three degrees of a sign rising – is not really the issue. What is at stake is whether the astrologer has an attitude which allows the non-using of astrology, as well as its using.[10] With the horary strictures, this conscience of the astrologer has itself become symbolised, and their use operates as a form of ethical participation in symbols.

SYNDERESIS OF THE STARS

At a certain point in practice astrology's ethic and its participatory symbolism come together. If we indeed seek the anagoge in astrology, then it is here that it is to be found, because the ethical symbol is, I believe, a pre-requisite condition for prophecy. By astral prophecy I understand a possibility for astrology to act as a collective medium for a teleological symbol. This is what is being expressed by the story of the three kings and the Star of Bethlehem; or by the vast collective symbol of Christianity in the precessional Great Age of Pisces.[11]

So what is required of the astrologer who wishes to secure this knowledge? 'The more holy thou art, and more neer to God, the purer judgment thou shalt give', says Lilly.[12] Here is the essence of *a te..*, the pre-Enlightenment understanding that all higher knowledge and true science is profoundly ethical, which is indicated in the meanings of horoscope houses by the religious 9th of 'higher mind'. The knowledge of astrology is not separate from the action and conduct of the astrologer, and there is no such thing as value-free astrological interpretation.

Consider the following statement from Francisco Spina. This is given in the prophetical astrology writings gathered by Lilly in his *Mock Suns* collection:

> There is something super-celestiall that assisteth a man in foretelling of future events; for then by the Synderesis of the Stars, and of the Intelligences, we are able to prophesie of things to come...[13]

Prophecy is a function of *synderesis*, a rare term which appears to be of neo-Platonic origin.[14] It refers to the highest part of the soul, and it is the source of conscience. The Intelligences here are either the old gods, or an exalted species of the daemones. Why, according to Spina, does this function have to be super-celestial – that is, *above* the stars? We can set these Intelligences against the dead weight of the deterministic tradition of planetary influences bound into the Ptolemaic cosmos. A magic of Intelligences, such as that of Pico or Agrippa, escapes the deterministic bond by rising above even the circle of the stars. Spina is defending astrology's noblest possibility, but in order to transcend its self-imposed limitation he is drawn to employ the language of Pico and of magic.

The magical provenance of synderesis is obvious from Agrippa, who explicitly refers to it as the 'intellectual passion' of the soul:

> The Philosophers, especially the Arabians, say, that man's mind, when it is most intent upon any work, through its passion, and effects, is joyned with the mind of the Stars, and Intelligences, and being so joyned is the cause that some wonderfull vertue be infused into our works...[15]

LILLY'S 'PRESBYTERY'

It is hard to imagine how this could be demonstrated within the practice of astrology. As usual, however, Lilly gives us a lead. If any item of practical case-book horoscopy can demonstrate the infusion of 'some wonderful virtue' then it must be his 'If Presbytery Shall Stand?' By any criterion this is the most ambitious judgment in *Christian Astrology*.[16] It is also a rare astrological demonstration of symbolic participation as this steps into the realm of prophecy.

A major problem for us reading the judgment is that it is difficult to appreciate fully unless one can unpack it from the transient political details of Civil War England. It is not my intention here to give a full resume, or to arrive at some final verdict about the whole of the prediction. To treat this fully requires a careful work of historical-astrological scholarship.[17]

This is a horary employed in the broader service of mundane astrology. Questions of this sort have come to be known as 'great questions'; there are several ways in which the method of reading such a chart breaches the established methods of horary astrology, but in brief it is enough to say that the one asking drops out of the picture; their responsibility for, or influence upon the situation, is either slight, or has no determinative influence on the situation inquired about.[18] Many astrologers inspired by Lilly have attempted to follow him down this road, mostly with uninteresting results. Such horaries demand the highest discretion if they are to offer 'true resolutions', otherwise they rarely mean anything or come to much. But then Lilly cannot teach discretion to those who do not have it.

The figure was cast for 11th March 1647, and *Christian Astrology* was on the press before the end of the year, when the whole issue would still be red-hot. The question was asked by Sir Thomas Middleton, a member of Parliament and an army man.[19] The background was a politically unsettled situation in the aftermath of the Civil War. King Charles I had been defeated by the Parliamentary forces, but he commanded support in Scotland and Ireland. In Parliament there was a split between Independents (moderate Puritans) and the Presbyterians, who had a strong Scottish base. Charles was ready for a deal with the Presbyters and the possibility was looming for a Church-State government in England which would be rigidly Puritanical and Presbyterian. To add to the brew, the army was ready to rebel as it had not been paid for months since its return from the campaign in Ireland. Oliver Cromwell, hero of the army and of the Independents, had retired from active military involvement.

We may add to this background that the Presbyters of the day denounced astrology as the work of the Devil. Lilly had an account to settle with one of astrology's most implacable foes. I will not go through all of the finely crafted steps here, as my concern is limited to bringing forward the centrepiece of the judgment.[20] Lilly's discussion is partly aimed at establishing the radicality of the figure, an essential step for an interpretation that is to carry any weight. The core of the symbolism, the foundation of radicality in this chart, and the knot of fate, resides in the condition of the quesited, Presbytery. Lilly takes Saturn in Taurus in the 9th house of religious affairs as the significator for Presbytery. Here is his interpretation:

> The positure of Saturn in the ninth who is naturally of a severe, surly, rigid and harsh temper, may argue, the Presbytery shall be too strict, sullen and dogged for the English Constitutions, little gentle or compliant with the natures of the generality...

'Strict, sullen and dogged': I have never come across a better description of Saturn in Taurus. Having established the status of Presbytery from the 9th, Lilly finds its enemy also from the 9th, for Saturn *afflicts* the affairs of that house just as well as it describes those very same affairs:

> If you would know who shall most afflict, or who shall begin the dance, or most of all oppose it? Saturn represents the Countryman, for he afflicting the house properly signifying Presbytery shews the cause...

The Countryman was the epithet for Oliver Cromwell, the rough squire from the Fens of East Anglia. 'The Souldiery will distaste it', says Lilly, referring no doubt to the Mars. We infer that Cromwell will be back, leading the army. This is a bold step: there does not seem to have been an obvious indication in the spring of 1647 that Cromwell was planning such a move.

Why should Cromwell begin the dance? 'Religious Rites and Ceremonies is now standing to Direction', says Lilly, referring to Jupiter on its station, turning direct, strong in Cancer but threatened by the applying conjunction of Mars. There would seem to be a connection with Jupiter for the dance, turning, like religion, on its station and about to change signs. Lilly does not make this connection obvious, but look at his major move of interpretation. Saturn stands at one and the same time for Presbytery *and* for Cromwell afflicting Presbytery. Cromwell's beginning the dance and Presbytery's ill condition are *two sides of one and the same fate*. From this foundation the judgment secures its first prediction, that Presbytery will not survive:

> ... it will not stand or continue (statu quo): Remove Saturn, viz. Covetousnes,

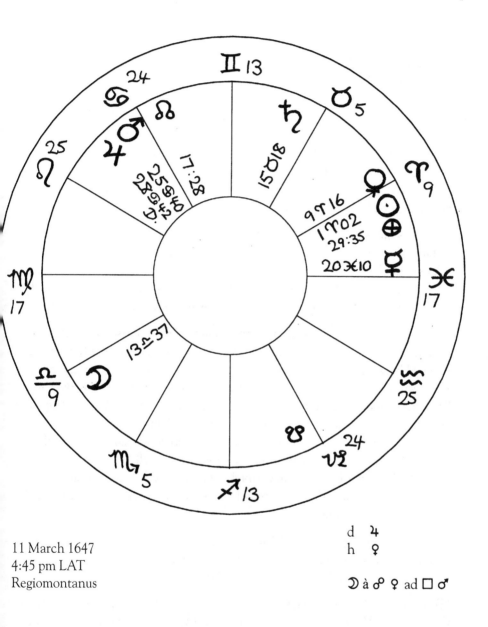

11 March 1647
4:45 pm LAT
Regiomontanus

FIGURE 28 'If Presbytery shall stand?'

Figure as given by Lilly's *Christian Astrology* p.439

Rigidnes, Maliciousness, etc. then there may be more hopes that it might, but yet it will not stand (*ita in fatis*).

'Thus in fate' Presbytery will not stand – and yet, it *could* still stand, *if* it were not for those failures that have rendered it 'little compliant with the natures of the generality'. Lilly loathes Presbytery yet I do not think it is gratuitous when he talks of 'hopes' for it. Springing up everywhere through his astrology is the hope that benefit shall prevail, and as he reminds us in his *Epistle to the Student in Astrology*, 'exprobrate no man, no not an enemy'. [21] Yet we also know the leopard will not change his spots and the Presbyters bring their own fate – and the opposition of Cromwell – on themselves.

Immediately following this decisive conclusion Lilly adds the striking prophecy for which the judgment is best known:

> Three whole years from hence shall not pass, ere Authority it self, or some divine Providence inform our understanding with a way in Discipline or Government, either more neer to the former purity of the primitive times, or more beloved of the whole Kingdom of England... for some time we shall not discover what shall be established, but all shall be even as when there was no King in Israel...

King Charles I was executed on 30th January 1649, almost two years later, a terrible act that few had contemplated even as late as the time of Lilly's judgment. England became a Commonwealth with Cromwell as its Lord Protector: as when 'there was no king in Israel'. Lilly completes the judgment by moving back to the Presbytery theme, suggesting that this will 'come to be handled by the Magistrate' and considered by the 'grand Authority of the Kingdom'.[22]

So far I have summarised the political dimension of this judgment, but there is another that is clearly of great importance for Lilly himself – the role of astrology itself. By the way it is described, we might wonder whether it is actually the *most important* dimension. After discussing features of the chart but before giving his final interpretation, Lilly declares:

> From these configurations we shall naturally frame our judgment, not positive or affirmative, but conjecturall, onely out of a desire that posterity may see there's some verity in Astrology, and the Clergies just cause to carp at the Art if I lye...

We need to take a step back to assess the significance of this statement. In *Christian Astrology*, Lilly reports several Great Questions, but this is the single public prediction that is still open when the book appears. His astrology is completely exposed to view at this point; if this prediction failed, it would spoil the whole text. This horary appears in the ninth house section, naturally enough for the question of Presbytery, but of course, astrology itself is a great ninth house question. Lilly is playing for high stakes. It is obvious that to take this sort of risk, he will feel as sure as he can possibly be about the efficacy of the judgment, which encourages the view that it has to be treated as part of a larger cycle of mundane predictions and prophecies, all pointing the same way concerning the dissolution of the monarchy.

Given this situation, Lilly sets the whole judgment *in the context of the test of astrology against the attack by religion*. His book is called *Christian Astrology*. He is going to demonstrate the verity of astrology by its power to show forth the changes in 'Religious Rites and Ceremonies'. If Lilly lies, it will be 'the Clergies just cause to carp at the Art'. Posterity and the passage of time will decide, and this Saturn in Taurus could certainly carp. Is it not therefore obvious that we should see astrology and the test of astrology as the Saturn in the 9th? I regard it as more than likely that Lilly was aware of this further lamination of meaning.[23]

THREE SIGNS IN ONE SYMBOL

We have now arrived at a remarkable point in the analysis, where it can be demonstrated with some plausibility that one symbol in the figure, Saturn, is the principal significator for no less than three major but apparently separate themes in the whole context of the interpretation:

– first theme: Presbytery and its failings
– second theme: the Countryman, who afflicts Presbytery
– third theme: astrology, challenged by Presbytery

Further, these themes become mutually identified and brought into unity in the interpretation. The first and second themes demonstrate that it is really Presbytery's own fate, a part of its inherent character, that draws upon it the enmity of Cromwell. The third theme unites with these in the form of the astrology which is the agent of revelation. Lilly knowingly uses this judgment to demonstrate astrology itself, and the symbolism declares this intention.

The reader who is not versed in horary or traditional astrology will, in some measure, have to take on trust the emphasis I have placed on the Presbytery judgment. It is a beautiful and eloquent play of symbolism, a joy in all its parts, and we can be sure that Lilly delights in its radicality. He is fully aware of the import of his prediction, and prepared to put the credibility of his astrology on the line with its publication. It is his answer to the religious critics of astrology by showing them the announcement of the heavens in relation to the religious and temporal governance of the nation; there can hardly be a higher calling for astrology. It is all too easy in hindsight to lose the sense of the gathering storm of destiny that inspired Lilly in laying down this extraordinary claim, with its specificity of detail and its barely concealed timed forecast of the demise of the king. It is appropriate to term work of this class as 'prophecy', for there is here something that in its effects and implication goes entirely beyond our usual haphazard attempts at astrological prediction.

There is a gift at work here, the recognition of which is vital for the truth of astrology. It seems so obvious to state, yet here again I suspect that it will only be fully apparent to the traditionally-oriented astrologer. This judgment is undoubtedly inspired, yet the inspiration does not depend on spontaneous imaginative association, and still less on what we might ordinarily conceive of as dislocated consciousness or divine frenzy. It is prophecy brought back within the orbit of intellect, and worked through and through with rational inference from the principles of astrological symbolism. We may say that the interpretation is *returned to the stars*. It is seen to have its own self-generated logic of symbolism, while at the same time speaking authentically from the authority of its tradition. This cultural transmission in turn allows the judgment to be revived and realised within the intellect of every other astrologer coming anew to it.

Because the judgment, while guided by spiritual inspiration, is at the same time worked through rational inference from symbolism, Lilly can in all honesty declare that 'from these configurations we shall naturally frame our judgment, not positive or affirmative, but conjecturall...'[24] His concern is not to demonstrate that he has supernormal faculties, and it would defeat his object if we were to imagine that the prophecy springs solely and wholly from him. This would be to separate the mind of the astrologer from the daemon of astrology. Lilly's task is to show that his judgment belongs to the objective form of the craft, and is therefore part of the heritage of every astrologer who cares to study it. It is on this basis that he proclaims the craft, makes his invitation to posterity, and issues a challenge to the carping clergy. We uncover here the irreducible mystery of divination in the meeting-point of subject and object; the prophecy is established *a scientia*, and inspired *a te*.

QUESTIONS AS COME NOT UNDER THE VULGAR RULES

What has led Lilly to a prophetic horary of the order of his 'Presbytery'? Who has guided or taught him? Many astrologers before and since have exercised their skills in mundane astrology, using the inceptional figures for nations or other collective ventures, but Lilly's great question horary approach is entirely unorthodox. He is making a prediction concerning great affairs of state, but not as an objective judgment from the reported moment of an act or political decision carrying direct consequences for the matter asked about. His prediction stems from the moment an influential querent happens to ask him about this affair of state. Thomas Middleton, the querent, is a Member of Parliament, so he may indeed have considerable influence, but he does not have the right to speak for Parliament or seek an oracle for Parliament. Lilly takes the place of the oracle, and raises Middleton's question and his own response to the status of an oracular exchange. We are to assume that the heavens have decided to elect Lilly himself as medium for an answer given collectively to the whole nation. Put this way, we can see what a bold claim is being made by any astrologer who puts himself up in this way.[25]

As we have already discussed in Chapter 6, there is enough of a problem in working out how the heavens can organise the precise significators in a horary where the matter really does directly concern the actions of the querent, as in the case of Lilly's 'Fish Stolen'. But the circumstances of Presbytery are even more improbable. Does this mean we can simply speculate about anything we like, near or far, part of our business or none of our business, and expect to get an answer from the heavens?

The answer to this rhetorical question is 'no, we cannot': there is some unique coming-together of circumstances that permits a meaningful horary in these rare cases. Some of these circumstances are obvious, such as the status of the astrologer – and Lilly did indeed have high status at the time of this question, and when he produces his judgment, he will be listened to. His judgment will therefore 'count'. Other elements of these circumstances are less obvious, and bear on the unique gift, like the touch of grace, vouched to the astrologer in that moment.

As we start talking of 'grace' and 'unique gifts' then we enter an order where a simple-minded approach to the rules of astrology must break down. There can be no rule to contain such an act, and no textbook can teach it. It is only by demonstration and example that we may be inspired, as so many students have been by Lilly.

Lilly is fully aware of the dilemma, and he is equally aware of how vulnerable to criticism his approach must be. He is after all claiming a unique inspiration in developing great question interpretations. This uncomfortable awareness erupts into his text in an intriguing way in *Christian Astrology*, in the 'Prince Rupert' judgment.[26] It is significant that this appears to be the first in time of his published great questions, and it is over four years prior to the Presbytery judgment. I have no record of any earlier horary of this type, and it could well be Lilly's initiation into the practice.

Here is the question: 'If Prince Rupert should get honour by our Warres, or worst the Earle of Essex? What should become of him?' It was posed in November 1642 by 'a very great wel-wisher to the Parliament', and Lilly briefly refers to the traditional rule that the querent shall be signified by the ascendant and its ruler. He immediately moves away from this signification, because for the rest of the judgment the ruler of the ascendant becomes irrelevant in this role. Lilly's move is unorthodox. He confesses to a struggle of interpretation: 'The very truth is, I was twenty four hours studying the resolution of this question...' This is not only because of the political significance of the subject matter; I believe the struggle reflects the uncertain genesis of a radical and potentially disintegrative reworking of horary method, with little justification in the tradition.

Concerning the judgment, it is sufficient to say that Lilly correctly predicted that Rupert 'should gain no honour by this War' and had no prospect of worsting the Earl of Essex. For our discussion, what is significant is Lilly's spirited defence of his method, in his opening words:

> This Question fals not under the notion of vulgar rules, or must the Astrologian expect particular Rules to governe his Fancy in every Question; it was well said, *A te & a scientia*, for I doe daily resolve such Questions as come not into the vulgar rules of Guido or Haly; and yet I was never to seek a sufficient reason in Art, whereby to give a good and satisfactory answer to the Proponent, &c. as many hundreds in this Kingdome well know, &c.

This strikes a defensive and also defiant note, a justification against censure, either imagined or real. He is justifying the very ground of his interpretation to his fellow astrologers and to posterity.

Let us be clear exactly what Lilly proposes. Firstly, his approach is not governed by the ordinary (vulgar) rules, since we will find nothing like it in our traditional authors; and secondly those same rules cannot provide us with guidance in every 'fancy', that is, in every single move we are inspired to make. Indeed it would be an error for the astrologer to imagine that the whole of any interpretation, and its direction in detail, can be assigned to conventional rules. The good and satisfactory answers Lilly has given to large numbers of inquirers cannot be wholly decided in this way. This does not however mean that the interpretations cannot 'after the event' be expressed as reasons of art, which are the accepted and conventional meanings of symbols, and the rules by which these are manipulated; what is important to realise is that at the moment of astrology, the inspired instant of origin of a symbolic seeing, a statement of conventional meaning does not sufficiently explain why the astrologer chose *this* particular expression of the symbolism as opposed to several other feasible expressions.

The worth of this project is proven by the success of Lilly's practical astrology-in-the-world, to which numerous clients can testify; but his theoretical justification is a statement of authority from tradition: 'it was well said, A *te & a scientia*'. With this invocation we are carried to the heart of the debate about the nature of astrology.

PTOLEMY AND PSEUDO-PTOLEMY

In order to take up the debate we must move between contradictory and competing interpretations of one and the same phrase, 'by you and by the science'. We start by putting aside Lilly's understanding, discussed above, and returning to the primary and classical interpretation, which is ultimately derived from the theoretical construction given to us by Ptolemy in the *Tetrabiblos*.

A *te & a scientia* is the opening phrase of the Latin translation of the *Centiloquy*, the hundred aphorisms attributed to Ptolemy. Their origin is disputed, although they had probably been gathered in their current form by the eighth century AD.[27] They are said to be 'fruits' (*karpos*) of the *Tetrabiblos*, but they include horary and other teachings that are clearly inconsistent with that text. The problem of historical origins, and the question of the intentions of the Greek author(s), are however less important for our present discussion than the fact that the Latin translation of the *Centiloquy* carried considerable authority for mediaeval and renaissance practitioners, and became a focus of debate.

Here is the first aphorism, in the form best-known to the English-speaking world, in Ashmand's translation:

> I. Judgment must be regulated by thyself, as well as by the science; for it is not possible that particular forms of events should be declared by any person, however scientific; since the understanding conceives only a certain general idea of some sensible event, and not its particular form. It is, therefore, necessary for him who practices herein to adopt inference. They only who are inspired by the deity can predict particulars.[28]

Our key five-word phrase has expanded into a twelve-word clause: 'judgment must be regulated by thyself, as well as by the science'. It is a fair translation according to the orthodox reading, yet the idea of being 'regulated', by which Ashmand probably understands rational inference, introduces its own nuance which may cloud as much as it illuminates.

From the standpoint of a classical and Aristotelian interpretation, the aphorism determines the scope of what we may properly know through our astrology. It demarcates the science proper both from speculative inferences on the one hand, and from supernatural or divinely-inspired intuition, clairvoyance and prophetic gifts on the other. Supernatural gifts are not denied, but it is asserted that for the astrologer the discernment of particulars, by which is meant the details of the transitory and contingent accidents and events of life, can only ever be a matter of speculation. The detailed working out of the heavenly pattern of influence is not therefore directly available as an object of knowledge in astrology. Where an affirmative and definite prediction of particular forms of things is achieved, then any certainty we attribute to such a prediction comes from some other supernatural inspiration, and is not within the capacity of the natural science of astrology. The impossibility of predictive certainty arises because the primary influences created by the universal order of the celestial bodies are, in any particular instance in the world below, competing with various secondary and contingent causes.

What is entailed in this cardinal distinction is a definition of astrology as *a science of causes, rather than an art of signs.*[29] The heavens are the primary and originative influence on all things without exception, but for any particular circumstance they operate as one set of efficient causes amongst many. Amongst the competing causes is the free and unconditioned choice of the human actor. This is why, in the quintessential dictum of an Aristotelian astrology, 'the stars incline, they do not compel'. Because of this, any particular judgment is 'regulated by thyself', in Ashmand's expansion of the terse Latin *a te*. This may be taken to mean that in practice discretion and common sense must be employed, to allow for the various contingent and essentially unpredictable possibilities in any given situation, since *scientia* itself cannot provide a rule for all eventualites.

We may note that, when read in this way, the first aphorism is philosophically consistent with Book I Chapter 2 of the *Tetrabiblos*, which discusses the limits of prediction of particulars and the nature of inference. It goes beyond Ptolemy only in the apparently rhetorical embellishment of the last sentence, concerning the possibility of divine inspiration granting a prophetic prediction of the particular forms of events. Ptolemy himself does not bother to add such an embellishment, but there is no reason to suppose that he would have rejected it. Taken in conjunction with the *Tetrabiblos* this aphorism represents a consistent interpretation of rational inference, rather than positive knowledge, at the basis of judicial astrology, and in general conforms to an Aristotelian epistemology.

THE HERMENEUTIC TURN IN RENAISSANCE ASTROLOGY

In the extensive bibliography to *Christian Astrology* we find a reference to Giovani Pontano's commentary on the Centiloquy; this commentary in turn throws a brilliant shaft of light on Lilly's approach to the *a te* formulation and his justification for great questions. We cannot determine whether Pontano's text in particular was the definitive influence, but from our reading of Lilly we infer that it is probable that, at the very least, this is one of his primary sources.[30]

Pontano's treatment of astrology represents a discussion that was well-known in renaissance intellectual circles, concerning what may be broadly defined as the relation of science and intuition. In all significant respects the distinction between speculative and radical/realised interpretation indicated in Chapter 15 mirrors this old debate.[31] Pontano, as we shall see, takes this discussion into a powerful analysis of astrology. I have termed this a 'hermeneutic turn' because it offers a fundamental reorientation of our description of how meaning is derived in astrological interpretation. This turn unambiguously establishes judicial astrology as divination. It is also a 'return' because it restores our connection to the participatory and sacral roots of astrology.

Pontano gives the Latin version of the first aphorism, *A te & a scientia...* etc., and then gives the following commentary:

> To be a doctor or a moral philosopher is a matter not just of knowledge, but also of a certain way of working (*operatio*), which is the healing ability of the doctor and the action of the moral philosopher; and this way of working appears to be honest, virtuous, and rational. We say the same about the astrologer: if he has knowledge not just of the heavenly bodies, but also of those things that may be portended from them, then prediction is his. And indeed, this knowledge of the future, which it pleases the ancients to call divination, seems to be attained both by a certain natural instinct, as well as by study and discipline.
>
> On account of this, prediction of the future is seen to be two-fold: one (part) is referred to a particular power innate to man, a natural impulse free of all artifice; the other (part is referred) to discipline, consisting of reason and observation. The first of these appears to be stimulated by the stars, but it is not of those things which may be spoken of, and indicated by celestial motions, through reason or deliberation. These unbidden motions, not tempered by human art or reason, we are accustomed to call inspired by a deity (*fanaticos*)[32]; and those who are moved in this way we call first inspired, then raving; indeed, the vulgar call (these motions) demoniacal spirits. The prediction from all of these (motions) of which

I have spoken is to be immediately referred back to the stars (*praedictio statim referatur ad stellas*).

Pontano mentions phenomena of prophecy and divination outside of astrology, in order to show that the distinction between the two parts of divination has been recognised from antiquity. He then makes a crucial observation concerning the knowledge of the astrologer ('mathematician'):

> Those who are in a frenzy either do not understand what they utter, or do not know from which cause they predict: in a word, they are ignorant. But, since the mathematician depends at first on reason and then on observation, he understands what he says, and is by no means ignorant of the manner in which he predicts; these predictions originate from knowledge of the stars.[33]

What exactly is Pontano's move? He has taken his theme from a debate outside the field of astrology, concerning the relationship of intuitive knowledge to the knowledge granted by science. He reads this polarity into the *a te* and *a scientia* pair of the Centiloquy. But something important has been displaced by this move: for Ptolemy rational inference is regulated *a te*, it is part of the discretion and common-sense of astrological practice, since it does not belong to the positive and definitive knowledge of science. For Pontano, rational inference does not belong to *a te*, and instead he locates it as simply another part of *scientia*, which consists of 'reason and observation'. But unlike Ptolemy he includes as *a te* a non-rational and unpredictable inspiration giving direct knowledge of the particular forms of things, a knowledge which is entirely excluded from astrology in the *Tetrabiblos*.

By this move Pontano reworks a potential ambiguity in the Centiloquy into a reversal of Ptolemy's intention in the *Tetrabiblos*. Where Ptolemy must *exclude* direct knowledge of the particular forms of things from the possibility of astrology, Pontano *includes* this knowledge as the *a te*, and thereby elevates it to logical equality with the mode of knowledge derived from scientific principles.

The analogy with medicine is a fruitful one: the art of healing means nothing unless the universal principles of medicine can be appropriately applied by the doctor in the particular case of *this* person and *this* sickness here and now. It is exactly this skilful uniting of scientific knowledge and a concrete and particular manifestation that constitutes a certain way of working (*operatio*) that justifies the title 'doctor'.

The virtue that grants us this gift with respect to the particular forms of things is not therefore derived from any discipline, reason or observation, it is not logical inference, but is 'a particular power innate to man, a natural impulse free of all artifice'. Here is the root of *a te*. It is spontaneous and unpredictable in its working, and we are therefore unable to discern the sources or reasons for its working. Nevertheless, for Pontano, it too, like all things in the sublunary world, must be stimulated into action by the stars, even though its mode of working is not reducible to any law, or open to examination by science. In the commentary he goes on to include a brief Aristotelian cosmological digression on the origin of all change in the world, all motions and all generation and corruption of beings induced ultimately by the movements of the Sun and stars. Even divinely inspired intuition is to be seen as part of this same cosmic power.

What is perhaps most difficult for the modern astrologer to grasp, and of the greatest consequence for the understanding of our practice, is that this intimate genius, natural to us and closest to our innermost intuition, is at the same time *divinely moved and prompted*. Pontano is careful to remind us that this movement in our very own being is also a movement of the daemon, and the language is that of religious ecstasy. Here we recover the subtle meaning of divine breath (*numine afflati*) in the first aphorism, with a nuance that is lost in the translation as 'inspired by the deity'.

Pontano therefore gives us an origin of divination that is at one and the same time innate in us, and natural, and yet also inspired by the divine. This is what is meant by *a te*. But what of *a scientia*? Despite its divine origin astrology is to be distinguished from ecstatic modes where the diviner is in a frenzy of possession. It is essential for the science of astrology that the inspired element in any symbolic seeing, and therefore in any interpretation, should be 'referred to the stars' and brought back into reasons of art. The astrologer, although inspired, is not cast into a divine frenzy because he or she must at the same time employ discretion, inference, and reason. In this moment the astrologer must *choose*, which brings us back to the ethical relationship with the symbol, and renders the interpreter responsible for the interpretation. By this understanding astral divination is carried back into reason, astro-*mancy* into astro-*logy*. In the moment of astrology there is no gap between the two.

By corollary, if no coherent interpretation is sought then the astrologer enters the realm of the clairvoyant or scryer, using the horoscope images like specks of light in a crystal in order to evoke a vision that is quite independent of the crystal.

In order to appreciate Pontano's position, we should bear in mind the common broadly Platonic understanding of soul as being layered, turned at one and the same moment to both the Intelligible realm of eternal Being, and to corporeal and temporal reality.[34] As soul expresses its knowledge in language and thought, it moves in two modes, on the one side conceptual and literal, and on the other side intellectual, a division that is reflected horoscopically in the polarity of the 3rd and 9th houses. In the practice of astrology both modes reunite as one.

On this basis we may begin to discern the implications of a statement from Marsilio Ficino which, in describing the divide between science and inspiration, is close in spirit to Pontano. The passage occurs in the *Disputation against the Judgment of Astrologers*, which underlines the fact that, despite the evocation of Ptolemy, it runs against the grain of conventional astrological opinion:

> Through whatever art future things may be investigated, they are foretold more completely out of a certain gift of the soul (*dos animae*) than through judgment (*judicia*). Here often those unlearned in the art judge more truthfully than those who are learned. About which Ptolemy said, knowledge of the stars is both from you and from them, as if he were saying that you find the truthfulness of judgment not so much through scrutiny (*inspectio*) of the stars, as by a certain foreknowledge innate to you (*praesigium tibi naturale*). It is explained that you will follow this knowledge at one time through your diligence, and at another time you may possess it through the stars' beneficent action.[35]

Ficino's interpretation rests its case on the first aphorism of the Centiloquy, and it follows the pattern of Pontano's overturning of Ptolemy of the *Tetrabiblos*. Prima facie we may speculate that with respect to the Centiloquy it is a broad paraphrase of Pontano, which has however been assimilated and recast within Ficino's own philosophical programme. Notice, as in Pontano, that the 'beneficent action' of the stars is itself the source of astrological inspiration. At the same time, Ficino teaches that this spontaneous and unpredictable knowledge is innate to us: 'preceding all human faculties of reasoning the gods implanted in the soul an experiential faculty of knowing', which he describes as 'a certain touch of divinity'.[36] This faculty of knowing is both divine and yet natural to us, which is why the inspiration of our astrology is *dos animae*, a gift of the soul.

* * *

I opened this book with the terrible condemnation of divinatory astrology by the renaissance magus, Pico della Mirandola; and with the equally terrible implications of the legend of the prediction of his death, laid against him by three astrologers of Florence. I have ended this book with one of the most beautiful examples of mundane predictive astrology in the late European tradition, which is at the same time William Lilly's rejoinder to our critics. Somewhere in between is a hermeneutic turn that heals the divide in Western thought between a magical-religious and a deterministic conception of the moment of astrology.

This book is therefore a reply to Pico, some five hundred years late. It is a gentle irony that his own teacher, Marsilio Ficino, should point us towards the most persuasive of all possible interpretations. And if we are to respond to our many critics, and speak truthfully for ourselves, then perhaps we too must return to questions of divination and the soul, and give up a certain absolute and literal claim on which our practices sometimes appear to be founded. By this act of sacrifice, something more precious may take its place:

> There came up a water bird, whose head shone with vivid peacock-blue colouring; and it swam to the land and walked about, shaking itself free of water and growing larger and more brilliant as he watched.[37]

* * * * * * *

NOTES

1 I acknowledge that my use of the phrase reverses Al-Biruni's stated intention (see ch.6 p104). The reversal is a picture in miniature of the dilemma of our Ptolemaic tradition.

2 C.G.Jung, *Aion: Collected Works* 9, part II (Princeton University press, Princeton, N.J., 1968) section 51, p27. The English edition gives the 'ai' spelling of 'daimon', which I have here altered for consistency.

3 See ch.9 note 21.

4 The death prediction against Pico is discussed in Chapter 1, with technical details in note 29. My disagreement with the Florentine astrologers is not simply a criticism that they have a particular knowledge granted to them through their astrology, and they then choose to use that knowledge badly. Such a criticism is an exoteric interpretation of astrology's ethic which is true enough within its limits, but does not go to the heart of the matter, since it seeks to distinguish the apparently objective knowledge (ie a forthcoming nominally fatal direction in Pico's horoscope) from desire. The desire of the astrologers is in wishing for, taking up, knowing, and giving voice to a judgment that will effect their desire. Who knows what is set in train in such an act? From the divinatory perspective, the objectification of the act of knowing onto an external fate to be suffered by a victim shows a radical failure to understand the nature of the astrological phenomenon, namely that its grain and fibre flows from the context of meaning in which it is taken up.

A technical note on the Pico direction: the astrologers predicted Pico would die 'before the completion of the 33rd year of his life' (see p15), and he in fact died in his 32nd year. Let us put aside any doubts about the origin of the version of Pico's horoscope being used (17 Libra asc), and take it exactly as it is given. We note that the primary direction of ascendant to Mars for the 33rd year of life depends a) on the computation of Mars, given in Guarico as 12 Scorpio to the round degree, but by modern computation 13°49' Scorpio; and b) on the use of Ptolemy's measure of arc to time of 1 degree = 1 year. Because of the unreliability of the original planetary calculation, the dating of Pico's death from the direction of Mars is out by a full year. Correctly computed it falls near the end of the 34th year, two years after Pico's death. This renders the prediction much less convincing, and if we are to found our interpretation on the 'real' astronomical factors, then the facts of the case certainly do not sustain the legendary status claimed for them.

Concerning the use of Ptolemy's measure, this is the classical method prior to the seventeenth century; but by Lilly's time dissatisfaction with its results had set in. Maginus (1604), proposed an equation of each year of life to be measured by the arc in right ascension of the Sun in 24 hours on the day of birth. Valentin Naibod (1619) equated the arc at the rate of 59'08" (the mean motion of the Sun in RA in 24 hours) for each year of life in all nativities; Lilly commends the method and it has been authoritative in primary directions ever since (see the informative discussion in Lilly *Christian Astrology* republished Regulus, London, 1985; pp708-715). The only serious later rival to Naibod is the method of Placidus (true solar arc in RA).

The point in quoting these various measures is that none of them can rescue the arc of direction as given by the astrologers of Florence; all the established alternatives to Ptolemy lengthen the number of years equated by the arc of 33°53'. Naibod's method places the direction in the 35th year of Pico's life (age 34y 5m), and Placidus puts it in his 36th year.

A conclusion concerning technique: I do not intend to evaporate the prediction against Pico as if it is in some way *technically* mistaken; its failure is of a different order. My remarks do not set out to belittle the craft of these astrologers, or to open a debate about 'right' and 'wrong' measures of direction. The death prediction remains a striking and undeniable instance of symbolism which must have seemed compelling to those who framed it; for them it was a true answer from the heavens. But we observe that the answer revealed is entirely a function of particular techniques and calculations utilised by the astrologers; through these techniques they have assigned meaning and received their sign in return. The sign they see is far from being simply 'out there' in the heavens; it is much closer to home in the imaginal assignation of symbolism, craft and computation that constitutes the divinatory method of astrology. The working of divination remains a mystery however we approach it; but the lesson of this exemplary prediction is that what we like to think of as objectivity in the craft of astrology is something of an illusion, since the desire and the imagination of the participants are the vital components.

5 Lilly's frontispiece engraving in *Christian Astrology* gives an unambiguous interpretation of the prophetic relation of astrology to Christianity. See my discussion in the afterword in the Regulus reprint (Regulus 1985). Like many astrologers of his time, Lilly was taken with Kepler's studies suggesting the Jupiter-Saturn conjunction of 7BC as the Star of Bethlehem. On the evidence of the engraving he intends us to understand a millenarian backdrop to his predictions of the end of the Stuart line as indicated in the Jupiter-Saturn conjunction of 1643, which fell in the last degrees of Pisces. The relation of Christ and kingship was a common and traditional problematic. For a discussion of Lilly's treatment of these themes, see Ann Geneva *Astrology and the Seventeenth Century Mind* (Manchester U.P. 1995), especially ch.7. pp208-212.

6 See ch.9 p167.

7 Dennis Elwell, *Cosmic Loom* (Unwin/Hyman, 1987; revised edition Urania Trust, London 1999). See for instance ch.8, 'Become what you are!'.

8 It is usually assumed that these are evidence of a fate laid out for us, and this in turn bolsters a notion of astrological determinism. But the evidence actually suggests that the intervention of consciousness is crucial and may work to change the 'fate'. On this important topic see

Michael Shallis, *On Time* (Burnett Books, 1982; Penguin, 1983), especially Ch.9: 'precognition does not necessitate loss of will to alter a possible future event'.

9 William Lilly, *Christian Astrology* (1647 and 1659; reprinted Regulus, London, 1985) p.289. Lilly is an unrivalled guide to the deeper questions of astrological practice, but it must not be assumed that everything he does should go without criticism. On another question of death I believe he errs – the judgment 'What Manner of Death Canterbury should dye?' (ibid., p419). Whether or not he is in error to make the judgment in the first place, it is an error to allow students with less discretion than him to assume they have this type of fate-judgment at their command in third-party horaries. It is significant that this interpretation that so jars is about a Church figure. The underlying motif of *Christian Astrology* is to demonstrate against Christian opponents that astrology shows truthfully in sacred as well as in secular matters.

10 Strictures: this distinctive naming of certain of the traditional 'considerations' is a quite modern development. I would add that the deterministic attitude in horary tends not to abide with the concept of 'strictures', and the katarchic or magical-religious attitude tends to embrace it. The best discussion of the function of the strictures is given by Marc Edmund Jones in his *Horary Astrology* (Shambhala, Berkeley/London, 1975).

11 Great Ages and the Star of Bethlehem: see, for example, Maggie Hyde, *Jung and Astrology* (Aquarian, London 1992), especially ch.1.

12 William Lilly *Christian Astrology* op.cit., 'Epistle to the Student in Astrology', which follows the Table of Contents at the front of the book.

13 Spineus (Francisco Spina), *The World's Catastrophe*, transl. Ashmole from the 1625 Latin edition, edited by Lilly, 1647. See A.Kitson, 'Notes on Lilly's *World's Catastrophe* and *Mock Suns* Collection', *Astrology Quarterly*, Vol 58, no.3, Autumn 1984.

14 The *Oxford English Dictionary* quotes what is presumably the first recorded instance in English, from the allegorical poem *The Assembly of Gods*. This gives the following description of the battle of Virtue and Vice (lines 932-938):

> Macrocosme was the name of the felde
> Where thys gret batayle was set for to be.
> In the myddes thereof stood Conscience, & behelde
> Whyche of hem shuld be brought to captyuyte.
> Of that nobyll triumphe iuge wold he be.
> Synderesys sate hym withyn closyd as in a parke,
> with hys tales in hys hand her dedys to marke.

Mirroring the human world below, the battle is conducted on the heavenly field of the Macrocosm, with Synderesis keeping an account of the deeds of Conscience (*tale*: account, reckoning); the word also indicates a stirring or prick of conscience. This text is attributed to John Lydgate, and has been published as *The Assembly of Gods* (Early English Text Society, University of Chicago, 1895 reprinted Oxford University Press, 1957). Lydgate elsewhere defines synderesis as 'the higher party of Reasoun, whereby a man shall best discerne his conscience to governe' (see OED reference). The commentator of the 1895 edition, Oscar Triggs, has in my view misunderstood the allegorical mode adopted by the poet (see his comments and 'correction' of the word *macrocosm*, op.cit p84). Lydgate was an erudite Benedictine monk: he lived from c1370 to c1471.

15 Henry Cornelius Agrippa, *Three Books of Occult Philosophy* (James Freake's translation published London 1651, reprinted Cthonios Books, 1986), Book I, pp. 140,149. See also this translation in a modern edition with annotations by Donald Tyson (Llewellyn, St.Paul, MN,

2000) pp197-209. Aggrippa's interpretation is consistent with that of with Lydgate, since he terms intellectual apprehensions which follow goodness, justice and truth 'intellectual passions, or synderesis'. In neo-Platonic vein he describes the tripartite division of the soul or mind into Sensual, Rational and Intellectual, giving three orders of passion of the soul, with corresponding orders of influence in the world (ch LXII); he shows how these passions work themselves on the body and soul (ch LXIII,LXIV), and on the body of another (ch LXV); how the passions can be conformed to the stars (ch LXVI), and how the intellectual passion may join with the stars and intelligences (ch LXVI, quoted).

16 Lilly, *Christian Astrology* op.cit pp439-442

17 The context and substance of Lilly's Civil War predictions has been excellently and sympathetically researched by Ann Geneva op.cit. She demonstrates the pattern of prophecy developed by Lilly in his almanacs, and has clarified our understanding of his methods. She has, however, not given consideration to the Presbytery horary.

18 Great Questions: in the first edition of *Moment of Astrology*, I attributed this naming to Lilly, but since then I have failed to locate the source, and it is probable that it is not Lilly. The method differs technically from ordinary horary in that (1) like all third-party horaries the perfection is no longer understood to involve the circumstances of the querent, or the significators for the querent, and (2) uniquely for great questions, houses are not derived from the ascendant as the querent. These questions may be termed 'great' in the sense that they imply a collective asking on a matter of collective importance, where the asking is not on behalf of anyone but everyone. In the Presbytery horary, although it is possible to retrace the role of the querent represented by the ascendant, and this may be of real political consequence (see note 25), this nowhere enters into Lilly's judgment and it does not enter into the consideration of perfection. From the point of view of the katarche, the line of initiative in this case is indirect and not direct, because despite his undoubted implication in the matter, Thomas Middleton is not seeking an answer as to what *he* should do in the situation, and certainly Lilly's treatment of the theme carries it entirely beyond the scope of the querent's power of decision and into the realm of the nation's fate. This universal nature of the judgment is its hallmark, even if as we may suspect Lilly knows and wishes that Middleton will carry the prophecy to others in a position to influence events: as I have suggested that knowing participation, truly and ethically prompted, is itself a ground condition of synderesis. The universal character of a Great Question is why houses and planets take on a wholly universal signification – thus in this judgment the 9th shows religious matters in a national context, and not the religious concerns of the querent. Although in conventional horaries rooted in the querent's initiative we will often see a valid crossing-over to universal house symbolism, nevertheless the primacy of the querent = ascendant is still retained. Great questions therefore mark a decisive departure from more orthodox traditional method. Where Lilly has gone, others have tried to follow. Very few modern astrologers attempting this experiment seem to know what they are doing or to be aware of the extraordinary and deluded inflation to which it is prone. See Chapter 8, p162 and note 18.

19 see Lilly's Diaries: ed. Katharine Briggs as *The Last of the Astrologers* (English Folklore Society, 1974) Ch. XVII p78.

20 There is an abstract of the judgment in *Mundane Astrology* by Baigent, Campion and Harvey (Aquarian, 1984), pp.357-60.

21 William Lilly, op.cit., see note 12.

22 The striking nature of the prediction, 'three whole years from hence shall not pass..' invites us to seek the relevant time symbolism in the figure. I have to admit that in my earlier discussions on this theme, I refused to accept as anything more than a secondary testimony a

signification that now seems to be of primary importance: the three years to the new dispensation are shown by the three degree application of Mars to Jupiter. This does look like a king facing the axe. As always with horoscopes there are elements that can be interpreted several ways, and in some of the details of his judgment concerning the initial decline of Presbytery Lilly may not be right. I suspect he is not far wrong, either; but such considerations require further historical work to decide.

23 Confirmation of Lilly's understanding of the significance *for astrology* of the Presbytery judgment will be found in his diaries ed. Briggs op.cit. ch. XIII p52; in this same passage is found an invocation of Conscience and Divine Providence as inspiring *Christian Astrology*, very much in keeping with the idea of 'synderesis of the stars'.

24 William Lilly *Christian Astrology* op.cit. p440.

25 The following illuminating interpretation was first suggested by Richard Eden, in a discussion at the Astrological Lodge of London. In the horary, Mercury, ruler of the ascendant for the querent, goes straight to the trine of Mars. It is a detail that is not commented on in the text. Weak (or perhaps disguised) though his significator is, do we not see here Thomas Middleton going straight back to the army with news of the judgment? Lilly is far from being a mere observer speculating on great public affairs, and he almost certainly has a good idea of the effect his judgment may have. At this time he carried an extraordinary reputation for his predictions on behalf of Parliament. He was nearer to the role of 'official oracle' than any astrologer seems to have been since antiquity. This means that he is implicated and actively participating in the possible resolution stemming from his astrology (see discussion in note 18). Great Questions raise in an extreme form the problematic issue of what has sometimes been called the 'mandate' of the astrologer, that is, what is granted to the astrologer to rightly judge, and to resolve through the judgment. This granting belongs to grace, to the daemones, or to heaven.

26 William Lilly *Christian Astrology* op.cit. p452.

27 Origins and influence of the *Centiloquy*: see the discussion in Jim Tester *A History of Western Astrology* (Boydell, 1987) esp. pp92-3,153-5. Hugh of Santalla's translation into Latin was made in 1136 (op.cit. p152).

28 *Ptolemy's Tetrabiblos, or Quadripartite* translated from the Greek paraphrase of Proclus by J.M.Ashmand (London, 1822); reprinted by W.Foulsham & Co.(London). Here is the Latin text as given by Giovani Pontano *Commentationem in Centum Claudii Ptolemei* (Basle, 1531):

Ptolemaeus I.

A te & à scientia. Fieri enim nequit, ut qui sciens est, particulares rerum formas pronunciet: sicuti nec sensus particularem, sed generalem quandam suscipit sensibilis rei formā: oportetque tractantem haec rerum coniectura uti. Soli autem numine afflati praedicunt particularia.

29 Astrology as signs or as causes: for a further discussion of the issue see Chapter 3, section headed 'some other element' (p55)

30 Giovanni Gioviano Pontano (Jovianus Pontanus) *in centum Ptolomei Aphorismes commentatio* (Basle, 1531). Credit for seeing the connection between Lilly and Pontano, and recognising its significance, goes to Vernon Wells.

31 Science and intuition: the renaissance debate on the relation of these modes is briefly but usefully discussed as a background to Jerome Cardan's astrology in Anthony Grafton *Cardano's Cosmos* (Harvard University press, 1999) pp172-3. Pontano's discussion makes the relevance to craft astrology of the science-intuition theme abundantly clear, as does the lucid observation from Ficino on 'astrology as a gift of the soul'. The uncovering of this theme

serves as yet another indication that however new the 'moment of astrology' thesis may seem, it is rooted in a tradition of thought, and is not essentially new except in the sense that it has taken up the question of astrological divination in a post-Ptolemaic cosmos. Renaissance astrology was still in the late maturity of the mythic and physical frame of that cosmos, and it is this fact that principally demarcates the formal distinction between the project of astrology then and now.

32 *fanaticos:* belonging to a temple, inspired by deity, religiously frenzied; by transference reduced to our modern meaning of 'frenzied' (cf. Greek *en-theos,* god-filled, hence enthusiasm); from *fanum -i,* a place consecrated to a god, holy place. There can be no doubt from the context that Pontano intends the word in its primary classical sense of god-filled.

33 I am indebted to the Latin Translation Group consisting of Chantal Allison, Clare Crawford, Sophie Page, Louise Ronane and Vernon Wells. The text was obtained courtesy of the Bodleian Library, Oxford. The translation given here is closely based on the provisional translation of Pontano's commentary on the first aphorism undertaken by the group; any errors are likely to be mine. See dox reference for more details of this text.

34 see note 15 for Agrippa's neo-Platonic threefold division of the soul as sensitive/sensual, rational, and intellectual. The two modes of thought mentioned here refer to the rational and intellectual parts of the soul. It appears that following Pontano and Ficino we would see the gift of divination as implanted in the sensual soul (and therefore a 'natural gift') as well as being inspired by the intellectual soul. Ficino's *inspectio* is a function of the rational part of the soul.

35 Marsilio Ficino, from his Commentary on Plotinus *Opera Omnia* (2 vols. Basle 1576, facsimile Turin 1959) p1626: translated by Angela Voss, who alerted me to this significant connection with Pontano. There is surely something shocking here for all astrologers who put faith in learning, technical wizardry, and passing exams – ie a large number of us. If Ficino is right, that 'often those unlearned in the art judge more truthfully than those who are learned', then within the main part of the tradition, the nature of technique and the role of expertise have been entirely misunderstood. I suggest that an honest assessment of our experience confirms what Ficino says, however uncomfortable it is to admit it. Even the feeble results from scientific testing in astrology tend to back this opinion, as has been suggested in Chapter 4 p000 (*Conclusions from Results of Research vii:* 'The perception of astrology is founded in *no special technique* – experience does not improve it').

36 Angela Voss 'On the Knowledge of Divine Things' *Sphinx* vol.6 (London Convivium for Archetypal Studies, 1994) p150. Angela Voss discusses Ficino's treatment of the divide between two modes of knowing in his Commentary on Iamblichus, where he 'distinguishes between *notio,* or a pre-eminent, intuitive sense innate to the soul, and *notitia,* or conceptual mental activity'.

37 Alan Leo's dream: see Ch.9 p169.

APPENDICES

APPENDIX 1

An Outline of Pico's 'Disputationes'[1]

Pico makes clear that he is distinguishing astrology from astronomy. His target is 'divinatory' astrology, the making of particular judgments concerning unknown or secret things from the horoscope, as for instance in the practices of natal, horary, and electional astrology. His tone throughout is scathing; when, he asks, have astrologers ever been honoured, or had statues and memorials put up for them? Their writings are so silly that one may wonder whether the astrologers themselves really believe what they say. Pico speculates on why people want to believe in astrology. He suggests that we don't fear things where the cause is obvious, but where causes cannot be established we seek some answer, and we imagine that Fortune and chance occurrence is related to the secret causes of the stars.

I will summarise Pico's major themes under seven broad headings. These concern (i) the authority of astrology's tradition, (ii) physical basis and primary data, (iii) foundation of the symbolism, (iv) primary logic of astrology, (v) application of the theory to horoscopes, (vi) astrological predictions in practice, and (vii) religious and ethical considerations.

[i] The Feeble Authority of Astrology's Tradition

The Old Testament prophets, as well as the Fathers of the Christian Church, are witnesses against astrology. Most of the great philosophers had no faith in astrology, and amongst these may be cited Pythagoras, Democritus, Seneca, Cicero, Plato and Aristotle. Certain works that have been attributed to Aristotle and Plato are false, and there have also been in more recent times false interpolations in the works of Albertus Magnus, in order to lend credence to astrology.

Some defenders of the subject say that even if astrology is not a science it should be granted the prerogative of an art, by virtue of the great antiquity of its tradition. But astrologers themselves have a weak understanding of history, and Pico disputes the reputedly long history of observations of the Chaldeans and the Egyptians which make no sense against a Christian chronology derived from the Old Testament. Certain effects might be observed under a particular constellation, but in order to check the relationship between these effects one would have to wait a thousand years for the planets to return.

In any case, the observations of these early astrologers were crude and inexact, and amongst the ancients, only the Sun and Moon were thought to have any effect. Since refinements in the subject are the result of recent theories, one cannot prove astrology an art simply by asserting its long history.

Another type of authorisation for astrology claims it as is a *revealed art*, given by divine inspiration. But how is this to be demonstrated? Was it revealed to the Egyptians, or to the Chaldeans, or to the Arabs? Was it revealed to Adam, who passed it on to his successors? How did the Hebrew patriarchs, who knew no mathematics, practise this art? The learning of the Chaldeans and Egyptians was limited. Lacking philosophers, in their idolatry they imagined that all things came from the stars. Instead of revelation we should trace many astrological notions back to primitive religious belief.

[ii] *Uncertainties in the Physical Basis of Astrology*

The number of heavenly spheres is in doubt; some authorities say nine, some ten, and there are many uncertainties about the movements of the heavens. Astrologers disagree about many parts of their doctrine, such as the question of the exaltations, and the theory of House division. Uncertainty about the correct moment for the beginning of the year affects a major part of astrological practice (ie. mundane astrology and the 'horoscope of the year', from solar ingresses). The inconsistency between astrologers shows that the subject is not really a science, and even some of the astrologers themselves realise this.

Astrologers are confused about the powers of the fixed stars. They use some but they say others are too small to be effective, yet they consider Mercury, the smallest of the planets, to be very important in the birth horoscope. Astrologers use tables and books that are known to be in error. Even if astrology were true this lack of diligence would render the subject false in its application.

[iii] *Illogical Basis of the Symbolism*

Pico takes the signs of the zodiac to be the basis of astrological symbolism. If these can be shown to be absurd, astrology is absurd. Even the number of the signs is uncertain, since the Chaldeans combined Libra and Scorpio into one sign. The signs are obviously established for the convenience of mathematicians, and their supposed qualities are really determined by the images projected onto them by astrologers. There are no animals in the sky; the zodiac figures are the fabulous creations of astrological madness. Pico denounces astrologers for 'profaning the heavens, the portico of God's temple, with a menagerie of inane animals'.

Pico returns repeatedly to this theme of the illogicality of the symbolism. He wonders on what basis the signs are given to parts of the body, and he finds no numerical or logical reason for the distribution of the twelve houses of the horoscope to brothers, friends, death and the like. He scorns the idea that some planets are malefic. Saturn is consonant with earth, is earth evil? Mars is consonant with fire, is fire evil? Is black bile (Saturn) not just as necessary as blood (Mars)? Most physical afflictions, observes Pico, arise from bad customs and not from bad planets!

[iv] *The Primary Logic of Astrology*

Astrologers believe there is some mysterious necessitating cause that comes from the heavens, but the influence of the sky is widely spread, and many influences attributed to the planets are really the result of the Sun's light and heat. The signs of the zodiac certainly have no share in the potency of the sun. The fact that the heat and light of the stars vivifies all living matter does not prove that the sky is animated. Since motion and light are common in the sky the effects of the planets must be common, and it follows that nothing particular depends on them. Even if there is a general effect, says Pico, the sky's influence is *universal* and not *particular*. The more particular and material a thing is, the less universal is its cause. If the sky did indeed determine the particular details of things then the natures and careers of people born at the same time and at the same place would be identical, but since this is not so, we see that the source of differences is material and earthly, and does not come from the stars. And if it should happen that two people with the same birth charts did in fact have the same careers, that would be no proof that their similarity was governed by the stars.

The latitude in which man lives will determine his life and career but this is not an astrological effect – men who are born on the coast usually follow fishing or sailing; those born in fertile lands are often less industrious than other men.

Consistent with his unwillingness to see any particular influence from the sky, Pico does not even allow the effect of the Moon on tides.

[v] *Application of the Theory to Horoscopes*

Pico brings out the practical problems in deciding on the moment for the horoscope. Is the foetus not alive when its heart begins to beat? He also criticises the ambiguity of inceptions. Astrologers cannot even agree whether the horoscope of a king should be taken when he is acclaimed or when he is crowned. They take the horoscope of a city when the first stone is laid, but it would be more reasonable to take it when the city is inhabited and its legal code formulated.

He also questions the notion that an infused force allows the natal configurations to take effect later in life, as with directions – if the stars cause things, then the effect should be strongest at the inception.

Pico ridicules the idea that a woman can conceive only when the stars are in harmony with those of her husband, and he points out the illogicality of putting the efficient cause (birth and the horoscope placings at birth) after the effect by describing the fortunes of ancestors from the horoscope placings of the child. Astrologers cannot even predict the child's sex before its birth so how do they presume to know about all these other matters?

[vi] *Failure of Astrological Predictions*

Farmers, navigators and physicians are always more skilful in their predictions. Astrologers claim they can enable men to obtain a favourable end and avoid a bad end, but they cannot advise correctly about the embracing or shunning of an action. Various men who scorned astrology have reached their chosen goals by their own efforts, while others following astrology ended miserably. Pico has numerous anecdotes showing astrologers missing the mark with their predictions. Since so much that is predicted doesn't come to pass, we may assume that whatever does turn out according to predictions happens by chance. People also have a habit of recording the hits and forgetting the misses.

Pico declares that he had studied the weather predictions during the winter he was writing the *Disputationes*. The astrologers' predictions were right for just seven out of 130 days[2] If they can't even tell the weather correctly how can they make predictions about the futures of men?

[vii] *The Religious and Ethical Question*

Pico attacks the heresy that assumes religious changes are due to planetary conjunctions, which was a common theme from the Arabic astrologers, and he also shows that astrologers disagree about these in any case. And which constellation or conjunction had lasted the 5,000 years that the world was pagan? Bonatti (Guido Bonatus) had even taken Christ to be subject to the natal horoscope, and derived his character and mission from the planets. All authority shows that God affects men through the angels. We act freely and not through stellar influence. Even if God foresees what we will do, he foresees also the act according to our choice.

Pico challenges the notion that stars can be 'signs' in terms of religious history, and he doesn't allow that they could be *both* causes and signs. He follows the line of the Church Fathers, that the star of the Magi was not a true star but a temporary miraculous manifestation created by God for an express purpose.

NOTES

1 Pico's *Disputationes* has not been translated into English, and my summary is drawn from secondary sources. The most important of these is the extensive abstract by D.C.Allen, *The Star-Crossed Renaissance* (Frank Cass, 1966), pp.23-4. See also Jim Tester, *A History of Western Astrology* (Boydell, Woodbridge, Suffolk, 1987). Various references will also be found in E. Garin, *Astrology in the Renaissance: The Zodiac of Life* (Routledge & Kegan Paul, 1983). Garin has translated the *Disputationes* into Italian, with parallel text (Vallecchi, Florence, 1946).
2 This figure for weather predictions is of course absurdly low; Pico hasn't used a criterion of success or failure that allows a .5 probability of success on any one day. The intuitive grasp of probabilities that is so obvious to the modern mind is not common in pre-modern times.

Lessons from the NCGR-Berkeley Double-Blind Test of Astrology

The NCGR-Berkeley 'Double-Blind Test of Astrology' stands as an exemplary demonstration of bad science, and a warning to astrologers of the penalties of naivety. Its story should be drummed into all who entertain a simple-minded notion of what constitutes research in our field so that, in future, this sort of nonsense may be nipped in the bud.[1]

The test was run in 1981-2 at the University of California by Shawn Carlson, in full co-operation with astrologers associated with the National Council for Geocosmic Research (NCGR). The test design was approved throughout by astrological advisors, although NCGR have denied ever approving the experiment, and the initiative appears to have been taken by their local chapter under the lead of Tony Joseph, veteran of the 1975 replication of part of Vernon Clark's tests.[2] The results were published in detail by the U.K. scientific journal *Nature* in December 1985.[3] The authority of this publication, coupled with the novelty value of the study ('astrologers disprove astrology' etc), ensured that it received wide press comment, all of it dismal.

Carlson's experiment manifestly broke down both through poor design and through freak circumstances that are outlined below, and this breakdown is self-evident on even a first reading of the report and figures given by Carlson. Yet despite this it was accepted uncritically by *Nature*, together with the author's tendentious and unscientific assertion that the results 'clearly refuted' astrology. We may suspect that, had the results appeared to favour astrology, then the editors of this august journal would have scrupulously sifted through for the slightest ambiguity in order to destroy it – if the study had not gone straight into the bin at first sight. Its uncritical publication is evidence, if any were needed, of an unpleasant fact of life: that when it comes to our neck of the woods we must expect brazen double standards from the high priests of contemporary science.

In the following analysis, I will describe the study in its own terms, before giving my comments. The experiment was designed to test the astrological proposition that

> the positions of the 'planets' (all planets, the Sun and Moon, plus other objects defined by astrologers) at the moment of birth can be used to determine the subject's general personality traits and tendencies in temperament and behaviour and to indicate the major issues which the subject is likely to encounter.

The experiment was conducted in two parts, using rigorous double-blind technique.

Part I: Subject Selection of Own Natal Interpretation

In the first part of the experiment, natal charts were distributed to the astrologers, with no statement of the sex of the subject. Each astrologer was required to prepare brief interpretations in a predetermined format, on personality and temperament, relationships, education, career-goals and current situation.

Following this, each volunteer subject was sent their own natal interpretation plus two others belonging to other subjects, and was asked to choose which of the three fitted them best. They also had to make a second choice.

The result   The test subjects proved unable to select their own horoscope interpretation, thus giving a poor result for astrology. However, Carlson finally decided that the conclusion from this part of the test might not be valid. This is because in a separate test on the subjects it was discovered that the subjects themselves could not even recognise their own psychological profile, the CPI mentioned below. If they could not recognise a psychology profile of themselves, perhaps they might not recognise a genuine astrology profile, either.

My comment   Apparently for these reasons, Carlson did not draw any conclusion from this part of his experiment and subsequent critics and astrologers have tended to ignore it. However, it is actually highly significant because of a most peculiar breakdown which occurred during the experiment, which has not to my knowledge been taken up by any other critic of this double-blind test. I have a suspicion that this breakdown is the real reason why Carlson backed off any conclusion. I will return to this shortly.

Part II: Astrologers Match Natal Horoscope and CPI Profile

The personality of the subjects had been assessed by the use of the California Personality Inventory (CPI). The astrologer had the horoscope of the subject and three CPI profiles, only one of which was correct. The astrologer had to make a correct match between the profile and the chart.

The result   The astrologers did no better than chance, so there is no evidence that they were able to match a horoscope to a CPI profile.

My comment   This was a wholly unsatisfactory experiment, as many critics, including the psychologist Hans Eysenck, later pointed out.[4] As mentioned above (Part I: The result) another part of Carlson's experiment had demonstrated that the subjects could not with any degree of significance pick out *their own* CPI profile, and the astrologers did no worse than the subjects themselves. There is no reason to assume in advance that astrologers are competent to match the results of a personality inventory to a *person*, let alone to the *horoscope* of that person. So why on earth didn't he reject this part of his experiment as faulty, just as he had rejected Part I? Yet it was on the basis of Part II that Carlson felt able to conclude that astrology was 'clearly refuted'.

One does not need to be a statistics buff to see that the experiment is wobbling, and that Carlson is making inconsistent and irrational decisions about which part of the experiment to accept or reject.

However, let us accept the Part II result, just as Carlson did. Even if it is a fair result in terms of the experiment, what does it actually mean? What can we reliably infer from it?

A Basic Statistical Problem: What Does the Sample Represent?

The NCGR-Berkeley test shows up an issue of outstanding importance for research in astrology, which is nowhere properly understood in the current scientific astrology literature. I am referring to a fundamental principle of statistics which Carlson has sailed through obliviously. I hope the reader who is not at ease with statistics will still bear with me. Getting this right could forestall problems about the correct interpretation of experimental results, if astrologers continue to engage in this type of research.

In statistics the word 'population' refers to the whole group of items, people or objects out of which a sample is drawn. Inferences can be made about the population, once we see how the sample behaves. So we may take a sample of two dozen ball bearings from a batch of 10,000 (the 'population') and if half of our sample is faulty, we infer that around 5,000 ball-bearings altogether could be faulty. A key issue is always whether the sample is a true 'probability sample', that is, 'random'. If I only pick nice, shiny ball-bearings for my sample, it will give a false indication of flaws in the 10,000 if shiny ball-bearings tend to be better finished in the first place.

With the idea of the probability (random) sample established, the NCGR-Berkeley experiment may be queried in this way. What is the 'population' that is to be sampled? We note from the carefully worded 'fundamental thesis of natal astrology' that, like all other Vernon Clark-style 'blind trials', the experiment is not concerned with correlations between planets at birth and temperament, etc., but directly with the capacity of astrologers to interpret. We can see that in statistical parlance, the *population* that is being sampled is '*[all] formal astrological interpretations of natal horoscopes by practitioners recognised as competent by NCGR*'. Having identified the population, we must ask: *is the sample representative of that population?* It seems to have been assumed by all parties that the sample was 'representative', but note that this problem is *not even considered*. When the advising astrologers agreed that this was a 'fair test', what did they think they were testing? Did they think this a fair test of astrology for a small batch of test subjects in the limited context of the experiment? Or did they realise that they were actually being asked to confirm that results *within* the experiment would be a fair representation of *all* natal interpretations – including those *outside* of the experiment? It would hardly be a nit-picking detail to work out in advance which of these two ways a result is going to be interpreted. Put in the way I have above, it would seem absurd to suggest that this experiment gives a 'probability sample' of all interpretations outside of the experiment, yet that is precisely the way in which Carlson manages to interpret it.

Before we can work out what the result of statistical analysis really means, it is essential to question the differences between the sample (that is, natal interpretations made in the test) and the population which the sample is measuring (that is, natal interpretations in general). Are one or more of their differences *significant* with respect to the characteristics of natal interpretation which are being tested? If we can answer 'yes' to this latter question, then the status of the sample as effectively random is in doubt. The sample might no longer be representative of the population. Now what does that mean for a typical astrology trial of this sort? If the astrology test differs significantly from real life, this does not invalidate the test as a one-off phenomenon but it would affect our ability to draw conclusions about 'natal interpretations in general.' *The non-appearance of the astrological phenomenon in the experiment could not be validly interpreted as the non-appearance of the phenomenon in general in the world.*

An interesting corollary of this may be expressed metaphorically in the dictum that you only have to find one unicorn to prove the existence of unicorns. A positive result for astrology in an unrepresentative sample such as the NCGR-Berkeley experiment would still succeed in suggesting the possible existence of the astrological phenomenon (or psi-Neptune).

Failure to understand the limitations of sampling is a frequent source of poor statistical method and spurious conclusions in the social sciences. Bad statistics are the handmaiden of scientism. What often happens is that methods that are one hundred per cent sound when applied to ball-bearings and gas molecules are naively applied to the subtle domain of human affairs, thus envisioning human beings and their actions as variants of ball bearings. Shawn Carlson falls into this classic mistake. It has to be said that most of the discussions about astrological statistics, including those in Dean's *Recent Advances in Natal Astrology*, show little awareness of the philosophy of probability sampling.

It does not require much effort of imagination to realise how different is horoscope interpretation under test conditions from consultation with a client. The most profound difference is introduced by the double-blind procedure which produces zero contact between astrologer and test client. In life, astrology and clients emerge within a definite context of meaningfulness for both parties. The interpretation will 'matter' for both. In the test, the only context is the experiment and it is only the experiment that matters. Instead of a human being the astrologer is looking at the chart for a sexless random code number. It is not clear *for whom* the interpretation *matters*. Nobody will be moved one way or the other by the interpretation. In this sort of test the astrologer is even 'blind' with respect to the experimenter, whose enthusiasm for the project could make the astrologer's work important. I do not need to go further with this description, neither do all the distinct differences need to be carefully itemised. From whatever direction the issue is approached the fundamental nature of the difference is obvious.

Here we come to a cleavage point concerning the definition of astrological judgment, for if astrological interpretation is no more than a rational assessment of some relatively unambiguous 'objective astrological facts', then all my observations above amount to very little. Interpretations should not alter in essentials between ordinary life conditions and test conditions. This assumption could be called the 'simple view of astrological facts', and it belongs to a natural-astrology conception. However, if astrological interpretation involves a complex phenomenon arising in the context of *perceived meaning*, that is, what *matters* for us, then it belongs to divinatory astrology. But observe the original statement of the aims of the experiment: it is trying to capture divinatory astrology. We can tell this because its definition of astrology includes the interpretive dimension: '...the positions of the planets... *can be used* to determine the subject's general personality traits...'

Once we hold rigorously to this interpretive definition, then we can logically infer from the results attained one of two possible outcomes: either a) the positions of the planets cannot 'be used to determine the subject's general personality traits', or, b) the experiment has failed to establish a probability sample and its design has therefore possibly neutralised any interpetive divinatory-astrology phenomenon in the sample selected. Notice that Carlson does not even consider the logical possibility of both of these outcomes; he therefore does not establish grounds for concluding that answer (b) given above is incorrect. His final negative conclusion results from an misunderstanding of the protocol of inference from statistical sampling.

Of course, Carlson can believe or have a hunch that answer (a) is correct, just as I believe from the evidence of careful and long study of astrology that answer (b) is correct. We can pit our views and our hunches one against the other, but let us be clear that this particular experiment doesn't solve the matter for either of us one way or the other, and giving it and all tests similarly constructed the authority of solving the matter is a logical error and cloudy thinking: when it appears in the form of an experiment it is bad science. The illusion of authority claimed for such illogical thinking is the hallmark of scientism.

CATCH-22: IF IT'S INTUITION IT'S NOT ASTROLOGY

Hidden in the veil of Carlson's scientism is a deadly catch-22 for the astrologer. Geoffrey Dean had already laid down a clear marker in this direction.[5] We can be sure that, had this experiment come up with a plus result for astrology, the critics would have said that its stated interpretive dimension allows 'intuition', or telepathy, or some other paranormal faculty, and intuiton or any psi-faculty is somehow not astrology – hence the NCGR-Berkeley experiment could not 'prove' astrology to its critics even if the astrologers had succeeded!

In attempting to validate divinatory astrology it has become apparent, on the basis both of this and of many similar cases, that of their very structure such experiments tend to isolate the test situation from the reality in which astrology is found to occur. The exception may be when these experiments are conducted in a genuine spirit of discovery, with the intention of opening up the phenomena, rather than shutting them down. It seems that unless tests of this sort are being conducted with the sympathetic genius of a Vernon Clark they are pointless, and even in these exceptional circumstances a large question mark must be placed against their worth, since it is not clear what any result is supposed to *mean*. Perhaps for a few they may provide a momentary glimpse of the unicorn, but by now we should surely have learned that in the court of modern science all such sightings are destined to be shouted down and explained away.

PSI AGAIN?

In the first part of Carlson's experiment, a control group was established to enable checking of the main data for 'Sun-sign bias'. Each subject in the sample had a matching Sun-sign partner in the control group. This partner had a dissimilar chart and was born at least three years earlier or later. The control group 'match' received no astrological interpretation of his or her own chart. Instead, each control subject was given the interpretation of their partner, plus two other incorrect interpretations. Although the control subject was told one of the charts was his or her own, in fact none of the three was their own. The control subject then had to choose the interpretation which was the best fit and then give a second choice.

The reason for this Sun-sign control group was to check the possibility that the subject might already have an astrological self-image through a knowledge of Sun-signs, and might respond positively to key words for their sign. This would load things in the astrologer's favour. To compensate for this, for astrology to score a hit, the group of 'real' subjects would have to do significantly better than their control group partners who would equally be picking up on the identical Sun-sign description. Yet as we shall see, this control group played a funny trick on Shawn Carlson and the astrologers.

The test subjects themselves picked their own interpretations no better than chance. By chance, these 84 individuals should have chosen their own interpretation around 27 or 28 times, and this they did: 28 out of 83. Clearly the astrologers' interpretations weren't making any impact. However, by chance one would expect out of 94 individuals in the control group, around 31 or 32 of them would pick their partner's interpretation. How did the controls do? They picked their partner subject's interpretation 42 times out of 94, which is a surprisingly high figure.

For the lay person this might not mean a lot. But from a statistical point of view it is an eyebrow-raising figure for a control group. It is over 90-1 against getting a result as high as this by chance (2.3 SD, standard deviations from the norm). Eyebrow-raising, but not a complete upset. In statistical testing of this sort, it is customary to pre-set a statistical figure for significance, so that a result is declared 'significant' and not chance if it jumps over that hurdle (in this case 2.5 SD). This particular figure has not quite jumped the hurdle (2.3 SD). But hidden in Carlson's figures, and conveniently *not* reproduced for publication, is a devastating figure which can be very simply tallied from his published table. The control subjects ranked the 'right' interpretation, for their twin, in third place very infrequently indeed, as if they could tell which was a completely *unfitting* interpretation. They ranked the right interpretation in third place in 18 out of 94 cases (2.9 SD). This would be expected by chance less than once in 520 such tests. The magic figure for statistical significance has been crossed and the control group has broken down as a control by showing apparently non-random behaviour. We could take it as plain bad luck. Carlson calls it 'a statistical fluctuation'. I believe it is a characteristic result of the (mis)application of statistics to the human domain, which refuses to be squeezed into a logical strait-jacket. Here this has induced an irregular and unstable context-psi phenomenon, crossing between the 'twins'.[6]

My interpretation of psi must be taken with the necessary pinch of salt since there is no way it can be proved, and in any case it is, for the purposes of the present discussion, secondary in significance to the main conclusion concerning the misunderstanding of probability sampling and statistical inference. However, I cannot help taking this possible twist of context-psi as a curious little highlight against the unrelieved futility of Shawn Carlson's scientistic shambles.

NOTES

* A more detailed description of the methods of the trial and a tabulation of statistical results, is available on-line in the *Moment of Astrology* dox file – see Preface for details.

1 The test was originally discussed in *Astrology Quarterly* vol.59, no.4, Winter 1985/6.
2 According to information I have received from both Erin Sullivan and Robert Hand, Tony Joseph never checked with his colleagues on whether NCGR were happy with the way the research was being conducted. Erin Sullivan originally participated but withdrew when she was not satisfied with the test design. Completely wrong progressions were given on at least one of the test charts, but Carlson did not acknowledge that this put a question mark on the way material was being prepared.
3 *Nature* vol 318, December 1985 p419-425 (Macmillan Journals, Basingstoke, Hampshire).
4 Professor H.J.Eysenck, 'Critique of "A Double-Blind Test of Astrology"' in the journal *Astro-Psychological Problems* (published by Françoise Schneider-Gauquelin, January 1986). Eysenck rejects Carlson's experiment as a faulty application of the CPI.
5 Geoffrey Dean on the non-acceptability of evidence that 'astrologers work' as a proof that 'astrology works' – see chapter 4 pp62-3.
6 Context-psi as a ground for meta-statistical interpretation: of its nature such a suggestion seems impossible to pin down, but it is essential than any astrologer attempting objective and empirical research should maintain an open mind and an exploratory attitude to this possibility. Jung's attention to the curiously meaningful (although, taken overall, statistically non-significant) behaviour of samples in his astrological marriage experiment, and his exploration and explication of the phenomenon, is paradigmatic and a starting point for further discussion – C.G.Jung, *Synchronicity: an Acausal Connecting Principle* Routledge, London 1972, and in Collected Works vol.8. The case is discussed by Maggie Hyde in *Jung and*

Astrology (Aquarian, London, 1992) ch.7; this work, with its analysis of the ambivalent components of synchronicity, is revolutionary in being the first to take on board the implications of Jung's suggestions for the practice of astrology.

I suspect that wherever the human soul is bottled up into logical categories for the purposes of scientific testing, then this same unpredictable phenomomenon will tend to occur, as if to disturb the scientist and remind us of something more important. Jung names this Mercurius, the 'synchronicity trickster' (see note 20 to chapter 4 for the trouble I have at this point in distinguishing the symbolism of Mercury from Neptune).

APPENDIX 3

Some Thoughts on Horary Astrology:
Charles Carter [1]

If any of the great astrologers of the past were to attend a session of our meetings nothing would probably strike him more than the scant attention paid to horary astrology, which played so large a part in the work of the seventeenth century students and has only really shrunk into the background during the last fifty years or so. Of course it has its devotees, but quite eminent and experienced astrologers of today have not only been sceptical of the merits of horary prognostication, but have even rejected it outright.

One of the reasons for its popularity in the past was no doubt the paucity of other material. Clocks were not common and not very accurate; and trustworthy data for natal work were hard to come by.

I find it difficult to believe that there is *nothing* in horary astrology, though my own experience with figures cast for me by horarists has been unfortunate. In fact, they have usually been downright wrong and never strikingly right.

We must admit that the theory of horary figures is obscure, to say the least.

It has been said that the map is cast for the 'birth of an idea'.

That applies to some cases.

Suppose Edwin, meeting Angela, asks himself, 'Shall I marry that girl?'

This *is* the birth of an idea, at least so far as Edwin is concerned. Angela, sly minx, may perhaps have asked *herself* the question, but we will put that possibility aside. We will say, 'Never before has the question "Will E. marry A." entered a human mind.'

Now I see no reason why a chart for the moment of that question should not be valid and produce a clear answer. There is no doubt about it. Either he will or he won't marry her.

But other queries are not so simple.

Suppose the thought enters my head, 'Will the favourite win the Derby?'

It may be the first time I have thought of this, but we may be sure thousands of other people, at all sorts of times, have asked themselves the same question.

Why then should my question furnish a valid answer?

Where do these thoughts come from?

Socrates believed in his Daemon or Genius, which gave him injunctions as to how he should act at several critical times in his life; and I suppose any of our readers will accept, at least as a hypothesis, that such a conception is true. It is immaterial, at any rate for our present inquiry, whether we call this being the transcendental self, genius, guardian angel or what you will. Such a being knows far more about our future than we – the lesser self – can foresee. And it is reasonable to suppose that if it wished to communicate something to the lesser self it would use whatever method seemed appropriate. Often this would be, as in Socrates' case, by direct 'voice'. Then there were the ancient oracles and divination by the flight of birds, and so forth. To an astrologer it might well speak by means of horary astrology.

Of course we can trace the reason for many of our thoughts. We hear, see or smell something that calls up a train of ideas by association. There is, I believe, an entertaining parlour game based on such associations. Or our friend who is interested in the Derby may see a newspaper headline that prompts his inner inquiry as to the fate of the favourite.

But many thoughts are not so easily accounted for. They seem, as it were, just to float into our minds.

Now we may venture on the hypothesis that, just as other ideas are plainly stimulated by our outer experience, these may be picked up telepathically.

Our Genius would not be likely to communicate with us except occasionally and on important matters.

Then we must ask, as regards other thoughts which might prompt a horary question, what are the entities that 'put the idea into my head'? It appears that upon their character depends the whole value of the idea and the likelihood that it might be illuminated by horary inquiries.

Believing as I personally do that the world is full of immaterial or semi-immaterial beings of varying grades of intelligence, it seems to me that we must protect ourselves against silly and even mischievous intrusions upon our mental integrity.

Furthermore, some horary practitioners may have a natural or acquired ability to contact trustworthy entities, whilst others may lack this quality. Even so, I cannot see how a valid figure can be cast for the moment *they* receive the idea, which is not their own, but the querent's.

The practitioner may find half a dozen letters of inquiry on his breakfast table, asking all manner of questions. He will open them more or less at the same time and obtain almost identical horoscopes. How can he read them all correctly?

It seems much more reasonable for the querent to tell the astrologer when the idea first came to him, the querent.

The only exception I would make is very serious cases when the astrologer is literally inspired by entities of a high order, as when the late W. Frankland was enabled to assist the police to find, if I remember rightly, a dead body.

One common-sense argument against some horarists is that if their claims were true, they and their clients would have the world almost at their feet; at least financially speaking. This does not appear to be the case.

Now although I have seldom consulted others in this way, I have cast numbers of horary figures for myself, when it was possible to assert fairly confidently that the time of the 'birth of the idea' was ascertainable.

What was the result?

Not, certainly, complete disillusionment.

But a firm conviction that, for some reason or other which I cannot discover and perhaps am not meant to discover, many figures are not be be judged; they must be thrown aside, discarded.

But, on the other hand, where the answer appears plain, that answer is trustworthy.

In such cases there is no need to bother much about house division or house rulerships; the oracle will speak clearly.

If Edwin casts a figure for the moment that the idea occurs to him that he might be happy with Angela, and finds Moon conjunction Venus not savagely afflicted, well, he will be. If he finds the same planet conjoined with Uranus, he won't be.

I cannot help thinking that the 'bloomers' that are, I fear, often made by horary astrologers arise because they *fear to discard.* They feel the map is a puzzle and as such a challenge, and they worry at it to get a straight answer, like a doctor who cannot make head or tail of the patient's symptoms but forces himself to pronounce a verdict. That, of course, is apart from the problem already mooted as to whether a map for the time a question is received by a practitioner can, in the nature of things, be reliable any way.

I write 'reliable' because I have already hinted that in my belief the Genius may make use of all sorts of means for getting information through to the ordinary consciousness. But such cases would be rare, at least for most of us.

Well, *is* there anything in horary astrology?

It is 6.45 p.m. GMT, June 21, 1962: why not put up a figure?

Sure enough, it looks radical. The prophetic Sagittarius rises; Mercury is exactly setting in its own sign but it is also square Jupiter, also in its own sign, and in the 3rd. Also Mercury has a nice couple of trines to Moon and Saturn.

I think horary astrology has given a pretty clear verdict in its own favour; but that square to Jupiter does contain a certain warning.

What do *you* think, dear reader?

NOTE

1 Carter's Horary Chart appears in Chapter 6, p.119. This study was published in the *Astrological Journal*, vol.5, no.1, December 1962, and is reproduced by permission of the Editor.

Frankland's 'Missing Father' Judgment: A Testimony of the Daemon

Apart from the tantalising reference in Carter's article no records appeared to be available of Frankland's horary work, until there occurred a fortuitous contact with his son, himself an elderly man, who had in his possession a few of his father's documents. One of these was a copy of an article in the London *Evening News* for Monday, 1 March 1926, titled 'Strange News from Lancashire'. This item was in turn commenting on the brief news item published in the Saturday issue, 27 February, under the heading 'Found By Aid of Stars – Coroner told of London Astrologer's Guidance.' Two local newspapers reported the inquest in detail, and the following account includes details from these sources.[1]

This is a fascinating and highly radical horary with intriguing symbolism, judged with discretion and skill, showing an effective outcome, and in the rare category of astrological judgments that achieve public recognition. On all these counts Frankland's work certainly deserves the respect of his fellow astrologers. However, my reason for giving this case such extended treatment here is that it reveals a strange and illuminating twist.

THE STORY OF EDWARD WHITEHEAD

The dead man was Edward Whitehead, sixty-three years old, of Morpeth Street, Burnley. He was a colliery winder but had not worked since suffering a nervous breakdown the previous October. He had become shaky and had said he would not wind men up and down the pit in that condition. On Thursday, 18 February he stayed in bed all day and complained of stomach pains. About 4 am on Friday he got up and dressed, and went into the yard, for the back toilet. His wife also got up to make him some cocoa. About five minutes after he had gone out she went to see how he was, but found the yard door open and her husband gone. After an unsuccessful search she informed the police, and the disappearance was mentioned on radio on Saturday night.

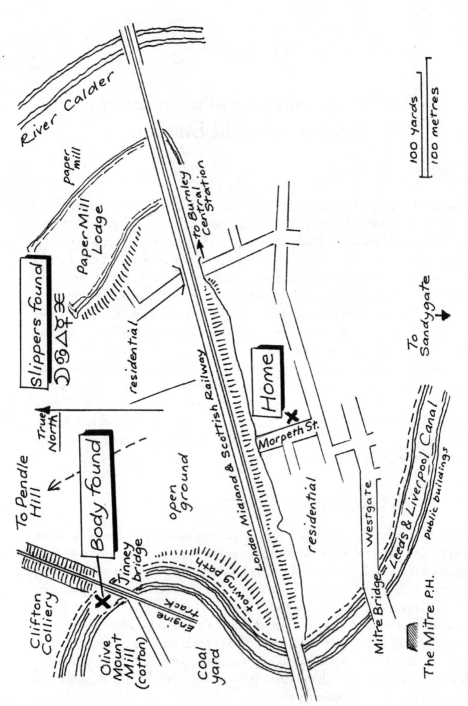

FIGURE 29 Frankland's horary: the geography of an astrological coincidence

About 4pm on Monday Edward Whitehead's son, Benjamin, found a pair of slippers belonging to his father on the banks of the Paper Works lodge [*lodge = reservoir. This lay several hundred yards to the north-east of Morpeth Street*]. The police began dragging there until Wednesday evening, with no success.

Following this fruitless search, around 8.30 am on Thursday, Charles Pollard, son-in-law of the missing man, obtained a dragging-iron from stables near the Paper Works lodge. He went to the canal between the Clifton jinney bridge and the Mitre Bridge. [*This is the Leeds and Liverpool Canal, skirting the area to the south and west in a crescent around 250 yards from Morpeth Street. The jinney bridge carried tracks for a colliery engine = 'jinney'*].

On being asked by the coroner why he chose this section of the canal, the son-in-law explained that on Monday morning, before anything was found, his wife telegraphed for help to an astrologer friend in London, namely William Frankland. Frankland was a Burnley man who had left the town about ten years before, but he did not know the deceased. He had asked for Edward Whitehead's date of birth and asked for the time he went missing, and sent his judgment in a letter. The son-in-law decided to act on the astrological advice after the fruitless search in the Paper Works lodge.

[*From various statements it may be inferred that the daughter left a message in the morning, and that Frankland later spoke on the telephone, requesting details. The time of the horary, 4:45pm, is therefore likely to be the time of the telephone conversation. The text of the letter, which is given in the next section, was reported in both the the the local newspapers*].[2]

CORONER (*referring to Frankland's letter*): According to this letter it says 'A little distance away south with a little west may be tried'. If I was going south from Morpeth Street I should go towards Westgate.
WITNESS: Due south is at the Mitre.

[*The son-in-law's reply makes no sense, since the Mitre Public House and Bridge is south-west of Morpeth Street. The Coroner is puzzled and will not let the point go*].

CORONER: If you were going to judge from this as his being possibly in the canal south of his own home, one would have thought you would have gone somewhere about Sandygate. What made you go where you did? That is what I am wondering.
WITNESS: I went to a friend of mine for a compass, and it was just a suggestion of his. I thought I would work from the Mitre Bridge and get a little west, as he said.
CORONER: It is quite a coincidence, and it looks rather strange you should get to

that part of the canal when the instructions in this letter, so far as I read them, are in an opposite direction.

WITNESS: I might have been a little out in my calculation. Pendle Hill is to the north, and I looked south, and the canal was the nearest water, so I worked from there to give it a trial, and the whole thing came out unexpectedly.

[It thus transpires that although the son-in-law has interpreted the astrologer's statement of 'west' in the way that could be rationally expected, he has treated south as if this was oriented not from the home of the deceased, but from Pendle Hill. Lying somewhat east of north and under six miles from Burnley, Pendle Hill is the outstanding landmark for the region, and a cardinal reference point for directions. However, anywhere in that area is south of Pendle Hill. The son-in-law's own home in Waterloo Road was a mile to the south-east of the Mitre Bridge, and does not therefore appear to enter into the reckoning].

CORONER: Did you start at the jinney bridge?

WITNESS: I had tried on the side of that bridge which is nearest the Mitre for about half-an-hour, and thought of moving nearer the Mitre, but decided to try on the other side of the bridge first. I threw in only three times before I found him. It was a marvellous thing. I could not pull the body out as it was too heavy, so I called out to a mill on the opposite side and they telephoned for the police.

CORONER: Is there any explanation as to how his slippers were found on the Paper Works lodge bank, and the body being found in the canal?

WITNESS: As long as I have known him he has always been full of that sort of thing, and very jocular. The conclusion I came to was that he had thrown his slippers down there, and moved away somewhere else. Where the slippers were found was very muddy, and if the man stood there he would have gone down about a foot, and the slippers would have been buried.

It was reported that the dead man was found with a silver watch, a pound note, 14s 6½d in loose cash, a metal chain, and a gold medal attached to the watch. The Coroner returned a verdict of 'suicide whilst of unsound mind', due to ill-health.

Further Comments from William Frankland

The judgment, given in quotation marks below, was published in the *Burnley Express and Advertiser* of 27 February, together with the statement that Frankland's letter 'was written before any discoveries were made in Burnley'. The additional material was not published, but appears to have been added by Frankland at the time:

On the 22nd Feb., 1926, I received a message from a young lady in Burnley, informing me that her father was missing, had left the house, two days previously, and had not been seen since. Could I throw any light upon the matter? Having by experience become convinced there is a relation between the Symbolism of the Heavens and human life, I cast what is called a Horary Figure or Map of the Heavens for the moment I received the query.

Also having asked for the data of his birth, I calculated the influences operative upon his life at that present period, which are termed in Astrology 'Progressed Directions.' These are calculated for the number of days, from birth, equal to the years of the native or person concerned.

From these two, the Directions and particularly the Horary Figure I gave judgment to this effect:-

'That there was probably death by water, in a stream or canal; South and a little West; not exactly near the home but at no great distance; in a place where there are sheds, tools and boats, at a rather barren place.'

This judgment was arrived at, firstly, because the Directions then operative, were very adverse and could prove fatal. Sun square Saturn, Sun square Jupiter, and others. Secondly, and most important, because in the Horary Figure I found that the 4th House, which represented the Father, had the planet Saturn therein, square to Neptune, a very depressing influence, and which also marked the Figure as a true one.

His significator was Mars, the Ruler of that House, exalted in Capricorn. This is generally counted a good position, but intuitively I took this to indicate that, for good or ill, he accomplished his object.

Mars was opposed by the Moon in Cancer in the 8th House, counting from the 4th. Now this 8th House represents death, so I judged death.

Cancer represents Water, but of the *running kind*, Cancer being an active sign, stream or river, so there is indication of death by stream or canal.

Mars being his representative, and in Capricorn, I judged the direction to be South which Capricorn suggests, and a little West, being on the Western side of the Map.

The distance was not great, Mars being in a Succedent House.

The type of place was judged by the sign in which Mars was placed, namely Capricorn. This sign is gloomy and Saturnian, but commercial, so I judged canal, boats, etc., for the stream, and barren place with sheds, tools, or commercial requisites near.

The Judgment was simply scientific, combined with intuition which is of course always necessary in the judging of symbols.

The chief aim was to mark the Significator and judge conditions such as were indicated by any influence directed thereto, remembering that in his Directions the influences were very adverse.

When Frankland describes his judgment as 'simply scientific' I think we must take this to mean that it is founded on a shared convention of astrological method based in a rational process of interpretation. Any other astrologer can piece his or her way through the judgment and trace its logic. The fact that Frankland has woven the threads of symbolism in the exact way he has, and with such success, is the additional component of intuition. However, the whole case is very far indeed from anything that could be called 'science' in our modern age. This mysterious intuition has had to run its path not just through the daughter prompted to make the question, and not just through the astrologer framing his interpretation, but to the eventual key recipient, the son-in-law who was moved to get the dragging iron. All these parties have to play in to the context of the symbolism for this horary to become true.

Now it is true enough that this particular case is a rather typical instance of the confusions of Neptune, but my years of study of cases of astrology inclines me to suggest that it is nevertheless representative of many other occasions of the working out of symbolism. The puzzling picture of events that emerges in the to and fro of discussion in the Coroner's inquest presents us with a potent illustration of the intractable serendipity that is the working of astrology. We cannot say that the astrologer's judgment gives a straightforward objective truth of the location of a body. Indeed, it would not be a great problem for the sceptic to pick away at the inconsistencies of the 'information' yielded by the astrology, unitl we were left with little apparent justification for the son-in-law to search exactly where he did. Yet he really *did* find the body, undeniably guided by the astrologer's judgment. The son-in-law has had to 'take' the astrologer's words creatively and intuitively in his own way, and frame them in his subjective geography, against the brooding presence of Pendle Hill.[3] Only then could he chance upon – or be led to – the body. The 'moment of astrology' in this case is woven into the *psychic reality and active participation* of one of the people involved. Here is the daemon of astrology, leading desire to its goal through symbol and auspicious coincidence.

NOTES

Frankland's horary is given on page 121.

1 Coroner's records for this area and period have not been kept, and my sources are therefore the newspapers, the *Burnley Express and Advertiser*, 27 February 1926, and the *Burnley News* of the same date. There are differences of coverage and also slight but unimportant inconsistencies in the reportage, and I have collated the two separate accounts in describing the case. The *Burnley Express and Advertiser* mentions that Frankland 'took up the practice of astrology about ten years ago. He is stated to have been extremely successful, and to have assisted the police in many ways.' This tantalising unlocated reference appears to be a case of dramatic embellishment by the reporter. More puzzling is the mystery over Edward Whitehead's birth data. Searches have not so far revealed a birth that could match these details. It is possible that his age was wrongly given throughout.

2 The overlap of times makes it possible that the daughter knew of the discovery of the slippers by 4:45pm on Monday, and she could have informed Frankland of this. This, however, seems unlikely; there would be every reason for Frankland to make some indication of this in his reply. The *Burnley Express and Advertiser* makes a point of stressing that the astrologer's letter was written before 'any discoveries were made', which although not strictly correct leads in the same direction, by showing that the reporter believed that Frankland had no positive information to suggest that the missing man was drowned.

3 The more closely the details are examined, the more curious is the weaving of symbolism and serendipity. A detail that might not be obvious on first consideration is Frankland's linking of Cancer and canals. These usually hold calm, still water which is moved only when a boat passes. The River Calder fits the bill for 'running water', but not the Leeds and Liverpool Canal at Burnley. Frankland has been led by a traditional connotation of Saturn and industry, reinforced by Mars in Capricorn, to give him the suggestion of a commercial setting. A canal, unlike the fixed body of water of a 'lodge' or reservoir, carries commercial traffic and it is this movement that may in this context make it cardinal water, Cancer.

It is tempting to ask whether the astrologer has missed some clue that would have given him a more exact compass direction. Frankland has used the traditional attribution of directions to signs as his basis (south for Capricorn, the sign of Mars as significator for the dead man), modified by mundane hemisphere (to the west of the meridian). He would have had a better result by dropping the sign indication and going wholly for the house and quadrant of Mars, which gives a broad north-west indication. However, that is to be clever after the event, and anyone who has attempted this type of exercise from a horary will recognise how frustrating and inconsistent the method can be, even in strikingly radical figures such as this.

Frankland seems to have assumed that his directions should be taken from the missing man's home, and this is how it has been understood by the son-in-law. Accordingly I have searched for various possibilities of a theoretical direction to match the 33° north of west bearing of the jinney bridge from the house, but have not found any convincing exact solution from the horoscope. In any case, all speculation of a technical nature is in danger of missing the essential point. However Frankland has finally arrived at this conclusion, nevertheless the judgment is just what is required to convince Charles Pollard that the body must be in a stream or canal, after it was not found in the obvious place, the Paper Mill Lodge. Of all locations 'at no great distance', the River Calder is ruled out because it is east, definitely not indicated by the judgment. The tow-path south from the railway embankment to the Mitre Bridge bordered a residential area at that time, so we must look north of the embankment to match the description of the 'barren place' given by Frankland. It is probable that the description of 'sheds, tools and boats' narrowed the choice to the area close to Olive Mount Mill and the coal-yard around the jinney bridge. But to arrive where he does the son-in-law has to negotiate his way, consciously or unconsciously, around the explicit direction, 'south and a little west' from the dead man's home.

From around 50 yards south of the jinney bridge the curve of the canal brings it in line with the visible of Pendle Hill. By treating this line as the north-south axis Pollard can visualise this location as 'south' (of Pendle) and 'a little west' from his starting-point.

As a final note to this case study, I must thank Harold Frankland for his generous assistance, and Iris Verity for her extensive researches in Burnley.

Ashmole on Astrology: Commentaries from the Theatrum Chemicum Britannicum[1]

Iudiciall Astrologie is the Key of Naturall Magick, and Naturall Magick the Doore that leads to this Blessed Stone.

> *Trust not to all Astrologers, I saie whie:*
> *for that Art is as secret as Alkimie.*

Astrologie is a profound Science: The depth this Art lyes obscur'd in, is not to be reach't by every vulgar Plumet that attempts to sound it. Never was any Age so pester'd with a multitude of Pretenders, who would be accounted (and stick not to style themselves) Masters, yet are not worthy to weare the Badge of illustrious Urania. And (oh to be lamented!) the swarme is likely to increase, untill through their Ignorance they become the ridiculous object of the Enemies to Astrologie; (would that were all,) and Eclipse the glory of that light, which if Judiciously dispens'd to the World would cause admiration; but unskilfully expos'd, become the scorne and contempt of the Vulgar.

He that understands no more of Astrologie (nor will make a further use of it) then to quack with a few Tearmes in an Horary Question; is no more worthy to be esteemed an Astrologian then Hee who hath onely learnt Hebrew may be accounted a Caballisticall Rabbi. Tis true, he may be so fraught with words, as to amuse the unlearned, with the Canting noyse thereof, but what is that if compared to the full and intire knowledge of the Language? Yet of this sort at present are start up divers Illiterate Professors (and Women are of the Number) who even make Astrologie the bawd & Pander to all manner of Iniquity, prostituting Chast Urania to be abus'd by every adulterate Interest. And what will be the issue (I wish it may prove no Prophesie) ere long Astrologie shall be cried down as an Impostor, because it is made use of as a Stale to all bad Practises, and a laudable Faculty to bolster up the legerdimane of a Cheate. And besides having now growne famous by the true Predictions of some of her able and honest Sons, shall grow into as much disgrace and infamy, by the unskilfull Prognosticks of ignorant Illegitimate Bastards: who rather then they will accuse themselves when they faile of truth in their Judgments, will not stick to condemne Astrologie it selfe as defective and lame, in what their slothfull negligence or ignorant blindnesse was not able to finde out. And therefore Norton here speaks truly, that Astrologie (take it with all its Comprehensions) is as Secret or Misterious as Alchimy, and as difficult to be throughly and perfectly understood.

There are in Astrologie (I confesse) shallow Brookes, through which young Tyroes may wade; but withall, there are deep Foards, over which even the Gyants themselves must swim. Such is the Doctrine of Nativities, Directions, Annuall Revolutions and what else depends thereupon, belonging to Man, the little World: and beyond these, those of Comets, Eclipses, Great Conjunctions and Revolutions, that refer to the greate World. These are subjects of Eminency, and being judiciously handled Magnifie the Art. But,

> Many men weene[2] which doth them reade,
> That theie doe understonde them when theie doe not indeede.

I know some few Artists have satisfactorily manifested what excellency of Skill there is in Judging an Horary Question, and how much of truth may be drawne from that branch of Art; But they are those that are throughly read in all other parts of Astrologie; for such only are able to give a true Resolution to the Querent, and from the events of their considerate Predictions, bring Honour to the Art, and gaine Reputation to Themselves.

NOTES

1 Ashmole is commenting on Thomas Norton's *Ordinall of Alchimy*. 'Theatrum Chemicum Britannicum... containing Severall Poeticall Pieces of our Famous English Philosophers, who have written the Hermetique Mysteries in their owne Ancient Language' (London, 1652).
2 *weene*: to surmise, conceive or conjecture.

APPENDIX 6

Reworking Sibly's Horoscope for America[1]

The horoscope for the American Declaration of Independence given in Ebenezer Sibly's *Occult Sciences*, first published in 1784, has long intrigued and frustrated researchers. This is the earliest known astrological record of this momentous event, and is an item of interest for the historian as well as the astrologer, since it appears to testify to the hour of the declaration's signing. The source of frustration is that, try as we might, we cannot make the engraved horoscope data consistent with any single time and place on 4th July 1776; furthermore, there are no simple computational errors we can seize on which, when put right, allow us to make sense of the data. Data and planetary positions show apparently irretrievable inconsistencies.

The data mismatch falls into two orders. The first is that the time stated, 10h10m pm, cannot yield the stated cusps in London whether we treat the data as LMT (local mean time), GMT (Greenwich mean time), or LAT (local apparent or sundial time). The MC of the engraved chart is 13° 12′ Sagittarius. This requires a time of around 9:53 pm mean time, or 9:49 pm local apparent time, and nowhere near 10:10 pm as stated.

The second order of error involves the stated positions of Sun, Moon and planets. A comparison of planets in the engraving and their modern computation yields the following results: the Sibly Moon is 3 degrees out, at 24 instead of 27 Aquarius, short of its true position by five hours of motion; and the Sun is given as 13°08′ Cancer, but this should be 13°19′ Cancer; the time discrepancy here is four and a half hours of solar motion. Mercury is difficult to read, but it appears to be at least two degrees adrift, some three days of retrograde motion beyond its correct position.

Any thought that this is something to do with the state of ephemerides in the 18th century must be put aside. In his book we find a sample page from White's Ephemeris for June 1784; this falls well short of modern standards but it nevertheless shows a high order of accuracy for the Sun, differing from modern computation only within the order of a few seconds, and an accuracy to within two minutes of arc on the Moon. Mercury, Venus and Mars show errors ranging up to four minutes of arc; the traditionally troublesome factors for the ephemeris-maker are Jupiter and Saturn, and in White's Ephemeris these reach a quarter of a degree in error. The discrepancy in the Sun's position in Sibly's figure is especially telling, since the Sun is a secure cornerstone of all navigation, timing, and ephemeris construction, and where the calculation is carried to the minute of arc from an accurate ephemeris, as in Sibly's figure, then 10' adrift would show an indisputable failure of competence for any astrologer in the modern or early modern era.

THE SCENE OF THE CRIME

We are faced with a situation resembling an accident or crime scene, where someone involved has hastily rearranged a few items of evidence in the hope of throwing investigators off the trail. The first outsiders on the scene are accordingly misled, and jump to one or more wrong conclusions, but their explanations remain unsatisfactory. It just doesn't hang together, and however we approach the problem, it seems intractable. The breakthrough comes with the recognition that several apparently crucial pieces of data are misleading and should not be taken at face value – only then can a careful evaluation be made, sifting through which elements are reliable and which are unlikely. The moment we take this sceptical view, then provided there is other supporting circum-stantial evidence, we will have reasonable hopes of discounting false leads and arriving at a plausible reconstruction of the original scene.

In our present example, the original scene is the horoscope actually cast by Sibly. The misleading clues are key pieces of published horoscope data, and the culprits are the printer and the engraver. Once this can be demonstrated as a plausible possibility then we have a way of proceeding, and everything else begins to fall into place. But before we examine the most important evidence, it is instructive to look at how the horoscope is laid out in the engraving, for this gives a revealing clue. The planets in the fifth house have been squeezed in, and the Sun is compressed to the point of illegibility. There is hardly space to put in the zodiac positions in this house, and the execution gives the appearance of not having been well thought through from the start. It is possible that the picture went through two distinct stages, with the skilled artist producing the picture and being instructed to leave white space for the horoscope diagram to be entered separately – and as it turned out, he did not leave quite enough space. The people involved were unlikely to have any understanding of horoscopes, or at best a confused understanding, so they would be working from what would be to them cryptic and incomprehensible material. The chain of instructions may well have passed through several pairs of hands: from Sibly to the printer, the printer to the engraver, or vice versa, with the potential for error compounded at each stage.

There is a telling indication in the mis-spelling of 'Independance'. Sibly is an educated man, his spelling is careful and consistent, and in his lengthy discussion of the astrology of the American revolution he uses the forms 'independence' and 'independent', and nowhere the 'a' spelling. The word appearing in the engraving is no longer Sibly's choice, and cannot even have been proofed by him. We may infer that he had no control over errors appearing in the final engraving.

There is convincing circumstantial evidence to back this suggestion throughout *Occult Sciences*, where typographical mistakes pop up repeatedly in horoscope diagrams. Further, these are mostly errors of the sort that a person unacquainted with astrology would not readily identify. One instance in particular rivals the American Independence horoscope in the scope of its errors: this is the figure used by Sibly to illustrate for the student the principles of casting the horoscope (p197). I can count no less than seven typographical errors; in addition one item is missing completely, the Part of Fortune, although this is elaborately described in the text and its place in the horoscope clearly referred to. Several of the errors are gross: Mercury is missing, but there are two Jupiters; and the MC is given as 31°02′ Gemini (the IC is 13°00′ Sagittarius). In the list of aspects in the centre of the figure, a Moon-Jupiter square has become a Venus-Saturn square, and Venus has been turned into Mercury. This represents a surprising degree of typographical sloppiness, and there is clearly no possibility that Sibly proofed this horoscope, since these errors spoil his efforts in this section of his text. If the typesetter has created such havoc here, we may take it as quite feasible that the same thing has happened to the horoscope for the Declaration of Independence.

Our investigation brings us to the reasonable assumption that unless it can be demonstrated otherwise, any apparent inconsistency in the data must prima facie be assumed to be typographical, rather than computational. It follows that we cannot take as a valid representation of Sibly's original workings any single piece of data, or stated position, or numeral, in the engraved American Independence horoscope. At this point the focus of our detective work changes. Because typographical errors are arbitrary and in effect random, they are likely to prove superficial and unable to disguise the interwoven numerical fabric of a full horoscope computation. Even if we are faced with a battery of such errors, we should be still be able to restore Sibly's original, provided we take account of the method of astrological computation of his era, and follow the approach he uses in his other examples.

RETRACING SIBLY'S STEPS

At this point it is worth establishing some details of which we can be fairly sure. The first is that an accurate longitude of Philadelphia, and therefore the correction between London and American timings, was readily available to navigators and geographers in Sibly's day, and he explains and demonstrates the conversion of geographic longitude to time in his textbook. We may have to allow a difference on the MC of perhaps 3 or 4 minutes of zodiacal longitude depending on the exact statement of Philadephia's geographic location, but it is unlikely to be more. The only real query is whether Sibly took a rounded 5h west correction to Philadelphia, or the more precise 5h 00m 36s from the Greenwich meridian. Even here, we are not looking further than a cumulative 9′ arc range of possibilities on the MC of the horoscope relocated to Philadelphia.

From my researches, it looks as if Sibly usually took the Greenwich Meridian as the London meridian – we know that in his day Greenwich served the purpose of regulating time for London; and since much of the commercial city is less than half a minute in time west of Greenwich, this is a good solution for both ordinary time keeping and practical astrology.

The greatest confusion has always attached to the statement of time, 10h 10m pm. Most later astrologers coming to the problem have not appreciated the significant differences that occurred in the 19th century both in computational approach and in ephemeris design. These changes came in response to the adoption of standard time meridians, especially the Greenwich Meridian. The methods we find in Sibly are in an ancient mode of practice predating mechanical clocks, deriving the hour of the horoscope directly from observation of the Sun. Sibly is in a changeover period where modern clocks and accurate ephemerides have become the norm, but where astrology's computational foundations have not yet adjusted to new demands. Misunderstandings arise when we read backwards onto older methods from our own modern ways of working. Without going into unnecessary elaboration, the following paragraphs give an outline of the approach in Sibly's day.

1) The astrologer will start, as we do, with the raw data of the reported time of an event. When this time has been taken from a mechanical clock, then it will be set for local mean time – in the case of London, this is GMT. The next step is to use an

ephemeris computed from a reference meridian (probably Greenwich) to find planetary positions.[2] For horoscopes for the whole of England the astrologer does not need to fuss with the time correction to the ephemeris reference meridian – it requires a 6 degree change of geographic longitude to alter the Sun's stated position at local noon by just 1 minute of zodiacal longitude. This is why before the 19th century astrologers do not usually need to bother with a geographic longitude or its equivalent – it makes no practical difference, and it does not come into their horoscope computation at the ordinary working level of accuracy.

2) The zodiacal longitude for each of the Sun, Moon and planets is found by interpolating for the given LMT, as a proportion of the time between noon prior and noon following the birth or event, much as in a modern manual calculation.

3) From this point the computation follows a different route to that taken in modern times. Once the Sun's zodiacal longitude is found to the degree and minute of arc, this is converted to right ascension using a standard table equivalent to the MC and Sidereal Time entries in the modern Table of Houses.[3]

4) The astrologer returns to the raw data LMT value which is now corrected by the 'equation of time' to give the sundial time or local apparent time (LAT). White's Ephemeris gives this value, to the second, for noon each day. The equation of time is the difference between the mean time clock and the sundial, for the same meridian; this variance can reach 16 minutes either way depending on the time of year.[4] The local apparent time is identically the 'hour angle of the Sun' from the local meridian, expressed in hours and minutes along the equator.

5) By combining the hour angle with the RA of the Sun, the astrologer derives a key piece of computational data, the RA of MC, right ascension of the Midheaven. It is equivalent to the LST, local sidereal time, of our modern workings; it may be expressed in degrees or in hours and minutes. Its formula is RAMC = HA of Sun + RA of Sun, where the hour angle is measured 0-360 degrees or 0-24 hours from the previous noon.

6) From the RA of MC, the Ascendant is computed with the aid of a Table of Ascendants, under the appropriate Pole of the Ascendant. The Table of Ascendants is equivalent to the Asc and Sidereal Time entries in a modern Table of Houses. The Pole is a vital element of computational data, and is therefore commonly entered on the diagram; it is equivalent to the geographical latitude of the place.

An important point to make clear is that in this way of working we find three items of computational data commonly given with a horoscope. These are the civil date; the pole or geographic latitude; and the RA of MC, or alternatively LAT, the hour angle of the Sun, which latter is Sibly's practice. Unlike modern practice which works from standard time meridians, the raw data of the LMT of the event is commonly not given.

We are therefore inclined to treat the statement of time in the Declaration of Independence horoscope as a reference to the hour angle of the Sun in London, or on the Greenwich meridian, and not to a civil or mean clock time. But the printed version is obviously in error: the hour angle of the Sun, or local apparent time, is 9h49m post meridian, and not 10h10m. This is the single most misleading error in the figure.

We can only speculate as to how the engraver, or some other intermediary, half-understanding horoscope data, perhaps even trying to improve on it, has managed to mess this up. It could well be that in conversation a figure such as 'ten before ten' (ten minutes to ten) has been mis-heard and its origin misunderstood. It is also a matter of speculation as to how these errors were dealt with after the initial printing; it is difficult to imagine Sibly letting them go, and it is quite possible there existed a separate printed insert for corrections, which either failed to arrive or failed to survive in the few editions of *Occult Sciences* so far studied by astrologers.

But these speculations in the end lead us nowhere. Our only secure position is to work off what we have established as the astronomical foundation of Sibly's published horoscope. This is where we apply detective work. Since the angles and Placidus cusps of the horoscope are completely consistent, this assures us that the stated MC is indeed Sibly's computed MC. From this we can work back to find the correct hour angle of the Sun, which is 9h49m16s post meridian (pm); there is only one position of the Sun in right ascension and in zodiacal longitude that yields this exact hour angle and corresponding MC. The reason we can be so confident of this assertion lies in what we have established already as the method of computation used by Sibly. The Sun's position is not, as in a modern manual calculation, a secondary factor derived from some more primary data (ie the GMT of the horoscope) but is itself primary data on which is founded the computation of the MC and the horoscope houses. It follows that once we have the date and the MC we may directly determine the solar position on which that MC is based.

This reveals to us immediately the typographical error that has dropped a digit from the longitude: Sibly must have computed the Sun as 13°19′ Cancer, or possibly 13°18′ depending on rounding, and not 13°08′. The erroneous Sun position in the engraving cannot yield the hour angle, the RA of MC, the angles and the Placidus cusps displayed on the angel's scroll.

Here are the nuts and bolts of Sibly's computation: from the engraving the MC is given as 13°12′ Sagittarius. The RA of MC is 251°47′. The Sun we are taking to be at 13°19′ Cancer, which is RA 104°28′; from this we determine the hour angle of the Sun as 147°19′ (251°47′-104°28′). Converting the hour angle to time gives us a local apparent time of 9h49m16s p.m. The equation of time to LAT is +4m02s, which gives LMT London/GMT 9h53m18s p.m. The Sun at this time on 4th July 1776 is at 13°19′ Cancer, bringing us back to the starting point and solving the computation for one unique midheaven and moment, MC 13°12′ Sagittarius at LMT/GMT 9h53m18s p.m. Within a possible orb of rounding error of a few seconds, this is the moment taken by Sibly to represent America's declaration of its independence from Britain.[5]

SORTING OUT SIBLY VARIANTS

The above discussion should enable the reader to discriminate between the Sibly derivatives proposed over the years to solve the problem.[6] Sibly's original is cast for London, because his intention was to show this extraordinary turn of events from the point of view of Britain's destiny. As an inceptional figure for the fledgling United States, the figure must be relocated to Philadelphia. It is this relocation that creates the primary Sibly horoscope for America's Independence, giving an MC in Philadelphia 26°19′ Virgo, and an asc. of 8°47′ Sagittarius. I am sure that like the London original this will be found to be a significant figure, deserving of careful study.

NOTES

1 The original version of this discussion appeared as 'Making Sense of Sibly' in COA Bulletin no.22 17th Sept 2001. It was soon after renamed to avoid confusion with Susan Manuel's earlier article by this name – see Nicholas Campion Book of World Horoscopes (Cinnabar Books, 1996) p415. Further discussion relating to this material is available on-line in the *Moment of Astrology* dox file – see the Preface for details.

2 Computing from a reference meridian: that is, the positions of the planets will be given for noon LMT on that meridian. Note that for most purposes in astrology it makes no practical difference to the zodiacal longitudes of the planets if we use the same (Greenwich) ephemeris when we are a few degrees east or west of Greenwich. Liverpool is 3° (twelve minutes of time) west of London, but we will have the same Sun degree (to within a minute of arc) at noon LMT Liverpool as at noon LMT London. The most affected factor is the Moon which will be

out by around 6' arc between London and Liverpool, but for ordinary astrological purposes this is slight. As it happens this matches the uncertainties and the order of error of the Moon's position in White's ephemeris.

The method taught in *Occult Sciences* for calculating the horoscope follows the approach given above, and does not require any consideration of the geographic longitude of the place. Where careful accuracy is being established, for instance for a highly rectified birth horoscope, then the astrologer of Sibly's day will be able to make a further small time correction to allow for geographic longitude from the reference meridian for the Moon and for the Sun, where this latter is being computed to the second of arc. This order of exactitude appears to be the exception rather than the rule, however.

3 The sidereal time is equivalent to the right ascension of the corresponding zodiacal degree in the MC column. Therefore to find the Sun's RA, look in the MC column for the Sun's degree, and its corresponding RA, expressed in hours and minutes of arc, is found under Sidereal Time. The hours and minutes of arc may be converted to degrees and minutes by multiplying in the ratio of 1 hour = 15 degrees.

4 The equation of time in modern astrology: this is most likely to be encountered in using Planetary Hours. See for example a table showing the approximate value for any day of the year in Llewellyn George *Improved Perpetual Planetary Hour Book* (Llewellyn, St.Paul, Minn., 1975) p178.

5 The only variations in the modern recomputation of planetary positions between the Sibly London chart for 9:53:18 p.m. GMT (asc. 19°49' Aquarius) and the later Rudhyar rectification given on p268 are as follows: in the earlier Sibly chart discussed here, Mars is 21°22' Gemini, Venus is 3°05' Cancer, Sun is 13°19' Cancer, Moon is 27°00' Aquarius; night Part of Fortune is 6°07' Cancer.

6 Another approach to the problem posed by the engraving has been offered by Susan Manuel, and taken up by Nicholas Campion in his *Book of World Horoscopes* (Cinnabar Books, 1996) p415. Manuel believes that the engraved horoscope is an amalgam of transits for 4 July noon in Philadelphia and cusps for the Cancer ingress in London. Now Sibly does indeed set great store by the ingresses, and demonstrates the symbolism of the breach with the colonies in the preceding Aries ingress for London. Both ingresses are, in Sibly's own words, 'calculated with great accuracy and precision'. They appear just two pages away from the 'Revolution of America' engraving – but the Cancer ingress shows different cusps (MC 11 Sag 30) to those of the horoscope in the angel's scroll. Since in addition there is no indication of the method Manuel proposes in Sibly's text about the American Revolution, or in the main body of *Occult Sciences*, then I believe that her hypothesis is untenable. She has been misled, as have earlier researchers, on the reasonable but invalid assumption that the data shown in the engraving faithfully represents Sibly's computations and therefore his computation errors. Once that step is taken, every attempt to resolve the problem ends up making nonsense of Sibly.

Case Study: Stella

WHAT SHOULD I DO ABOUT
THE PREGNANCY?

This horary question marked a qualitative change in my practice of astrology; it was the first really 'serious' horary question that I had taken on. The question was asked by one of my students in an Adult Education class on astrology. She had already consulted the I Ching and got hexagram 54, the Marrying Maiden, with no change. Although this was in many ways descriptive of her situation, as is often the case when we are in emotional confusion, we are unable to interpret our own oracles. Unable to see any clear direction, she was still confused and phoned me for guidance. She explained her situation and asked me: 'What should I do about the pregnancy?' I knew that I should take it as a horary. I told her that I would look at the matter and be back in touch with her.

Before proceeding with the case, it is instructive to dwell on the nature of the decision, resting entirely with the astrologer, that firstly one will take up an issue at all, and secondly, which symbolic method will be employed. In this instance it would have been an option to back down from divination altogether. After all, in teaching a local authority evening class in astrology I had not explicitly offered myself as mentor of my students' souls or guide to their destinies, so I should not feel duty bound to take on board such an intimate and important issue. It would be feasible to move more or less directly to the counselling role, and perhaps something useful might be accomplished in this way. However, my student had not approached me in the generalised role of the counsellor, but more specifically for my experience in matters of divination, and I don't remember having a moment's doubt that I should take her dilemma on board and at least consider whether I could offer a view derived from symbolism. There are some requests whose genuine nature is obvious, and then the astrologer feels called. When you hear that call, choice hardly seems to come into it. This experience is the first foundation of radicality in all astrology.

The second phase of this initial decision concerns the method to be employed.

Hidden within this apparently straightforward choice are several shades of possibility of different practices of divination, the nuances and differing requirements of which have hardly been recognised, let alone discussed, in the tradition of astrology. Here, as the querent is herself using divination, I could have taken up her own response from the *I Ching*, and worked through this further. This would have opened up into a special type of consultation, with the possibility of a further decisive test of divination by the querent. This approach of 'divinatory supervision', which is in effect a process of consultation together with supervision of the client's own symbolic practice, in my experience works well, especially with the *I Ching*. Here, however, the urgency of the situation, and the state of the querent, made appropriate the greater objectivity and decisive intervention that may come from a judgment given by another diviner. The need to separate out an effective symbolism also suggested in this case that if a horary were to be taken, it should be for the time the question was put to the astrologer, rather than for the time of the original divination, which had now become compounded in the mother's confusion. As to whether horary or natal astrology should be employed, the choice is usually clear. Natal astrology is well able to show the overall strategy for a period of life, as well as revealing those deep conditions of the soul which have become constellated in a particular issue. It may be expected to offer some revelation of both the ultimate setting and the scope of a crisis, and its ramifications for other dimensions of the native's life. However, even where the natal horoscope does give an exact symbol and timing for a point of decision in life (which is far from always the case), by virtue of its breadth and depth, natal astrology is often ill-suited to the signification of the actual line of good or ill fortune flowing from a particular decision. It may show the problem, but not the likely outcome. Radical horary has an unmatched capacity to signify the actual *here* and *now* of a life situation. Depth, and importance of the issue are not the criteria. As in the case under discussion, horary can address the supreme issues of life. A major difference is that natal astrology is effectively open-ended and widens out to symbolise the whole life-project, while horary is dedicated to true and false in the matter at hand. This distinction is reflected in the differing requirements of natal and horary practice. Natal work is usually more ponderous and technically substantial and requires more extensive discussion with the client, whereas effective horary can be short, sharp, to the point, and then finished with.

This digression on the initial process of decision undertaken by the astrologer could make it appear more difficult than it really is. In practice, these matters are frequently decided in a moment, as the astrologer moves intuitively to an appropriate response to a client's request. In an important sense, these things decide themselves. After all, I may decide on a horary and then find it's not on, either through a stricture or through ambiguous radicality. In this way my craft of astrology will be prompting me, either to refer the client elsewhere or to consider natal astrology, if both I and the client are willing for that commitment.

The choice of horary, with the implication that one will focus on the here-and-now crisis and hope to offer a resolution one way or the other, requires of the astrologer a crucial process of reflection, which is traditionally the first and most important part of the 'considerations before judgment'. Invariably in horary we pause and ask, what does this question mean? How come the querent has to ask me this? Before leaping in to the symbolism of the horoscope, as far as possible the astrologer needs to understand how the question has arisen in the context of the querent's present situation, as well as the implications of any decision the querent may take. In paying heed to the story, and to how the querent presents it, the astrologer will usually soon be assured of the first foundation of radicality, that the question is sincere and not simply speculative, and that the one asking genuinely intends to follow through into action what is understood. Only then is there any resolution through symbolism.

To return to the dilemma of the pregnant woman, here was the situation as I understood it from our first conversation. She lived with a man by whom she had given birth to several children. There was little money to spare, and another mouth to feed could be a problem. The woman had been participating on a trial run of a particular version of the birth-control Pill, but whether through her own error or a failure of the Pill itself, she was now pregnant. Her doctor had made it clear that he would facilitate an abortion and there was no need for her to consider having the child. The man with whom she lived, and father of the child, was strongly against her extending the family. In fact, he declared that if she went ahead to have this child then that was it, he was off. All things considered, therefore, it appeared unreasonable for the mother to want to go to term. In human affairs, however, reasonableness is far from being the deciding factor. It so happened that the querent enjoyed the process of motherhood and wanted this child. Hence her dilemma, exactly as she stated it in the moment that enshrines the horary: 'What should I do about the pregnancy?'

Before going ahead with an interpretation, it is worth pondering the issues involved. This question concerns the life or death of an embryo, a potential human being. Is the astrologer in a position to give such a judgment from the stars? This was an ethical dilemma for me. I did not wish to be asked to give this sort of judgment. At that time I had definite views concerning the matter of abortion, which I am less certain about now. I felt that on the whole abortion was wrong unless there were obvious reasons concerning the health of the mother or the possibility of a seriously handicapped child. My own feelings would be very much against having to deliver a judgment from the stars that there should be an abortion of a healthy foetus from a healthy woman simply on the grounds of pressure from a husband and a doctor. Nevertheless, in accepting the horary I was taking on the possibility that I would make such an unhappy judgment if that was clearly the showing of the horoscope. It is in such ways that one's faith in astrology is tested and purified. As to my dilemma, as so often happens, the symbolism moved in a different direction to the preconceptions of either client or astrologer.

Once the question has been accepted, and its context and implication pondered, the astrologer comes to an important interpretive decision, the resolution of which is not always obvious if the question has an ambivalent form. What is the querent's *desire* in the matter? The astrologer must ask, given this querent and this question, *to what* a horary perfection will refer. In the current question the querent has chosen not to express a simple and straightforward desire to have the child. She has not asked 'Should I go ahead with the pregnancy?', in which case a perfection means 'yes'. But neither has she asked 'Should I go ahead with the abortion?', in which case perfection also means 'yes', subject to the appropriateness of the symbols to such an act. What does she want? Like the baby in the story of Solomon, her wish is cut in two by the choice that has to be made, and the wording places her in a limbo of indecision between unbearable alternatives. In this case I had no clear idea before I cast the map of what a perfection would mean. In such cases the astrologer takes a stand in the ethic of interpretation and has to let the symbolism of the horary bring light to the concealed line of good fortune. If the map is going to work at all, the significators will reveal the meaning of their own perfection.

So we turn to the chart (Fig30). Scorpio rises, the sign of life and death, and Mars is the significator for the querent. The question of pregnancy is traditionally taken from the 5th, the house of the child. As Aries is on the cusp, Mars is also the significator for the quesited, the foetus. So we have Mars showing both the querent and the quesited, and itself located in the 5th. This indeed appears to present itself as a 5th house question! In cases where the ruler of querent and quesited is the same planet several horary authorities say that 'the matter is in the hands of the querent'. What could be more appropriate? Mother and pregnancy are as one – it is completely the mother's decision whether she does, or does not, have the child. Mars is strong in Aries, but it is moving to the serious affliction of a conjunction with the South Node. This is the threat to the very existence of the foetus (Mars, lord of 5th), which is also the sorrow of the mother (Mars, lord of ascendant). Pluto, as co-ruler of the ascendant and therefore a secondary significator for the querent, offered a testimony to this affliction of Mars. Placed

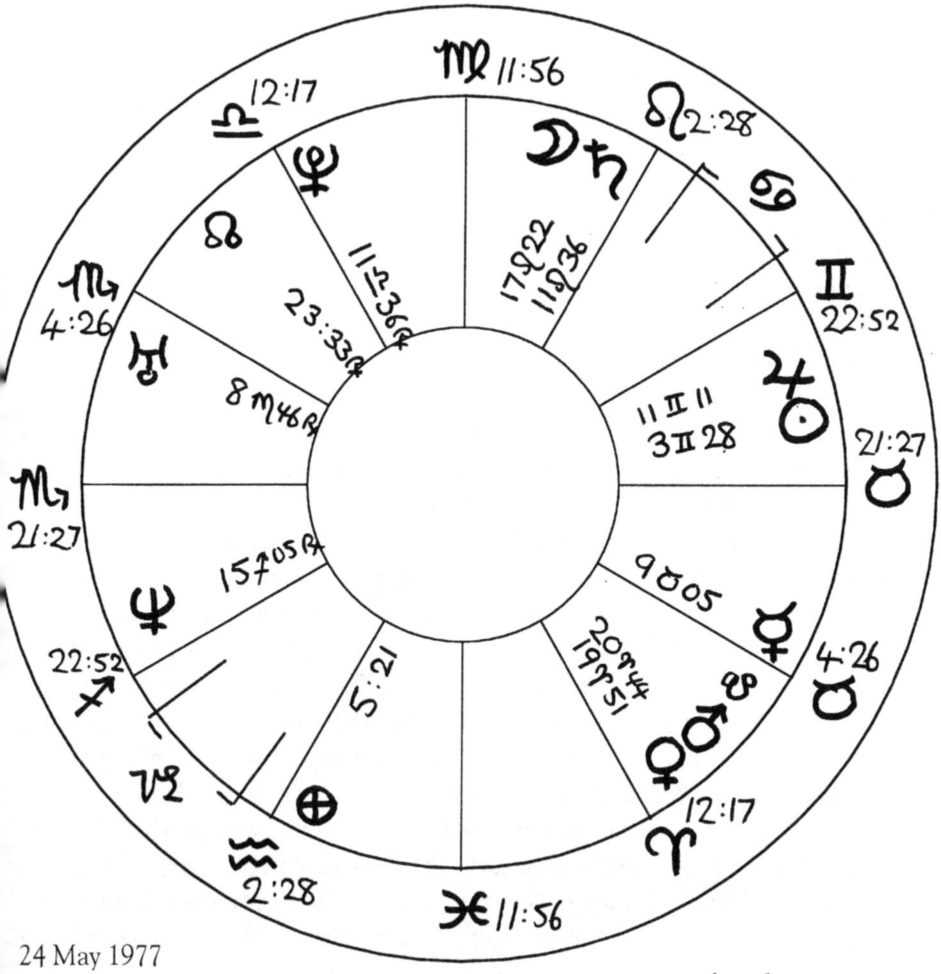

24 May 1977
7.45 pm BST
London
0W10 51N30
Topocentric

d ♂
h ☽
☽ à △ ♆ ad △ ♂
⚷ 3♉24

FIGURE 30 'What should I do about the pregnancy?'

right on the 11th cusp it was in opposition to the 5th, threatening the foetus. This is at the same time the destruction of the querent's own hopes and wishes (11th), and the threat of abortion.

Venus is with Mars in the 5th, and this must be the father of the child, the woman's husband, ruler of Taurus on the 7th. The detriment of Venus in Aries shows the man in a discreditable condition, and under the power of Mars, his pregnant wife. A detail she hesitantly divulged on our second conversation graphically illustrates the selfish attitude symbolised by Venus in Aries. Apart from the poverty of the family, the man was moved at least momentarily by a more primal desire. He did not want his woman to be sexually 'out of commission' for yet another spell of pregnancy.

The Moon's role is nearly always decisive in cases where querent and quesited are identified by the same significator, and this question lies within her universal symbolism of babies and births. At the time, I could not make much sense of her house placing, although I wondered whether this reflected the ethical dilemma involved in a judgment from astrology (9th house), especially given the afflicting conjunction from the detrimented Saturn.

It is the Moon's applying aspect, however, which has overriding significance in this map. She applies trine to Venus and Mars, with *Venus* standing in the way of the perfection of significators, Moon trine Mars. The symbolism is obvious: the real question is about the *husband*. That is why the Moon goes to Venus, ruler of the 7th, rather than to Mars, ruler of the 1st and 5th. The trine with Mars would be the woman doing what she willed with the pregnancy, but Venus *interposes*, and her desire becomes wholly qualified by the husband. Pluto can now be re-taken in its placing on the 5th cusp from the 7th – literally, the husband's attempt to destroy his own offspring. Now if we follow the horary principle that the form of both question and answer shall be directly symbolised in the significators, then the querent's dilemma is recast. The true question, the one that is faithful to the significations, is revealed: 'Will my husband stay with me, if I go through with the pregnancy?'

This move recasts not only the querent's dilemma but also mine as the astrologer. No longer am I seeking a fate judgment, a decree from heaven about what should and should not be done about the pregnancy. Nor am I looking for the predictive possibility that there will or will not actually be a full-term pregnancy, as if it is already decided in the stars what this mother will do. The scope of prediction is entirely switched to the issue of the likely behaviour of the husband, and to resolving the crisis of his threat, which is at the heart of the dilemma. Once that is decided one way or the other, the mother knows where she stands and out of her own free will she must take the decision that is hers alone. It is by such a turn of the symbolism that we discover the way in which horary, like all divination truly understood, tends towards the enhancement of human dignity and freedom.

In the ordinary course of events we would expect the Venus-Mars conjunction to be made in the sign of Aries, which would bring husband and wife to come together in whatever they decided, although there would still be the potent maleficity of the South Node, afflicting them both. However, their conjunction was not made until the planets entered Taurus, so from the horary point of view, we do not see the means for them to come together on this current issue. If anything is to be effected, it will not be by Venus and Mars unaided. It was, however, my judgment that the two would be brought together with the help of the Moon. But to explain how this is so raises a fascinating detail of horary craft.

At the time, I shared with a few other horary astrologers the clouded reading of the tradition that was so characteristic of late twentieth-century Western astrology. Lilly's authority was partially obscured by Zadkiel's nineteenth-century emendations. The few horary authorities later than Zadkiel, working in the main without the benefit of Lilly's original text, all offered confusing accounts of the traditional structure of the subject, so that unresolved ambiguities already inherent in the received tradition were compounded. This showed right down to the technical definition of 'translation of light'. Up to that time I had understood that a swift planet might come from behind two other significators, and applying to each of them in turn, would join their light. So in the present case, I thought the Moon would pass the light of Venus onto Mars as she applied first to the trine of Venus, and then moved to the trine of Mars. By this symbolic reasoning, I judged that husband and wife would be joined in the matter, and that he would not leave if she went ahead with the pregnancy. Her will would prevail over him.

In addition to this main symbolism, there was a further indication that the couple would stay together. Mercury's separation from the opposition of Uranus also appeared significant in the light of events described to me. Mercury has some relationship with the 7th, as part-ruler, and it is also the dispositor of two male planets in the 7th. The husband had lately threatened to leave – Mercury opposite Uranus, Uranus lord of the 3rd, Mercury lord of the 8th; an expressed threat to end things. Uranus of his nature is also a planet of divorce and disruption. However, I felt those words had no power of future fulfilment, since the opposition was separating. This was an important testimony to the main theme of the judgment.

When I phoned the woman back I gave the following opinion: that whatever she decided, her husband would not leave her, and his threat was empty. I did not offer a judgment as to whether she should or should not go ahead with the pregnancy.

It was in this second conversation that the mother told me something that moved me deeply, revealing that the birth had already been presaged in the most ancient and primordial medium for divination, the dream. On the night the child was conceived, as she later realised, she had a dream about a baby girl, and the girl was called 'Stella'. If she had told me this *before*, it is very likely that I would not have bothered to set up a horary – what was required to be understood was already there before her.

With this news an obscure element in the horary fell into place: the Moon's placing in the 9th, the house of prophecy. Although I missed it at the time, just as impressive for a prophetic dream is the Moon's separating trine from Neptune in visionary Sagittarius. The Moon makes the dream real as she carries light from Neptune onto the significators in the 5th, onto Mars and Venus, the man and the woman.

So it came to pass in November that the mother gave birth to a baby girl. Father and mother stayed together, and they named the child Stella. For my own interest, I attempted to work out the date of birth from the horary, but I was completely wrong in the prediction I made for myself. Obviously that wasn't required for the effective resolution of the horary – all that was needed was for a single important issue to be interpreted by me and understood by the mother.

However, there is a marvellous and unpredictable connection between horary and birth, which gives yet another dimension to the interpretation. Baby Stella was born with Jupiter rising, exalted in Cancer (see Fig.31). That is the image of the great protector. Jupiter is the sender of dreams, and the baby is protected by the gods. A second notable configuration is that of the cazimi, the close conjunction of Sun and Uranus, trine to the Ascendant. As both Jupiter and Uranus are sky gods, we begin to see the significance of the name Stella. The peculiar suggestion that this child has already, at her conception, announced her own name is reflected in the Moon in Leo, ruler of the ascendant, in the 3rd house of names – a typical Moon Leo flourish.

I have occasionally noticed in natal maps some curiousity about the name or nickname when there is a 3rd-1st connection involving the Moon.

The Moon, showing the girl who has named herself, is at 19°50' Leo. If we look back at the horary, the horary Moon is also in Leo but Venus is at 19°51' Aries, so the natal Moon is just 1 minute of arc from the trine of horary Venus, highlighting it as the key to the horary. This interpretation is decisively confirmed by the powerful testimony of the natal day Part of Fortune (and therefore night Part of Spirit) at $19^3/_4$ Aries – exactly on the Venus of the horary.[1]

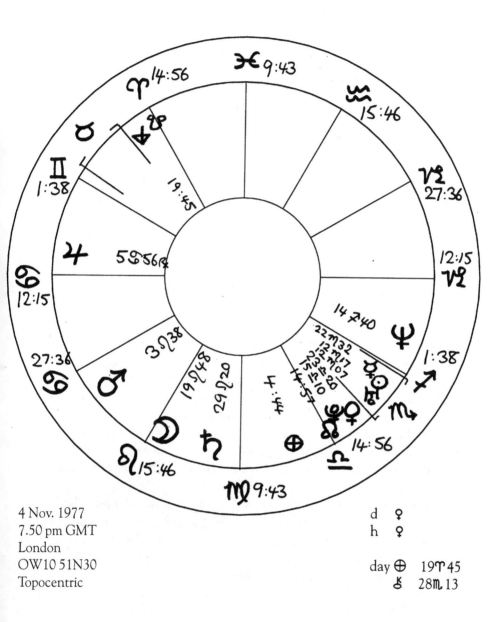

4 Nov. 1977
7.50 pm GMT
London
0W10 51N30
Topocentric

d ♀
h ♀

day ⊕ 19♈45
⚷ 28♏13

FIGURE 31 Stella

From these connections we attain an unequivocal understanding of what constitutes perfection in the horary – it is the Moon to Venus *alone*, not the Moon to Venus then Mars.

I should add that this horary arose at a time of formative debate amongst the small group of us concerned with the restoration of horary. It made clear the significance of 'interposition', which has been inadequately treated in modern horary. Venus here interposing between significators shows the real structure of the question, and allows a re-framing or re-taking of the question to allow it to express the line of good fortune for the querent, but without imposing a fate solution.

The matter was already in train for the querent from the time of the conception and the dream, but the husband's threat interposing divided the querent's desires against herself – her husband and the situation of the family against the foetus. The role of the astrology seemed to be to support the indication of the dream and resolve the interposing issue, thus leaving intact the mother's free decision, undetermined by the symbolism. With the interposing issue being clarified, whether for good or for ill, the resolution of the main question returns to her decision and her initiative.

This case therefore shows once again the principle of divination in general and horary in particular that enables us to move away from the fate-prescription *judgment* – what will happen, or what is the heaven's law about what should happen – to *resolution* in the free-will prescription – in doing what you desire to do, understand what is involved. Horary offers a concrete and sometimes startlingly exact description of reality, yet never forecloses on it ahead of the free decision that is still possible in a situation. Yet there was also in this question a significant element which concerned purely technical craft problems of translation and interposition, part of the debate amongst a small group of horary astrologers at the time.

So I also learned from this example the way in which the astrology which arises seems to match the level of one's current practice, as if it is a thoughtfully conceived invitation to monitor and develop the astrologer's technical and symbolic methods. In an important sense the most vital astrology that we experience refers also to the practice of itself.

NOTE

1 The Part of Fortune by day and night (see discussion on this in the Preface): Stella's natal horoscope is an exceptional case where my relatively recent decision to distinguish fortuna by day and night is sorely tested In the first edition of this work, Stella was presented with

fortuna at 19°45' Aries, which was my practice at the time, and it is a most powerful testimony to the deep connection of the nativity with the horary question. I have an open mind on the signification of the Part of Spirit, which is its complement; I use it only rarely, but have chosen to show it here to maintain the originally observed symbolic connection, which so moved me at the time. Just as a tradition moves on collectively, so each practitioner's practice changes and re-forms. We are bound to make and re-make these decisions to include and exclude various factors, since we are always selecting a tiny set of symbols from an infinite range of possibilities. Conflicting forces of authority, community and a desire to create must be satisfied, yet in the final analysis there is no arbiter of right or wrong other than the inspiration and fruitfulness of the choice itself. All that is required is that we see what seeks to show itself through whatever symbolic forms we have taken up.

Index

a te & a scientia, 303, 308, 318-9, 321
Addey, John, 48, 58, 75, 92, 97, 181, 228
   Astrology as Divination, 290
   Cheam Road zodiac, 220-1
affinity effect, 208, 227
Agrippa, Henry Cornelius, 13, 20, 310, 327, 330
Al-Biruni, 104, 122, 304, 325
Albertus Magnus, 101, 278, 290, 333
allegory / allegoric
   see also entries under fourfold hermeneutic
   anagoge underlies, 284, 291
   'as if' interpretation, 289
   astrology and, 279, 282-9, 296, 298-9
   Biblical, 228, 278, 280, 290-1
   Dante, 281-2
   divinatory, 277, 285, 289, 294
   extended metaphor, 285
   Mercury & 6th house, 279, 284
   objective, 283, 285, 298-9, 308
   and real-isation, 285, 293-4
   and symbol, 286-8
Allen, D.C., 18, 20, 21, 339
Allport, G.W., 24
Ambrose, 290
anagoge
   see also entries under fourfold hermeneutic
   9th house, 284
   and astrology, 282ff
   Biblical, 278-280, 291
   and Bodhisattva, 302
   function and process symbolism, 297-302
   images unbind images, 301
   interpretation of Being, 286
   resists interpretation, 284
   synderesis and prophecy, 309
   teleological, 284, 297
   underlies allegory, 284, 291
Anderson, W., 291
anti-astrology signature, 26-7, 36-9, 83, 115, 204, 206, 304
Aphek & Tobin, 301
Appleby, Derek, 41, 158-9, 165
Aquinas, 279

Aristotle, 8, 89, 96-7, 135, 142, 174, 304, 333
Asclepius, 141
Ashe, Geoffrey, 219-20, 228
Ashmole, Elias, 147, 162-4, 166, 359-60
astro-cartography, 221, 228
astrologer
   mandate of, 329
Astrological Association, 50, 58, 123, 181, 230
Astrological Lodge, 123, 165
astrology
   alchemy, 162, 297
   astronomy, 28, 96, 135, 170, 240, 252, 286, 333
   blind trials, 59, 62, 66, 74, 296, 341
   chess analogy, 289
   cosmobiology, 47
   divinatory, 199
   divinatory allegoric, 285
   double conception, 59, 74, 79, 91, 187
   esoteric/exoteric, 168, 182, 252, 255
   gestalt defence, 53, 55
   great questions, 328
   hermeneutic, 230, 279, 282, 284, 321, 324
   horary *see separate entry*
   humanistic, 86, 92, 94, 161, 189, 262, 304, 307
   katarche *see separate entry*
   metaphor, 19
   midpoints, 47, 175
   mundane, 97, 163, 242, 257-9, 262, 272-4, 311, 315-6, 324,
   natal, pre-assigned radicality, 204, 231
   natural vs. judicial/divinatory, 74-9, 91, 189, 257, 303, 342
   neo-Platonism, 4, 12, 92, 307, 310
   psychoanalysis, 35, 76, 118, 222, 278, 296-7
   psychological, 44, 53, 90, 95, 97, 161, 222, 262, 287, 299, 304
   religious observance, 284
   ritual, 142-3
   scientific, 25, 34, 44-6, 48-9, 56, 91, 189, 340

astrology (*cont.*):
  signs vs causes, 7-8, 55-7, 74, 78, 81, 92,
    257, 303, 320,
  takes, 123, 227
  types of text, 13-4
  Uranian system, 47
  work of devil, 180
Aubrey, John, 183
augury, 8, 110, 124, 127, 130-2, 134-7, 173,
    176-7
Augustine, 11, 175, 179-183, 279, 290
auspice, 8, 127-8, 139, 178

Bailey, E.H., 249
Barclay, Olivia, 165-6
Barley, Alfred, 168
Beard, Mary, 141-2
Bellanti, 14-5, 20
Berégovoy, Pierre, 199
birth
  induced, 58
Boddhisattva, 302
Bok, Bart, 22-3, 26, 31, 40
Bonatti (Bonatus), 14, 20, 106-7, 122-3, 336
Bottéro, J., 142, 182
Bouché-Leclercq, 130, 135, 142, 176, 183
Bowden, Mary E., 20
Brooke, Elisabeth, 18, 361

Caine, Mary, 219, 228
Campion, Nicholas, 227-8, 240, 253-4, 272-3,
    275-6, 328, 367-8
Carlson, Shawn, 42, 338-45
Carter, Charles, 33-4, 40-1, 52, 58, 109-113,
    115-8, 120, 122-3, 160, 164, 181-2, 196,
    198, 201, 347, 350-1
Cassirer, E., 19
Causabon, Isaac, 18
causal-temporal origin, 83, 94, 102, 106, 110,
    176, 209, 231, 289
  see also doctrine of origin
Chiron, 41
Chrysippus, 142
Cicero, 141, 333
Cirlot J.E., 227
Clark, Vernon, 57, 59-66, 68-74, 76, 78-80,
    340, 341, 343
Coley, 107, 122
comets
  Hale-Bopp, 242, 254, 260-1, 275
  Halley, 259-60
Company of Astrologers, 181-2, 302

conscience, 307-10, 327, 329
  see also synderesis
context-psi, 76, 78, 214, 222, 344-5
continuous correspondence, 88-9, 96, 102
Corpus Hermeticum, 2-3, 18
CPI *California Personality Inventory*, 339-40,
    345
Cromwell, Oliver, 311-2, 314-5
CSICOP, 43, 57
Culpeper, Nicholas 139, 143, 165, 215-6, 218,
    228
Cumont, Franz, 134, 142, 182
Curry, Patrick, 18, 167, 181

daemon
  of astrologer or querent, 111
  bad, 309
  corrupted by astrologers, 181
  daemonion (sign), 179, 305
  djinn (genie), 179
  etymology, 183, 305
  and Ficino, 3-4, 179
  guardian angel, 117
  guides astrology, 168
  lord of horoscope, 179
  Neptune, 118
  and Socrates, 110, 348
  and theory of horary, 116
  time does not bind, 117
Dante, 277, 281-2, 291
Dawkins, Richard, 43, 57
De Vore, Nicholas, 97
dead sheep and flamingo, 209, 212-4, 218
Dean, Geoffrey, 45, 52, 57-8, 61-4, 66, 68, 70,
    73, 79, 80, 189, 201, 227, 253, 342-3,
    345
decumbiture, 138-141, 143, 165, 176, 208,
    215-6
definitive direction, 249
Delphi, 129-131, 134, 141-2, 264, 266-7, 269,
    301-2, 364, 367
destiny
  negotiable, 131
  not negotiable, 173
Diana, Princess, 232-3, 235-243, 245-9, 253-
    6, 261, 263
divination
  Mesopotamian, 141, 142
doctrine of origin, 87-91, 94-5, 110-1, 117,
    125, 135, 137, 177, 231, 285, 289
Dorotheus, 124
Dunbar, H.F., 290-1

Ebertin, 47, 57
Eden, Richard, 329
election of the will, 106
Elizabeth I, 190-1, 193-5, 199, 222
Elliott, Roger, 232
Elwell, Dennis, 41, 56, 58, 94, 97, 196, 198,
    201-2, 227, 243, 245, 254, 307, 326
  on suicide, 202
equation of the orders, 75
ESP, 79, 253
ethical symbol, 301, 305-10, 372
Etruscans, 129, 134, 135
Eudoxus, 96
Evans, 147, 179
Exodus, 279, 280, 282
Eysenck, Hans, 70-3, 80, 340, 345

Faculty of Astrological Studies, 59, 181
fate and destiny, 182
fate-threads, 172
Ficino, Marsilio, 2-8, 10-13, 17-20, 24-5, 39,
    164, 174, 178-9, 183, 307, 324-5, 329-30
  notio and notitia, 330
Figulus, Nigidius, 134-5, 142, 174
Flint, Valerie, 183
Fontenrose, J., 142
fourfold hermeneutic, 277-8, 292, 294, 296-7,
    299, 303, 308
  in astrology, 282ff
  see also entries for allegory, anagoge,
    tropology
Frankfort, Henri, 142
Frankland, William, 111, 120, 122-3, 349,
    351, 353-5, 356-7
Freud, Sigmund, 286, 297, 302

Gadbury, John, 15-17, 20, 38
Garin, E., 18-20, 122, 339
Gassendi, 16, 20
Gauquelin, 34, 44-50, 52-3, 55, 57-9, 62, 64,
    66, 74-5, 79, 91, 97, 194, 252, 290, 345
  plus zones, 201
Geneva, Ann, 274-5, 326, 328
Goldstein-Jacobson, Ivy, 41, 100-1, 122
de Gournay, Norman, 36-7, 41
great questions
  see horary
Greene, Liz, 97
Guarico, 20, 325
Gurney O.R., 141

Halliday W.R., 143

Hand, Robert, 48, 50, 57-8, 142, 161, 166,
    170, 345
Harding, Michael, 95, 97
haruspicy, 124, 134, 142, 174
Harvey, Charles, 49, 58, 199, 220, 227-8, 328
Heaton, John, 300, 302
Heidegger, Martin, 284
herbalism, 3, 18, 165
hermeneutics, 277-80, 282, 284, 290-1, 296-
    8, 308, 324
  see also fourfold hermeneutic *and* interpre-
    tation
hermetism, 13, 92
Herodotus, 131, 142
Heydon, Christopher, 16
Hillman, James, 183
Hone, Margaret, 287, 291, 294
Hookham Michael, 302
horary
  analytical method, 28, 33-4
  daemon, 111, 117-8, 120, 122, 356-7
  of fearing, 309
  fear to discard, 112
  feeble, 163-4, 359-60
  great questions, 162, 166, 311, 314, 317-8,
    321, 328
  and katarche, 125-6, 135
  medical, 139, 215
  moment, 100-2, 106-110, 123, 209, 215
  mutual reception by degree, 35, 156
  non-deterministic, 17, 148, 150, 308
  non-Ptolemaic, 98, 103-5, 124, 135, 256
  participation, 138. 145-6, 165, 208
  perfection, 41
  psychological, 161-2, 166
  radicality, 83, 153
  revival, 90, 113, 144, 160, 161
  ritual, 136
  strictures against judgment, 107, 111, 208,
    309, 327, 371
  subsumed by natal theory, 113
  in *Tetrabiblos*, 319
humanism, 2, 13, 20, 25, 40
Humanist, 22ff, 39, 44, 57, 204-5
Hyde, Maggie
  astrology as ritualised discourse, 186
  atemporality, 251, 255
  decumbitures, 165
  Diana's death astrology, 242, 275
  goldsmith dream, 299-300
  Hale-Bopp, 260, 275
  participation of astrologer, 299-300, 346

Hyde, Maggie (*cont.*):
  psychological astrology, 97, 287, 299
  resolution vs. judgment, 164
  synchronicity I & II, 76-8
  takes, 205
  twins, 183
  universals and particulars, 287
hypothesis of seeds, 87-90, 94-6, 100, 102
  seed moment, 94, 165

I Ching, 108, 187, 209, 288, 291, 308, 369-70
Iamblichus, 142
Ibn Ezra, 103
illusion of technique, 40, 164, 296, 326
incubation, 143
interposition, 151, 378
interpretation
  see also hermeneutics
  literalist vs. symbolist, 256-7
  profile, 72-3
  speculative vs. realised, 292-6
  symbolic-historical, 258
Jerome, Lawrence. 22-6, 40, 278
Jerome, St. 278
Jones, Marc Edmund, 276, 327
Jones, Alan, 165
Joseph, Tony, 61-2, 340, 347
Jung, Carl, 54, 76-8, 81, 96, 165, 178, 180,
      182-3, 222, 239, 278, 286-8, 292-3, 297-
      9, 301, 305, 325, 345-6

Kagami, Ryuji, 260, 275
katarche, 106, 124-8, 132, 135-9, 141-5, 148,
      150, 160-1, 172-4, 177, 208, 216, 221,
      228, 328
Kekule, 187
Kemp, Chester, 230, 254
Kepler, 20, 48, 50, 58, 75, 326
Kingsley, Peter, 143
Koestler, Arthur, 196-9, 201-2
Kollerstrom, Nicholas, 275
Kurtz, Paul, 22, 26, 36, 57

Lawson, J.C., 143
Lemay, Richard, 122, 141
Leo, Alan, 18, 168-9, 181, 330
  curse and blessing, 182
  dream, 169, 324
  Esoteric Astrology, 182
  karma of astrologer, 168
  organised astrology, 181-2
  star angels, 168

Leo Bessie, 18, 182
Lewis, Jim, 228
Lilly, William
  9th house judgment in anti-astrology map,
      30, 41
  a te & a scientia, 303, 318-9, 321
  Christianity, 306, 315, 326-7
  Civil War predictions, 258-60, 274, 311-4,
      316-8, 328
  considerations before judgment, 107
  demonstration of astrology, 14
  discretion, 114
  fish stolen, 98ff, 124, 145
  great questions, 311, 314, 317-8, 328
  lamination of symbol, 152, 315
  magic, 145-8, 162-3, 165
  marriage horary, 145-6
  medical horary, 139
  'neer to God', 310
  non-deterministic, 148-50
  participation, 145-6, 150, 152-3
  prophetical astrology, 148, 310, 316, 326
  psychological horary, 164
  radicality, 115, 315
  revival of horary, 162, 165
  vary your rules, 146
Lindsay, Jack, 142
locating significance, 302
logic of inclusion, 220
Lull, Raymond, 203
Lydgate John, 327

machine of destiny, 173, 181, 262
magi, 306
magic, see under astrology
Maginus, 326
Maltwood, Katherine, 219, 228
Manilius, 46, 173, 182
Mardonius, 131
Marx, Karl, 205-6, 227
Masha'allah, 107, 122
Mayall, Margaret, 26, 31, 37, 40
Mayo, Jeff, 104, 122
Mercurius, 77, 80, 346
Merleau-Ponty, M., 201
method-switch, 112, 123
Metis, 302
midrash, 278
Mikes, George, 198, 201
Milburn, Joseph, 276
Morin de Villefranche, 16, 20-1, 104, 126,
      291

Morton, Andrew, 235, 237-9, 253-4
Mursilis, 133
mutual detriment, 30
mutual reception by degree, 35, 41, 156
mythopoeic thought, 142

Naibod, Valentin, 326
Nasr Seyyed Hosein, 122
National Council for Geocosmic Research, 46, 50, 338
NCGR-Berkeley Double-Blind Test, 64, 338, 340-1, 343
negotiation of the symbol, 294
neo-Platonism, 3, 4, 7, 8, 10, 12, 328, 330
Neugebauer & van Hoesen, 141
Newton, Robert R., 97
North John, 141
Norton, Thomas, 163, 360

Omarr, Sidney, 40
Origen, 278-9, 290

Paine, Thomas, 270, 271, 275
Palchus, 125-6, 137, 141
parapsychology, 63, 76, 80, 82, 118, 209
Parker, Derek, 274
participation, 62
    symbolic, 145, 150, 153, 305, 307, 310-11
part of fortune, 41, 183, 378
Pausanias, 131, 136
perfection (horary), 41
Phillipson, Garry, 79-80
Pico della Mirandola, 1ff, 38-9, 164, 169, 174, 181, 184, 204, 306, 310, 324, 325, 333-7
    death prediction, 14-18, 20, 324-6
Pico G.F., 20
Pingree, D., 141
Placidus, 122
    directional measure, 326
Plato, 3, 4, 8, 10, 142, 171, 182, 305, 333
    etymology of daemon, 183, 305
Plotinus, 3, 4, 7-8, 10, 12, 19, 330
Plutarch, 183
Pontano Giovani, 321-4, 329-30
Pontis de Tyard, 21
potter's wheel fallacy, 174-5
Porter, David, 123
prediction
    scope of, 261-3
Press, 50, 51, 52, 58, 61
Pritchard, J.B., 141
Project Hindsight, 142, 166

projection, 11, 221, 224, 308
prophecy, 33, 103, 115, 163, 211, 258, 280, 284, 286, 306, 310-11, 314, 316, 322, 376
psi-Neptune, 75-6, 78, 80, 82, 104, 118, 228, 341, 343
psychoanalysis, 228, 302
Ptolemy, 37, 81ff, 101-6, 124, 134-5, 142, 170, 174ff, 205, 257, 304, 319ff
    Centiloquy, 103, 122, 319, 321-2, 324, 329
    directional measure, 20, 325
    on disease, 183

Qabalah, 10, 290

radicality, 31, 35, 83, 107, 115-6, 122, 153, 165, 212, 216, 218, 231, 240, 269, 276, 293, 312, 315, 369, 371
radix, 231
Rantrovius, 15
Rectification, 230, 245-250, 253, 264, 267, 269, 271-3, 276, 368
red-and-black fallacy, 70-3
refranation, 34,
    in anti-astrology signature, 41
Relf, Anthony, 143
resolution vs judgment, 329
Rudhyar, Dane, 92-5, 97, 189-190, 201, 262, 267ff, 275-6, 307, 368

Sabian symbols, 271-2
Sasportas, Howard, 97
Savonarola, 10, 11, 25
Schmidt, Robert, 142, 143
Schumacher E.F., 201
scientism, 33, 42, 74, 186, 189, 304, 342-3
second sight, 219, 292
secret mutual connivance, 77, 222, 227, 299
self-referencing, 123, 208, 222-3
Serapio of Alexandria, 124
Seymour, Percy, 46, 57
Seznec, J., 21
Shallis, Michael, 201, 228, 255, 326
Sibly, 262-7, 269, 271-2, 274, 361-7
Sieggruen, 47
significance
    participatory, 133-5, 137-8, 177-8, 187-9, 214, 221
    theoretical, 133, 177, 251

Silberer, Herbert, 297-9, 302
Socrates, 110, 179, 183

Solte
  Scorpionic America, 276
Soudines, 134
Spina, Francisco, 310, 327
Star of Bethlehem, 306, 310, 326-7
stated-time horoscope, 238, 248-250, 264
stoicism, 17, 101, 134, 142-3, 171, 173-4, 176
Stone, Alby, 172, 182
suicide, 52, 56-7, 61, 66, 122, 198, 202, 354
  New York Study, 50-2, 54, 56, 58, 62, 64,
    79, 195-6, 198-9, 202
sun-signs, 22, 53, 75, 252, 296
  bias in tests, 344
superstition, 23, 33, 47, 172
symbol
  defined, 291
symbolic attitude, 6, 187, 209, 219, 243, 262,
  292
synastry, 77, 200, 216, 218, 229, 232, 235,
  241, 253, 261
synchronicity, 54, 76-8, 81, 180, 211, 293,
  299, 345-6
synderesis, 281, 309-10, 327-9

taboo, 172, 182
takes and re-takes, 203-9, 214, 216, 218, 221-
  2, 224, 227-8, 258,
  299
talismans, 3-4, 136, 147-8, 162
Tarot, 108, 288
templum, 132, 136
Tertullian, 278
Tester, Jim, 20, 329, 337
Thatcher, Margaret, 190, 192-5, 199, 222,
  260
Theosophy, 92, 168, 181-2
Thornton, Penny, 238, 253
time
  causal-temporal origin, 142, 227, 254
Tobyn, Graeme, 122, 143, 215, 216, 218, 228
transference, 222-3, 227, 299, 330

translation of light, 163, 375
triads of houses, 291
tropology / trope (= moral level), 279ff, 308
  see also entries under fourfold hermeneutic
  12th house, 284
  blind in tests, 296
  contextual, 283
  function and process symbolism, 297-300
  knowledge and action, 283
  and psychological astrology, 283
  solstice, 280
  synchronicity II, 299-300
trutine of Hermes, 87
twins, 174-5, 182-3, 220, 345

unique case of interpretation, 184, 188, 190,
  194-5, 199-203, 207, 232, 253, 257, 288,
  303
Urania Trust, 42

Vettius Valens, 142, 173, 182
Voss, Angela, 7, 13, 19, 330

Walker, D.P., 18
Wang Yang-Ming, 291
Warde-Fowler, 141-2
Watson, Gordon, 158, 206-7
Wells, Vernon, 205, 227, 329-30
Wharton, George, 275
Witte, A., 47
Wolfson H.A., 290
world soul, 4
World Trade Center attack, 262-3
wrong chart working, 230, 231, 232, 235, 248,
  250, 251

Yates, Frances, 18, 20

zodiacs
  Glastonbury & Kingston, 218-221
  Cheam Road, 220-1

Further Studies in Astrology

For links and information, visit the website of the **Advisory Panel on Astrological Education** (A.P.A.E.) at www.apae.org.uk

The APAE, founded in 1980, is the lead body in UK astrological education, representing the great majority of reputable schools and larger societies. As well as advising education authorities and other official bodies on the qualification of astrologers, it serves as an organisational forum and means of communication for the community of astrologers.

****

The Company of Astrologers

Major themes in this book have been developed and explored in cooperation with colleagues at the Company of Astrologers. The Company is a non-profit body founded in 1983 to promote the practice of astrology as a way of insight and self-knowledge. It offers studies in astrology and divination, a programme of meetings in London, and a regular e-mail Bulletin of articles and contemporary astrology.

For more information visit http://coa.hubcom.net (or up-to-date link on *Moment of Astrology* dox webpage). You can e-mail the Secretary on admin@coa.org.uk; write c/o PO Box 792, Canterbury, Kent CT2 8WR, England; phone +44 (0)1227 362427.

****

Katarche
Correspondence Course in Horary Astrology

The Katarche course is a correspondence course covering horary theory and practice in considerable depth. It is suitable for students who already have some background in astrology. The course and qualification is recognised by the Company of Astrologers. For more information, please write c/o the Company of Astrologers, address above, or see details on the COA website.

****

Moment of Astrology dox

Useful and updated links will be found on this book's dox file (web-based document extension and reference) at www.astrodivination.com (see the Preface to the Second Edition for details).

CPSIA information can be obtained
at www.ICGtesting.com
Printed in the USA
BVHW042159250521
608161BV00010B/185

9 781902 405117